Praise for Joseph W. Naus's

THE PALSGRAF REVELATION

"Joseph's follow-up memoir, The Palsgraf Revelation, is as open, honest and raw as his first. His prose skillfully conjures the addict mind. An incredible read."

—Rich Roll, host of Rich Roll Podcast and Author of *Finding Ultra*

"If you've ever been knocked down so hard by life you could not fathom how to get up, *The Palsgraf Revelation* gives you an unflinching glimpse of what it takes. There are few writers who capture what it means to live and die and somehow live again in Los Angeles as viscerally and cerebrally as Naus. He paints with words and breaks your heart in the process."

— Nick Guthe, Filmmaker

"Welcome to the most fascinating and truthful memoir of the life IN recovery. Beautifully written, painfully vulnerable and unabashedly realistic. A must must must read."

— Amy Dresner, Author of *My Faire Junkie*

"Joseph Naus has the rare ability to crack your heart open like an egg with his deeply evocative work. To read *The Palsgraf Revelation* is to be submerged in the tender, painstaking beauty of what it takes to climb from the darkest chasm of an addiction bottom to find a spiritually meaningful life."

— Heidi Ferrer, *GirltoMom.com*

ALSO BY JOSEPH W. NAUS

Straight Pepper Diet

On Death, Four Short Stories (Fall 2020)

Joyce & Larry –

THE PALSGRAF REVELATION

A MEMOIR OF LOVE, ADDICTION, RECOVERY AND PRACTICAL SPIRITUALITY

You are powerhouses

by Joseph W. Naus

of God's light &
I love you both.

Love
Joseph Naus

K. M. PUBLISHING

Los Angeles, California

Story Editor: Alison Palmer
Copy Editor: Catherine J Palmer
Cover Design: KMP with Rachel Lopez-Bagan at Play Grnd
Book Layout: KMP

Published by K.M. Publishing

Printed in the United States of America
ISBN 978-0-9862833-1-4 (paperback edition)
ISBN 978-0-9862833-2-1 (ebook edition)

10 9 8 7 6 5 4 3 2 1

Publisher's Cataloging-In-Publication Data
(Prepared by The Donohue Group, Inc.)

Names: Naus, Joseph W., author. | Naus, Joseph W. Straight pepper diet.
Title: The Palsgraf revelation : a memoir / by Joseph W. Naus.
Other Titles: Memoir of love, addiction, recovery and practical spirituality
Description: Los Angeles, California : K.M. Publishing, [2020] | Sequel to Straight pepper diet.
Identifiers: ISBN 9780986283314 (paperback) | ISBN 9780986283321 (ebook)
Subjects: LCSH: Naus, Joseph W. | Lawyers--California--Biography. | Recovering addicts--California--Biography. | Spiritual life. | LCGFT: Autobiographies.
Classification: LCC KF373.N38 A3 2020 (print) | LCC KF373.N38 (ebook) | DDC 340.09209794--dc23
Library of Congress Control Number: 2020900162

AUTHOR'S NOTES:

12-STEP ANONYMITY. I respect the tradition of personal anonymity at the level of press, radio, and film, which is the principle of all 12-step recovery programs that are based on the original 12-step program, and thus I have not identified myself or anyone else as a member of any specific 12-step program. And while I understand that inferences can be drawn, none are intended. **SPONSOR/SPONSEE & 12-STEP MEETING ANONYMITY.** I believe the 12-step sponsor/sponsee relationship is sacrosanct and confidential. Therefore, not only have I changed the names of sponsees and sponsors in this book, but I have either received permission to recite certain facts regarding my interactions with these individuals or have altered the non-essential details in such a way that the essence of the scene is retained but the facts have been rearranged or otherwise altered to protect sponsor/sponsee anonymity. I have made similar amendments to protect the confidentiality and anonymity of 12-Step meeting participants. **QUOTATIONS.** With the exception of the quotations from court hearings, which are taken verbatim from court reporter transcripts, and in the tradition of the vast majority of American published memoirist, quotations are intended to indicate dialogue and not verbatim statements of myself or others. My intention is not to recite exactly what was said but what was conveyed and the essence of how it was conveyed. In doing so, I referenced my memory, my extensive journals, and I interviewed some of the people involved to corroborate certain events and details.

PUBLISHER'S NOTE:

The actual names of all non-public and some public individuals have been replaced to protect their privacy. Further, in light of the history of memoirs, particularly in this genre of memoir, the publisher feels that it is important to note that this is a true memoir, only subject to limited amendments to protect identities as indicated in the author's notes above. While we understand that perceptions of people, places and things are subjective, facts are still facts. The publisher has verified the truth of the basic facts of this text, by for instance, examination of certain government documents, employment documents, interviews of witnesses, social-media cites, photographs and historical references.

Dedications

Mom
(1953-2016)

To those who attempt to take the next right indicated step and to those who help them do so.

To all the addicts in my phone who can no longer answer my calls. I'm so sorry you aren't here anymore. I wish we could go to one more meeting together, have one more coffee.

We have no might against this great army, but our eyes are upon thee.

—KING JEHOSHAPHAT, 847 B.C.

PART I

The Body (Effect)

ONE

A perfectly neutral female voice commands me, "Enter your seven-digit code and press the pound key." I follow her instructions, pressing each button with breathless caution, as if clipping the wires of a time bomb.

"C'mon, c'mon, c'mon," I plead aloud, "not today, baby."

There's a long pause as if the recorded woman is contemplating her decision. I imagine she's twisting her face up in deep thought. After an excruciatingly long silence, a man's stern recorded voice reveals my fate, "Minnesota Vikings, I repeat, Minnesota Vikings."

"Ah fuck."

Yesterday, Oakland Raiders, today, Minnesota Vikings. That's the way it goes. The Probation Department's random phone-line drug testing system has chosen the Vikings group of probationers to test today. I close my eyes, take a deep breath, hold it, and let out a long sigh. Man, I had solid plans today. I was going to re-re-watch the entirety of Season One of *The Office*, breaking between each episode for cigarettes and coffee.

I hate Santa Monica. It's where it all went terribly wrong for me. I hate driving to Santa Monica, too. It's only 15 miles away, but it can take a couple hours to get there. It usually doesn't, but I can't be late, so I usually end up arriving an hour early. When I moved out of Keri's place on the Westside of Los Angeles, bordering Santa Monica, to Echo Park on the Eastside of Los Angeles, I begged Maya, my probation officer, not to transfer my case to the downtown Los Angeles Probation Office.

Maya told me she doesn't think I should be on formal probation and she treats me more like a colleague than a criminal. I'm on three probation tracks simultaneously—sex offender, drug/alcohol, and violent offender—so she could have me jumping through hoops like a circus dog, but she only makes me do the things she can't avoid. She even fudges the weekly home visits. But she can't get around the drug and alcohol testing. Judge Von Silkman was unequivocal at my sentencing hearing. "For the next five years you are going to five AA meetings a week, and you will be tested, and if there is even a hint that you are drinking again, you are going to prison."

Prison. Nope, not me. If I decide to drink again, I'm buying a handgun with my bottle of Jack Daniels so I can blow my head off when I hear that knock on the door. "Knock, knock. LAPD, Open Up!" Ain't happening. I've got my cigarettes and I've got my coffee. Those'll do just fine. I don't really think about drinking anymore. Instead I think about that quick trip to the bottom of the Grand Canyon. Suicide. It's like a back-up parachute, but if I pull the chord on it, it ejects a pair of scissors so I can cut the strings. Why would anyone do that? Maybe because they are descending upon an alligator swamp and they'd prefer to die from the fall than from being eaten, maybe that's why.

I'm on the 10 Freeway, halfway there. Downtown Los Angeles is miniaturized in my rearview mirror. I've got the radio on just loud enough to drown out any unwanted engine noise, but not enough to drown out the noise in my head.

Santa Monica is breezy and sunny, below a flame blue sky, as it was when I moved here four years ago, as it was when I cruised through here on my way to Pepperdine Law in Malibu in the summer of 1994. Across the street from my destination is an ultra-modern building that houses one of the world's most prestigious neoliberal think tanks. Young, trim, smart people, men with better-than-typical khakis, and women with black rayon palazzo pants and cream silk blouses walk briskly, shoulders squared, backs straight, in and out of the think tank's custom glass doors.

I join dozens of others in the snaking security line to enter the Los Angeles County government building that houses several courtrooms and the Probation Department. As I get closer to the entry, my anxiety rises to a steady hum just below my skin. I have the same thought I had the last time I was here to see my probation officer, and each time before that. Am I going to get arrested going through security for possessing contraband? Did I leave one of those knife-like envelope openers I don't even own in my pocket or that money clip with the tiny pocket knife Grandpa gave me that I haven't seen in years? Or maybe someone slipped a tiny baggy of crystal meth into my pocket?

I place my papers, wallet, cell phone, keys, and sunglasses into a blue rubber basket and set it on the conveyor belt. This will go smoothly. I have nothing to hide. I watch my stuff move down the conveyor belt. It stops under the x-ray, it's seen on the monitor for what it is—nothing—and then the conveyor belt jerks my stuff forward. I walk under the metal detector arch. I wait for the beep, but there is no sound. I smile at the security guard carefully.

I walk down a long hallway past several women sitting on benches tucked away in little alcoves, past the domestic violence service window, and through double doors into a large waiting room. I sign in and sit down. The fluorescent lights are oppressively bright. There is an outdoor smoking area through a sliding glass door. Through the glass, I observe a uniformed bailiff conversing with a detective. The detective wears a chrome revolver holstered below his armpit and stands quartered to me. He speaks so demonstratively that his cigarette bounces, leaving little trails of smoke behind each intonation. I imagine the bailiff saying to the detective, "Really, you beat him to death with the butt of your pistol, and you weren't even sure he stole the packet of ramen noodles?"

A couple walks in. They are tatted and slinky in an American Apparel kind of way. He's the criminal. She's here because he's here. She sits several chairs to my right and he saunters up to the counter. He stands and rocks back and forth, hands forcefully stuffed into his ultra-tight jeans. He occasionally glances back at her, apologizing with his face. A probation officer bursts through the door.

"Hands up!" the officer orders.

"What's up?" the young probationer says.

The probation officer doesn't respond. He grabs his charge's wide boney shoulders and whips him around, presses him to the wall, and kicks each foot out wide. He whips cuffs out from a leather holster attached to his belt at the small of his back and slaps them on the probationer's wrists. It's all one big, bad, pro move.

"You tested dirty again. Opioids."

The officer holds the boy out toward his girlfriend. She begins to cry and then shouts.

"You fucking asshole! You fucking fuck. I came here with you—"

Despite being handcuffed, the boy lurches forward as if he's going to embrace her, but the officer turns him away and marches him back toward the door into the inner probation office. The boy cranes his neck and yells to her. "I didn't, baby. I didn't!"

The girlfriend marches out of the room. Her tear-diluted mascara and eyeliner bring a raccoon to mind. The waiting room is now silent and empty.

I've got nowhere to be, I just don't want to be here. These notoriously overburdened probation officers, they press one wrong button on their county-issued laptops and we probationers, we the presumed guilty, return to jail.

Officer Maya steps into the room. I hope she doesn't have handcuffs. Maybe a false-positive drug test came through and the boy and I are both victims.

"Quickly, Joseph," Maya says. "Let's get this done and get you out of here." She beckons me to follow.

I hand her my court cards—little green index cards indicating which AA meetings I've been to, the date, and a signature from each meeting's secretary. Maya slaps them down on the copy machine, prints them out and then leads me through a maze of cubicles to hers, back by the window facing the people waiting in the security line to enter the building.

"Ok, you are testing today, right?" Maya asks.

"Yep."

"You got your most recent registration for me?"

"Yep. Here you go," I say, handing them over.

She examines my sex offender registration papers.

"Hey look, you even got my name right," she says, and keeps scanning. "No job yet?"

"Uh, yeah, not yet," I report.

"Restitution?" Maya inquires.

"I paid it a long time ago."

"Oh yeah," she says, apparently recalling.

Officer Maya is a pretty, light-skinned black woman around my age. She's got two kids, both young teens. She must be a single mom. She wears no wedding band, and the photos of her and her kids are sans partner.

A head of blonde hair pops over the grey cubicle wall, followed by a woman's bulging eyes.

"Maya, you want to go to Third Street for lunch?" she asks, then sees me. "Oh, sorry, didn't know you were working."

"I'm almost done," Maya replies and taps away into her computer keyboard. "You gotta start looking for work, Joseph. And I don't know how long my supervisor is going to let me keep you. But today, just test and I'll see you next week."

"Thank you," I say, and smile at her. She smiles back in a way she wouldn't if she thought anyone could see us. It's nothing much, just a little kindness. I follow her back out to the waiting room. She asks a male probation officer to test me since she can't. He gives Maya a mild ration of grief but agrees, and I follow him out to the waiting room bathroom and smile a goodbye to Maya. She stands next to her blonde friend and responds to me formally, "Goodbye Mr. Naus. Remember, I'll need employment progress next week."

I stand at the urinal trying to pee into a pill-bottle-sized container without touching its edge with the head of my penis. The man stands over me. He's not casual about it. He stares at my cock, completely asexually, I presume to thwart the possibility of me cheating on this pee test. I stall out.

The probation officer sighs dramatically and says, "We doin' this or not?"

"I got it. I got it," I reply.

I close my eyes and imagine a wooded mountain stream, flowing steadily. After a few beats, urine begins to flow. I feel the plastic container heat up from my pee. I cap the sample, initial the sticker that seals the cap, and sign a form. I thank the man and hurry out of the building.

As I alight into the God-kissed meteorological perfection that is Santa Monica, I mumble a prayer, "Thank you, God," acknowledging my gratitude for completing such an unpleasant task without incident. I jump into my car, pull onto the street and am immediately sandwiched between two shiny Santa Monica Police cars. My anxiety returns. It says: Cops to Jail to Prison to Death. Cops to Jail to Prison to Death. I strangle my steering wheel, grit my teeth, and breathe deeply through my nose, until a couple blocks later and I'm loosed from the cop cars and back on the freeway. Relieved again, I crawl along the jammed 10 Freeway, one tire rotation at a time.

"Jesus fuck!" I say to myself. It has become my custom to think aloud in my car. "It's a design for living that works in rough going. Rough going? Who talks like that? An alcoholic stock analyst in the 1930s with a penchant for womanizing, cigarettes, and eventually, hallucinogenics.

Okay, okay. Don't kill the messenger. I'm the messenger now. Just call your sponsor and go to a meeting. Just call your sponsor and go to a meeting, Joseph."

I call my sponsor and he answers the phone, "Vinny, here."

"I'm going a little crazy here, Vinny," I say as if trying to prove my statement.

"Okay, okay. Take it easy, Joseph. I feel you man, but do you got a roof over your head?" he asks.

"Yeah," I answer.

"A little money in the bank?"

"Just a little, but yeah," I say.

"Food in the fridge?" Vinny asks.

"Yes," I admit.

I can hear office noise in the background. Vinny works at a giant downtown civil litigation firm.

"Then you're alright, today. Just do today. Right?"

"I guess, man. I don't feel alright."

"Jesus, Joseph. You made it through prison. This is cake. But you go home, read pages 86 and 87. Pray, meditate, go to a meeting. Take some steps to get a job. That's all you can do. You made it this far. Love you man, but I gotta go."

Vinny hangs up. I keep my eye on the car bumper in front of me. I'm traveling 10 m.p.h.

Vinny is right. I'm okay. Read the Big Book, pray, meditate, go to a meeting. Take some action to get a job. It's all I can do. I know the routine. I've been doing this, under great duress, for over two years now. "Lack of power," the Big Book says, "that was our dilemma." Was. It was my dilemma, but now I don't want to drink, and I sure as hell don't feel like going to a prostitute or massage parlor. Actually, the idea of relapsing terrifies me.

But what am I going to do? What do I want to do? How am I going to make a living?

No good comes of these questions. I'm not ready to answer them. I've got some time. I've got a few bucks in the bank from Yi & Naus, my law firm that existed what seems like a long, long time ago.

I turn up the radio as loud as I can stand it, to drown me out.

TWO

"No, I've never played golf," I responded to Tito. "I only play real sports."

He laughed at me, the way one laughs at a precocious young adult that's just finished reading a shoddy summary of Keynesian economic theory and now confidently explains the remedies to all socio-economic ills and to drive home his brilliance, starts every other sentence with "obviously." I knew this, because I had just graduated from the "obviously" phase, thanks to a carefully placed expression from Tito—a gentle, effective, wordless, "Is that so?" that made me rethink my use of the word, "obviously" and more generally, my overconfidence, particularly in the presence of accomplished lawyers and judges, decades my senior.

Despite my response, Tito invited me to play golf at Arrowhead Country Club, where he and his family had been members for many years. Tito was the first and only Mexican-American member. I knew this because Gary, Tito's youngest son, told me so, one of the many times I'd been assigned to drive him somewhere. Gary referred to Arrowhead Country Club as, "a bunch of fucking elitist pigs." I accepted Tito's invitation, despite having never held a golf club before. It dawned on me later, while summarizing the rambling eight volumes of deposition testimony of an orthopedic surgeon who clearly understood he was being paid $700 per hour that I'd better figure out how to play golf before I showed up at Arrowhead.

How hard can it be? I'm an accomplished kickboxer, a solid tennis player, an adequate basketball forward and an arguably competent soccer fullback. Fat old men play golf. I can run a six-minute mile, bench press my weight eight times and squat twice my weight. Of course I'm going to be good at golf. Why wouldn't I be?

My mouth held the word "Wow," as I stood in the entryway gawking at this gigantic golf store. I worked at a sporting goods store for four years prior to working for Tito and I thought we sold it all, but golf equipment never even crossed my mind. Was there even a golf course in Moreno Valley? There were racks of brightly colored cotton polo shirts and shelves of glowing white sleeves of golf balls, dozens of different brands, displays of chrome shafted irons and giant-headed metal woods with rubber grips. Putters leaned in racks around a tiny faux putting green with mini flags stuck in holes. And the shoes! Someone took the world's ugliest dress shoes and added vicious little metal spikes to their soles. Why on earth would golfers need metal spikes when soccer players and football players need only plastic?

"Can I help you?" asked a tall doughy yet skinny young man in a burgundy polo with a Roger Dunn logo on it that matched the sign on the front of the store. His name was Brad, and he was clearly one of *them*, those kids who were too weak to play other sports in high school.

"Yes," I responded. "Why do these shoes have metal spikes that look like they could kill someone? I mean, overkill, right? Two hundred-pound running backs turning on a dime only use rubber cleats."

"I don't know, man," said Brad, with an I-just-work-here tone. "Uh, do you like, want to buy some?"

"Do I need to?" I responded.

"I guess," he said. "I mean everyone that plays golf wears golf spikes."

After several trips back and forth to the stockroom, Brad finally suggested he just grab any size thirteen he could find. It turned out there was only one pair, a hideously preppy, dark brown and light tan, suede saddle shoe, made by a company called FootJoy. I tried them on. They were not particularly comfortable. He asked how they felt, and I responded with a quip about the irony of the brand's name. Brad looked at me blankly.

"So, do you, uh, want them?" he asked indifferently.

He was clearly not being paid commission.

"I uh, well, I guess so," I responded. My lack of choice and need for golf shoes had united Brad and me in indifference.

Next, Brad led me to the *new* golf club iron sets, and after I looked at the price tags and let out an involuntary gasp, he showed me the *used* iron sets. Seeing that, like him, I was taller than average, he showed me a set of used Taylor Made-brand irons that had extended shafts. He explained that I'd need extended shaft irons because I was tall. Brad mumbled something about protecting my lower back, "lie angles" and, I think, "elective loft." As with my joyless FootJoy shoes, I had a choice of one or none.

At least I had a choice of golf balls. Brad came out of his shell a little, and while chuckling, he recommended I buy the most inexpensive balls because I'd be losing most of them anyway. Brad said something about me being a beginner and thus spin and compression were not an issue. I dismissed this as the blathering of the sadly unathletic but chose his recommendation of Top Flight brand balls anyway, since they were cheap and I liked the name.

Brad pulled air in through his teeth and nodded, as if readying himself to tell me something he knew I didn't want to hear. "You're probably going to need more than three balls."

"You sure?" I asked. "I don't think I've ever lost a single basketball. You think I'm going to lose more than three of these?"

"Who sold you those?" my golf instructor Chuck asked rhetorically. He pulled my three-iron from the Ping brand golf bag Tito gave me, twirled the club by its neck, looking at the head from all angles. "This'd be good for spreading butter," he said, laughing, and then walked off, leaving me puzzled.

Chuck wore a white visor that read, "Lynx," which I presumed was a golf brand, and he strutted as if we were at Augusta National and not a shitty muni-course in San Bernardino. I wanted to ask him what exactly he meant by his butter comment, but Chuck left to attend to a student wearing a short white tennis skirt and a terrifically taut white polo that demanded attention.

After a few minutes, Chuck stood in front of us, the dozen-or-so students in his "Beginner's Golf Group Swing Lesson—Learn and Have Fun!" class and welcomed us insincerely.

"Turn to the person to your left and shake their hand," Chuck instructed.

I was the only man and there was no one on my left, so I had no hand to shake. I glanced at Chuck, presuming he'd come over and shake my hand. Instead, he had everyone turn in the opposite direction, freeing him up to behand the woman in white, and giving me a turn to shake someone's hand.

"Next," Chuck instructed, "one of you take your seven-iron—that's the iron with the seven on it—and point the grip at your partner as if it's your hand."

Chuck then demonstrated for us how the right hand holds the club. "In the fingers, not in the palm," he said, walking up and down the line. Then he folded his left hand onto the club. Chuck's hands looked like a big wad of fingers around a black goose neck.

I held my seven-iron, pretty much as Chuck instructed. He went down the line and readjusted nearly everyone's grip, mine last. He completely rearranged my hands and fingers. It felt like I had two left hands, and they were wrestling. As soon as he returned to the woman in white, I reattached my hands to my club, and held it like a baseball bat. I couldn't possibly hit a ball holding the club as Chuck had instructed.

Chuck explained the address position with great detail. It was mostly all the stuff I'd learned in basketball, boxing and tennis, what is commonly referred to as an "athletic position." Twenty minutes later, after an exhausting and incomprehensible review of the multiple stages of the golf swing, we were finally given some old beat-up range balls to hit. These were not the candy white balls displayed in packs of three like jewels at Roger Dunn's Golf Shop.

I dragged a golf ball out from a green plastic bucket and perched it on a patch of grass. I drew my Taylor Made-brand three-iron. I took a smooth practice swing. I waggled myself into the perfect athletic position. Then I swung as hard as I could. *Whoosh.* I missed the ball completely but did manage to detonate a small dirt bomb. My ball sat there unblinking, mocking me. I looked to see if anyone had seen what I'd done. Thankfully, they were all preoccupied with their own bad swings. I set out for my revenge. I swung again, ripping across the air with all my might, hitting several inches behind the ball. The ball dribbled forward, maybe five yards. The older lady next to me was calmly swinging her nine-iron and pretending not to notice the turf removal program I'd instituted next door. Once more. This time I hit the ball with the part of my club that connects the club head to the shaft. A nasty vibration shot up through my arms and the ball skidded dead right, ripping through the grass.

"Nice shank," Chuck quipped from behind me.

And so it went, over and over. There were swings where I completely missed the ball—others where I dug holes behind the ball, under the ball, right of the ball. I hit balls off the hosel and off the toe, again and again.

"Jacob, right?" Chuck asked me, but continued without pause, "Jacob, why don't you bench that three-iron and pull out your pitching wedge."

He stood there watching as I perused my golf bag, trying to figure out what club he was referring to.

"It's the one with PW stamped on it," Chuck advised.

I pulled it out.

"May I?" he inquired.

I handed it to him. He silently showed me the grip again. I nodded impatiently. He waggled into place as if there existed a perfect spot just for him. He raised the club back above his shoulders and then swung back down through the ball in one effortless, elegant motion. It sounded like a hammer crushing an egg. The ball took off like a jet and landed like a helicopter 30 yards past the 100-yard sign. Awestruck, I wondered if I'd ever seen a more elegant athletic movement than Chuck's golf swing.

"You see? It's about technique, not muscle," Chuck said and handed me back my pitching wedge.

THREE

It's just before 6 a.m. and still dark out. I sit in my parked car, facing the Los Angeles Police Department's Skid Row station. A one-armed black man limps by on the sidewalk, gesturing violently, and yelling at someone only he can see. Another man lies akimbo atop a dirty blue tarp on the station's lamp-lit grassless lawn. I'm still tightly gripping my steering wheel. My car beeps at me to remove my key from the ignition.

"C'mon, just do it," I plead to myself.

But I can't move, not yet. I feel as if gravity is focusing all its attention on me, trying to pull me down into hell. All the pain, all the fear, it's back. It grows from my chest. For the last couple weeks, as this day approached, the fear has grown exponentially, and now it's taken over. It's in my blood. My guts twist. My head pounds. I sweat toxic droplets. I want to swallow my eyes back into my head so I don't have to see this. My skin tingles with anxiety. I just wish someone would come save me. Tell me this isn't real. Please God, please.

Today is my birthday.

I walk down a short hallway into a shabby lobby. There are two cops in dark blue uniforms sitting on stools behind a long built-in desk that seals them off from the rest of the room like bartenders at a rough bar. There is a swinging half-door on one end, behind which a cop stands looking at a clipboard. Men are lined up on a floor-mounted bench with their backs against the wall. They are all obviously homeless.

"Can I help you, sir?" the desk sergeant asks me.

"I'm a PC 290 registrant," I reply.

He looks me up and down. His forehead creases, as if confused. "Alright," he says. "Sign in and Officer Romero will be right with you."

I do as I'm told and find a spot near the men at the end of the bench, but then the stench of dried piss and feces is so strong that I have to move or I'll vomit. I find a place to lean against the wall several feet away between a broken payphone and the out-of-service bathroom. Officer Romero quickly processes one man after another. As I learned from my probation officer, homeless sex offenders have to register every 30 days. So it makes perfect sense that this police station, in the middle of the largest skid row in the United States, is packed, even before sunrise. I'm the apparent anomaly, as usual.

The desk sergeant deals with other homeless men who come in and out of the station, each with varying levels of insanity and all of them complaining of thefts and assaults. He speaks to them loudly as if they don't understand English and makes inquiries that ensure he'll be doing no paperwork: "Do you have a written inventory of all the items that you claim were stolen? Do you have a written statement from any witnesses?"

I hear my name. "Joseph Naus," Officer Romero announces.

"Yes, Officer," I say. I stand and slowly move toward him, moving carefully. I feel as if any wrong move may cause me to have some type of emotional outburst—tears or screams.

"You are here for your annual registration?" he asks.

"Yes sir."

I hand him my driver's license and then go lean against the wall. I repeat the Serenity Prayer in my head over and over at a frantic pace, but it makes me feel worse. I'm whistling in the dark, and I know it. Officer Romero said "annual" registration. That's right, Joseph. It's annual, and it's forever, as in for the rest of my life. Every year, forever, no matter what.

Officer Romero is gone much longer than he was with all the other registrants he's handled since I've been here. Joey D. Ramirez and

Alexander Jones both scribbled their names on the list after I did and they are both long gone. But he's still back there, with my California driver's license, the one with the photo of me with my neck, linebacker-thick, from lifting weights in preparation for prison.

I gaze across the lobby at a plastic-framed poster for the 1996 Los Angeles Marathon, sponsored by Acura. In 1996, I was in my third year at Pepperdine Law School. I knew something was wrong with me. I knew I was different because if people felt like I did, suicides would be as common as jaywalking. I thought it—whatever it was—would end once I had money and a career, once I was finally safe. I didn't know I was a burgeoning addict. And I sure as hell never imagined I'd end up here.

I'm still waiting for Officer Romero. It's been too long. Something is wrong.

I feel the dread more than usual. The dread is the foundation of my fear. It's the answer to the questions, "Is this really happening to me?" and "Am I really going to be punished for the rest of my life?" But the fear is what's making my teeth chatter. It's on the surface. It's the knowledge that I could get snatched up like a kidnapping victim at any moment. I've seen it happen. I saw it happen at rehab. I just saw it at Probation just the other day. The cops can do whatever they want. They might have a reason, or they might not. I don't have any Constitutional rights. I'm not a real citizen anymore. I'm a felon of the worst kind. These cops could slap handcuffs on me and drop me in general population at Twin Towers Jail because they didn't like the taste of their breakfast burrito—or because they did.

I close my eyes and repeat the Serenity Prayer, but again, it doesn't work. Instead, I can hear Steven shrieking. He was just a child. The sheriffs at Twin Towers did nothing to protect him. And I remember the sound of jaw meeting concrete when a muscle-bound sheriff hand-cuffed a man, picked him up by his arms and dropped him on his face. Then there were guards at Chino prison, casually watching a man bleed to death right in front of me. But more than the violence, it's their eyes that haunt me. Not all, but many. The police officers, sheriffs and prison guards didn't hate us for the crimes we'd committed. Hate, I could understand. Rather, they excised us from their definition of human. We had become something far less.

I should leave. I should leave right now. I'm not in custody yet. They'll arrest me now and make something up later. They'll say I didn't register on time or that I didn't register the right way. Failing to register as a sex offender is a felony. I'm a two-strike felon. They could send me to prison for the rest of my life. I may never be free again.

I can smell my acrid stress sweat. I breathe in short little bursts. I close my eyes again and tamp my breathing. Take it easy, Joseph. C'mon, man.

I feel a presence. I open my eyes. A cop is standing in front of me.

"Here you go, Dwight. See you in a month," the female cop says, handing registration papers to Dwight, who's standing next to me. Dwight mumbles, "Okay boss" and limps away, leaning heavily on his four-pronged cane.

That's it. I'm leaving. I can't just stay here and wait for Officer Romero to arrest me. But I can't seem to move. The desk sergeant holds a telephone receiver a couple inches away from his ear to let his fellow desk cop listen in. "No, sir, you can't file a vehicle theft report if you don't own the car... I understand, I understand... Have her file the report..."

Officer Romero appears from the back and stands next to the female officer, who is crossing off names on a clipboard. Officer Romero eyes me as he speaks into her ear. She looks at me and conspiratorially turns to him and nods.

"Mr. Naus," Officer Romero says and walks toward me.

Keep cool. Keep cool. Answer his questions directly. Don't show fear. You've done nothing wrong.

"Yes," I say, deciding to drop the "sir." No need to be overly submissive. That's what all the criminals do. I'm not a criminal.

"Do you own a car?"

"Yes."

"Is it here?"

"Yes," I intone directly, with just a pinch of defiance. "It's parked right outside."

He gestures for me to follow him to my car. I do so. It's a red 1998 Honda Accord I recently bought for $6,200 cash with some of the money I had left from my law practice. The salesman told me it was owned by a little old lady from Redlands, and he might have been telling the truth. I open the car for Officer Romero. He opens the glove box and then shuts it without examining it. I presume he was looking for a handgun.

"When did you buy the car?" he asks.

"About a month ago," I say.

I follow him back in. He asks me what I do for a living. I tell him the truth: Nothing. I do nothing.

Officer Romero hands me my registration form and tells me to check the information for accuracy. Listed are numbers that were assigned to me upon my becoming a permanent enemy of the United States of America.

CII—Criminal Investigations and Identifications Number

FCN—Department of Justice File Control Number

CDC—California Department of Corrections Number

FBI—Federal Bureau of Investigations Number

OACN—Originating Agency Case Number

The rest is familiar: Name—Joseph W. Naus; Social Security; Date of Birth—1971; Height—6'4"; Weight—220; Eyes—Blue; Tattoos—None; Employer—None; Vehicle—1998 Honda Accord, Red, VIN 1HGD560SA35294, CA Plate 3JKL568; Address—504 Thumber Lane, Los Angeles, CA.

"It's all correct," I tell Officer Romero, "except my weight. I'm 200 now. Also, you inverted my address. It's 405 Thumber Lane, not 504."

His eye-roll and exaggerated sigh reveal that Officer Romero is not accustomed to registrants checking his work. He compares my original registration to the new one he's prepared, I presume to confirm that I erred on the original form, but then realizes he made the mistake. He mumble-groans and disappears again.

A new batch of homeless sex offender registrants has refilled the bench. They are just like the old batch.

I sit on the bench, wait and study the 1996 Los Angeles Marathon, sponsored by Acura, poster, and try not to think.

Officer Romero reappears. His eyes are indifferent. He doesn't have the dehumanizing eyes, not yet, at least. And I think if he was going to arrest me, he'd have done so by now.

"Okay, let's get your photo and fingerprints and get you out of here," Officer Romero says.

I'm greatly relieved to hear him say that he wants to get me out of here. I'm in complete agreement, and while my dread is fully present, the terror that I might be snatched away at any moment has mostly subsided. I can almost breathe again.

He directs me to stand for my portrait while he tinkers with a digital camera.

Should I smile? Should I play it straight? Teeth or no teeth? Frown? If I smile, it'll look smug. Or will it say, "I didn't do it, but I'm dealing with it?" If I frown, it definitely says, "I got caught. I'm depressed, because I did it, and I got caught." Teeth are a sign of aggression. Wrinkles outside the eyes reveal an authentic smile. This photo will be accessible to anyone with an internet connection. Billions of people will have access to this photo. I've got to nail this.

"Okay," Officer Romero says, "got it." And he dismounts the digital camera from the tripod.

He didn't say "cheese" or anything. He took my portrait while I was thinking about how to pose. Damn! I've been denied the opportunity to strike the perfect balance between acceptance and innocence.

I expertly roll my right thumb across the ink pad, left to right, smoothly on the pad and then smoothly on the paper. I've done this so many times since my first arrest. It creates a perfect impression of my thumbprint in the little box on the bottom right corner of the registration form. I have a wishbone-shaped scar across my thumb, which makes the imprint instantly identifiable as mine. I opened a can of tennis balls before a high school tennis match and the edge of the lid sliced open my thumb. I left an uninterrupted trail of blood through the campus, from the tennis courts to the nurse's office.

Officer Romero lays the 290 registration form down on the counter and hands me a pen. I sign the front and initial the back in the requisite 19 spots. If I read each line of micro-font, I'd be here for another hour. Each paragraph is warning after warning:

You must register annually within five days of your date of birth, forever—Happy Birthday! You must register if you step foot in any school, anywhere, forever.

You must register any time you move, forever.

You must notify law enforcement of any new vehicles you own, forever.

You must stand in the public square of every town you enter and scream, "I'm a registered sex offender!" forever.

If you engage in sex, you must write "Registered Sex Offender" on your chest in black or blue medium point Sharpie, forever.

"You can read it later," Officer Romero barks, done with me.

I hand the form back to him. He disappears and then reappears seconds later with a copy of my completed sex registration form. He hands it to me with my driver's license. He calls out the next name on the list.

I trot to my car. I have to get out of here. I'm 35. If I live to 80, that means that at the very minimum, I'll be required to register as a sex offender 45 more times. I get in my car. Two cops in a patrol car are parked to my left, blocking my view as I back out onto the two-lane one-way street, with homeless people darting all over like barrels in *Donkey Kong*. Meanwhile, the racing thoughts are gathering in my brain. I crank up the radio. It's a commercial for car insurance. What am I doing? I won't be able to hear anything. I'll back into traffic, cause an accident, and kill a homeless person. Then I'll definitely go to jail.

I turn off the radio. I take a deep breath. Focus. I look in my mirrors and slowly back out. I see the dirty chrome of a shopping cart in my driver's side mirror, and I depress my brake firmly. A crazy-eyed, filthy woman with street-imposed dreadlocks yells at me and waves her hands and lets go of the shopping cart, which is packed with junk and buoyed by garbage bags. Her cart follows the crowned slope of the street and settles softly against my bumper like a boat at dock. I wait. She continues to yell, not exactly at me. The cops look back and then the one in the passenger seat pops out of the patrol car and yells, "Move along!" She does. I back out and head down Sixth Street.

It's the walking dead down here. These people haven't fallen between the cracks, they've fallen off the face of the earth into a waterless toilet. There are so damn many men with limbs missing. Where are their limbs? A man squats, shitting on the edge of the sidewalk. A younger man passes. He wears dirty white leather Nikes. They lift off his heels like flip-flops, because his shoelaces are missing, probably because he's just gotten out of jail. He pinches his nose demonstratively with one hand and holds up his beltless, baggy jeans with the other. The farther north I drive, the fewer dead men and women I see until, in the shadow of the federal court building, there are none left. Several gleaming white Homeland Security SUVs are parked in front of the green marbled skyscraper. It wasn't that long ago that I was inside it representing a real estate client in a bankruptcy hearing. I forget exactly why. I just remember the building being echoic and empty, the judge ready to pounce at my slightest procedural misstep.

I make it to Cesar Chavez Avenue. And there stands another reminder, Twin Towers Jail. In its brutish walls is enough reinforced concrete to blunt an atomic blast but not nearly enough to dampen the waves of the fear and pain of the souls inside. Most of the men I was with there are still incarcerated, either as sheriffs or inmates. Some of the inmates have been shipped to one of the 33 prisons in California and are now part of the brutal society of over 100,000 incarcerated men. Some of the guards have served their sentence as jailers and been promoted and now spend their working days feeding the pipeline with fresh bodies.

Cesar Chavez turns into Sunset at Figueroa. Further west, I pass Beaudry and now I'm in Echo Park. On the northwest corner is a Japanese church complex, including a 10-story high-rise. It's my favorite building in all of the Eastside. It's solid concrete and must've been built in the '70s. Each story has a balcony that wraps around the entire floor. I'm proudly reminded that I've long opined to yawning girlfriends that it's a shame that any high-rises are built without balconies. The building is boarded up, waiting to be revitalized. I theorized it was condemned because it wasn't earthquake retrofitted. If I were still a lawyer, I'd consider putting together a group of investors to buy it and turn it into condominiums.

I make it back to my tiny apartment. It's still early morning. I survived my annual sex offender registration, but it took all I had. I feel like the loser of a 10-round street fight. I just want to be alone, so I can sleep, smoke and drink coffee, watch *Scrubs* reruns and eat pints of ice cream—for a week. I sit on my couch and stare at my fresh sex offender registration form while my coffee maker gurgles and dribbles into its glass pot. There is so much information on this form, but there is no place to document my fear and desperation.

Happy birthday to me.

FOUR

Like a pup clumsily trying to keep up with a full-grown dog, Joseph followed the long-striding Manuel across Sunnymead Boulevard and into the alley behind the Safeway Market. They were going to meet up with Joey and his girlfriend, Julia at "the corner." The corner was a juvenile hang-out spot at the corner of a block wall that separated Safeway Market's property from the acres of dirt fields that bordered its rear and west sides. With the ease of a gymnast mounting a pommel horse, Manuel hopped over the wall from the Safeway side, behind the semi-truck loading docks, to the weeded field, an eight-foot drop. Joseph, not willing to make the leap, shimmied down so he hung over the wall, his shirt hiked up and his belly scraping the rough cinder block, and carefully dropped to his feet. A bunch of junk gathered at the corner of the wall—three stacked tread-bare car tires, several two-by-fours, a couple sheets of plywood, an old freezer—formed a half-shanty and served as a place to climb over the wall back to the Safeway side. There were empty beer bottles, stamped-out cigarette butts, and the wall was shoddily tagged with blue spray paint and primer, something far less than graffiti. Beyond the fields of hard taupe dirt and hip-high, hay-colored weeds, beyond temporary chain-link fences with windscreens, stood enormous construction sites with hundreds of tract homes in various states of unbuilt, as was the nature of the City of Moreno Valley in the early '80s.

"Fuckin' A, dude," Manuel said to Joey, as he and Joseph approached Joey and Julia.

Julia stood atop two wooden pallets. She was bent at the waist, the side of her face pressed into the back of her hands which pressed flat against the wall. Her dress was hiked above her hips and panties bunched at her knees. Joey stood below her with his face pressed up and under her butt. Joseph observed in shock that it looked as if Joey was making out with Julia's butt. Manuel moved in for a closer look as if it were the only thing to do, and Joseph stood frozen, considering how he could get back over the wall without Joey or Julia seeing him.

Like a mechanic sliding out from under a car, Joey emerged from under Julia's butt to greet Manuel. "What's up dude?" Joey said enthusiastically. "Who's this?" Joey said, pointing at Joseph with his chin. "He looks like he's still in junior high." Joey smirked at Joseph.

"Uh duh, that's because he *is* still in junior high," Manuel said sarcastically. "That's Joseph. He's alright."

Joseph smiled awkwardly at Joey and then at Julia, who was waiting for Joey to continue what he'd been doing. She returned Joseph's smile with a look of boredom and mild irritation. Joey looked at Joseph as if he was deciding whether to let him live. Joseph had never met Joey, but he'd heard a lot about him. He'd heard that Joey was going into his senior year at Moreno Valley High School and that he was a bona fide bad-ass dude. The kids of Alessandro Middle School, where Joseph attended, spoke of Joey in revered tones, like cowboys around a campfire passing down the legend of Jesse James. It was rumored that he'd done a stint in juvenile hall for beating up his basketball coach and that he'd had sex with a super-fine English teacher, not to mention the entire cheerleading squad.

"Dude," Manuel said to Joey. "Joseph's the one I told you about that might help us out."

Joey snickered, then said to Joseph, "Oh, hey, what's up dude?"

Joseph didn't answer and Joey didn't wait for him to. Joey went back to what he'd been doing before Joseph and Manuel had arrived.

After a few moments Manuel said "C'mon, dude" to Joseph as if there weren't two people having sex between them. "Let's go steal some Cokes from Safeway. We'll talk to Joey about you later."

With one bounding step, Manuel sprung off the stack of tires over the wall, practically vaulting Joey and Julia. He reminded Joseph of a praying mantis, his legs so long that if he sat on a couch, his knees would cover his ears. Joseph looked at Julia apologetically, twisting his face into a micro-gesture, as if to say, "Sorry to interrupt. Nice to meet you."

Joseph followed Manuel into Safeway, his body pulsing with adrenaline and his brain bubbling with what he'd just witnessed. He also thought of what it might be like to burgle a home with Joey and Manuel. Manuel said it was easy. He said they did it during the week when kids were at school and their parents were fifty miles away at work. He told Joseph he could make sixty bucks each time, and get whatever he wanted—a Walkman, Nintendo, Atari, even a rad BMX bike.

Joseph recalled the time he'd gone with Manuel to Manuel's home and met his foster parents. He'd hoped to recover the bike Manuel had "borrowed" from him. The meeting was so strange. They lived in a two-story house in a new housing tract. Manuel's parents had stood on the stairs waiving politely down with forced smiles on their faces, as if Manuel was their captor not the foster kid they took in two years earlier. Manuel was bigger than both of them. He was like a feral cat, but criminal and 200 pounds. Joseph suspected they were just waiting for Manuel to turn 18, so he would move out and leave them alone, and they could forget all about their altruistic foray into parenting.

"It's easy, dude. Just grab one, open it and walk out like you came in with it," Manuel instructed, as they cruised down the Safeway aisles. Manuel led Joseph down an aisle past dog and then cat food, to the back of the store where there were 6-packs of chilled soda. He was terrified. He thought of the time he was caught shoplifting from the Sav-A-Minit, 5 years ago, when he lived in Riverside and was in second grade. Manuel twisted a Coke from its 6-pack and walked down the toilet paper aisle. He boldly cracked open the can of Coke, took a swig and looked over at Joseph, seeing Joseph hadn't grabbed a Coke.

"You're such a little pussy," Manuel said, disgusted. "Go back and get a Coke."

He thought of Joey and Julia. "Pussy." It was an actual thing, a strange thing, not just a word his friends used in every sentence. It was an actual body part.

"I'm not thirsty," Joseph responded, wondering if he could get in trouble as an accomplice to Manuel's shoplifting. It reminded him of that dark office he'd sat in at the Sav-A-Minit with the two-way glass, waiting to see if he was going to juvenile hall.

"Don't be such a little faggot," Manuel said, standing outside of the Safeway. He gulped the remainder of his Coke, crushed the red aluminum can with his hand, dropped it to the asphalt and smashed it into a disc with his foot. It made a satisfying sound. A woman pushing a full cart of groceries with a small boy riding in the cart, his legs dangling, looked at Manuel, as if to say, "Young man, you pick that up right now!" Manuel ignored her, and Joseph picked up the can and smiled at the lady apologetically.

"Maybe we should just forget you helping us," Manuel said, baiting Joseph. "If you are too much of a pussy to steal a can of Coke—"

"I'm not a pussy," Joseph, said, almost sure of himself. "I just wasn't thirsty, and why risk getting caught stealing for a can of Coke? I'd rather make some real money so I can buy a new bike—you know, to replace the one I had."

Manuel stopped walking in the middle of the parking lot and turned to Joseph. "Look, dude, I'm sorry about your bike. I just meant to borrow it. I'll get you another one, or you can get one for yourself when we pick a house to do, okay?"

Joseph shook his head in mild agreement.

"Let's go see if Joey is done boning Julia," Manuel said.

Uh, I want to, but I've got to go home," Joseph lied. He never had to go home.

Joseph stepped back, fearing Manuel might punch him. But Manuel just looked at him, chuckled and sarcastically said, "Right, dude, go home," high-fived him, and walked off. Joseph felt as if he'd re-pinned a grenade. Being around Manuel scared Joseph, but excited him, too. Manuel acted as if he could kick anyone's ass and do anything he wanted.

Her name is Julia, Joseph thought. He mouthed her name: Julia.

Joseph saw his reflection in the window of the Schwinn shop, where his dad had bought him his first Takara BMX bike during the summer before first grade, the first time Marie and he had lived in Sunnymead, which later became the City of Moreno Valley. His dad had randomly showed up in an old truck, looking rugged and scary, but handsome too. He was blonde, with thick deeply tanned skin, and his eyes were so water-blue they didn't seem real. Joseph was reminded of the guy that played *Cool Hand Luke.* Joseph's dad wore a red-on-white can of Budweiser beer and a red and white pack of cigarettes the way men in old movies wore a hat and cane. Like Manuel, he was big and always on the verge of anger. It would take nothing for him to crush Joseph, but Joseph's dad's meanness was different than Manuel's. Where Manuel's was just plain viciousness, Joseph's dad's, although it was scary, seemed to come from frustration. Even when he was yelling at someone or something else, he was really mad at himself.

As the apartment came into view, Joseph recalled the day Joseph's mom's deadbeat boyfriend, Carlos, had returned nearly a year earlier. He recalled the sinking feeling he had when he heard the familiar hard, rapid knocking at the door. He knew before he knew. When Joseph had opened the door, he saw Carlos holding an empty plastic milk jug and an army-green duffel bag. Carlos didn't say hello or ask Joseph how he was. It was understood that they both wished the other didn't exist. Carlos had parked his car in the empty parking space, where the car Marie didn't own should have been. It was a far cry from the muscled-up Chevy

Nova he'd driven when Joseph had first met Carlos, the car he'd used to win Joseph over, for a week or two. He'd taken Joseph for a ride, racing down Second Street by the Alley. Marie had been happy, and that made Joseph happy, because Marie didn't smile much since the time before she'd met Carlos, since that time when Joseph came home to the Alley and had found police cars at their front door, shattered beer bottles, and Marie, her face swollen and her body wrapped in a blanket, when he'd been whisked away in a police cruiser without explanation. Marie, with a cautious smile on her face, had said it was okay for Carlos to take Joseph for a ride as long as they didn't go too far. Carlos had gunned the Nova's V-8 engine, pinning Joseph's head to the car's passenger seat.

The little car parked off to the side was befitting of Carlos's gimpy return: a sun-beaten, oxidized-red VW Rabbit, hood up and engine billowing steam.

"She's not home," Joseph recalled himself saying, hoping against hope that Carlos would turn around and go away forever.

Carlos had said something about needing to fill his water jug. Joseph wasn't able to muster the strength to tell Carlos that, no, he couldn't come inside. And when Marie came home an hour later, neither could she.

Not only did Carlos no longer have a cool car, or a car that ran, for that matter, he didn't have a job either. Now he made his living on what Marie referred to as SSI, which Joseph understood was free government money given to Carlos because he had grown up in a Catholic orphanage.

Despite Marie's protest, Joseph had immediately called Grandpa and told him that Carlos was back. It was only fair. Grandpa had paid for Joseph and Marie to move for the very purpose of getting away from Carlos and the Alley. Grandpa didn't comment to Joseph, just asked how Joseph was doing, to which Joseph, replied, "fine" as always, and then Grandpa asked to speak to Marie. Joseph handed the phone to his mom, went to his room, and pressed his ear against the door and listened to one side of the phone call. Marie had said: "We can't make it on our own." "He's changed." "He apologized." "He's got a steady income." and the words, "rent" and "bills" were repeated several times each. The last thing he recalled her saying was, "Don't worry Dad, it'll be different this time."

After Marie was done talking on the phone with Grandpa, she gave the phone back to Joseph. Grandpa said he'd be picking him up on Friday and taking him to Oceanside for a week before the end of summer and the beginning of eighth grade. Joseph was elated. He'd have to deal with Grandma's insanity, but they'd be going out to eat at Anita's Mexican food restaurant. Grandpa would make pancakes some mornings and others they'd have Grape Nuts cereal, and, for lunch, Grandpa would make cheese sandwiches. Even when Grandma was yelling and cussing, there was always food. And he and Grandpa would go swimming in the ocean just before it got dark.

Joseph jimmied his key into the lock of the apartment. He could hear the television and knew Carlos was on the couch within a couple feet of the door. He walked into the apartment, his mind swirling with thoughts of Julia and the things he could buy if he started burglarizing houses with Joey and Manuel.

"Quiet, your mom's still asleep," Carlos said, without looking away from the television.

Joseph didn't acknowledge Carlos. It was nearly two o'clock. He just went in his room, ducking through the doorway. The apartment was a lightless cave, perfect for Marie and Carlos. It was a two-bedroom apartment and yet it was too small to be a one-bedroom apartment. Each room was the size of a jail cell, like the ones in Alcatraz Joseph had seen on television.

He sat on his bed, thinking of how much he despised Carlos. All he did was sit on the couch and tinker with his stupid stereo. It was the only thing Carlos owned or cared about besides for his guns. Since he almost shot his toe off a week ago, lying on the bed aiming through the backdoor at a squirrel and accidentally pulling the trigger, Carlos had been spending less time with his guns and more with his stereo. He had a Techniques-brand record player and matching Techniques components, all stacked up in a glass-faced console. The speakers were nearly as tall as Carlos and looked ridiculously out of proportion in the low-ceilinged, tiny apartment. Carlos's console stack included a Laser Disc player that played movies. The weird thing was that Carlos didn't like movies or music. He only owned one album, Michael Jackson's *Off The Wall*, and one movie, *Beastmaster*. Joseph was into heavy metal music and admitting to liking Michael Jackson would have been a worse offense than admitting to liking Wham! or Frankie Goes to Hollywood, but he secretly danced in his bedroom when Carlos played Michael Jackson's *Rock With You*. *Beastmaster*, on the other hand, Joseph openly admitted, was one of the best movies ever made, second only to *Star Wars*.

As he sat on his bed, leaning on the wall with his head between a poster of Bruce Lee in a yellow jumpsuit and another of Farrah Fawcett in a red bikini, he fantasized about kicking Carlos's ass. Joseph stood up and looked in the flimsy full-length mirror that leaned against the wall, its concave shape distorting him so he looked thicker. He imagined himself as Bruce Lee. He thought of bursting through his bedroom door and facing Carlos.

"It's time for you to pack your things and leave, Carlos! You've been here long enough."

Joseph imitated Bruce Lee, watching his distorted reflection in the mirror. With his right hand, he thumbed his nose, held out his hand, and then beckoned Carlos to fight with an inward wave of his four right fingers.

"You," Joseph whispered dramatically, "are a coward. You cannot defeat me. Leave now or face my fists of fury!"

Joseph tightened his arm into an "L" and made a tight fist, his arm vibrating with mock confidence and power. He shifted into a loose boxing stance, his hands hanging off his shoulders like hooks off a fishing line. He shuffled back and forth, imitating Bruce Lee imitating Muhammad Ali, but with abbreviated steps, so not to trip over all the books, plastic toys and dirty clothes that covered his bedroom floor. He stopped, stood still, and peered at his distorted reflection. He was embarrassed at what he saw. Sadness filled him. He saw a wimpy little boy fantasizing about doing something he knew he didn't have the courage to do. He saw a boy that had nothing. Unlike his school friends, he wasn't good at anything. He wasn't good at BMX like Erik. He didn't play the guitar like Rex. He couldn't run fast and play soccer like Andy. He wasn't popular with the girls like Scott or popular with everyone like Kevin. He wasn't even that good at school anymore.

Joseph lay down on his bed and looked up to the water-stained popcorn ceiling. He thought that he had to do something or things would stay the same. He'd go to Oceanside with Grandpa and have fun. Then he'd come home, and he'd feel that let down he always felt when returning home from Grandpa's or Aunt Suzie and Uncle Billy's. He'd see the permanent apology in his mom's big brown eyes, as if she was saying, "I'm sorry you have to come back here." He always felt like she wanted him to assure her that he hadn't told Grandpa or Aunt Suzie how bad things were at home. But she knew better. She knew it was against their only family tradition. They never asked Joseph anything other than, "How's your mom?" and he always said the same thing, "She's fine." Joseph knew not to talk about certain things. He knew, above all, not to cause a hassle. Whatever the problem, it wasn't important enough to cause a hassle. He didn't talk about his mom's arrests, or methadone or Valium, or why his mom's face was swollen when all those cop cars were outside their door in the Alley. Just like Grandpa never talked about why Grandma threw a knife at him the night he'd hung the Christmas lights "like a fucking idiot" or why she exploded and cussed at waiters in crowded restaurants or why she slept past noon. These were things you didn't talk about no matter what, even though, Joseph sometimes thought, they seemed like the only things they should be talking about.

He always told his mom he loved her, but that didn't mean anything. If he really loved her, Joseph thought to himself, he wouldn't have been a coward and let Carlos back in. Now, there was nothing he could do for her. He couldn't even help himself. Once school started, things would be a little better. He'd have his friends. He'd spend the night at Scott's and Kevin's as often as he could. Their parents would feed him dinner. He'd scrounge up 15 cents for day-old Devil's Food donuts at the donut shop before school and another 10 cents for milk at school. He'd pretend he wasn't hungry. He'd live his double-life, acting as if his life was like his friends' lives, that everything was "just fine." After so many excuses, Joseph's friends didn't even ask to come over to his house anymore, let alone sleep over. None of them knew exactly where he lived. He wasn't sure they'd still be his friends if they did.

I have to do something, Joseph thought to himself. At the same time, he was trying not to think of Manuel and Joey, but it was right there, the only real choice he had. It was terrifying to think about climbing into a window and roaming around a stranger's home. He envisioned himself riding a stolen BMX bike, holding the handlebars with one hand and with the other, holding a giant black bag of loot over his shoulder. Manuel was right. During the middle of the day, Moreno Valley was full of thousands of brand-new tract homes. The parents that owned them were a hundred miles away or however far Los Angeles is. Their kids would be in school, clueless. Joseph knew firsthand. He'd been in these extravagant homes with clean garages and electric garage door openers, kitchens the size of their apartment with dishwashers that did the dishes for you, and so many rooms it was hard to keep track of them all. These were the homes of his friends' parents. They were stuffed with brand new furniture, big TVs that had remote controls, Atari, Nintendo and Intellivision video game consoles, and sleek stereos and portable boom boxes. There were bright yellow Sony Walkmans just lying around for the taking. There were extra-wide refrigerators, the fancy kind that dispensed water and ice, packed with lunch meat, cookies, frozen pepperoni pizzas and burritos, and half-gallons of rocky road and chocolate ice cream. Joseph recalled the morning after a sleepover at Erik's, seeing that Erik's dad left quarters and dollar bills in a little dish by the door where he kept his car keys. Dollar bills just lying there! Erik had grabbed a couple dollars and stuffed them in his pocket as if it was nothing. These people, Joseph thought, had so much money and stuff that they can't even keep track of it all. They won't even notice it's gone, and if they do, they won't care, they'll just buy more.

It's achingly hot in here, but I've got a thing against AC, so I'm sweating it out. I'm grateful for this place, my little hovel. It's a cute little apartment that one of my 12-Step buddies, Shannon, lived in for several years. The owner, Gabbi, lives upstairs. She's a nice woman, about my age, mid-30s. She bought it several years ago, when buying property in Echo Park was the equivalent of buying Microsoft at its IPO price. She's one of those smart people who has her shit together. She's the landlord with the view of downtown Los Angeles, the high ceilings, the French windows, and original hardwood floors, and I'm the tenant in the hovel—albeit a nice hovel—downstairs with the low ceilings, and about 400 square feet. Gabbi could have rented this place for much more, but Shannon referred me, so I'm paying the same rent he'd been paying for the last five years. She wanted to rent to a man. It makes her feel safe. Ten years ago, this neighborhood was no safer than Kandahar. Many of the homes, including this one, still have barred windows to prove it. Shannon told me that when he first moved here, he could only go one way on his street because the Echo Park Locos that congregated at a house on the corner wouldn't let him pass the other way. It's a narrow street, and the first time he tried to drive through and was blocked by the Locos, he had to reverse his truck a full block while they threw beer bottles at him. Another time, when he was on foot, several of them chased him back home.

I've got to get to my meeting. I don't have time to smoke. I only smoke when I have time for at least three in a row. I jump in my car. I drive by the old Echo Park Locos house. It's not much of a gang house anymore, just a couple guys in white t-shirts and Dodgers hats sneering at me and waiting for *mi madre* to submit to gentrification and sell the house for 20 times what she paid for it. Every time I drive by it, I picture Shannon running with an entire gang chasing him. I don't doubt it for a second. Shannon is a modern-day adventurer. I'm jealous of him. Everyone loves Shannon, especially the ladies. He has a pint of Southern charm with just a shot of the accent. And, no matter how many times he relapses, he always seems to make it back without too many consequences, just a bunch of funny stories. The only time I've ever seen him sad was when he told me about his best friend, the lead singer of a multi-platinum selling rock band. They lived and partied in New Orleans. Shannon sold coke and pills and used as much as he sold. His best friend, the rock star, overdosed and died. That was nearly 10 years ago, and Shannon has been in and out of the Program ever since.

I drive down Sunset, thinking of Shannon. I pass the giant podiatrist's clinic sign. I get lucky. Today I get the Happy Foot side of the rotating sign. I hope Shannon gets lucky, too, but I have a feeling I'm not going to see him again. He's off to Australia, indefinitely, because it's the epicenter of hang gliding, his newest obsession. "Shit," I say aloud to myself, breaking my thought-trance. "I'm a felon. Australia won't even let me in their country."

Not that I'd want to go. I feel uneasy crossing La Brea, let alone leaving the country.

I find a parking spot a couple blocks away, which gives me time to think. I have to make a conscious effort not to speak my thoughts aloud. I spend so much time by myself, and I've gotten in the habit of letting my thoughts leak audibly.

You have to have one hell of an incredibly demoralizing story not to be able to tell it in the 12-Step rooms, where "I used to suck cock for crack" gets little more than a nod and a smile. When I tell my story, I just say I had a DUI and then a year later I was convicted of a violent felony assault I committed in a blackout. I throw in the lawyer shit, too. That's what they remember. "Oh, you're the lawyer guy."

I'm pretty sure Shannon didn't tell Gabbi, my landlord, my full backstory. She knows I'm in the Program, but no way he told her I am a registered sex offender with a conviction of assault with attempt to commit rape, who was convicted of breaking into someone's home in the middle of the night just a couple years ago. That'd give her nightmares. But she's safe with me. God dammit, she's safe with me. I don't know what I'm doing with my life right now, but I know one thing, I'm going to make sure she's safe whenever I'm home. There's that. At least I can be of use to someone.

I read somewhere, probably on my sex registration form or maybe when I was researching Penal Code section 290, or maybe Keri told me: I'm not allowed to go online and look at the registry website, Megan's Law List. Everyone in the world can go online and look at my mug shot, my zip code, my date of birth, my convictions. Everyone but me. I'm told there's a map with red dots signifying the location of registered sex offenders. I am one of those red dots. I've been told by friends who have looked—and gingerly reported back to me—that there are a lot of red dots in this area of Los Angeles. I envision a sea of red dots, so many red dots. I'm just a drop of blood in a puddle of blood.

I sit in the dark in the back row of the back room of Café Tropical in a meditation meeting. Meditation, not particularly described in the original literature, but referenced in the Eleventh Step of the Twelve Steps: "Sought through prayer and meditation to improve our conscious contact with God as we understood Him, praying only for knowledge of His will for us and the power to carry that out." So we sit for 20 minutes in the dark with our eyes closed, meditating. It seems from the original literature that Bill Wilson was not talking about this closed-eyed emptying-of-the-mind type of meditation but rather a contemplation of the day's events, but whatever, it works for me. In fact, it worked really well before I went to jail. I'd sit in this room and close my eyes and find some relief in concentrating on my breathing and nothing else. It was a respite from the variety shit-show my life had become starting July 26, 2003, the day of my arrest. When I was in Chino prison, I was meditating—zenning out in my cell for hours at a time. Now, back in this room, it's comforting, but not as much. My desperation is not as sharp now as when there was an hourglass counting down to my entry into the abyss of the California Department of Corrections. There is still an hourglass counting down to my demise—the one represented by my bank account—but I can add sand.

I hear muttering outside the door. There are always homeless people outside Café Tropical. They bang their bottles and cans against their shopping carts. They mutter fragments of conspiracy theories. They speak to the dead. They are, I think, a not-so-subtle reminder of our future without Recovery.

As I sit in the dark with my fellows, my mind flips through a deck of 12-Step-isms:

Stinking thinking

Put one foot in front of the other

Chop wood and carry water

You can't fix a broken brain with a broken brain

God is everything, or God is nothing

Do what's in front of you, and let God take care of the rest

My disease is doing push-ups

F.E.A.R. fuck everything and run

Stay sober and help another alcoholic

Page 67-68 or is it 86-87? That's it. That's what I need. I can't keep spinning in my head, thinking of the horrors that may or may not materialize as the result of my newfound life status, my résumé de horror. Listen to the speaker, go home. Do what it says. Just do what it says. Do what the old drunk stock analyst Bill Wilson says. The one who died of emphysema, the one who so emotionally abused his long-suffering wife, Lois? Yes, yes. That's the one. Just do it. Shut up your head.

My mind is churning with ideas. I used to fight it, try to quiet my mind, but not so much anymore. I just as often let my mind run. I philosophize.

I think about the story that I've heard so many times since I got sober. There's a woman on a subway, and these kids are acting wild, bumping into people and screaming. Their dad just sits there and does nothing. The woman becomes annoyed and admonishes the man to please control his kids. The man apologizes and explains that he doesn't know what to do, that he and his kids just came from the hospital where their mom died. Great story, right? You never know what people are going through. Great. That's Stage One of Recovery. But then, after hearing that story over and over and recalling it every time somebody cuts me off in traffic, and thinking, "Don't get mad, remember the subway story. The driver that just cut me off probably has his dying kid in the car and he's rushing to the hospital," I began to question it.

Stage Two of Recovery: I call bullshit. When it seems like people are acting like assholes, it's usually because they *are* assholes, not because they are in some unlikely dire situation. So instead of pretending that the asshole who cut me off on the freeway isn't an asshole, I've decided to simply forgive the person for being an asshole, mostly because I can emphasize with being an asshole. I've cut people off on the freeway. I broke into a stranger's house at night and attacked him. If I can't forgive someone for cutting me off on the freeway, how can I possibly forgive myself for all the things I've done?

Then there's Stage Three of Recovery. This is where the heavy-hitter spiritualists reside, like Buddha, Jesus, the Dalai Lama, and KRS-One. It is simply this: Don't judge at all. Observe it, learn from it, store the information away, but don't judge it. That doesn't mean that one can't react. That is a decision one has to make for oneself. I like to think of Stage Three as having more to do with efficiency than morality. It's often best to act like one of those GPS driving gadgets my friend has in his car. It tells him the fastest way to get where he's going. When an accident occurs on the freeway, the device doesn't express an opinion as to who was at fault or why the accident happened or what the punishment should be for the liable driver. It doesn't get mad. It reacts. It simply recalculates the best driving directions based on the new path. It doesn't judge, because judging doesn't serve its purpose.

"Compare and despair," is within the realm of Stage One and Stage Two. Ever since my crash and burn, people, especially people in the Rooms, like to tell me that I'm lucky. They'll usually have a story of someone who had it worse than me. They'll tell me how a guy they read about or tangentially know killed someone drunk driving and now that someone is in prison for 20 years and living with the death of an innocent person on his conscience. This type of reverse "compare and despair" or as I call it "compare and rejoice" used to make me feel grateful. But then I started getting resentful at people who would tell me these things. I'd think about the myriad different ways my life could have played out better. Maybe instead of breaking into someone's home in the middle of the night in an alcoholic blackout, I could have simply been found out by a friend and encouraged to go to rehab before the whole "jail, prison, registered sex offender, and disbarment" thing happened.

Whether I think I'm lucky because I compare myself to a worse scenario, or I think I'm unlucky because I compare myself to a better scenario, it's still a comparison. And comparison is a type of judgment. Stage Three applies. There is no value in judging myself or what happened. It's inefficient. It doesn't serve my purpose of living my life here and now. Stage Three of Recovery is simply taking right action based on the facts as they present themselves. It's exhausting reminiscing over countless scenarios of what should or could have happened or who is more or less lucky than me. I've had too many concussions to dedicate this much of my brain to processing useless and even harmful thoughts. But how? How does one simply not judge?

It's a practice. It's a practice. That's where my meditation has landed me, repeating the phrase "It's a practice" over and over.

Delicate chimes from the meeting-timer's phone indicate meditation has ended. The lights come on. The Seventh Tradition basket is passed and I drop a dollar in it. The speaker states the most important lesson that can be heard in a 12-Step meeting: The message is in the Big Book. Nowhere else. Then she rambles on for 10 minutes about her Hindu meditation practice. I mentally check out upon the second mention of the word "chakra," which unfortunately, I know is not a Swiss heavy metal band but some Indian yoga bullshit. My complete and utter dismissal of the idea of even considering this hippy-dippy nonsense, surely Westernized to the point of being unrecognizable from its origins, almost guarantees that I'll be immersed in it or something similar in the near future. This is my punishment for "contempt prior to investigation," a condition that can only lead to "everlasting darkness" as stated in the III Appendix of *Alcoholics Anonymous*. Or, in other words, it's my karma—cause and effect—for judging.

"I'm just grateful to the Program for allowing me to find my true practice," the speaker concludes.

"Okay, okay," I hear you, I say in my brain. I'm trying not to think negative thoughts about her, like, it sure is amazing how all these attractive young women—and some men, too—get all spiritual and grateful after they come in the Rooms for five minutes, find a rich sober guy, and get married. It sure is nice to have your new worst problem be whether to choose the sporty but stiff suspension of BMW or the speed-bump absorbing suspension of Mercedes.

Joseph, what happened to Stage Three? No judgment?

I'm sorry. It's a practice. It's a practice. It's a fucking practice, alright?

I alight from the room into the fresher night air and realize how vile it smelled in there, so close to the most utilized toilet in Los Angeles.

My trudging buddies are gone. Peter drinks now and dabbles in pills. I can't even be around him, he's so crazed. I can't go a minute without hearing a list of his resentments about whatever, although we do manage to surf occasionally, but I insist on driving because he has, on more than one occasion, become psychotic in traffic. And in the surf line-up, he becomes insane with rage because someone dropped in on him and then paddles up to me with plans of retaliation, vaguely including me, the former kickboxer, to which I respond to remind him, I don't fight anymore, and I'm sure as hell not going back to prison because you seem to keep getting dropped in on. And by the way, I don't ever get dropped in on, so what's up? Ironically, Peter hates confrontation, so he changes the subject.

And then Mickey, he claimed he was HIV positive but then said he wasn't. He's doing pills and acting weird, posting weird shit on social media, looking all gaunt and pale. He has also dived into Scientology, and they aren't down with the A-and-the-A, so maybe that's it.

Clarence just stopped going to meetings. He's been driving down to Tijuana on the regular, but supposedly still sober. Oddly, when I talk to him, he seems to have his head on straighter than any of my other former trudging buddies.

Brandon, that kid that worked at the ad agency that got the DUI, the one I used to informally sponsor, I guess things got much better or much worse because he stopped calling.

Damn, even my old sponsor has withdrawn from the Program. I guess after a decade of meetings and endless service, he just got tired of it. He was my hero. He saved my life. But I had to move on.

I stand on the sidewalk in the middle of everyone. They smoke and talk and linger around, slowly dispersing. I used to get freaked out if I didn't have anyone to talk to, but now I kind of like just standing here observing. Don't pull out the cell phone, don't smoke—not hard, I almost never smoke in public—just stand here and be here. I'm a head taller than nearly everyone, so I'm literally standing slightly above it all. Breathe in and breathe out.

"What are you doing?" Paddy asks.

Paddy is so clearly of Irish descent he might as well have a leprechaun on his shoulder.

"I'm doing this zen thing, where I just *be* in a crowd," I respond.

"How's that working out for you?" he asks.

I've prepared my answer to this many times in my head.

"Better than freaking out about having no one to talk to, or pretending to be busy and jumping on the cell phone, or going to find someone to talk to when it isn't natural… not that talking to you isn't natural."

He chuckles. He's got a thick-skinned forehead. He's got big teeth, too. Seeing Paddy always reminds me that I wish I had big teeth.

Paddy withdraws a cigarette and beckons me for a light.

I offer my lighter.

"Thanks," he says. "You smoke?"

"Yeah, a pack a day. Like I'm trying to kill myself," I retort.

"Whatever dude, I'm just trying to not drink. I had a month and now I'm on day two again."

I've known Paddy for a while, but just from the Rooms. I give him rides. He goes to my men's stag meeting, and I pick him up and drop him off at the sober living complex he lives in by Filipino town. Our conversations always end up being braggadocio—what we used to have and how great we used to be. He and his hot South American girlfriend used to flip homes before flipping homes was a thing. I tell him about when I was an attorney and used to represent agents and homebuyers, that I was a real estate litigation specialist, that it's unbelievable how these mortgage brokers, some of whom I used to represent, make a killing on people's equity. Usually, about 10 minutes into our conversation, I'd hate myself.

Why do I have to impress Paddy? Why do I need Paddy to agree that I was so fucking great?

I drive Paddy home.

"Yeah, same place. It's hard living here," Paddy says. "I used to own multiple homes. I'd live in one and be working on two with my girl."

Don't do it. Don't do it. Joseph, shut up.

"Yeah, it's a big change," I say. "I never owned multiple homes but I can relate to a lower standard of living, that's for sure."

"Man, if I could just get some cash I could get right back in and double it," Paddy says, more as an out-loud proclamation than something he's telling me.

Don't do it. Shut up, Joseph.

"Put 10 percent down," Paddy explains. "Take some out for improvement and then just go to work and three months later, you sell it for 30 percent more."

"Yep, I know." I respond. "I used to represent REITs. You know what that is?"

What an asshole you are, Joseph.

"Nah," Paddy professes.

I explain what a REIT is and subtly include how unbelievably impressive I was. I hate whatever part of me is speaking right now.

I drop off Paddy and agree to pick him up for our Wednesday men's stag meeting. He salutes me, takes a deep breath and gets out deliberately. I watch him walk through the institutional yard with the institutionalized men, most, obviously fresh out of prison. The concrete, the worn grass, the pipe railing, everything overused, even the trees are depressed. I see a pair of Nike Cortez and high socks, white t-shirts, bad tattoos. A mix of men, most hustling, even if only with their eyes, trying to dig in a little spot for themselves, fighting their inevitable recidivation.

I did it again. Why can't I stop trying to inflate my ego when I talk to Paddy? I'll never do it again. I promise. I'll listen to him, make small talk, drop in some 12-Step-isms.

On the drive back to my apartment, I think of Paddy's sober living. It's just like prison, rehab, jail, The Boy's Club, the Welfare office, the Methadone clinic, and the barracks at March Air Force Base. It radiates a dull hopelessness. What is it? Is it the government's touch? It's hard to be homey in a place some people call work. Maybe it's that drag in time between a really poor move and the inevitable resulting checkmate. As we say in the Rooms, active addiction always leads to "jails, institutions, and death" or for most of the guys in the institution Paddy now calls home "jails, institutions, jails, institutions, jails, institutions and finally, finally, death."

I pull into my parking spot under the lemon tree, my car angled on the drastically pitched driveway so close I can almost touch my hood and my front door knob simultaneously. The lemons that dropped to the concrete several days ago are still on the steps rotting. No, I still don't feel like picking them up. I let them fester in my mind with the other minor chores that I neglect but spend a great deal of time thinking about: laundry, the bathroom, the dishes, all the junk that fills the backseat of my car, the papers from my court case, the papers from my long list of creditors, a great abundance of creditors, the vast, vast debt hanging over me—most of it non-dischargeable under Chapter 7 of Title 11 of the Bankruptcy Code. I just need a cigarette and a nicely sweetened cup of coffee. Then I'll take care of it and everything else. I'll start rebuilding the structure that is my life with the same intensity I employed in its demolition.

Stop, stop, Joseph. Page 86 and 87. That's what you need. Cigs and coffee first, then maybe a nap.

As I insert my house key into the knob lock, I see a stark white business card tucked into the door frame just above the brass-plated handle. I pull it out. L.A.P.D. Detective Jose Gonzalez. An embossed badge with gold coloring. A 213 phone number. There it is! There's that feeling. It's where the neck stops and chest begins, the air I breathe now being filtered through desperation and fear. The mind set afire with ideas. I knew it would be like this. Every time there is a crime, they are going to come talk to me. There will be detectives in my living room asking me questions, just waiting for me to say the wrong thing. "You aren't under arrest," they'll say. "We just want to talk to you." "What about?" I'll say. "We can't say… just a few questions, Mr. Naus."

Oh God, oh God. I live right by Elysian Park. I go running through it all the time. I can see it now. A woman gets assaulted in the park. A witness says she saw a tall blonde guy, running. Maybe talk to him. Check Megan's Law List. Bingo, check it out, Detective. Well, well, looky here—Joseph Naus. Tall blonde guy, lives right down the street, witness saw him running away from the scene. I think we got our man. Get a search warrant. We don't need one. He's on probation. Or, another scenario: young girl says guy asked him to get in car, she runs away, she tells mom, mom calls cops. Cops show girl mug shots of all the local registered sex offenders, including one, Joseph Naus. Is that him? You aren't sure, but it could be, right?

I open the door of my apartment. It smells of garbage as my dirty dishes have ripened in the heat. I prepare the coffee maker to brew, press the button and stare at the business card while the coffee maker hisses and pees strong coffee.

Why leave a card with no message? Hey, just in the neighborhood. Thought I'd stop by. Didn't have much to do, wanted to see how life is treating a sex offender like you.

They'll come over. One will do most of the talking while the other snoops around. Hey, hey, hey, you can't do that. Don't go through my papers. Why? You got something to hide, Mr. Naus. No, but come on, what are you doing? Why are you here? Why don't you let us ask the questions? I'll have to strike a balance. I can't be completely obstinate or they'll just abuse me. Search everything, take me downtown. They can do whatever they want. I'm on probation. No warrant necessary. They'll call my probation officer, Maya, and start raising hell, then that'll cause problems for her. She'll kick me off her caseload whether she likes me or not. But I can't let them walk over me. I'll call Keri, my lawyer.

I pull the coffee pot from under the brown stream and quickly pour my cup. Why was I thinking this was one of those models that paused when I pull the pot out? It's not. The solid line of coffee is striking the burner like liquid iron into a blast furnace. I replace the pot and finalize the mess. At some point, I'll stop using this sickly-sweet liquid vanilla creamer with the shelf life longer than my life expectancy, but for now, I'm hooked. I pour it in until my coffee is caramel-colored and thick as milk. I take my coffee mug outside with my Marlboro Light 100's, my lighter, and my ashtray. The tiny little raised slab on my porch, which doubles as the landlord's walkway to her home upstairs, has a little wood table and two tiny matching narrow chairs with a green umbrella. It's my perfect little smoking spot. Luckily my landlord works long hours, so I'm rarely concerned with the smoke rising up and entering her window. If she ever asked me not to smoke on my patio, it'd be a monumental situation. She's not home now, and so I sit in the shade with my coffee and cigarettes. I can relax. I'm okay.

I smoke four in a row, sipping my coffee, staring at the name. Detective Jose Gonzalez. It sounds made-up. Maybe it is.

I dial the number. It rings and rings and finally he answers, "Detective Gonzalez, Registration Unit." He speaks so loudly it's almost aggressive.

I can't return this aggression. I must strike a moderate, friendly yet firm tone, one that says, Yes, in this relationship I'm the criminal and you are the police, but I'm responsible and have paid my debt to society and all the preconceived notions you have about me are, for the most part, wrong. I am not a recidivist, I am not uneducated, I am not always trying to manipulate the system, I am not a liar, I do not drink or use drugs, I am not poor—at least not in that institutional way. While I understand that in your line of work, prejudging is sometimes a matter of your safety and even when not, is systemic in your community of police officers but given that you have risen to detective, it is important that you not make assumptions in situations like this one.

Yes, I need to strike a tone that conveys all these ideas clearly.

"Can I help you?" Detective Gonzalez asks. But what he means is, why have you called me and not said anything when I answered the phone?

"My name is Joseph Naus. I live at 405 Thumber Lane in Echo Park, Los Angeles. I'm on probation. Your business card was in my door. I'm not sure if you left it because you—"

He interrupts me. "Thanks for calling. I'm just verifying you live where you are registered."

"I do."

"Okay. Thanks for calling," Detective Gonzalez says and hangs up.

I hold my phone in front of me. An observer would say I look as if I'm holding a device I'd never seen before. I am not satisfied with Detective Gonzalez's seemingly glib and uninterested response, but I'm relieved that he won't be cross-examining me while his partner rummages through my mail or my dresser drawers, as they do on the ubiquitous TNT and TBS cop shows. I wonder, will these unannounced stopovers be frequent? I imagine I am the talk of the neighborhood. Everyone knows about me, and they are worried. They are worried about their safety. They are worried about their property values. I'm surely, if nowhere else but my mind, the topic of discussion among local real estate agents.

LOS ANGELES: EASTSIDER REALTY THREAD

TOPIC: WARNING: Joseph Naus. New Sunset/Echo Park Area Sex Offender Registrant

RealtyGirl79: I know. I just saw that. It's terrible. There is a school nearby and a park.

ReMaxWarrior: It's worse than there being a murder in the listing, but at least we don't have to disclose! :)

BrokerBadsley: Not yet, but the CalDRE is always improving their forms LOL.

TopSales258: That's a way to kill a commission. Write in the Transfer Disclosure Statement: Rapist across the street.

RealtyGirl79: LOL but NOT! I live close to there!

TopSales258: He'd be crazy to mess with you. ;) I remember how you handled that escrow cancellation on Upton Drive. Or should I say, attempted cancellation...

Enough! I have to stop thinking. I grab my royal blue hardback Big Book and turn to page 86-87: "When we retire at night... On awakening... As we go through the day..." It's all right here. Instructions. Instructions on how to train the raging wasps' nest that is the addict's mind. Wake up and do this. Pray, meditate, ask for God's guidance that I not be filled with self-pity or dishonesty. Make a plan for the day. Relax, don't struggle. Ask God for guidance. Pause when agitated. Remind myself whenever necessary, I'm not running the show. I'm not running the show. No self-will. What does this mean? It means: Get up and pray and meditate. Make a to-do list. Do it, and don't act like a selfish prick while doing it. If I get stuck, ask for guidance. Pray, meditate. The answer will come if I let it. Okay, back to work. When I'm done, review my day and determine whether I was resentful, selfish, dishonest, or afraid. Check, check, check. Do I owe an apology? If so, do it and make it quick-like and move on. Don't drift into worry, remorse or morbid reflection. Go to bed, repeat.

Oh my God, I have to stop my head.

SIX

"I'm giving you a couple extra," he says and carefully hands them to me.

They remind me of a mouthpiece for a high-tech bong, which reminds me of Amsterdam, which reminds me of bikes, bikes everywhere. His name patch reads "Rusty." It's an odd name for a Middle Eastern guy, I think, just before I recall that he told me his name the first time he hooked me up, and it damn sure wasn't Rusty.

"There's a new sequence," he informs me. There's a touch of geek-glee in his voice.

I sit in the passenger seat of my car and Rusty/Not-Rusty climbs in the driver's seat the way mechanics do, with the door open and a certain natural dominion that makes me question my car's loyalty.

He pulls the clear plastic nib off its black housing tube and blows into it several times. "One-one.... two and then three. Got it? One-one, two, long on the two, and then a quick three, until it beeps," he instructs.

I nod. He plugs the nib in and I try it. One-one, two... The unit *ainks* at me like the third strike on Family Feud.

"God dammit," I say and correct myself with, "Fuck, ooops," followed by a fumbling, "I'm sorry," which I revise to, "No, fuck, just sorry... sorry, sorry." I'm trying to cuss less, sometimes extremely unsuccessfully.

"No, no. You just try it again, you'll get it," Rusty says, his Middle Eastern accent coming out, as if he's talking to one of his children.

I think how kind it is that he's treating me so nicely. He's always smiling. I can tell he doesn't cuss as he mildly flinched at my vulgarity before refocusing on the task at hand. He has never treated me differently than any of his other customers even though he knows I have no choice but to be here and pay the state-mandated fee.

"Okay, I got it this time," I say, straightening with confidence.

I blow the sequence precisely—one, one, two... three—and the breathalyzer makes the good sound, *boooop*, which unlocks the ignition, allowing me to start my car without alerting the fucking FBI. Rusty looks over at me with a satisfied smile, a genuine smile.

I turn away as tears well up in my eyes, like when I watch an Olympics behind-the-scenes personal piece where the gymnast hugs her mom after attesting to her mother's years of sacrifice. I jerk my head away abruptly as if a bug flew into my nose.

"Oh, Jeez. What was that?" I say. I turn away and shake my head. "Must've been a bug or something—hold on."

For God's sake. What's the matter with me?

"You alright?" he asks.

"Oh yeah, it's nothing," I respond and turn back.

"Okay, try it one more time," he says.

I blow into the breathalyzer in sequence again, and it responds with the *boooop* again. I'm anxious to get out of here. I pay cash in a rush. I need to be alone with my thoughts and a cigarette and some coffee so I can figure out why the slightest kindness of strangers and sappy commercials make me cry.

"Thanks—"

"Momo," he finishes for me. "Short for Mohamed."

That's right. Mohamed. Momo. He probably started going by Momo after 9/11.

I drive back down La Cienega in a minor panic about how to get back on the 10 Freeway. It's tricky around here. As if to test more than just my sobriety, the breathalyzer beeps again. I pull it out and blow the sequence. Nailed it, I say, after the *booop* sends it back into submission.

I think: You proud of me Momo?

Yes, Momo responds. Momo flies above my barely-moving car. He sports a black cape over a safety-orange bodysuit with an oversized "M" on his chest, which looks like a "V" because the legs of the "M" wrap under his arms because he's so skinny. During the day, he's the lovable, honest mechanic, but at night, he's Captain Momo, flying above the streets. His sole superhero activity is distributing pamphlets regarding the statistical anomaly that is Muslim-extremist terrorism. A bright green piece of paper with a smiling cartoon of Prophet Mohammed riding a rhinoceros reads, "Did You Know More People Die of Rhinoceros attacks in the U.S. than by Muslim Extremist Terrorists?" and another reads, "Did You Know the Rate of Felony Arrests among Muslims in America is Half the Nationwide Average?"

I'm relieved to find the 10 Freeway on-ramp east. With a sigh of relief, I estimate that I'm no more than 30 minutes from coffee and cigarettes and solitude. Meanwhile, I drive toward the little skyline of downtown Los Angeles, and along with my many fellow Angelinos, I stop and go and stop and go. I open my sunroof and imagine Captain Momo flying above my car, joking about not needing to fly given the speed of traffic, about to drop a brightly colored flyer through my sunroof.

But Momo, I say, save your flyer for those who need it. I'm enlightened.

My dear felonious friend, Momo responds, you are part of the problem, too. Do you not believe that Muslims are more likely to commit acts of terrorism than non-Muslims?

I consider Momo's response when, *beeeep*, my breathalyzer sounds. I take a deep breath and clear my mind as best I can. I close the sunroof so I can concentrate on the breathalyzer while driving in stop-and-go traffic. I blow, I blow, one, one, two... and then I cough.

Aiinnkk, it squeals at me.

I have two more tries and if I can't execute the sequence properly, my car will shut down on the 10 Freeway, and there is no emergency lane, and I'll have to pay to have it towed, and I'll have to spend $1,000 to get it unlocked and reinstalled, and I'll have to deal with Maya, my Los Angeles probation officer, and the Riverside Court, who has jurisdiction over my DUI, which happened four fucking years ago. These are not the thoughts I need to have right now. I have one minute to try again, or it will auto-*aink* to indicate fail number two.

My breathing increases and the car in front of me, a black Mercedes SUV with tinted windows, slows abruptly. I slam on my brakes because I didn't anticipate it braking, because I couldn't see beyond it because of its tinted windows. All the clothes and papers in my back seat fly forward. Dammit, tinted windows should be illegal on SUVs. The fast lane is closed so we are merging over. A CHP officer stands by his bike, still wearing his helmet and waves us over to the second lane. I have the breathalyzer in my mouth. I'm not ready. In fact, the new sequence is gone from my mind and all I can think of is the old sequence.

What'd Momo say? One-one, two... three?

I begin to blow and on the beginning of three it *aiinnkks* at me, indicating a failed attempt.

"You gotta be fucking kidding me!" I say through clenched teeth and I pound the steering wheel.

DUI, CHP, panic, ambulance, fucked, jail, prison, cigarettes, massage parlor, fear, disbarred, death.

I crank the wheel and cross three lanes of traffic. Angry horns follow me. I pull over to the emergency lane just before an off-ramp. I shift to "park," yank the emergency brake to its last click, and take a deep breath.

I've got this. I've got this. It's no biggie. You aren't going to jail, it's just a little hassle. Please God, just uh... fuck it. Whatever your will. I'm going to try and whatever happens fucking happens.

I repeat the number sequence aloud—One-one, two... three. I go for it. It goes off smoothly and gives me the good noise, *booop*. Before I even have a moment to feel my relief, I hear a loud siren-blip, the way cops get your attention in Los Angeles.

The loudspeaker drones out something that ends in, "move your vehicle." I comply so radically I almost hit a tow truck attempting to jut into the slow lane. The nerves in my shoulders and arms are popping like little landmines under my skin. I shake. Back in the flow of traffic, I begin to laugh, softly at first, but then it builds into a manic kind of machine-like noise, *hak-hak-hak-hak*. This is not the belly laugh that helped me survive the two years after my arrest. This is my nervous system berating my brain and my brain passing it on. For a few moments, I'm just an observer of myself, not in the meditative way but in the dissociative, this-is-how-crazy-people-must-feel way.

"Okay, okay. It's all good, Joseph," I console myself aloud. "Just take it easy. Cigarettes and coffee coming up."

I turn my radio to 91.5 FM, the USC-associated classical music radio station. The DJ soothes me with his sincere and modulated introduction to a Handel piece. I calm down in harmony with long organ notes as my fellow drivers and I slowly follow the transition onto the 110, tracing the downtown Los Angeles skyline. A giant mural of several members of the Los Angeles Philharmonic, including most prominently, a bearded man in a long-tailed tux holding a violin—or is that a viola?—and a woman in a long dress with long hair holding a viola—or is that a violin?—a dozen stories high, on the side of a parking structure, look down with knowing smiles as if to say, "It's alright, Los Angeles, it's alright." They are lying, but I appreciate the sentiment anyway.

I place my 24 ounces of coffee on the 7-Eleven check-out counter/ recessed glass lottery tickets display. A display box of tiny orange bottles of energy elixir irritates me more than anything else in here, but I focus.

"A pack of Marlboro 100's in a box, please," I say, trying to mask the increasing urgency of the situation.

"We only have soft pack," the clerk says and slides them onto the counter, waiting for my approval.

This is not a big deal. Why does this feel like a big deal?

"Sir, these good?" he asks. "We are out of hard packs."

I weigh the relative hassle of going someplace else. I glance to my right through a glass display at several sweaty rolling flautas and hot dogs, as if they might possess a solution. I'm very fond of this particular cup of coffee and I've gone through a great deal of specific mixing of cream and sugar in order to achieve its perfection. I could buy the coffee here and then get cigarettes at House of Spirits. No, no, Joseph, the parking sucks there. It's a total crapshoot and I'm already so behind. I should have been smoking an hour ago. I can't suffer any further delays.

"Yes, thanks," I respond to the clerk. "Just the cigarettes and the coffee. Thank you."

I have to swipe my bank card because I don't have enough cash on me. This costs me more time. I rush out and zoom down Sunset Boulevard. I'm catching green lights. I pull into my driveway. I go inside, rummage through my trash, and find the empty pack of Marlboro 100's. I didn't crumple it and it's not sullied. I'm very fortunate. I deftly empty the cigarettes from their new container into the old one and pack them with several thumps against the heel of my left palm. I sit on my little patio, in my little chair, under the umbrella. My landlord isn't home. I'm all alone, safe and secure with my cigarettes and coffee.

I just smoke and think about smoking.

Smoking is the top preventable cause of death in the U.S. Twenty percent of adults smoke. A half-million die from smoking every year. I'd pay $20 a pack if I had to. Damn right I would. Phillip Morris, stock symbol, PM, dropped like a rock after the first billion-dollar punitive damage award against it in 1998. I know because I bought it on the dip. It was my first stock purchase. I knew the punitive damage award wouldn't stick and I was right. But more telling, I knew from watching my mom and from my own experience that PM would rise again. Nicotine addiction is unbelievably powerful. And sure enough, PM rose again! She renamed herself Altria, stock symbol, MO, spun off Phillip Morris, and people starting calling her "Big MO." Big MO made a deal with the government, paid the lobbyist who paid the politicians, started investing in vaping and e-cigs, and then Big MO expanded into China, India, and countries where people can't or won't sue Big MO for intentionally selling a product that when used exactly as intended causes the user to die a horrible death. Go, Big MO, go!

I pull cigarette number four from its 20-unit magazine, light it, take a deep drag, ash into a plastic water bottle filled with my freshly lit cigarette's stubby cousins, all drowning in sickly orangish-yellow water.

I recall a woman at a Nicotine 12-Step meeting saying that if you soak a pack of cigarettes in water and then drink the water, you'll die of nicotine poisoning.

So what. There are a lot of ways to die.

I take a long, deep drag. My throat feels as if it's lined with high-grit sandpaper, and my lymph nodes are sore and swollen. I blow out a plume of smoke, and I sigh with pleasure.

SEVEN

The Saturday night Café Tropical meeting is a social meeting for me. It starts at 7:30, but I won't even go if I can't get there by 6:55. I refuse to fight for parking while hoping there's a seat left. I get there early, I save a seat, I get my five-dollar café mocha, which I don't mentally cringe at because the Trop lets us 12-Steppers use their back room for free. I heard the owner's son died of an overdose, and the owner was so grateful to the 12-Steppers for the time his son had sober that the owner recorded some type of property covenant in the chain of title allowing the back room to be permanently used for 12-Step meetings. While I did hear that, I would wager nothing on its truth, not a cent.

"Large café mocha, please," I say to the ever-present manager Donato.

"How are you, Yosef?" Donato says, with an omniscient Cheshire Cat grin. The Trop is a Cuban Café, so I'm betting he's Cuban, but I know he's actually whimsical elfin. We've never traded more than a dozen words at a time, usually about something odd and asexually flirty. Like Clarence, he's another person I wish I was closer with.

"Sober and alive, happy to be here," I respond, thinking how lame that sounds before the final syllable passes my lips. But then I reassess, and become okay—actually, pleased—with my response.

"Whatchur saying you guys have?" Donato asks, nodding to the back room. "Happee, choyus and free?"

I laugh. He winks. Donato makes me happy. He's got a big child-actor's head with thick curly brown hair and big dark eyes. Sometimes he'll just stare at me in this way that makes me break into laughter like we share a secret, and even though I don't know what it is, I know it exists. And then he'll just grin and keep doing what he was doing, usually carrying supplies between the storage room and the main café. Donato has no barnacles of irony, exaggeration, or sarcasm to protect himself. He's just serving up strong Cuban coffee and flaky guava cheese pies and making everyone smile. It's his beautiful little ministry.

The 12-Step meeting's secretary steps out of the door onto the smoke-filled, crowded sidewalk of addicts and announces, "Meeting time."

We funnel in through the door and squeeze into our seats, knees clasped and shoulders narrowed, some 60 of us 12-Steppers. Two years ago, I came into this room as an alien in a business suit, sitting in the back, feeling the weight of the consequences of my failures, trying to survive, looking around wondering how the hell I got here. Some several hundred meetings later, after surviving incarceration and the complete stripping of my life, I know nearly everyone in here. Maybe 10 of the people in this room came to my sentencing hearing. They helped save me from more prison time.

The Chapter Five rarely-have-we-seen-a-person-fail reading, which begins nearly every meeting after introductory and housekeeping announcements, is read by a gravely-voiced, strange old man who regularly says nonsensical things to the delight of the I-hate-this-Program-but-it's-saving-my-life-punk-rock contingent. Me and my trudging buddies call him "Burning Babies" in reference to a quote from one of his more acidic shares. He's over-enunciating the word "God" during the reading, to the delight of his fans. I've heard this Chapter Five reading so many times, I could probably recite it from memory if that part of my brain still worked. It has a hypnotic cadence that Burning Babies is trampling for comedic effect, which makes me want to strangle the life out of him with the straps of his own ironic fanny pack.

I scan the room. The number of beautiful women in here is amazing. You wouldn't find this ratio at the hippest bar in Silver Lake. It's undoubtedly a major factor as to why I have to get here a half-hour early just to get a seat. These are not your Bill-and-Bob looking addicts. There's your hipster in '70s high-waisted jeans and threadbare vintage t-shirt, no bra, obviously, with feathery long hair parted right down the middle. Then the suicide girls wearing black on black on black, knee-high stockings, and school-girl pleated skirts. There are two colorfully tatted former strippers leaning into one another, one tall with red hair and the other short with black hair. There's the Iranian-American woman who always sports an are-you-kidding-me? miniskirt. Some of the women are more understated, but they've all got miles of style. They are almost exclusively artists: novelists, screenwriters, decorators, photographers, models, cinematographers, art production types, actors, comedians, painters, and musicians. And for every beautiful woman, there is a male counterpart, including a couple of musicians and actors of note.

As Burning Babies nears the end of reading Chapter Five, just as everyone joins in for the finale, "... and God could and would if he were sought!" she walks in. I know I've never seen her before because there is no way I could possibly have seen her and forgotten. She has caramel-colored skin. She has big hair with loose curls, like the non-threatening black women in national commercials for detergent and department stores. She wears baggy, worn jeans low on her hips, rolled up above the ankles, with a flowery blouse. Everyone watches her enter as she makes her way to the front of the room. It would be impossible not to watch her, and she's obviously used to the attention. The eager young woman who has saved her a seat in the front-row couch hugs her and greets her enthusiastically but silently, like a mime might do. She settles in, allowing the room to refocus on the secretary and the speaker. The speaker gives her an enthusiastic wave with cupped fingers, the way one waves to a baby, over-mouthing, "hi-ayee."

After the speaker, a moderately famous, self-described anxiety-riddled Jewish comedian, gives his 15-minute pitch, chips are handed out for lengths of sobriety. Then there's a two-year birthday celebration—or "anniversary," as every prick from New York has to remind us they are called in New York—and finally the speaker picks the first person to share. The comedian chooses *her*. Her voice is raspy. She sounds like a late-night radio DJ that might dispense hushed love advice. She's smart and funny, and she drops some deep-cut spirituality laced with unabashed references to "love" and "God." When most people in meetings say the G-word, they say it as if they fear they will be pelted with fruit, but she says the G-word as if she's talking about her cool roommate. I've never heard anyone in a meeting speak like she does.

Per the meeting's rules, we aren't supposed to clap between shares, but people do for her, uproariously in fact, and then we all quiet down awkwardly when we, as a group, recall we aren't supposed to clap, and then we laugh at the awkwardness of the breached rule caused by the quality of her share. After all this, she looks around the room to pick the next person to share and looks back behind her. Her eyes meet mine, but only passively, like a spotlight steadily crossing a stage of choir singers, looking for the soloist. She chooses a handsome man-boy two seats to my left. He, of the ultra-cool-without-trying variety, thanks her for calling on him and repeats her name as if he knows her, Biblically.

Her name is Macy.

All I can think of for the rest of the meeting is her.

After the meeting, Paddy and I walk to my car. I don't wait for him to ask for a ride. I just tell him I'm going his way, even though I'm not, and does he need a ride? Yes, thanks. Okay, no problem. It's much better this way.

"You know that girl that walked in late?" I ask.

Paddy instructs me to go up and take a left on Santa Monica to cut across at Hoover. I wonder if I'll ever get used to these streets. I miss the grid layout of the Inland Empire. And, why the fuck would you name a street Little Santa Monica when regular ol' Santa Monica already confuses me by running in two different directions? And no matter how much I try, my brain won't accept the fact that the 10 Freeway runs from downtown Los Angeles dead west to the Westside, hence the name, but I swear it seems like it goes north. Goddammit, it feels north. My internal compass hasn't been the same since my DUI car accident and seems to have gotten even worse after the beating I took the night of my second arrest.

"You mean Macy, with the big hair, right?" Paddy responds after giving me driving directions.

"Yeah, her."

"Yeah, wow, right? A lot going on there," Paddy says in an uncharacteristically vague way.

"What do you mean?" I prod.

"Dude. I saw her speak Friday. She's deeper than most... Nice rack, too."

I chuckle and stop myself from saying something mildly judgmental like, "Aren't you the bastion of sobriety?" which is a solid little victory for myself, because the truth is, I was thinking the same thing about Macy and her nice rack, I just didn't say it because it seemed a little crude. Actually, I think to myself, that's not true. I don't care about being crude in front of Paddy. Sealed-diary truth is that everything I say and some of what I think is edited in light of my sex offender status. I'm training myself to speak and even think carefully or I will surely find myself being interrogated by a detective. There is a big difference between a pre-conviction Joseph commenting, "nice rack" about a woman to his friend and post-conviction Joseph the Registered Sex Offender commenting, "nice rack" about a woman to his friend. The former might be viewed as crude, while the latter might be judged as criminal intent.

"You needed to take a right back there," Paddy says as I turn left onto Hoover.

"Fuck, okay, I'll hook around on, what is that... Melrose?"

"No, dude, Melrose?" he says, stricken by my inability to navigate to the giant institutional sober living where I've picked him up and dropped him off a dozen times.

I decide not to explain my broken-compass-because-of-my-DUI-accident theory, which is probably mostly erroneous anyway. It's just another story I tell myself.

"Right here, dude," Paddy instructs urgently.

I brake abruptly and pull off to the curb.

"You alright?" Paddy asks.

I consider whether or not to tell him that I spend the majority of my time in a fantasy world and that I'm wondering if I won't soon slip into it permanently.

"I'm fine, cool," I say. "How are you?"

Paddy has no intention of getting out of my car anytime soon, so I roll down the windows for some air and then shut off the ignition. It's perfect out and the little breeze feels fantastic, despite the mild sewer smell wafting in. He's recapping his resentments: hot ex-girlfriend who left him, he can't get a job, he used to flip houses for big money, he can't get a girlfriend. I pretend to listen.

"It's rough man," I respond to Paddy. "I get it. But you're smart. You haven't been to prison like the rest of the guys in this place. And let's be honest, you have the advantage of being a white guy. Nobody presumes the worst about you. You can get a job and start over. You and I are lucky that way. Imagine if you were a black dude, fresh out of prison, like most of the guys in this place."

"I don't feel lucky," Paddy responds despondently.

"I don't feel lucky either," I admit, "and I hate it when people tell me I should feel lucky because something worse could have happened to me." I pause. "Sorry, dude. I should know better."

"Don't worry about it, dude," Paddy replies.

"But we know one thing for sure," I say, trying to inject some hope. "There is nothing that a drink can't make worse."

Paddy rolls his eyes. "You got all those 12-Step sayings memorized, don't you?"

"Dude, I'm no different from you," I retort. "I'm starting all over, too. I've got this fucked up résumé. You kiddin' me?"

"I appreciate it," Paddy says. "But let's be honest. You are you, and I am me."

"Look, man," I respond. "It may be cheesy, but I'm trying to live by all these 12-Step sayings, because I need to change. Yeah, I am me, the guy that burned down my life." I feel the heaviness of this fact in my chest. My checking account balance flashes in my mind. I squeeze my face with my hands.

"But I never had it going on like you," Paddy says.

He gets out of my car, shuts the door, lights up a cigarette and stands, leaning on my car with his elbows on the roof. I watch him through the sunroof's dirty tinted glass. His eyes bulge.

I feel desperate, powerless to say anything helpful to him. I think of the Big Book, the chapter entitled, "Working with Others." What does it say? Fuck, I can't remember. I've read it so many times. Why can't I remember?

I press a button and the sunroof slowly slides open. "Just keep coming back, Paddy," I say.

Paddy stares through me.

"Nice work, Joseph," I mumble to myself, sarcastically.

He drums my car's roof twice. "Alright, Joseph. Thanks for the ride, man."

Paddy walks toward the rear entrance of a depressingly-institutional building. I have to say something. I burst out of my car and stand above it. I'm pinned against my car door by passing traffic.

"Paddy!" I holler.

He turns back, squinting at me. He moves a few steps closer, but not enough to commit to a conversation.

I shout out a couple of 12-Stepper platitudes, none of which penetrate him, all of which I'm embarrassed to be shouting out in the open. I feel inept, helpless, stupid.

He bails me out. "Thanks dude," he says. "I really appreciate it." He crushes his cigarette in the patchy crabgrass, turns and walks away.

I drive off. I pull up to a stoplight. There is a beautiful young woman in a little white Honda beside me. I don't want her to see me talking to myself so I bring the conversation back into my head.

Maybe Paddy is going to relapse. Maybe he already has. Every time I get an inkling someone relapsed or that they are drunk, stoned or high on opioids, it turns out I'm right. Maybe he's just depressed. Why wouldn't he be? He's my age. It's tough starting over in your mid-30s. It's not like some of those 20-somethings in meetings, especially if they didn't end up with a criminal record. Hell, they're probably better off in the 12-Step culture than with their non-addict peers. They've got a new way to live that works. They are powerful people. Paddy and I, we are powerful too, but we've got wreckage to deal with.

I've got a little over 10 grand left. That's a lot of money for someone who has an income and doesn't live in Los Angeles, but for someone who doesn't have an income and does live in Los Angeles, that's only enough to live on for a couple months, maybe four if I stretch it out. I'm prone to convenience spending, so I know the reality is that I've got two or three months, tops. I shouldn't be doing what I'm about to do, but I want to. It makes me happy.

I drive up Hillhurst Avenue past Los Feliz Boulevard. The street narrows and splits, one side for those coming into the park and one side for those leaving it. Between the lanes is a wide grassy median with mature oak trees. On both sides of the street are large homes, some are modern with flat roofs and lots of glass, some are old adobe types, and some have the feel of old Hollywood. I think to myself, maybe Fatty Arbuckle or Charlie Chaplin lived up here, back when silent movies were shot in Echo Park. Just past the last of these homes, where Griffith Park begins and just short of the outdoor Greek Amphitheater, is a nine-hole muni golf course called "Rosy," short for Roosevelt. It's the middle of the day on Tuesday, so the course is uncrowded, and it's only $12 to play.

I walk up with my old golf bag in tow. I've been hauling this bag around with me from town to town since Tito gave it to me in 1991. It was old when he gave it to me. I also have the same golf shoes I bought back then, ugly suede bucks I bought at Roger Dunn in San Bernardino. They used to fit. I don't know how my feet got bigger, but they did.

Clarence walks toward me from the parking lot.

"What's happening, Clarence?" I ask.

"I'm alright, Joseph. Enjoying your freedom?"

"I sure am. Still sober." I say this to invite a response as to whether he is still sober. Like Peter, my pre-prison, early-sobriety trudging buddy, he was always a bit half in the Program, at least that's what I thought. But Clarence doesn't take my bait, he just smiles. He's wicked funny. Clarence has this joke he tells: "I was talking to my mom the other days, and she says, 'Terrence, how are you doing?' And I say, 'I'm fine, mom, but my name isn't Terrence, it's Clarence.'" He could tell that joke, delivered raw and deadpan like he does, a dozen times in a row, and I'd laugh as if I just heard it for the first time. Underneath a façade of calm, Clarence is smoldering angry and full of resentment. He's a classic Big Book-style addict. He was the lead guitarist in a rock band that only the drastically cool have heard of. The lead singer committed suicide just when the band started getting mainstream fame. I forget what Clarence said. The lead singer either hanged himself, shot himself or OD'd on heroin, the usual, but Clarence didn't like the guy much, at least that's the impression I get. Clarence lives off an income property in Los Feliz that he bought back when he signed a record deal for his own band, which he started after the singer offed himself. He's kind of got it made, except for living with that alcoholic head of his. I like Clarence a lot, but we aren't close. I'm not sure he's close to anyone. He and Peter go way back to their Orange County punk rock days when Peter played in The Teenagers and was a notorious raging drunk. Peter played me one of Clarence's songs. I was waiting to be unimpressed, but I swear it sounded like The Beatles.

"That's Clarence," Peter told me. "He recorded it, and even played all the instruments, maybe except drums." Peter said "Clarence is huge in Austria. Sometimes he still tours there."

Trenton and Paul arrive together, and our foursome follows a foursome of geared-out Korean ladies, which ensures this will be a long nine holes, which is fine with me. I love spending time with these guys. I volunteer to tee off first. I take a big vicious practice swing and swish the air. Trenton snickers something about John Daly. I don't know who that is, so I don't respond. Trenton is from Boston and moved out to Los Angeles with his wife to practice law, but he burned out on it the way addicts do and now he teaches instead. His law degree is from BU and he's got a masters in something from BU too, and he's getting another one in Computer Science. I met Trenton a couple years ago at a meeting, and ever since we've hung out pretty often. He's got this giant Jew-fro and rides his bike everywhere. He's all about computers. I call him when I become tragically frustrated and am contemplating a personal control+alt+delete. He helps me out, sometimes even takes over my computer remotely, which blows my mind, and then tells me never to let anyone else do that. And then he plugs open source as if he is trying to recruit me into some operating system-based cult.

Rosy's Hole One is a straight-ahead short par-four with mature pine trees right and some room left. A really good player could drive this green. I pull my driver, the Taylor Made 360Ti that Will recommended I purchase back before we opened our law firm, Yi & Naus. He told me it was the greatest deal ever, so I rushed across town to some giant golf store in West Los Angeles. It's a mean-looking thing, all shiny black with red accents like a black widow. I take another major league prac-tice swing, then step up to the ball, take a deep breath, and take a rip-ping swipe. The feel of contact with the ball is something akin to taking an axe to a steel pipe. The vibration is painfully wrong. It's all fucking wrong. My ball starts right and keeps going right, depositing itself deep in the weeds, 40 yards out and up the hill.

"Fuck! God dammit! Mother fucker! Jesus Christ! Every mother-fucking time, errr!" I yell and my cussing fades off through my bit teeth. It's hot red suppressed anger, not that good, funny kind, but the vicious type—the kind that reminds me of my dad.

"You might want to hit another one," Paul says, chuckling.

I'm embarrassed by my shot but more so by my reaction. Why can't I keep my mouth shut? I'm terrible at golf. Why do I think I should play well?

Clarence tells me to just take a Mulligan, which is a free shot, as if the first one didn't happen. I do so, and I hit the identical shot in the identical place, but this time I'm able to limit my reaction to only one "God Fucking Dammit!"

Paul tees up next. Paul is Trenton's sponsor. He's got his absurdly famous, rock star friend's old clubs, which are brand new and expensive. Paul hits a glancing, five-iron that starts left and fades right, but it ends up in the middle of the fairway. Paul has the perfect disposition for golf and life, for that matter. He enjoys the walk and has no expectations. If he hits a bad shot, he doesn't act much different than if he hit a good one. Paul's impeccable golf attitude irritates me.

Clarence is up next. He uses an old wooden-headed club. If cc is a measurement of volume, which I think it might be, and my Taylor Made 360Ti driver is 360 cc, his wooden driver is probably a fourth the size, 100 cc. He takes a couple practice swings, stands over the ball, waggles his club, and takes a smooth swing that seems slow, but when Clarence hits the ball it makes a mellifluous crack sound. The ball flies high and starts a little right and then draws back a few yards. It's a beautiful thing, right in the middle of the fairway about eighty yards short of the green.

Trenton's swing is a spastic thing, comically ugly. After he hits and cusses, and hits again and cusses, he and I go look for our tee shots, all four of which are buried in the same area on the hillside.

"At least we are fucking consistent," Trenton says. "I didn't know Clarence was so good."

"Yeah," I say. "He's like a bad-ass guitarist and super good at baseball, too. What an asshole, right?"

"Completely," Trenton says. "Don't invite him again."

The round, especially the time spent waiting at tee boxes between holes, becomes a small uninhibited men's stag, 12-Step meeting.

In response to my complaints about not being able to get a job before I've actually tried to get one, Paul says, "Just do what's in front of you, and let God take care of the rest." Despite being born and raised in Los Angeles and being a drummer in an iconic Los Angeles rock band, Paul has a Southern manner that makes cliché 12-Step axioms seem like original gems of wisdom.

"Yeah you are right," I respond. "I should spend less time worrying about getting work and more—or actually, any—time trying to get some work."

"Chop wood, carry water," Trenton says cheekily.

As if in a Stepford Wife trance, Clarence speaks at quarter speed, "Let... Go... Let... God..." Fully committed to his gag, he holds his face in an empty-eyed, slack-jawed stare, which reminds me of the Andre the Giant "Obey" posters that were plastered all over Los Angeles. After a few beats of perfect facial paralysis, Clarence shakes his head as if he's been suddenly awakened from hypnosis. He acts confused, as if to say, "What just happened?"

I laugh with my whole body, and all the double and triple bogeys, skulled chips and three-putts sting less. A couple triple-bogeys later, I contemplate asking him to tell us that joke about his mom calling him Terrence again but decide not to. I commend myself. It's a rarity that I'm able to keep my mouth shut. It's more and more the case that the sound of my own voice, especially when re-reiterating some worn-out opinion I don't even care about, makes me cringe. Is there anything more annoying than someone who takes a 12-Step anniversary cake at a meeting and shares and then shares again? Shouldn't that be illegal or something? Yeah, wring that rag out again, Joseph. You are a couple months away from bankruptcy. Do you really want to spend your energy complaining about 12-Step meeting faux pas? What about people who don't put a buck in the basket when they've got a $5 latte in their hand? It's maddening. Shut up, Joseph. Just shut up.

By the time we get to the eighth hole, my dream of breaking bogey golf is dashed again. Given my score, maybe I should dream of playing double-bogey golf first.

I stand on the tee box. "Hit a cut-shot starting at the observatory and let it drift back toward the hole, about 175 yards," Clarence instructs me, as if I have any idea how to hit a cut-shot. I'm not even sure what a cut-shot is, although I'm guessing it's a slice that doesn't hurt my ego.

"Shall do," I reply.

I'm the last to hit. Trenton's ball is up the hill in the trees right. Paul and Clarence are in the fairway, Clarence ideally, and Paul acceptably. So far, it's a repeat of Hole One, but not for me. My shot is going to be straight and long.

I approach the tee box gingerly, so as to not disturb the golf gods. I'm going to follow Clarence's lead, nice and smooth. Let the club do the work. I make a rhythmical practice swing. Yes, yes, Joseph, that's nice. I waggle like I saw Clarence do. I dig in my FootJoy spikes, take one last deep breath and take my three-wood up to the top of my backswing. I take a vicious slash at the ball. My clubhead digs into the ground several inches behind the tee as if my intention was to dig the tee out like a weed. My ball, my sixth ball actually—the first five having been deposited somewhere in the trees and brush of the previous holes—dribbles 25 yards up and right and into the scrub brush.

I yell "fuck!" gutturally, which, at least reduces the volume from the more high-pitched variety I unleashed on the first tee. My anger quickly recedes into a spectrum-wide embarrassment. Why does this make me so mad? I tee up another little white dimpled devil and take a swing exaggeratedly slow in order to make a show of the fact that I have to swing this slow just to make flush contact with the ball. To my surprise, a nice little crack sends my ball flying nicely up the fairway.

A little chorus of mumbling compliments arises from my playing partners. This is the first time in the round that I have produced anything resembling a golf shot.

"Even a broken clock is right twice a day," Trenton quips.

EIGHT

I stand atop the landing of an old set of concrete stairs that lead down to Sunset Boulevard. It's just around the corner from my apartment. The sun is high, it's winter-warm, and the air is clear. The sparse downtown Los Angeles skyline is several miles away, but it feels as if I could reach out and touch it.

I turn back and admire the rows of seven-story tall, palm trees that line both sides of Laveta Terrace. When the Santa Ana winds blow, they sound like an ocean storm, and they're just as loud, and they bob and bend, but they never break. Today, however, their shaggy tops only lightly sway in the breeze.

I'd be surprised if this staircase hasn't appeared in an old noir movie or two. It's wide, concrete, and bordered by thick trees. At night, it's lit by old-timey street lamps built into its low sidewalls, reminiscent of the movie poster for *The Exorcist*. During the day, it's a portrait of Los Angeles civic architecture.

I climb down the first flight of stairs, and a man comes into view on the first of three landings. He lies atop a bed of cardboard and is wrapped tightly in a dirty grey blanket. I walk lightly so as not to wake him. The stench of dried body odor and stale beer reminds me that I picked a lemon blossom from the tree that canopies my driveway. I pinch the lemon blossom between my fingers and hold it under my nostrils and breathe in the sweet smell.

I make my way down to Sunset, walk down the boulevard past the dollar store, the second-hand clothing store and the athletic shoe store that seems to have no customers or employees. The four corners of Sunset Boulevard and Echo Park Avenue are bustling. A Latino street vendor selling bags of cut fruit, the hipsters and the homeless, the Latinos and all kinds of people less visually classifiable, they're all out and about. I cross Sunset at Echo Park Avenue. The *tee-tock, tee-tock* sound notifies the blind that the crosswalk light is green. I hop forward to avoid a cop car turning left. Its driver, a man with a tight haircut and aviator sunglasses, waves out his window to me in apology.

I stand in line on the sidewalk at the Bank of America ATM. I feel good. And then I realize that since I left my apartment 15 minutes ago, I've been in my body. I haven't been thinking about me and my fears. It's definitely better this way. Every moment that I'm not thinking about my hideous label, my crash-and-burn, or my myriad other problems is a victory for my mental health.

Someone, I think it might have been Shannon, told me that this particular Bank of America was once the most robbed bank in America. I can feel it. I can see their ghosts. They park on the street and leave the motor running. They burst in shouting obscenities. They wear women's nylons squeezed over their faces, distorting their features monstrously. I can see the reddish vapor trails from their violent adrenaline. I can hear sirens and terrified customers.

Maybe I've watched *Point Break, Heat* and *Reservoir Dogs* too many times.

I've never been inside this Bank of America, but I always peer in through the glass en route to the ATMs. It's gigantic. The ceiling must be three stories high, imposing like the old savings & loans that used to be the pillars of most towns. Now all the banks are like fast food joints. The massive line of teller windows is all hidden behind 20-foot-high, thick Plexiglas, with little sliding pockets for the customers to slip their paychecks to the tellers. It's as if the bank doesn't want its customers coming inside. It's continually eliminating these pesky, costly human interactions. I comply and use the outdoor ATM. There are two of them, one empty, and yet there is a long line inside. The customers must want to see a bank robbery firsthand. They are tired of all the cinematic dramatizations. After my failure to enter the correct PIN twice because I'm really enjoying my bank robbery daydream, the ATM spits out my two twenties and a receipt. I brace myself to look at my balance. Oh God, I've dipped below $8,000. I have less than $8,000 worth of days left until my final demise.

Macy and I stand on a colorful terrace overlooking Sunset Boulevard just west of Café Tropical. We are guests at a crowded 12-Stepper party hosted by a mutual friend from the Saturday night meeting. Our mutual friend—she of the old-timey hats, the kind that require bobby pins—has decorated her large apartment Mexican shabby chic. There is an unfinished wood table, potted cacti, and mosaic tiles in pale orange, cornflower blue, and sunlight yellow.

Night is finally overtaking day.

At her request, I tell her my birth date, and Macy reports the only thing I know about astrology, which is that I'm an Aquarius. She tells me Oprah is an Aquarius too, and that we are mass communicators and ambitious. My belief in astrology rivals my confidence in Voodoo, but I eagerly answer her questions as she inputs my answers into a program on her phone that will, she tells me, provide us with a full report of my tendencies and future prospects.

I was so happy to see Macy here. These 12-Stepper parties can be brutal. My usual survival technique involves finding another uncomfortable partygoer and locking eyes with them for a couple hours. Then we take turns dumping every sordid detail of our lives, including exactly how we came to be addicts, our family and romantic relationships, which rehabs, jails, and psych wards we've attended, which meetings we go to, what we love and hate about each and every meeting we go to, and who we sponsor and who sponsors us and which of the 12 Steps we are on—all until *I*, and I'm quite sure *they* feel the same way, would have preferred to have stood alone in the middle of the room staring silently at the wall. The emotional hangover from these 12-Step mass data dumps, which I can't seem to avoid, involves my skin slithering off me and hiding in a closet while I recount the conversation and its awkward end.

After she has finished imputing all my information, Macy fiddles with her phone, but ultimately reaches the conclusion that she can't tell me the results now because of poor cellphone reception and will have to email me my astrological forecast later.

I tell myself: I'm not going to do that cowardly thing I've done in the past where I talk to a woman I like here and there and insert myself into her life, always looking for hints of whether she likes me, so that when I do ask her out, I already know the answer. It's dishonest. I'm not doing it. You man-up now or you fucking leave her alone.

I give her my email address. She punches it into her phone. A friend of hers, another stylish 12-Stepper, approaches with a purposefully exaggerated zeal, and hugs Macy. Macy introduces me, and her friend nods and smiles at me and then returns her attention to Macy.

"Girl, you are the queen of the cute top and jeans," she says.

I nod and smile in agreement. Macy says something self-deprecating and funny. I can feel the door of opportunity closing as the conversation shifts and Macy readies to leave.

Fuck it.

"Excuse me. I'm sorry to interrupt...," I say, and they both stop and stare at me. "I know you have to go...," I say to Macy and turn to the woman and awkwardly explain. "She told me she had to go around eight, and it's 8:15... anyway." I pause and turn back to Macy. Her eyes are giant brown orbs and twinkling just a bit. Her lips are pursed. "I uh... May I have your number, your phone number... please?"

Macy's friend squares her shoulders to me as an affectation. I smile lightly at her and then Macy.

This is one of those moments. Don't turn away. You have nothing to be ashamed of. Just stand here in the discomfort and let her know your intention with your eyes. Jesus, that's a lot of positive-affirmation bullshit to ask a girl for her number, you fucking sissy.

Shut up, Joseph.

"Yes, of course," Macy says softly. She digs in her purse. It's a modern version of a suede hippie purse like my mom had when I was a kid. Macy hands me a torn piece of paper.

"Okay, thank you. Okay..." I stop, tongue-tied.

"I'll talk to you soon," Macy finishes for me in her calm, low, radio voice.

I rush away. The tops of my ears and cheeks burn red hot.

It'll be easy to get a job as a paralegal or legal secretary. Some solo practitioner is going to get the deal of her life: a seven-year attorney who has worked at big firms and who ran his own show, for the price of a paralegal, and all they have to do is put a little clause in their retainer agreement to let their clients know a disbarred attorney may be working on their file, and also, let the California Bar know! It's just a standard form. The attorney that hires me will make a killing. I can write motions that they'd have to pay some first-year attorney twice what they're paying me, and the motion will be far better. I keep repeating and refining this story of petrified bullshit as if it'll become true if I say it enough. Truth is, I've never gotten a law job without some connection. Does anybody just apply to an ad and then get a job? Nah, that doesn't happen. I've cut ties with almost all my lawyer friends and colleagues, and most lawyers wouldn't hire me if I paid them, because the thought of communicating with the California Bar, let alone advising them that you've hired a disbarred lawyer, gives them nightmares.

I've made the calls. I've emailed and even faxed my résumé to dozens of lawyers and firms, all over Los Angeles.

Crickets. Loud and constantly chirping crickets.

$5,861.32.

The number keeps going down. At the beginning of every month, it goes down by $1,500, and I'm not even paying my student loans, and just the minimum on my credit cards. Fucking vipers. I haven't charged anything on these cards in years. I just pay the minimum. I've probably paid the principal twofold. As if they know I'm thinking about them, my phone rings. It's my credit card company.

"You're calling me, and then you put me on hold and then I have to verify who I am?" I say with heavy sarcasm. "You called me!"

"It's for security reasons, sir."

"You only have a job because the United States Congress has been bought out by corporate America and gives predatory corporations exceptions to laws against usury! I bet you don't even know what usury is."

"Usury, sir?"

"Yes, usury! A loan shark charges 20 percent, he goes to jail. Citibank does it, and their stock goes up. Usury is in the Bible!"

"Sir, I don't make policy. I'm just calling to remind you that you are late on your payment."

"That is bullshit. Everyone just passes the buck. What's your name?"

"Michael. Employee Number 1542."

"You sure don't sound like a Michael-Number 1542. Let me talk to the guy who does make policy. You are part of the problem, you know that, Michael-Number 1542? I'll fucking pay when I get the money!"

I hang up.

A neighborhood cat, black with white-tipped ears, sits atop my futon, staring toward me nonchalantly, pulsing his underhanded paw like a sea anemone, claws stretching out.

I think of how unsatisfying it is to press "end call" on a cell phone instead of slamming a receiver down. I stare into the cat's green eyes. He looks right into my eyes.

"I know, Black. I know... No, I'm not calling my sponsor. Why would I? I know what to do. Step Nine, Step Ten."

I scratch Black between his ears until he bites me. I'm suddenly exhausted. I pick up my cell phone, which is now five pounds heavier, and dial the number to Citibank. A half-hour later and after several tries and a silly number of button presses and long holds, explaining to each call-center rep that I have to talk to Michael Number 1542, I'm miraculously reconnected to Michael from India or maybe Bangladesh, Employee Number 1542. He makes me go through the whole social security number, card number, and address verification process, which I endure with deep breathing.

"Michael, I just called to apologize for yelling at you," I say.

"Sir?"

"I'm the guy that said you are part of the problem and usury and all that..."

"Oh, yes. What can I help you with sir?"

"Nothing, I just called to apologize. Is there anything I can do to make it right?"

Michael holds the silence for a moment. I wonder if he's considering his training and trying to reconcile this unusual situation. I imagine there is a supervisor overseeing every call on some Big Brother phone system in some giant room in Calcutta, the only Indian city I can think of. It probably flags unusual conversations.

"Would you like to make a payment, sir?"

"No thank you, Michael. Have a good day."

I press "end call." The phone feels lighter, but I'm still tired.

You happy, Black Cat? Huh? Maybe next time instead of being an asshole and apologizing for it, I can just not be an asshole in the first place?

Black Cat jumps down off the couch and stands next to the counter where I sometimes feed him. I pull out the box of Purina dry food I bought at the bodega, and Black gets excited, dancing back and forth, his tail up, wagging.

"That shit about usury is true, Black Cat," I say as I pour the brown star-shaped kibble into a saucer. "You know I'm right."

$3,872.55

"I know what you are thinking, but it's not that," I say to Black Cat, who I'm refusing to let out until I finish talking this through with him. It's the least he can do. I've been feeding him every day since I made amends to the Citibank employee, Michael from India. "I'm okay with the whole worker amongst workers deal. So what if I was a lawyer? I believe a hard day's work is honorable no matter if it's digging graves or managing the cemetery. It's just scary. You don't fucking know. You just want me for my Friskies. I'm going to do this, Black. Meow if you're with me."

Black Cat responds to his name by staring at me and then returns his focus to the front door, but he does not meow.

"Fine, go on," I say and open the door. Black Cat darts out and down the driveway between my car and the city trash cans and then crosses the street and disappears under my neighbor's chain-link gate.

I pick up my phone, find Ken's number and call him.

"Joseph," Ken answers. "I'm so glad you called. We have a lot to go over."

Ken launches into his legal issues. "My accountant fucked up the paperwork on the Mexican union contract on the maquiladora—costing me money every day. He's an idiot. You can take that over. And there's my Fullerton rental, the one you handled the arbitration on, remember that one?"

"Yeah," I respond.

"I'm trying to sell it and the, uh... fucking tenant... suddenly discovers mold, mold which he doesn't seem to be able to find to show me, of course, after I tell him he needs to vacate in a few months. He's stopped paying rent. Just evict him, and then—"

"Ken," I interrupt. "Let me just stop you. I can't do any of this stuff. I'm disbarred. It's not that I can't go to court and do trials. I can't practice law at all, even if it's only transactional work."

"Nonsense," Ken responds. "My accountant isn't a lawyer, and he handles the maquiladora corporate legal filings. It's just paperwork. Same with my broker. She's handled tenant issues for me before. She's not a lawyer."

"No, Ken. I can't. Believe me. I could go to jail for practicing law without a license. Brokers and accountants can do certain things within their fields that is technically the practice of law. It's like an exception to the law against practicing law without a law license."

"No shit?"

"No shit."

"So why'd you call? Just to say hello?"

"I need some work, Ken. I can do whatever. I need a paycheck."

I wait while he sounds out non-words, *mmm, hmm, mmmmhhhmmm*. After a final short *hmm*, there is silence.

"Ken?"

"I'm thinking... Uh, look, I'm sorry, man. I don't have anything. I'll let you know if I do. Gotta go."

He hangs up. I feel buzzy and anxious. Oh, fucking fuck! This isn't good. Ken was my ace. I expected him to have something. He has so many businesses. Skid Row floats to the top of my mind. Dudes I know from rehab, mostly junkies like Gerard, ended up there. Their Skid Row stories were hard to even listen to. I don't know how to do that. I couldn't survive like that. I'd go into the forest like Grizzly Adams and try to make a go of it like that. I'm not sure I could do the begging thing. That's probably what Gerard said, too, but he did it. I still have a nice suit. I could hold a cardboard sign that reads "Illegal Legal Advice from Disbarred Lawyer." I bet that'd get some traction, just like those homeless guys that hold signs that say things like, "Honestly, I just need a beer." This isn't that fucking funny, Joseph. You are getting close to the end of the line. I recall when my mom and I lived in the Alley, when I used to go down to the Santa Ana riverbed and collect cans, and there were these homeless encampments, before I'd ever heard the word homeless. I think about driving down to Malibu and just swimming out to sea... just keep swimming and swimming. Maybe this is too much for me to handle. Maybe I need to pull the plug.

I dig out the crumpled ATM receipt from my pocket.

$3,872.55.

"Can I take you out to dinner?" I ask Macy over the phone. I'm nervous but try to sound confident, just not too confident.

I can tell from the first word out of her mouth that her answer is no. Did she just give me her number because I put her on the spot? It didn't feel like that. She explains she's just ending a relationship and isn't in the right place to be dating, but she likes me and wants to be friends and appreciates the invitation. I sense a sliver of an opening when she tells me she particularly appreciates me not playing games when asking her out like most guys do. I have nothing to lose at this point, so I put up a fight. As a concession, she says we can have coffee.

"My intention was romantic," I say. "I mean, not that I don't want to have coffee and be friends, but my intention was, you know, to go on a date."

I can tell this sentiment hits her by the tone of her response. Macy agrees to meet me at the Bright Spot, Echo Park's official hipster diner.

Even though I'm not picking her up, it's a date. I say, just to make sure, "It's a date, right?" Macy giggles and says, "Yes, it's a date."

NINE

I'm on my way to Arrowhead Country Club with Tito. He's driving his Mercedes. He presses hard on the gas and then brakes, gas and brake, jerking the car like a broken Ferris wheel. I want to explain my drive-like-water-runs theory, but I don't, because I'm twenty years old and just happy to be here. I love being around Tito when we are alone in the office dealing with some big lawsuit. Just being around him makes me feel better than I've ever felt. I want to be the best I can be, because he chose me. Maybe I make too big a deal of it, but I've had lawyers come up to me and ask in this conspiratorial tone, "So... how do you know Tito?" I tell them my story, how I met him at a luncheon where I'd won a scholarship based on an essay I wrote, and Tito was there awarding his annual memorial scholarship for his eldest son who passed; that later, I'd gone to his office and said I would work for free, that I just wanted to learn; that it quickly turned into a paying gig. I don't tell them I think Tito sees a little of himself in me: a kid that came from nothing, less than nothing, and is pulling himself up by his bootstraps on the way to becoming a trial lawyer. Or, maybe that it has to do with Tito's eldest son, who was going to become a great legal talent like Tito, but died of a rare disease while attending Berkeley's law school, Boalt Hall. And I don't talk about how I imagine that Tito is really my dad, and how great that'd be.

Tito nearly rear-ends a truck and I grab the oh-shit handle above the passenger window. We drive by beautiful homes: Colonials, Tudors, Cape Cods, Modern Ranches, all adorning Arrowhead Country Club's golf course like melee diamonds in the settings of a giant jade broach. The grass and trees are lit by the low winter sun, and the sky is electric blue, and the air is cooled by the snow-topped San Bernardino mountains, which look close enough to reach with two solidly struck five-iron shots. I've picked up street prostitutes a few miles away, down on Baseline Street. I squeeze my face and crush this thought. I banish it. Never again. Today, in this great year of my life, in 1992, I'm going to play golf for the second time ever, at a private country club. I've got my new-used clubs, my golf spikes, I've been to the range a half-dozen times. I'm ready to wow Tito and his son, Tomar, and a lawyer from the office, Jaime Paleco.

Tito is treated like a celebrity here, even more so than at the courthouse where the other lawyers and judges have to keep the gushing to a minimum. It takes 15 minutes just to make it through the clubhouse, as Tito is greeted by every member and employee we cross paths with. He always says, "This is Joseph, my assistant, a debate champion who will be attending law school soon," in reference to my Model United Nations victory. Everyone is some big shot. He owns a string of car dealerships. He's a judge. She's a surgeon. That was the mayor. That's Mitch Meyers, you recognize his surname from the opposing counsel's letterhead on that big quadriplegic accident case I just settled. Oh, and he's the senior partner at "White Guy, Rich Guy and Old Guy, Attorneys at Law." "Oh, it's a pleasure to meet you, Joseph!" they all say.

Jaime, Tomar, and I wait at the first tee box for Tito, who is getting some last-minute instruction from the club pro. Tito is holding his driver, and the pro is standing behind him, holding the clubhead and directing its path in the backswing. "Back and up, yep, that's right Tito, very nice, back and up."

The first hole is a dogleg left, which, Tito explains, means the hole is shaped like a dog's hind leg, the fairway going up and then left to the putting green. Tito tees up first. The head of his driver is the size of a pug's head. He steps up and uses his ball to plug the tee into the ground.

Tito points the head of his club down the fairway like Babe Ruth pointing to the outfield. His practice swing is violent and spastic and wholly un-athletic. His real swing is even more vigorously spastic, but sends the ball flying down the fairway a couple hundred yards. He looks back at us with a cocky grin.

I'm next.

"Go ahead, Joseph. Hit it right down the center of the fairway," Tito instructs me.

I've sweat through my white polo. What happened? I was so confident. I was looking forward to this tee shot, this round. It's a beautiful, green, perfectly manicured course. But now I'm terrified.

"Jaime and, uh, Tomar, go ahead," I say, walking back to the electric golf cart, pretending that I forgot something in my golf bag.

Jaime steps between the tee markers, plugs his ball onto the tee the same way Tito did, using the ball to press the tee into the ground. Jaime takes a nice fluid swing at the ball. His ball curves from left to right and rolls out 20 yards past Tito's. Tomar does the same and his ball flies even further.

I try to tee my ball up like Tito and Jaime, using the ball to drive the tee in the ground, but I can't seem to get it right, and I'm shaking. I'm shaking! What the hell? I clumsily set the ball on the tee. It tumbles off, because I've got the tee angled. I pull it out and replace it. I look back at Tito. He looks concerned, his eyebrows raised, arms crossed on his chest. Tomar gives me a reassuring half-smile.

I take a practice swing. It settles me a little. That didn't feel too bad. Nice and smooth. I look down the fairway, take a deep breath. Then I rip the club back and tear a gash in time and space as I give it everything I've got. I hit the ball solidly, but the clubface was wide open and the ball fires into the dense bushes with such force it actually makes it through, dribbling off into a portion of the golf club's property that is not intended for golf balls.

"Go ahead and take a Mulligan," Tito instructs.

I don't look back. I'm tingling with embarrassment and shock. I knew I'd do better than that. I just knew it. What the fuck just happened? I re-tee a new ball, a nice shiny Top Flight 1, and I take another swing. This one travels an equal distance forward and right, for a net total of about 50 yards. I squeeze my mouth shut and try not to scream fuck. I walk over to the cart, lock-mouthed, and resist slamming my driver down into my bag. I get in the cart, and Tito drives me to my ball. It's about 150 yards behind his ball.

I swing my iron and displace more fairway than had I swung a flat-head shovel. I take three more hacks, and I'm still behind Tito's ball. Holding a tight smile, Tito shows me how to fill a divot with the sand-filled bottle attached to the cart.

"That was four, young man, not counting the Mulligan, so actually, six," Tito says. "Why don't you take a break, and I'll hit."

Jaime and Tomar are already on the putting green waiting, staring back at us. Tito pulls out a five-iron and takes a swing that is a smaller version of his driver swing. I am suddenly much less critical of it. His ball lands just short of the green and trickles on. He smiles at me, winks, and then laughs. I follow by skulling my ball three more times. I'm on the green in seven strokes, nine if you count the Mulligan. I walk to my ball which is 10 feet from the flag. I see Tomar and then Jaime cringe at me as I walk to my ball. I look at them confused, then back at Tito, who is walking up after pulling the cart up to the side of the green.

"You just walked over everyone's line," Tito says.

"Line?" I respond.

Tito explains what it means to walk on someone's line while Jaime and Tomar putt out. I manage to three-putt from 10 feet for a 10, or 12 if I count the Mulligan.

"Par for me," Tomar reports, as he writes down the scores. "Birdie for Jaime here, par for dad, and Joseph... well, I'll just put an X..."

❖   ❖   ❖

She opens the door to a security gate leading into a small parking lot, freshly asphalted. Her car, one of a couple dozen, is parked under a numbered off-white painted carport. It's a Toyota 4Runner, blue and beaten. The apartment complex is set atop a thin strip of property on a hill in Silver Lake. She's wearing those jeans again: faded old Levi's 501s rolled up above her ankles and so loose, her hips barely keep them on. She wears strappy platform sandals and a billowy blouse. I follow her. She walks briskly and doesn't look back, as if she has someone waiting on the phone or maybe just wants to get back inside. I follow, my head on a swivel, taking it all in: the smell of eucalyptus trees, the hum of the freeway, louder than its proximity. We walk down a short flight, take a right down a covered outdoor hall and stand in front of her apartment door.

"Welcome to my home," she says, turning to me and then opening the door with a long right arm like a doorman.

I smile at her. Her smile is broad, with big teeth, nicely imperfect, like handmade jewelry.

I stop only a few steps inside and gawk. "Wow," I say.

There is a kitchen to my left, separating the rest of the room with a counter. To the right are steps leading downstairs. The rest is a high-ceilinged rectangular box with a large window at the end. The floor is stripped to the floorboards and painted a dark flat Prince purple. There is a shabby-chic wood table with mismatched wooden chairs, a gold-upholstered mid-century couch. The television sits on an industrial-style metal cart. A giant white-on-black lithograph of a cowboy in an advertisement hangs on the wall. I walk deeper into Macy's loft apartment and she follows beside me, like a museum guide. I'm in awe like a college kid visiting the Met for the first time. I turn and stare at the giant stark cowboy painting. I know almost nothing about art, but I know this is something.

"It was my ex-husband's. I took it when I left," Macy says and smiles mischievously, knowing she just revealed a whole new line of questioning.

Macy sits on a piano bench behind a black vintage electric keyboard on a black metal stand that forms the shape of an X. I walk to the window. It's dark out now. We are suspended hundreds of yards up on a hillside in Silver Lake over the 5 Freeway, a giant traffic artery with several lanes running north and south. Running alongside the freeway is the Los Angeles River, and beyond I see twinkling lights of yellow white and orange, which is Atwater Village and then beyond, the city of Glendale. The backsides of the mountains of Griffith Park are hulking shadows to the north.

It is beautiful. I feel relieved, calm. I want to open the window and glide out above it all, like Peter Pan. I slide open the window a little, and the hum of the freeway is much louder than I expected. I look over at Macy, expecting her to say something, but she doesn't. I shut the window. She plays several somber notes on her electric keyboard. It fills the room. I sit on her gold couch.

"Your place is amazing," I say to her. I notice that she is wearing more makeup than the last time I saw her. Her hair, this giant beautiful mess of loose curls in caramel, black, brown and blonde strands, is lit by the lamplight so that some of the blonde curls appear electrified.

"I didn't know you were a musician," I say, looking around at some of the gear surrounding her: a mic and stand, an acoustic guitar, and small amp.

She begins to play a song. It's slow and soulful and sparse, every note has its own life. And then she sings, slowly, fully. Her voice is clear and raspy, sad and beautiful, and completely unique. Oh my God. It's fantastic. Gooseflesh starts on my forearms and spreads up to my shoulders. I stare with my ears and eyes, and after a while I gasp because I forget to breathe. She finishes the chorus, something about fossils, and then plays the last long note and then there is silence. She looks up at me with a soft smile.

I'm stunned.

"Why in the hell aren't you a star?"

She giggles and saunters over to the couch and sits next to me. She tells me how she made this album with a previous ex-boyfriend, how they'd played some good venues and that one of the songs was the title track to a movie, but ultimately, it petered out. She still likes to sing and plays occasionally at home but performing wasn't her thing.

Her horror story childhood rivals mine. Dad was a pimp, mom was a prostitute that has since disappeared. She was raised by a wonderful foster family. Her face softens when she talks about them, The Stensons. She enjoys saying their name. Then her dad gets out of prison and whisks her away, and when he goes back in, as cons tend to do, she ends up being raised by a very fashionable and artistic but cruel former high-end prostitute.

Macy has a son. She shows me his photo. It breaks my heart. He's so beautiful, with hair like an angora bunny, and toffee skin, and dark, innocent, sadly shaped eyes.

Macy's been married three times. Her son's dad is a good man and a good father, just not the man for her. Before that she was married to another good man, but she was not in love with him. It was really more of a father-figure thing, she eventually discovered. Then, just recently, she married the opposite kind of man. He's elfin-handsome like Beck, a stylish Ivy-leaguer, lives in a giant loft in downtown Los Angeles, a place she calls "skid row adjacent," which I love, as it just rolls off the tongue. He's a commercial director, makes a lot of money, spends all of it and more. She has come to realize she married him for wrong reasons and that became readily apparent when, just months after their honeymoon, she bumped a table, which activated a keyboard, which lit up a screen, which revealed a profile on a sex hookup site. It was his profile, and he was quite active. She's dispassionate about him as she tells me the story, as if she's relived the experience so many times, she's beaten all the drama out of it. This discovery, this end of a short marriage, it was all very recent. She just moved in here. The Prince purple paint is barely dry.

I tell her about my childhood. Born to teenagers; dad leaves when I'm six months old; mom is a heroin addict, gets arrested scoring with me in car when I'm six, goes on methadone, kicks dope but becomes a shut-in depressive; welfare, etcetera.

I'm reciting this on cruise control, but all I can think of is "Registered Sex Offender." She has a kid. He's six. She'll probably just kick me out, say it's too much. It is. I'm too much. I'm way too much. She's got enough problems. But I like her.

I continue. "... mom's shitty abusive boyfriend, and I pull myself up by my proverbial bootstraps and go to college and graduate from Pepperdine and practice law but then my addictions, my addictions, my addictions..." I don't reveal the details of the night of my self-inflicted apocalypse. I go with my standard "violent assault committed in a black-out." Then rehab, jail, sober living house, prison, and now here I am.

"Oh my God," she says with mock urgency, "we are doing that thing where we tell each other way too much..." She stands up and walks over toward the kitchen. She turns on music. It's some B-side romantic Prince. She sits down next to me a little closer. She rolls her shoulders to the music. I place my hand on hers. Her skin is soft. She has long narrow fingers.

"You're so pretty," I say. I try to stay cool. I don't want her to know my heart thinks I'm sprinting.

She smiles and slides a little closer to me. I caress her hand. We both know the next thing that should happen. I must make the first move. I can't let her move in for the kiss first. That would be a mistake I can never undo. I have to prove to myself that I'm not a coward, that I won't take the easy way out, that I'm willing to endure discomfort. But I'm not moving. I'm scared. I'm sweating. Just do it. C'mon. Just do it. It's getting really awkward.

And then I kiss her, softly. Her lips feel nice. I'm relieved. I do it again, this time with just a little more hang time. That's the turning point, I think to myself. Once you've kissed a woman, it's a whole different thing.

"That was nice," I say and immediately regret it because it was only to break the awkwardness. The truth is I'm uncomfortable. Normally, I'd be pressing to move this along to the sex part, but I have no intention of doing so with Macy. In fact, I won't. It just wouldn't be right.

"I think I knew I was going to kiss you from the moment I saw you walk into the Tropical," I say.

"Oh, is that right?" she says coyly, calling me out on my stated overconfidence.

"I didn't mean it like that. I guess I should've said, 'I knew I wanted to'," I reply.

A pounding on the door startles us both.

"Macy, Macy! Open up. I know you're home, please," a man's voice yells.

The hairs on my forearms rise like needles in a pin cushion. I look to Macy. She mouths "sorry" and walks over to the door. She tells him to leave. He begs her to open up, and then she tells him she has company. And she says it in a way that lets him know what she means. He becomes angry and demands that she open the door.

My stomach burns. My chest jumps. I'm frozen. This is bad. He's asking her to just open the door a little. This could end badly. I don't want to go back to jail. Oh my God. I don't want to go back to jail. If she opens that door and he sees another man with his wife, he's going to go crazy, and I'm not going to have a choice but to fight, because there is no other way out except the front door, and I don't want to get stabbed or shot by some irate ex-husband. Cops will come, then they'll check my license, find out I'm on probation and a registered sex offender. They'll say,

"Ma'am, you're kind of lucky this happened. You were probably minutes from being raped." Then Macy's ex will pretend he's the hero. I'll be led away in handcuffs, and I'll be back in Twin Towers, probably in general population. I'll be fighting Vatos again and this time they'll have shanks.

"I'm not letting you in," Macy says to her ex. "Leave now. We'll talk later, but not now." Macy looks back at me with an apologetic smile.

And then he leaves. And my heart begins to settle down. My armpits are cold with sweat. She walks over and pours me a glass of water and apologizes and then spins her iPod to Talking Heads' *This Must Be the Place*. It's nice, but I'm done. I feel like I've accomplished my goal, and now I just want to get out of here. I hate this about myself. I haven't changed that much. What I want more than anything is to be by myself with my drug of choice. It's just that now my drug of choice is coffee and cigarettes instead of alcohol, prostitutes, and cigarettes. Macy and I talk and kiss, but my mind is out the door and soon my body follows.

I sit at a rectangular fold-up table in front of a stage the size of a large patio in a church basement. Rows of flesh-colored, metal chairs are lined up with one aisle down the middle. I counted 68 people, but there are some on the stage and in the kitchen and milling around the door smoking, so I'm not sure of the exact count, but it's a hell of a lot of people to be staring up at me. I've sweated through the vintage salmon-colored Levi's cowboy shirt I commandeered from Keri's brother, so I keep my arms tight at my side. My dried stress-sweat is, at this point, chemically pungent.

This is a 90-minute 12-Step meeting with a 10-minute break, and I'm the speaker. It's unusual for a speaker with only a couple years sober to share at a meeting this size, but my story is dramatic, so I get asked a lot. The rule is don't turn down a 12-Step request, so I don't. When I'm asked, I show up. I do the deal and follow the traditional 12-Step format:

One, What I was like; Two, What happened; and Three, What I'm like now. It's just a story in three acts. The circumstances of my life have been a well-shaken porta-potty since the last time I took a drink, nearly three years ago on July 26, 2003, but, thanks to this Program, I've had many moments of love, serenity, laughter, and joy.

I give them my usual pitch: I had a rough childhood; I pulled myself up by my bootstraps; I became a successful lawyer; then my vices became addictions. I tell them that after I rolled my car off the freeway at 85 m.p.h. and was arrested for a felony DUI, my solution was to move to a neighborhood in Santa Monica where I could walk to bars. I say, "Clearly, driving was my problem." This gets the usual laughter, and I feel like a hack comedian. Then I tell about the night when everything changed for me. I hit them with my log line: "On Tuesday I woke up a successful lawyer, but on Wednesday I woke up handcuffed to a hospital bed charged with attempted murder." They go wide-eyed. They ooh and ahh. Anyone who wasn't paying attention is paying attention now. I repeat, for what feels like the thousandth time, my carefully worded summary of my crime: In an alcoholic blackout, I broke into a strange man's apartment and woke him up in the middle of the night. We fought. He chased me out of his apartment, and then he and his neighbor beat the hell out of me, splitting open my head. Luckily, I was the only one seriously physically injured. I was charged with attempted murder because I placed the man in a deadly chokehold. I don't recall any of it. I only know what happened because I've read it in the police report. I didn't know the guy and I'd never been to his apartment. Then I tell them how I went to jail, rehab, and prison, lost my Bar license, and fought to survive for two years, all the while getting clean and sober. I tell them that I think this Program gives all of us a chance to recover, not just from drinking alcohol but from the spiritual malady that is addiction, that it's the center of my world, the last house on the block, and that I owe my life to it.

What I don't share is that I'm a registered sex offender, that I have no idea how I'm going to support myself, that I'm going broke, that I'm terrified people will find out I'm a registered sex offender, that I'll die alone and homeless, that suicide is back on the table. And I don't tell them that giving up porn and prostitutes was far more difficult than quitting drinking. And I sure as hell don't tell them, if I am being totally honest with myself, that I believe I'm as much of an active addict now as I've ever been. I've simply transferred all my addictions into the mother of them all, nicotine, cigarettes, smoking, and that I think a lot of them have too, and if we don't stop, we're going to die from it, like our founder Bill Wilson did, and that this fact is horribly ironic and sad.

During the meeting's intermission, as is customary, my fellows line up and thank me. Several ask me something along the lines of, "Can you ever get your Bar license back?" I smile softly, pretend the question doesn't make my guts twist and tell them, "I'm not sure, maybe." Some people tell me they know a lawyer that might be able to help. I want to tell them that unless their lawyer friend is the Chief Justice of the Supreme Court, they are wasting their time. Instead, I am polite, and I smile, but inside I can't help myself: "Wait a second... I thought my chances of getting my Bar license back were pretty slim, but what is this you say? Your cousin's ex-wife in Victorville is a lawyer, and you'll talk to her for me!"

The intermission is over. People take their seats. And now it's time for sharing from the group. I hate this part. My fellows raise their hands and I call on them. They stare right at me. I battle with how much eye contact to return. They comment on my share, and thus they comment on me. They say, "Wow!" and "Thank God my bottom wasn't as bad as yours" and "At least you're not still in prison." I smile and I nod, but I'm churning inside. The muscles in my face tighten. I wish I had a mirror to see if I look as manic as I feel. My hands and feet are buzzing, more and more. I feel like I might lose control, burst out of my chair and begin laughing hysterically. I love the attention, but I can't have all these people seeing me.

I spend the last 10 minutes of the meeting just holding on. Thank God it's over. Everyone joins hands, and we pray out with the Serenity Prayer. A couple of my friends approach me. I mumble an apology for having to leave immediately. I bolt out the door, up the steps and into the parking lot. I feel slightly calmer in the quiet of my car, but mostly because I know I'm going to get my medicine soon, really soon if I navigate cleverly.

As I drive aggressively to 7-Eleven, I think of one of the readings from the meeting. "We don't regret the past nor wish to close the door on it." It's read at damn near every meeting. It's straight out of the Big Book. How does that work? How do I not regret the past? I did the Steps, but I'm feeling a hell of a lot of regret. And I'm feeling like slamming the door on the past. I think I might have been better off going to trial. Yes, it's true. I try not to entertain that thought. What's done is done. But I can't help it right now. Did I really say "yes" to living the rest of my life as a registered sex offender?

I pull into the 7-Eleven parking lot and am surprised at the amount of joy I feel upon finding a prime parking spot.

I place the 24-ounce, multi-colored, NASCAR-like embossed paper coffee cup with the corrugated cardboard heat-sleeve and black shiny lid with that little raised nipple on the counter and enunciate, with laser surgery precision, "Marlboro Red 100's in a pack, please."

With coffee secured in my car's cup holder and the unopened glossy cellophane-wrapped Marlboro Red 100's on my passenger seat, my anxiety lessens. I'm stopped at a red light on the corner of Alvarado and Sunset. It's ugly and beautiful with lights and people and ads and cars and that desperate energy of people who are barely surviving. There is a bus stop with people milling about, a tired Mexican woman, students with backpacks, unruly skateboarders and a man in dirty khakis bunched like an accordion into his worn black loafers. Across the street is a closed car wash, and a taco truck with fold-out chairs and a small line of patrons, mostly skinny, pale, white hipsters. An old pizza shop is on the opposite corner and across from that a mini-mall packed with shops: a smoke shop, a liquor store, a Burrito King counter with its big red-on-yellow sign. Hovering over it all are drooping electric wires, hunched white street lights, traffic lights. Even higher is a terribly large Apple iPhone ad with a silhouette of someone cool and free. Slightly lower and squatter is the ever-changing American Apparel billboard, with today's t-shirt-slanging nubile princess, looking more like a hostage than a model.

The light turns green, and I pull forward slowly following a police cruiser.

"If my life keeps going the way it's going, I will be amongst you very soon," I say to the crowd at the bus stop. I swig just a bit of coffee. I don't want to drink too much. This mix is a perfect combination of vanilla creamer and sugar, and I want to couple it with cigarettes, not waste it while driving.

The cop car stops abruptly, its sirens light and scream, and it screeches into a U-turn and heads back west down Sunset.

I pull into my parking spot and am relieved that my landlord isn't home to observe my chain smoking. I let myself into my apartment and quickly set up my smoking station on the patio chair. I light my first cigarette. I pull hard. The warm smoke fills my lungs. Relief. A police helicopter chirps above, and its spotlight darts about the hilly streets and homes, and then across my car, not 10 feet away. But it doesn't matter right now. Right now, nothing matters. I'm safe on my patio, under my umbrella with my cigarettes and my warm sweet coffee. I will sit and think and sit and think until I've smoked so many cigarettes in a row that my body revolts, my chest tightens, and I become sleepy and pass out. But that'll take an hour or more, so until then, I can think about how much I regret the past and how much I wish I could change it.

TEN

———————————

Trenton and I sit at a booth at the Bright Spot diner on Sunset. It's a classic diner made over with hiply ironic décor, my favorite of which is the creepy random family portrait that is framed and hung on the wall. The White Stripes's cover of *Jolene* plays in the background. Most of the waitstaff are tattooed, young, local residents, but today we get the waitress that came with the place.

"Seriously, I try not to sit in her section," I say to Trenton.

"She's so sweet. What's wrong with you?" Trenton asks and laughs, his big 'fro bouncing. His giant smile makes me happy.

Our waitress places two waters on our table. She's 4 feet 8 inches tall, with bright, white, short, curly hair and is so hunched over that she has to crane her neck to see us.

"You boys know what you want?"

"Oh no, sorry, give us a minute," Trenton says.

She walks off.

"Look, man," I whisper-speak. "She does the same thing every time. She'll give you extra fries, and she'll make a huge deal of it—this whole song and dance—but she never gets your order right. Never."

"Dude, c'mon," Trenton says and contorts his face like my words are painful to him.

"No, no, no. I'm not the bad guy here," I say. "I get it. She's 110 years old. But she's a horrible waitress. She is. It sucks that she's 110 and still has to work. Welcome to the new America. But that doesn't change the fact that she never, ever gets an order right…"

"Okay, fine," Trenton says and rolls his eyes.

The waitress returns, we order and then cover familiar ground. I tell him I can't believe he rides his bike from his condo in Hollywood to Cal State LA every day. He attempts to explain certain intricacies of open-source systems, like Linux, and why my desire to switch to Apple computers is the technological equivalent of supporting Jim Crow legislation. Trenton has a Juris Doctorate from Boston University and a Masters in something weird and is now teaching high school continuation classes while obtaining his teaching credentials and a Computer Science degree.

Trenton explains the absurdity of the Los Angeles Unified School District's student grading protocol and tells me that he's close to finishing a computer program that could streamline grading for the whole district.

"Really? Wow," I say, impressed. "How much are you going to make on that?"

Trenton's eyebrows raise, his mouth scrunches together, he tilts his head.

"I uh... I don't know. I never thought of that," he says.

"Money," I snap back. "You know, that stuff that keeps us from being homeless."

He bounces his shoulders and says, "I'll just give it to them."

Our octogenarian-plus waitress walks to our table balancing our plates of food precariously in front of her. Her eyes are below the level of my vegetarian chili, so it appears my chili bowl has a bright white head of hair like a Chia Pet.

"Oh my God, dude," I say. "That's a disaster waiting to happen."

She drops the plates and bowls down on our table noisily, like a weightlifter re-racking dumbbells.

"Okay boys," she declares as she stands back, recovering. "I gave you both extra, extra fries."

She stands still waiting for our reaction. I refuse to give her one. Trenton mumbles something, trying not laugh. She looks confused and walks away. I feel guilty and justified simultaneously. I hold up my bowl of vegetarian chili for Trenton's inspection.

"See, see? What'd I tell you," I say. He looks into the bowl. It's covered in diced white onions. "I'd have had a better chance of not getting onions if I said, 'please chop up a full raw onion and mix it into all my food. Mix it in to my fucking coffee while you're at it.'"

Our waitress returns. "Everything good?" she asks.

"Perfect," I say.

The conversation shifts to me. Trenton knows all the details of my story. We've been friends since he first got clean. We see each other at least twice a week. He attended my sentencing hearing with a couple dozen other 12-Steppers, when the judge freed me after my summer trip to Chino prison.

"I had no idea, man," I tell Trenton. "I didn't really think of how brutal it would be having this label. I was just trying to make sure I didn't spend 20 years in prison. I'm trying to just do the one-day-at-a-time deal. I figured I'd get hired by a solo lawyer who would be happy to get me, but the Bar reporting requirements. Lawyers just aren't willing to deal with it."

"That sucks, dude."

Trenton's not one for stock 12-Step advice, which I appreciate. I want to hear someone tell me the truth: This sucks.

"Can you imagine what dating is like for me?" I ask.

"Oh yeah," Trenton says, as if recalling something. "Are you going out with that chick, Macy? She's sort of hot in a Donna Summer kind of way."

"I was thinking more Lauren Hill," I reply.

"Does she know?" Trenton asks.

"No, dude. No."

"Fuck, man."

After larger than average slices of pie, over-the-top tip-bait from our waitress, Trenton and I pile up cash for the check. I count and stack it.

"Wait, wait, Trenton," I chastise. "You didn't even put in 10 percent tip."

"I agree with Mr. Pink," Trenton says.

"Fuck that."

"From *Reservoir Dogs*," he explains.

"Yeah, I get the reference, Tarantino."

"You said our waitress was terrible, and she was," Trenton protests.

"Of course she fucking was. She always is. But this place isn't paying her a living wage because of the ridiculous custom of tipping, which is just a way for them to avoid paying her so they can keep their prices down and lower their taxes. And the government allows this because of some fucking restaurant lobbying group that bribes politicians."

"C'mon, really?" Trenton asks.

"Look," I continue. "The hunched over 90-year-old should be retired, and I should be working. I got nothing against her. I got something against the government who makes someone like me permanently un-employable and someone like her still have to work."

Trenton looks at me and droops his eyelids, pretending to fall asleep.

"Are you done?" he asks.

"Yes," I say, decidedly.

"So... this is pretty much all about you not her, right?"

I pause, look up at him and my lips form a wry smile. "Uh... Yep."

Trenton tosses down two more dollars, and we leave the check and cash on the table and go outside. It's eleven o'clock at night, and I want to get home and smoke, but Trenton is trying to explain the bug he's working out on his grading program. He uses the terms interface and database more than I'm comfortable with. My mind wanders away from micro-Trenton to macro-Trenton. I recall the disaster he was when he came in to the Program. A couple years ago, he was an unemployed pill-popping, crack-smoking, meth-head. Now he's clean, and he's working with at-risk high school kids.

Trenton unlocks his road bike from one of three newspaper vending machines outside. It's a warm evening. Across the street, Taix, an old French restaurant, is hosting an event that is ending, and the last of the cars in its parking lot are being returned to their owners by men in red valet vests. I remember when I was invited to a fundraiser at Taix for that fascist motherfucker, Los Angeles Sheriff Lee Baca. I've since spent time in his jail and despise him even more.

One block west is the corner of Sunset and Alvarado, where there is slightly more activity near the bus stop.

"What are you going to do about it?" Trenton asks me as he stuffs his D-shaped bike lock into his oversized backpack.

"I'm going to do what I've been doing for the last three years. Page 86 and 87. What else can I do?"

Not to be outdone by my Big Book page reference, Trenton produces his Bible-sized cell phone and pulls up the electronic copy of the Big Book he proudly pirated. The screen lights up his face. While I wait for Trenton to find and read pages 86 and 87, I take in a quiet and dark Los Angeles. I gaze out over Echo Park lake, past the Hollywood Freeway to the city's skyline.

Then I hear guttural screams. I turn to see where the noise is coming from. I see people scattering away from the bus stop at Alvarado and Sunset, a block up Sunset, below the Apple billboard. Trenton stops swiping his cell phone screen and looks up at me curiously. Then I see a man in a white, ribbed tank top chasing another man in an oversized white t-shirt. I can hear their shoes slapping against the tarmac. The man being chased is 30 yards away and is crossing Sunset directly toward us. His pursuer holds out a pistol as he runs. *Tikew.* He fires the pistol. I drop to my belly behind the row of newspaper vending machines. Trenton hasn't moved, so I grab his ankle and pull.

"Get down!" I yell.

Trenton crouches to the ground, and his bike falls and clanks against the concrete. Trenton and I are head to head. *Tikew.* Another bullet fires. I hear it ricochet off the asphalt, and it makes a *ting* sound as it strikes the newspaper vending machine right above our heads.

I close my eyes, and I see a flash image of the glaring white lights of Twin Towers Jail's intake area. I see sheriffs' hulking bodies stuffed in khaki uniforms and inmates in bright blue scrubs. I open my eyes back to the dark where Trenton and I are hunched in this makeshift fox hole.

The pursued man swerves back to the sidewalk opposite us and runs past us. The gunman follows, losing ground. He tucks his gun into his waist. Trenton and I stand up in silence. The men are gone.

I observe myself. I feel relieved. Why? Is it because neither of us got shot? No. I know why I feel this way. It's because I think that if the man had been shot and killed, and I witnessed it, I'd be obliged to give a statement to the police. They'd take me downtown for a statement, and when they found out about my criminal status, they'd find a way to hold me. They'd take me away. I know it. I can feel it. They'll take me away again. I can see the handcuffs. They have that power. There is nothing I could do to stop them.

"Fuck," I say, breaking the long silence.

"Fuck is right, dude," Trenton responds. "I guess Echo Park isn't completely gentrified."

After a couple moments of wowing and head-shaking, Trenton pulls his phone back out and begins reciting page 86 of the Big Book.

"When we retire at night..."

ELEVEN

"Change the numbers?" I repeat back into my phone. J.D. and the janitor from *Scrubs* are frozen mid-argument on my television screen.

"Yeah, change the numbers," Keri repeats. She says she has to go and then hangs up. She always has to go. That's the nature of being a criminal defense attorney.

I mouth the words a few times. It rolls nicely. Change the numbers, change the numbers. Yes, change the numbers. It's like magic. Keri's going to do a magic trick. It means the District Attorney, at the recommendation of Judge Von Silkman, is going to change my conviction *post facto*. It'll be amended from Assault with Intent to Commit Rape to a Felony Assault. I'll still be a two-strike felon, but not a registered sex offender. And if I'm not a registered sex offender, I'll have a chance of getting my Bar license back. After all, my situation is the opposite of most lawyers disbarred for committing a crime. The California Bar looks into the facts of the crime and not only the label of the crime that the lawyer is convicted of. So if some lawyer pulled a gun on someone but got a sweet deal from the district attorney and was able to plead to a misdemeanor assault, she still might get disbarred even though the conviction was a misdemeanor, because the facts support a felony assault. But with me, the opposite is the case. The conviction—Assault with Intent to Commit Rape—is much worse than the facts. With me, the facts indicate I was in a blackout and out of my mind, and even the judge said on the record that I was obviously drunk out of my mind.

The victim, a man, said I was clearly drunk and that I said nonsensical things about being in Hawaii, and being in a fraternity, and something about a Volkswagen. I was clearly in some fantasy world, what the expert that would have testified had I gone to trial called a "fugue state." Nevertheless, I doubt the Bar is going to readmit a guy who is a registered sex offender. It just wouldn't look right. But if I wasn't a registered sex offender, I might have a chance.

That's what my life comes down to now. To have any meaningful relationship, whether it's a friend, a girlfriend, or an employer, I have to convince people to take a chance on me. I have to convince them that they should go against basic logic that dictates that someone who pleaded guilty to a violent sex crime probably committed a violent sex crime and is thus probably a dangerous person. And even if they take the time to listen to my story, and even if they believe me, it may not be enough. They might say, I believe you, but I just can't hire you, or I just can't be around you. It's not you, it's your label. I'm scared of everyone I meet, because everyone I meet has the ability to hurt me simply by typing my name into their browser and repeating what they see.

I pull up to Paddy's sober living complex. I wait for five minutes, but he's a no-show. I go inside. It has the feel of a jail's rec room. The men wear shower sandals and oversized white t-shirts. I give each one my best wide-eyed "A little help here?" look, but they all ignore me. Further down a hall, a group of prison-tough guys are watching *General Hospital,* which, I think must be recorded, because it's evening. I stand next to the reception window, and one of the men gets up with a reluctant sigh, trots over and goes through a door and reappears behind the window.

"I'm supposed to pick up Paddy to take him to a meeting," I report.

"Paddy ain't here, ain't been here for a couple days. He's AWOL."

"Oh yeah," I say. "You sure? White guy, kinda ruddy, about this high?" I say holding a hand palm-down near my chin.

"Yeah, man," he says, clearly irritated. "I know Paddy. He ain't here. We already gave his bed up."

I walk back to my car. A few guys from the house are gathered around talking, one leans on the hood of my car. Fuck, this is one of those prison situations, I think to myself. I can act hard, soft, or play it right down the middle. I pull out my key and stand up straight and walk to my car. The guy leaning against my hood stands up. He brushes off my hood as an apology. Maybe he thinks I'm a parole officer. I pretend I don't notice him until I'm right next to my car.

"You guys know Paddy?" I ask.

"Who you?"

"His sponsor," I lie, for the sake of simplicity.

"Oh yeah, man," he says, apparently accepting my credentials. "Paddy out. Out—like on a run, out. You feel me, chief?" He wipes his mouth with the back of his hand while eyeing me dramatically, as if this is some pre-rehearsed bit of business. Whatever, I get it. Paddy's gone.

$2,458.72.

Reading this number on the ATM receipt sends little waves of adrenaline down my legs. The energy sits in my calves, ankles and feet. I'm abuzz with anxiety.

"Oh man oh man oh man oh man," I say aloud to myself on the busy sidewalk, as if doing so will spread my anxiety about. But nobody even acknowledges me. They just keep walking as if I'm not standing on the sidewalk next to the Bank of America on Echo Park and Sunset, talking to myself, or no one, or everyone.

Above us is an Armageddon sky. An intense smell of stale beer and dried piss draws my attention to a man hunched with his back against the bank's exterior wall. I look west, across the cross-walk. People hustle across to make the flashing crosswalk light. I'm a head taller than any one of the 20 pedestrians in front of me, and except another homeless man standing against a wall by the bus stop, the only other white man

I see. The homeless man wears a long khaki raincoat and plays with a marionette, like the one my grandpa brought me back from Tijuana. A little boy at the bus stop takes notice of the man's marionette, and his mom dramatically pulls him away.

$2,458.72.

A shiver of fear runs through me. I'm scared. I can't be poor again. I can't go back there. I was never okay with it. I never got used to it. I was always blanketed in fear, ever since I was a kid. Fear was the air. I don't know how people do it, and I don't want to learn. I lean against the light pole, my eyes unfocused. I'm stunned into paralysis. The only energy in me is the anxiety buzzing below my knees. I could just stand here for hours. I pull the ATM receipt from my pocket and look at it again. $2,458.72. That's not much more than a month until I can't pay my rent. I'm no closer to a job than I was the day I got out of Chino prison. I rub the slick filmy ATM receipt between my thumb and forefinger. The feeling sends gooseflesh up my arms as if I just bit into a banana peel.

"Fine, Macy, fine. You're right. I'm not fucked! God's got me, and I live in a fantasy world where disbarred lawyers, two-strike felons get jobs."

Macy smiles softly. She's going to say something that is going to make me very angry. I can just tell. She stands up and walks to the kitchen counter. Her thrift-store triumph, knee-high, taupe leather boots, tap through an otherwise quiet apartment. I follow her with my eyes, waiting for whatever maddening thing she's about to say.

"Well?" I ask.

She pulls out a paring knife and begins slicing a green apple delicately with her long fingers.

"Either God is everything... or God is nothing," she says.

I grit my teeth. I take a deep breath. I try not to explode. It doesn't work.

"Easy for you to say! I'm a two-strike felon, disbarred lawyer. I couldn't get hired at fucking McDonalds!" I transition from speaking loudly to outright yelling. "You have no idea what it's like to be me—to be this fucked!"

I stand up and stare at her across the counter, waiting, challenging her to respond. She simply stares at me.

"Tell me, Macy. You seem to know everything! Tell me what I am supposed to do."

She sighs and takes a deep breath before she speaks.

"Joseph, you do whatever it takes! Whatever it takes!" She pauses and then continues excitedly, as if suddenly enlightened in this very moment. "If you humble yourself so that you are willing to do whatever it takes, the universe will respond, and you will be given opportunity."

"Oh Jesus fucking Christ. That's just fucking awesome, Macy," I say. "Look, no amount of positive thinking, no New Age bullshit, is going to get me a job. You have no idea how fucked I am!"

The truth is, of course, she really has no idea, because I haven't told her. I haven't dropped the atomic bomb. This is not the time. I need a cigarette now.

I grab my wallet and keys, and yank the door open.

"What are you doing? You're leaving?"

Macy's eyes dilate and her face droops and quivers. She's the daughter of a mom who left her at birth, and a dad who's left her for prison twice, once taking her from her loving foster parents. She's fresh off a divorce from a short marriage with a man who cheated on her. She doesn't have abandonment issues, she is an abandonment issue. I might as well just jam a finger in her open wound.

I slam the door in the midst of her repeating, this time half-tearfully, half-incredulously, "You're leaving?" Her tone is more revealing of her backstory than words can convey. They make me want to die only slightly less than I want, rather, need, a cigarette. I'm the same emotional infant I was before I got arrested. It should be illegal for me to be in a relationship.

I dash up the stairs and down to my car. Rowena, Glendale, Alvarado, Sunset, 7-Eleven, Sunset, home. With practiced efficiency, I'm back at my apartment smoking and drinking coffee in 15 minutes. Macy calls. I watch my phone vibrate on the wooden patio table. I sit in gut-wrenching guilt. The truth is, I'm pissed off, but I didn't leave Macy's because I was angry. I left because I needed to smoke, by myself, for hours. It's no different from when I was drinking except nicotine doesn't lead me to felonious blackouts. Granted, that's a big difference, but the internal workings are the same. My cravings for nicotine are far more acute and constant than my cravings for alcohol or prostitutes ever were. And it feels so harmless. I'll never be able to quit this. How can I with this much stress in my life? I'm no different. I see gaggles of smokers at nearly every 12-Step meeting I go to. It's accepted. Hell, there is even a butt-can commitment at most meetings. By 45 years old, I'll have that wet rattling in my throat. By my mid-50s, I'll be staring down lung cancer or COPD.

It's dark out now. I pull out another cigarette, number 17 since I got home two hours ago after my fight with Macy, and light it up. I take a long drag, then take a sip of syrupy coffee. My throat is sandpaper, and it hurts to swallow. About five cigarettes ago, I felt that weird gallop in my heart. I try not to think about it. I might as well finish the pack. There is nothing I'd rather be doing than sitting here by myself smoking. That's the pathetic truth.

Like every night I don't spend at Macy's, I collapse on the couch fully dressed. Then, at some point, in the middle of the night, I crawl out of my clothes and into bed. I sleep hard, and I dream. Sometimes I dream that I'm in Oceanside, and the waves are perfect, and nobody is out in the lineup, but I don't have a surfboard, and I keep trying to get one, but it never works out. I go to a surf shop, but it's closed. I try to borrow a surfboard, but something always gets in the way. I don't ever get a surfboard. Lately, I've had dreams of Los Angeles Twin Towers Jail and Chino prison. I dream of the prisoner named Lightning Bolts getting shanked, but somehow this time I'm involved. There is blood on me. And I dream of Steven, Steven the man-boy that traveled with me from Twin Towers to Chino prison—Steven crying, Steven moaning like an animal being slaughtered, Steven staring at me, teary-eyed, saying to me, "Why didn't you help me? You said you were my friend!"

Production. Macy suggests I get a job in production because in production no one cares about anything but getting the job done. She knows a little because her soon-to-be ex-husband is a director. Somehow, this makes sense, and just by being in the 12-Step rooms, I probably know a couple dozen 12-Steppers that work in production. I ask around, careful not to be too aggressive, but also keeping in mind that I'm on a steady march toward homelessness. These conversations, some with people that are slightly more than acquaintances, are clipped and hopeless. No one has a lead for a 36-year-old with no production experience. I can't even get a non-paying gig. Mike, not a close friend, but a friend, is a production coordinator, my last shot.

"It's brutal. You have no idea," Mike says, shaking his head as if bad memories are flooding in.

"Dude," I respond, "I have no prospects. I'm running out of money. I'm talking—I can't pay my rent status—soon to be homeless."

"I swear to God," Mike says, "I'd rather be homeless than coordinate another fucking commercial—almost had a nervous breakdown last time."

I search his eyes for the humor, holding my mouth in the ready-to-laugh position, but he's not kidding.

"It's that bad?" I ask.

"Damn close. It's insane. Eighteen, 20-hour days. One emergency after another."

"I don't care, man. I just need to work," I say with all the gravity I can muster.

"Dude," Mike replies, "I don't even have anything lined up for myself. I'm sorry. I got nothing."

I go home and contemplate what Macy said about "whatever it takes" and "God is everything or God is nothing" and that New Age stuff about the universe conspiring for my good. Some of it I believe, and some of it I don't, and I definitely don't fully understand it, but I do know that Macy is hustling and raising a kid, and she works her ass off, and she looks good doing it, with a smile on her face. Why not believe?

I log on to the Craigslist website. It has a designated section for production gigs in the Los Angeles employment section. I send out emails for a dozen ads. I receive a reply from a USC film student within an hour. I'm hired, whatever that means. I am to be a P.A., a production assistant; I am to be paid $50 a day for a week-long shoot. I am to meet for the production meeting tonight, no pay. So now I'm in the biz.

I have no idea what I'm doing, I tell Ahmed, the guy in charge, I know nothing, but I'll work hard. He doesn't respond, just asks if I have a car. That's good enough for Ahmed.

I'm in downtown Los Angeles in an alley in the Jewelry District that was originally created as a set for a studio, but now has actual businesses. It's very Disneyland. We are in the end of the alley in a Greek restaurant, which doubles as the entrance to several residential lofts. It's just after 9 p.m. I have a big heavy black walkie-talkie that I'm terrified to use. They all speak a language I don't speak. They say "sparky" and "grip" and "D.P." and "lock-down" and "ask crafty," and they tell me to get a "c-stand," and I just get in the way. I'm constantly in the way. D.P., she looks at me, after I stumble into a live shot, and she yells, "Cut! We are rolling. Are you fucking kidding me?" And she looks at Ahmed and says, "You couldn't get a real P.A.?" And Ahmed hustles me off the set and hands me off to Grip, which is someone who wears gloves and is angry, and Grip says, "Not my job," and does not look at me or Ahmed, and then Ahmed takes me to a woman who he introduces as "The Art Department," and he says, very frustrated at this point, "Just tell him what to do, and keep him out of the way."

And so she does. The pressure is off. I'm the idiot, not unlike when I was at Chino prison. I'm the anomaly again. So I do what she says. I learn how to use the walkie-talkie. I'm waiting outside in the alley in the cold. It's past 11. My job is to say "Quiet on set" and hold my hands up like the volunteers at a golf tournament. "Rolling," and then "Action" is called and "Cut" is called. They are moving on. "Moving on" is called. They are moving on from "dolly" to "sticks" and everyone jumps into action. It's just like when I was at Twin Towers Jail and placed in a dorm with a group of other inmates. As soon as the door buzzed, they opened it, went in, and they all knew exactly what to do. I had no idea.

And then someone barks my name into the walkie-talkie. I look at Sheri, The Art Department, panicked. Sheri nods as if to say, "You got this." I press down the button and respond as I've heard Sheri respond. "Copy that. On my way." This makes me happy. God dammit. Fuck you, it makes me happy. I run onto that fucking set like I'm a NASA engineer called on to the launch pad at Cape Canaveral. I'm hustling. I may be the oldest P.A. in Los Angeles, and I may not know "D.P." from "A.D.," but I'm going to knock this out of the park.

"What the fuck are you doing?" a big burly electrician says to me.

"They said we're in a hurry, to help move stuff," I say defensively.

"Don't ever touch the lights!" he yells. "How the fuck can you be on a set and not know that?"

My throat clenches and the muscles in my face twitch. My face wants to cry, but I refuse to let it. I stand up taller than I am and look down on the burly electrician. I square up, so we are chest to chest, and I stare into his eyes. "I'm sorry. I didn't know."

He softens and says, "It's a safety thing, man. Just be careful."

We work for 16 hours straight. Ahmed hands me cash, and tells me, "nice job." He has no idea how grateful I am for his words. I drive home feeling like I've climbed a great mountain. I sleep for five hours and get up and am back on set. This time it's 15 hours. And next day it's 15 and a half hours. I'm learning everything. When I'm not scurrying about, which is the job of a P.A.—scurry about at the whim of others—I'm scribbling notes in a pad I stuff in my back pocket. I write down how to talk in the walkie-talkie, which departments use which channels, the name of the equipment, the departments and what each does. By the fourth day, I've got the basics down. The crew is dwindling. No one is willing to work this many hours for such little pay, so if they get another gig, they bail out. Ahmed stops paying everyone cash every day in order to get them to stick it out, but that just makes it worse.

I'm hustling like my life depends on it. As the shoot falls apart, I'm tightening up my game. On the sixth day, we are at the Standard Hotel, shooting in a room without a permit. I'm helping smuggle up gear and wardrobe in my own suitcases. Sheri, The Art Department, is gone now. I'm The Art Department now, Ahmed tells me. The Art Department truck is gone, so I'm now stuffing my Honda Accord full of props and clothes and boxes of spray paint and markers and all kinds of colorful accoutrements.

The final shoot day is in Elysian Park. Our crew is down to Ahmed, two actors and three of Ahmed's friends from USC Film School, one handling the camera and one handling a windshield car shade that is being used as a light-bounce. A police cruiser stops by, and Ahmed tells them we have a permit. The cop says something about Film L.A., and that he'll be back, but then a car full of teenagers in a convertible low-rider passes, and the cop loses interest in us. We set up in another spot, requiring us to re-shoot several shots we already have "in the can," for "continuity." We finish after just over 10 hours, and somehow I end up driving Ahmed back to his car downtown. He pays me $100 for the final day and thanks me for sticking it out. I hug him, and he does not like it. He gets out of my car and says, "Okay then."

Sheri, The Art Department, calls me and hires me as an Art Department P.A. on a short film. She quits in the middle of the shoot because she gets a commercial gig, and I become the Art Department head again. I drive a big truck, and I'm trying to do the work of three people for $75 per day. We are shooting in the San Fernando Valley, and it's frying-pan hot out. I do the math. I'm making about five dollars per hour, but I'm learning. I learn how to shop for furniture and props at all the hidden-gem thrift stores in Los Angeles, one by the airport in Burbank and one at the intersection of the 5 and 110 Freeways on the Eastside by my apartment. I learn how to anticipate the director's needs—the most important skill relative to job security—what a director does, what a "call sheet" is, what "sides" are. Sometimes I'm even so tired that I forget to stress over the fact that someone on the crew might find out I'm a registered sex offender.

This gig leads to my first big commercial gig. I'm a P.A. It's for Starbucks. This is a whole other level of production. High dollar. I am one of five P.A.s. We are "P.A. Nation," and we hustle like it's a sport. Some of my fellow P.A.s are film school grads, and they all are looking to impress a grip, lead man, sparky, DP, anyone above them, which is everyone, so they can move on with their careers. They are killers. A call goes over the radio that the director needs a bottle of water. P.A. Jessica unsheathes her broadsword, decapitates me, impales P.A. Zach, does a one-handed somersault over a c-stand using her other hand to grab a bottled water from an ice chest, lands in a full sprint, and presents, on one knee, the bottled water, to the director. He mumbles, "Thanks," and his eyes never leave the camera monitor. He couldn't identify P.A. Jessica in a line-up next to five green aliens. P.A. Jessica returns to P.A. Nation, her fellows, despondent and mumbles, "Sorry." We completely understand.

I get on a roll of commercials: insurance, cars, fast food. The amount of money spent on everything involved, with the exception of my services, is astonishing. We are in the middle of Korea Town outside an apartment complex. The camera shot is of a young man picking up a young woman in his convertible Mustang. The light isn't quite right, so the commercial, which has a budget just shy of a million, goes an extra day. The grips bring in a crane, which lifts a 25-yard, square, white shade, which is framed in aluminum, that softens the sun's rays perfectly for the shot. There are over 100 people on this shoot. The higher they are on the employment ladder, the more relaxed they look. I try to look busy. I scurry around, pretending I'm on a mission. The Production Coordinator tells me, always look busy, always keep moving. So, I do. By the third commercial, this one for Del Taco, a trend emerges. On Day One, I'm the newbie that doesn't quite have everything down, and am outperformed by all the other P.A.s. The other P.A.s all go out drinking, even after 16-hour days. So Day Two and definitely Day Three, they are barely hanging on, some are even hiding out, pretending to be on errands, sleeping in the back of the Lead Man's truck, tucked in behind c-stands or pop-up tents. I don't have to do anything, just do the same thing I've been doing, and by Day Three or Day Four, if it's a long commercial, I'm often the last P.A. standing, or, at least, standing straight; Joseph-on-the-spot. It's another benefit of not drinking.

I just keep getting gigs. I even have to turn down a couple because they overlap. I get a call from a guy who is financing his own short film, and he pays me $150 a day to be the production designer. I even get to hire someone. I call a kid who was the Lead Man on the Anna Nicole Smith movie I worked on, who showed me the ropes. He's a tad irked that I'm hiring him, since he graduated from film school and has been working in the biz for several years, but he agrees to do it. It's a movie set in the '80s, so I get to use all my high school memories to design the bedroom of a gay teenage boy who is coming out to his family. We shoot in a giant mini-mansion in a gated community in the Valley, high up on a hill. The days are long, even for production. Like everyone on set, except the actors, I'm sleep deprived. One night I even spend the night because I'm too tired to drive. I sleep on an '80s foam green couch.

I'm a part of something. I'm making something. These people appreciate me. They appreciate how hard I work and how hard I try. I do the absolute best I can. I'm almost making enough money to pay my rent. I don't have to buy food, because food is on set. All I have to pay for is gas and cigarettes. Each new gig is like a new dream. It's all-encompassing. I can do nothing else. My probation officer calls and asks me to come in, and I tell her the truth. If I do, I'll lose this gig. It's that simple. Production isn't like other gigs. It's all or nothing. There is no taking time off. She says she knows all about it, and she comes to set and pretends she's a friend dropping off something for me.

On commercials, I'm hired as a P.A., but on small indie projects, I do Locations, Production Design, Art Department, and Wardrobe. They even had me helping out a camerawoman at one point. One time I become the A.D., the Assistant Director, on a small movie that we shot over four weeks. I started as a P.A., and as other people quit, I kept moving into new roles until, in the second week, I'm the A.D. I'm the manager of the whole thing. I keep it rolling. The director even has me calling "action" and "cut." It's a blast, but I'm making less than I do as a P.A. on big commercials, which still isn't enough to pay my rent.

It's the middle of the night. I've spent the last three days—15-hour work days plus a two-hour commute—working on a stop-action Advil commercial at the Ontario, California airport. A lady goes to grab her suitcase off the conveyor and the suitcase opens up while she grabs it and clothes go flying, and she's mid-fall, and the world stops, and the Advil spokesmen-dude rolls in and gives a clever Advil pitch. Fifteen-hour days, and the Coordinator, my boss, is hounding all the P.A.s to keep moving. I'm tempted to hide like most the other P.A.s do, but I refuse. I'm not sure why. I'd like to think it's integrity, but it's probably ego. It's like a goddam endurance event. We finally wrap at 1 a.m.

Usually, there's a little celebratory moment. Everyone claps and hugs, but this time everyone just falls away, relieved that this life-battle is over. Ten minutes later, I'm driving the production truck back to the rental lot in Hollywood. That takes an hour and a half. I drive off the lot, and in my backpack are two disk-shaped canisters of film. These are the result of a half-million dollar, three-day commercial shoot. All right here in my backpack. Anything happens to these, people's careers will be ruined.

The closer I get to Burbank, the quieter and darker it gets. They have those street lamps that emit orange light, and everything is commercial-perfect. All these businesses are closed. I could safely walk down the middle of the street. I turn off the radio and enjoy the silence. I do the math. Forty-five hours on set, 10 hours commuting and picking up the truck and returning it, plus this little jaunt. So about 55 hours divided by $200 a day. That's just about 10 bucks an hour. Could be worse. The other P.A.s do it because there are others on set that are making two grand a day and others, the director, the producers, who are making 20 grand a day. Everybody is there so they can add another zero. I guess I'm in the running, too. I could move up, maybe get in a union. It's unlikely but possible.

I park in the empty lot. I grab my backpack. A security camera mounted on the side of a concrete wall winks a blue light at me.

I think to myself that the possibility of a career working in commercial production would be an amazing gift. Somehow that nice thought leads me to visions of destroying these canisters of film: break the seals, let the film spin out from my car windows like fishing line from an ocean trawler; or, open the canisters and douse the film with lighter fluid and light them up and let the film burn in a toxic street-side mini-chemical fire; better yet, drive down to Malibu with a longboard and paddle out at Surfrider Beach and release them down to the sandy bottom of the Third Point break.

I stand outside the lobby of a large office building. A wall of glass separates me from a lobby desk, behind which sits a security officer. I pull on the door, but it's locked. The security guard looks at me. I hold up my backpack. The door buzzes, and I pull on the wrong door. The buzzing stops so when I reach to pull on the other door, it's no longer unlocked. I look through the glass door at the lady, and I raise my right index finger apologetically. She mocks confusion, presumably to let me know that she thinks it is strange that someone of apparently good health can't reach to open the door during the several seconds of buzzing that indicates the doors is available to be opened. It buzzes again. I open it this time, and on my way to the counter, I recall the buzzing doors at Twin Towers Jail. That thought leads me to think of Roman, the monster of a man I met at Twin Towers. I want to tell this lady about Roman, and I seriously consider it. As I walk across the lobby, I realize that I'm sleep deprived and that I shouldn't tell this lady about Roman.

"You must be from Addictive Concepts Productions," she says and holds open a large white envelope.

"Yep," I say. I pull the canisters out of my backpack and slide them into the envelope.

I sign something. She writes out a receipt and hands it to me. I walk out of the brightly lit lobby. I stand outside my car and call my Production Coordinator.

"The eagle has landed," I say.

As is the nature of Production Coordinators, she confirms every detail. Yes, I delivered both cans. Yes, I got a receipt. Yes, that's the correct address. Yes, I returned the truck. Yes, I noted the mileage. As she continues through her checklist, I think of how I would have been a better lawyer had I been more like a Production Coordinator.

"Great job, Joseph," she says.

"Thanks for hiring me. I appreciate it."

I drive while reveling in my attaboys. I'll be smoking in the dark in front of my apartment in 30 minutes or less. God, thank you.

Somehow I scrape the rent together. It's exhausting, but I know this is going somewhere. I just don't know if I can work this hard constantly. Then I get the call that P.A.s dream of. I get a call from a Locations Manager who worked on a Geico Insurance commercial I worked on. He liked me because I helped him out, 12-Step style, expecting nothing in return. He was flustered and needed to get a photo of a street corner for a possible location, and he needed it immediately. I just jumped in my car and did it for him. So then two weeks later, he calls. He asks me if I want to do some locations work. I say, "Sure, love to." But I think: "You mean, would I like to get into a union and make $600 a day, and be one of the people on the commercials that matters, and not be treated like a serf? Yeah, I say yes to that."

I get my first assignment. I drive five miles from my house, take five photos, and email them to him. The whole thing takes an hour, and I make more money than I make in three days of slaving away 15 hours a day. It starts out slow, and I still have to take P.A. gigs and other gigs. Also, I manage a theater for the Silver Lake Film Festival at the Los Feliz 3 and then for the Los Angeles Film Festival at the Billy Wilder Theater at the Hammer Museum. It's a nice break from the relentless grind of P.A.ing, but my pay barely covers gas and cigarettes.

I'm working my ass off, and I can't pay the rent. I refuse to borrow money from Grandpa again. I sell one of my surfboards to cover rent. This is crazy. Now, I'm actually making less than minimum wage, and I have no health insurance and no benefits and no regular work. The Locations Manager says the business is slowing. Commercial gigs are harder to come by. He hires me for the next gig he gets, this one for Bank of America, but he can only use me for one day because of the budget. I make $600, which is still pretty good. I just need to hang on. The problem is, even the indie gigs are getting more difficult to get. I have a theater management gig for the AFI Film Festival at the Arclight Hollywood coming up, so that'll pay next month's rent.

I catch 12-Step meetings when I can, and my probation officer has taken me off the random alcohol and drug testing list and only tests me when I come in for my regular appointments, which she has moved to every other week. She's fudging the weekly visits and even references the non-existent meetings. "Now last week when we talked—" she says. The first time she said this, I said, "We didn't meet last week. You mean the week before?" She half raised up and looked over her cubicle walls and then looked at me with her head tilted down, past her nose, like she meant business, and said, "No, no. I meant last week." I got on board. She was doing me a huge favor, after all. "Oh, oh, my bad. You're right. Of course, last week, yes, last week."

I knock on Macy's door. My anticipation amplifies as the sound of her boots' heels tapping gets louder until it stops, and she's standing in front of me. She wears a loose, earthy sundress and a loaded half-smile. It's loaded because yesterday on the phone I said, "I need to tell you something really important." I follow her to the couch. We sit. I take a deep deliberate breath. She doesn't say a word. The only noise is the hum of the freeway below.

"Okay, okay, look. I just need to tell you something... I mean you deserve an explanation about uh... the, uh, the thing I'm going to tell you, but that's not the only thing. Oddly, it is the really important thing in this one way, but in most people's mind, you know... it's not nearly as important as the other thing. So, I just want to emphasize—"

"Don't bury the lead," Macy says.

I laugh. "Yeah, I'm always doing that," I say. "Okay, here it goes..."

I tell Macy about my smoking. I'm ashamed of my smoking. I like to smoke alone. When I leave and tell her I've got to go home, it's because I need a cigarette. That's why I never stay too long. Macy is surprised. Is that all? You smoke. You don't understand! I smoke like a fiend. I'll smoke a whole pack, one lit off the other, until I pass out. I smoke alone staring off into the dark. I don't smoke like normal smokers. I don't look cool doing it. I don't want to be around anyone. I just want to be by myself. But I'm going to start going to a 12-Step program for smokers. They've got a program for that, just like for drinking. It's mostly filled with people from the alcohol and drug programs.

I can see the wheels turning in Macy's brain through her eyes. She doesn't care that I smoke. She does, however, care that I have a secret, that I have deep shame over it, and that I still have an active addiction. Nevertheless, she seems relieved. She probably thought I was going to tell her I was going to break up with her or that I'd been cheating or that I'd been drinking.

"But that's not all I wanted to tell you," I say. "This thing, is, well… it's shocking."

Macy bites her lower lip and crosses her arms.

"There's no other way to say it but to say it."

"Then just say it," Macy says.

"I'm a registered sex offender."

Macy's face travels through several expressions before it lands on a long, slow nod followed by, "Oh, wow…"

"Yeah, it's a lot to take in," I say. I'm tempted to rush in with words of explanation, words that will block, or, at least, reroute her paths of thought and conclusions. But no, I refuse. I let her sit with it and ask the questions she decides to ask. Yes, I'm on the web. Yes, anyone can look me up, and see that I was convicted of Assault with Intent to Commit Rape.

Macy works in TV news, and she's a single mom. She knows all about registered sex offenders and the Megan's Law List website. She has probably written copy for stories about registered sex offenders.

I tell her what happened on the night of my arrest. I tell her why I pleaded guilty. I tell her that I'm a recovered sex addict and that I used to go to massage parlors frequently. I tell her that I've had sex with over a hundred women, mostly prostitutes.

I wonder if I'll leave here today still in a relationship. The thing is, I think to myself, I haven't told her yet, but I love her. Otherwise, I wouldn't be putting either of us through this.

Macy was raised by her dad, a pimp. And when her dad wasn't in prison, Macy was raised by one of her dad's high-end prostitutes. As if that wasn't enough to cause Macy to run from a hint of sex addiction, she just left her husband after finding out he was a sex addict and had been cheating on her within weeks of their marriage. But the thing about Macy is she believes everything happens for a reason. She believes God has a plan for her. And more than anything, she believes in "leaning in."

Macy explains, "Of course I was attracted to you, and you to me." And as if it's as obvious as the sun in the sky, she says, "God put us together. It makes perfect sense. I'm no longer attracted to an active sex addict like my ex-husband, but instead to one who is in recovery. And just as you are part of my healing, I am part of your healing, too." For Macy, it's just that simple. Nothing is a mistake in God's world. We were meant for each other. God will take care of us.

Macy tells me she has to go pick up William and then do some errands.

"Good," I respond. "I need a cigarette."

TWELVE

During the summer, things had gotten worse and worse. Marie had been sleeping more and more and cooking dinner less and less. And Carlos was taking over the apartment. Joseph often came home to find Carlos's druggie friends lounging around, filling the tiny living room with a haze of cigarette smoke. Sometimes Carlos's friends, especially the men, eyed Joseph warily, as if he might be a narc. If asked about Joseph, Carlos would say dismissively, "Oh, don't worry about him. He's just my old lady's kid." Joseph felt as if he was a visitor in his own home.

Visiting Grandpa and Grandma's summer beach rental in Oceanside was a nice respite for Joseph, even though Grandpa had left Joseph with Grandma during the week while he drove back to San Bernardino, where he worked as the manager of a CED Wholesale Electric Supply store. After Grandpa left, in the mornings, a wiry man who dressed and acted young but had an old, worn face, showed up on a beach cruiser, collected money from Grandma and then a little while later, he came back with a full paper bag. She'd go in her room, and when she came out, she'd either be sloppy with emotion or angry. So Joseph would leave. He'd spend his days hanging out with a local kid who lived with his mom in the motel above the diner on the bad side of the pier, where Grandpa told him not to go. They'd go swimming in the choppy ocean, walking the pier and looking down at the surfers, or roaming the harbor. He'd often spy on families, wondering what the kids' lives were like. Did they live in a big house like his Aunt's or was it smaller, like

Grandpa's? Did they play soccer? Did they sit around the table and eat dinner every night?

After a week in Oceanside, Joseph's skin matched the color and glow of the varnished teakwood decks of the sailboats in the harbor and his hair matched the color of their bleached-white sails. It wasn't always bad with Grandma. She didn't always twist up her face in anger and cuss menacingly. Sometimes they watched *All My Children* and then went out to the yellow sand in front of their summer rental, posted up in low, fold-up chairs under umbrellas they stabbed into the sand, read paperbacks, and drank Grandma's sun tea from tea-stained glasses. They both read the squatty little paperback novels that Grandma bought at the grocery store every week, either scary titles with black and red book covers, or romance novels with drawings of buxom women peering longingly up at dashing muscular men. Joseph's trips to Oceanside had a distinct smell. There was the ever-present coconut-scented suntan lotion that Grandma rubbed on his back, which seemed to have been applied so much that Joseph thought if he was hugged too tightly it would ooze out of his skin. There was the salty air that thickened at night. And there were the noises, too, the gawking seagulls, the car stereos moving past him on the tiny street, The Strand that separated the window of the bedroom where Joseph slept and the beach. And at night, the sound of the waves was turned up to full volume, pushing and pulling, crashing and receding, soothing Joseph to sleep.

There was always plenty to eat in Oceanside. They only ate out when Grandpa was home, but Grandma always kept a variety bag of Hershey Miniatures at the ready, and she didn't like dark chocolate, so Joseph had all the dark chocolate he wanted, and sandwiches too. He must've eaten six cheese sandwiches a day with Fig Newtons and thick Frito-brand corn chips crusted with salt. At the end of his stay, Grandpa drove Joseph home so early that it was still dark out when they left. As always, they stopped at Sun City for McDonald's and Grandpa bought himself a coffee and for Joseph, a McMuffin, hash browns and orange juice.

In the days between returning from Oceanside and school start-ing, Joseph had begun visiting his Aunt Suzie and Uncle Billy without Marie. He'd never done this before. Aunt Suzie and Uncle Billy's house was invite-only, reserved for the occasional birthday party or barbeque. He knew they cared for him, but he also knew it wasn't okay for him to show up unannounced and uninvited, but he did it anyway. Joseph had become desperate, desperate for food, desperate for time away from Carlos and his drug buddies, desperate not to see his mom fading away, merging with her mattress. Aunt Suzie and Uncle Billy would feed him, and he'd pet their black Labrador, Ranger, and sometimes they'd let him swim in their pool. During his visits, Joseph saw the looks exchanged between Aunt Suzie and Uncle Billy. These were the looks of concern adults gave each other. He knew what these looks meant. They were the same looks his friends' parents gave each other when Joseph's friends asked if Joseph could spend the night again—just one more night. Joseph was a burden. Joseph was a hassle. He was uninvited and unwanted. So Joseph treaded lightly, and he gushed at Aunt Suzie and Uncle Billy's hospitality and, not long after eating, usually before they hinted that it was time for him to go, he'd announce that he had to go home, even though he didn't ever have to go home. He refused to accept a ride home when Aunt Suzie offered, even though it was a three-and-a-half mile walk home. The hard part was over, and it wasn't walking there in the first place, walking up the long, steep hill. It was knocking on their door, seeing the forced smile on his aunt's face, wondering if this would be the time she'd say, "No, you can't come in. We're busy. Next time call first." It wasn't the idea of Aunt Suzie and Uncle Billy not wanting him to come over that made his heart flutter before he knocked on their door each time—that much he already knew—it was the possibility that they'd act on their feelings and reject him, and the embarrassment that would follow. As he walked up the hill each time, he imagined how he'd respond if rejected, "Oh, I'm sorry Aunt Suzie. It's not a problem. I was just down the street at my friend Ricki's house. I'm sorry... okay... okay... see you later."

The last time he'd headed up to Aunt Suzie and Uncle Billy's, he quit halfway up the hill after convincing himself this would be the time they'd finally reject him. Luckily, a McDonald's had just opened at the bottom of the hill near the Perris Boulevard freeway ramps, so Joseph trekked back down the hill and ventured into the dining room and pretended he was a regular kid waiting for his mom to finish using the bathroom so they could order—he decided that's what he'd say if confronted—and he waited for someone to leave food on their tray and not empty it in the garbage bin. He kept waiting, it seemed like an hour had gone by, watching people devour their food and occasionally dump mostly-eaten Big Macs and a few random French fries. Just before he was about to give up and walk home, he scored big time when a frazzled mom wrangled several kids in green soccer uniforms to dump their trays. She strapped her purse over her shoulder and followed the kids. She left her own tray on one of the two booths the group had occupied. Joseph expected her to help the kids dump their trays and then come back for her own, but she didn't. They passed right by Joseph and out the front door, the woman shouting instructions at the kids. He moved quickly, but then realized a man in the adjacent booth was watching Joseph over the heads of his wife and young son. Their eyes met, and Joseph felt a shot of adrenaline go through him. He looked down, and began to change course, but then decided to go for it instead. He grabbed the tray, half expecting the man, to shout, "Hey, that's not yours!" or worse, "Thief!" but Joseph stayed the course. He prepared himself to dash out the door if need be. Moving as fast as he could, but without running, he turned and carried the tray back to the trash bin by the door. If he acted nonchalantly, as if he was just doing a good deed and clearing the table, surely the man would look away. Joseph was so pumped with energy, he could barely stop from screaming and running out of the packed restaurant. But he knew he shouldn't because then everyone would look at him. Someone would yell, "Stop him!" and Joseph would have no chance. Standing at the trash receptacles, he glanced back at the man to see if the man was still watching him, and sure enough he was. Worse yet, the man was pointing Joseph out to his wife, and she was turning to watch Joseph, too. For a moment, he again considered abandoning his plan. All he had to do was throw the trash away and stack the plastic tray. But he decided to carry on. If he had to make a run for it, he would. He knew exactly how to get through the housing tract construction site to the field where there was a hole in the fence, and he knew he could outrun this man, especially with a head start. Joseph wrapped up the half-eaten cheeseburger, fries, and apple pie into the ketchup-stained paper placemat, cartoon images of Ronald McDonald and The Hamburglar disappearing into the fold. Once he made it outside, past the glass entrance doors, he ran and he didn't look back. Once he was out of the McDonald's parking lot, he knew he wasn't being followed, but he kept running anyway. He pretended he was being chased like the good guys in movies, like James Bond. He dashed dramatically through the rough-graded dirt roads of the future housing tract, and around parked earth movers and stacks of lumber and piles of gravel, and then across a five-acre field of weeds. Once through the field, he ducked down and shimmied through the hole in the chain link fence. He looked back, surveying the area, making sure he was in the clear. Panting and smiling, satisfied with his heroic escape, he sat on the dirt and leaned against the fence. He unwrapped the placemat. Jostled together from the run, the burger was disassembled and the whole mess of food was coated in ketchup and apple pie guts. It was delicious.

With the start of eighth grade, things had been better. He was back in his routine. He'd get up in the morning and walk to the donut store and buy a 15-cent day-old donut. Often, if Joseph was the only customer in the store and her husband was in the back, the old Chinese lady that owned the store would give Joseph an extra day-old devil's food donut. The first time it happened, he'd thanked her, and she'd emphatically hushed him, and since then, she winked at him and he only smiled slightly in response.

Scraping up change had become more difficult since eighth grade started. He felt like he was too old now to beg for change from sympathetic moms in front of Safeway. The last time he'd tried it, a lady had become aggressive with him, asking him where his parents were, asking him for his address. He ran away from her and vowed not to beg for change anymore. He only asked Marie for milk money when Carlos wasn't around, but now Carlos was always around, so that source had mostly dried up, too. Sometimes he'd get so hungry that during school lunch break, he'd tell his friends he was going to the bathroom and he'd rush in and grab one of the welfare-kid free lunches. He'd gulp the mini-carton of milk and eat as much of the main course as he could—usually soggy pizza, macaroni and cheese, or some kind of ground beef and noodle dish—careful not to get caught. He couldn't let any of his friends see him eating with the poor kids.

Joseph had been spending the night at Scott's house two or three nights a week, which was really saving him, but then he'd heard Scott's mom get mad after Scott had casually half-asked, half-told his mom, "Joseph's going to stay the night again, okay mom?" She'd responded angrily, "No Scott, he can't! He can't stay here every night. He's a nice kid, but I already have two kids." Joseph knew this was coming. He knew he was a burden and a hassle. Unlike his friends, who were oblivious to the harshness of life, he knew how adults thought. Joseph wanted to apologize to her, thank her for all the nights she'd let him stay, all the cereal she'd let him eat, and all the times she'd set a place for him at her dinner table. It made him sick to think that he'd become a problem. But he couldn't let her or Scott know he'd been eavesdropping, pressing his ear against the door, and more importantly, he couldn't face the humiliation, so when Scott came in the room with a sour look on his face, about to tell Joseph he had to go home, Joseph preemptively announced he had to get home right away because his mom wanted him to go shopping with her. Joseph could tell Scott knew he was lying. They'd talked about going to Kevin or Erik's house, and Joseph had said nothing about going home. But Joseph was out the door in seconds, yelling back to Scott and his mom, "See you at school Monday, Scott. Thanks for letting me stay over, Mrs. Rowling."

Scott lived only a couple blocks from their middle school, so once Joseph reached the school, it was the same trip he'd made twice a day, five days a week since sixth grade. But it wasn't the same time he usually did the walk, which was in the morning before school and in the early afternoon after school. And there weren't kids around. It was chilly and nearly dark, and the sky was grainy. Joseph was so familiar with his path home that he knew every detail. He'd often notice when a car was missing from someone's driveway, when there was a new or absent barking dog, or when the liquor store's window had a new Marlboro advertisement where the Budweiser one used to be. The familiarity usually comforted him, but today he felt hopeless. It wasn't that he didn't think he could keep going. Joseph didn't need Marie to feed him. He could go days without eating, and he could always find a way to get food. It was that he didn't know if he wanted to keep going.

The one thing that made him special—without even trying—was now gone. He'd always been the smartest student in class. Up until last year, he'd known the subjects that were taught so well, he could teach them himself. In fact, when he was in fourth grade and hadn't filled out and returned the school registration forms because Marie said she was going to do it and she hadn't, Joseph ended up in the only classroom that was available, an ESL class. He spent an entire semester as a teacher's aide teaching Spanish-speaking kids English. And before that, when he was in third grade, he told his teacher, Ms. Molina, that he already knew everything she was teaching. She'd challenged him with an impromptu verbal quiz in front of the whole class, and he'd gotten every question she asked correct, even adding fractions, which wasn't going to be taught until the next year. Joseph thought she was going to get mad, maybe even write his name on the chalkboard, but she just smiled at him, and for the rest of the year, she sent him to the library on a teacher's pass for two hours each day. She told him he should read books and perfect his cursive, that the librarian, Ms. McKinsey, had beautiful cursive that he should emulate.

But now, for the first time since he could remember, there were new things to learn, hard things, and he didn't already know them, and so he didn't know what to do. There was homework too, and he'd never done homework. How? Where? When does one do homework? Last year, seventh grade, his grades had sunk only in science and math, but this semester, his only "A" would be in English. Soon, he thought, he wouldn't even be in the smart-kid classes with his friends, then he'd really be ruined. Next year, he'd be in high school, and he'd probably end up in all the classes with the juvenile delinquents, the future felons, like Manuel and Joey.

It was so dark that there were white stars on black sky by the time he made it to the apartment. The porch light was on, and under the porch light, leaning against the stucco wall, was the outline of a bicycle. Joseph trotted toward it, not believing it was his, but sure enough, there it was. He couldn't believe it. Manuel had returned his bike, the light blue ten-speed with handlebars in the shape of ram horns. It wasn't a BMX bike, but it was fast. It'd taken him the better part of an hour to walk home from Scott's house, but on his bike, he could have made the trip in 10 minutes. Joseph opened the front door, hoping his mom would be on the couch watching television—who knows? maybe even making dinner—and he could make a show of the fact that he had his bike back. He hadn't said anything about it being gone. She knew it was gone, but nothing was said. There was nothing either of them could have done about it that wouldn't have been a hassle.

Joseph unlocked the door and pushed it open with his bike's front tire. To his utter surprise, Carlos and Manuel were sitting on the couch. Carlos was holding a glass bong and Manuel, looking like a story-book giant sitting on a child's chair, was chopping up powder on a TV tray with a single playing card. They both looked back at Joseph as if he'd just walked into a fancy French restaurant wearing cut-off jean shorts.

"Your mom's at Bakers," Carlos reported, and then he took a hit from the bong, held his breath and continued speaking, as if he was a dying cowboy in a movie, trying to tell Joseph who shot him. "She's not getting you anything. She thought you weren't coming home." And then he blew out a cloud of smoke and coughed.

Joseph had no words. He wanted to ask why Manuel was hanging out with Carlos, but he didn't. The answer was obvious.

"Thanks for getting my bike back," Joseph said to Manuel, more as something to say than something he meant.

Joseph wheeled his bike toward his room. His bedroom door was open. His door was never open. Carlos and Marie never went into Joseph's room. One time Carlos had, and Marie yelled at him like he'd never heard her yell at Carlos before. He'd retorted, "I pay the rent!" and Marie had told him she didn't care. She said it was part of the deal. It was unlike her, but no matter how poor they were, Marie had always made sure Joseph had his own room, even in the Alley, where she slept on a hide-a-bed in the living room.

"Was someone in my room?" Joseph asked.

Carlos didn't answer but turned his head toward Manuel.

"I was just checking out your room, dude," Manuel said. "Nice posters. Bruce Lee and Farrah Fawcett—nice tits. At least I know you're not a faggot."

"Put that away before my ol' lady gets home," Carlos told Manuel.

Manuel rose off the couch. His head of bushy dark hair nearly touched the ceiling. He deftly wrapped up the powder into a sheet of paper, which he used to funnel into a miniature plastic baggie. He stuffed the baggie in his too-tight jeans and moved toward Joseph. Joseph turned red and fought back tears. He was scared and angry and a whole lot of other things he didn't want to think about. He just wanted Marie to come home and Manuel to leave.

"Dude, I was just fucking around. I know you're not a faggot. I saw you lookin' at Julia the other day."

Manuel pulled out his wallet and ripped the Velcro open and handed Carlos several bills. Then he followed Joseph to his room and stood under the doorway, leaning diagonally, filling it from corner to corner.

"Bruce Lee was bad ass," Manuel said, "C'mon let's go outside."

"I'm gonna stay inside, okay dude?" Joseph asked, immediately wishing he'd have stated it more strongly.

"C'mon man. I want to talk you," Manuel urged, "before your mom gets home."

Joseph relented, and Manuel grabbed Joseph's bike and wheeled it out.

"What are you doing?" Joseph protested.

"I just want to show you some tricks."

Outside, Manuel rode around in circles doing wheelies and bunny-hops. Joseph cringed. It was a ten-speed, not a BMX bike, and not meant for such rough treatment. He could almost see the rims bending. Manuel was acting manically.

"Dude, stop," Joseph pleaded. "C'mon you're going to snap the forks."

"You're such a pussy," Manuel said and then jumped off the bike while it was still moving, shooting it toward the front of the apartment. Joseph tried to catch it, but it smacked into a post that held the awning up over the front door.

Joseph tried to grab his fallen bike and go and hide in his bedroom, but Manuel jumped between Joseph and the front door.

Talking at the speed of blur, Manuel said, "Let's play slap fighting. You can be Bruce Lee." And before Joseph could decline, Manuel kicked him in the head with a snap roundhouse.

Joseph retaliated, but it was kitten versus tiger. Every time Joseph tried to emulate Bruce Lee and kick or punch Manuel, Manuel reached out and slapped Joseph across the face. After several slaps, Manuel finally stopped. Joseph was red and crying.

"You are such a little pussy," Manuel said.

Marie's silhouette came into view. She was a half-block away, swinging a bag of fast-food.

"Your mommy's almost home," Manuel quipped. "It doesn't hurt. I just tapped you."

"I'm fine," Joseph snapped back, wiping his tears. "I just—"

"I gotta go," Manuel said. "We are on for Tuesday. Meet me at my house at one o'clock. I got a place picked out. Bring your backpack."

"I can't," Joseph protested. "I've got school and I don't—"

Manuel interrupted Joseph, pointing at him. "You said you would." Manuel picked up Joseph's bike and mounted it. "If you don't show, I'm gonna kick your fucking ass."

"Dude, c'mon. Don't take my bike, please, c'mon," Joseph nearly begged.

"I'll give it to you Tuesday after we're done. Show up or your ass is grass."

Manuel rode off, standing atop the pedals and pumping the bike hard. His silhouette crossed an oblong cast of light and then he disappeared. Joseph readied himself to greet his mom, who was now walking up the driveway.

"Hi mom, how are you?"

"Everything's fine," she responded. "Was there a problem with that guy? Is everything alright?"

"I'm fine, mom," Joseph replied and then turned away so Marie couldn't study his face.

Joseph retreated to his room. Marie brought him a taco from Baker's. Joseph told his mom he loved her, like he always did, and she said she loved him, too, but this time it was different. This time it felt hollow and forced. Since he was a little boy, he'd always wanted to protect his mom. But he always failed. Right then, lying in his bed, he admitted this to himself for the first time. He was weak and pathetic, and he'd failed over and over. A few years ago, she'd been in the hospital, her skin and the whites of her eyes as yellow as vitamin-pee, almost dead from hepatitis. He'd done nothing to help her. He'd just stared at her through the hospital window. In fact, he remembered with a pang of guilt, he enjoyed getting to stay with Aunt Suzie and Uncle Billy while his mom was in the hospital and was sad when he had to leave after his mom had been released. It was almost as if he wanted her to stay sick! And then, of course, the event that changed their lives but had never been spoken of, she'd been attacked by a stranger in the middle of the night. Joseph had been too busy having fun, spending the night at his rich friend's home, to be there to protect her. He was eating pizza and playing *Star Wars* versus *Flash Gordon* with his rich friends while his mom was attacked by a strange man in her own bed. Joseph could never forgive himself for that. Never! He used to play a game with himself: What would he sacrifice to stop his mother's attack? He was willing to cut off his own finger. He'd thought about it so many times. He envisioned himself cutting his finger off with a box cutter. He'd do it, too. He knew he'd have to slice and gouge as hard and as fast as he could to cut through the bone and ligaments, but he'd do it. And if that wasn't enough, he was willing to let his mom's attacker do to him what he'd done to her. He thought of the faceless man, dark, and giant, crushing Joseph with his sweaty body, pressing himself into him, enveloping him until Joseph couldn't breathe, nearly suffocating him to death over and over, and then beating him, throwing Joseph across the dark living room, nearly breaking his back over the couch. Instead of Marie, Joseph would be the one standing on the porch that night, wrapped in a blanket, cops all around, asking questions, moving in and out of their apartment in the Alley.

Love doesn't mean anything, Joseph thought. Love was just a word. Love was a lie, like Christmas. In the past, the family would come together, the six of them. Everyone would be happy. There'd be food, and a Christmas tree and gifts under the tree at Grandma and Grandpa's nice little house, the one Marie and Aunt Suzie grew up in, their ghosts everywhere. It was cozy and safe and there was a big back yard with a giant shade tree. Joseph was the only child in the family, so he'd get endless attention and the lion's share of the gifts, but then suddenly, at the end of the day, Christmas would be over. Everyone would kiss him and hug him and tell him how much they loved him, but then, after Aunt Suzie and Uncle Billy or Grandpa dropped Marie and Joseph back off at whichever cockroach-infested apartment he and Marie lived in at the time, the lie would end, and he and Marie would be back dead center in the truth of their lives. Love was a lie. Money was the truth. Money is what they needed, not love.

Tomorrow, Joseph decided, one way or the other, he'd leave his mom. They'd failed each other, and all he could do was try to take care of himself. He'd come back when he had some money. When he became a lawyer, he'd buy her a house and a car and he'd give her a bunch of money, stacks of it, and he'd send Carlos away. But now, there was nothing he could do for her. He wasn't sure he could even do anything for himself, but he had to try.

PART II

The Soul (Law)

THIRTEEN

K en calls me and asks if I want to sell barbeque islands. I'm in a financial free-fall. I haven't gotten a call for a gig in three weeks, and two commercial P.A. gigs I had booked fell through. I think of Macy. She says, just say yes until you have so many choices you have to pick your yeses. Well, I don't have to pick. That's for sure. I say yes. Yes, I'll sell barbeque islands.

I meet Ken at the Los Angeles Convention Center in a hall big enough to race cars in. The ceiling is in the sky, and there are rows of booths that wind up and down the floor for a mile. It's a Home Show. Businesses come here to sell everything related to home improvement: windows, hot tubs, swimming pools, drapes, flooring, ovens, skylights, security systems, gazebos, pergolas, tool sheds, and of course, barbeque islands. Ken directs men who are setting up his company's display. There is a giant banner that reads, "Paradise BBQ Islands." The logo is oddly amateurish: orange and yellow script set atop a clip art palm tree. Ken's workers, wearing standard white polo shirts with the unfortunate logo, roll out bright green outdoor carpet and position barbeque islands with a small forklift.

Ken speaks fast and loud over the hubbub of activity and warning beeps from backing forklifts.

"People are equity rich," Ken explains, "so they are taking out home equity loans and buying these. It increases the value of their homes." Ken rushes over to the forklift driver and waves his hands wildly. "No, no. You'll crack the frame like that!"

I inspect one of the monstrosities already in position in the booth. It has a green marble countertop with a gigantic gleaming stainless-steel gas grill and eight matching knobs. It has a little brushed stainless-steel sink on one side of the grill, and the counter expands into a circle on the opposite side, and out of its center rises a palapa—an oversized raw wood umbrella, made to look like a palm tree, with palm fronds as covering instead of fabric. The marble countertop is stepped-up behind the grill and doubles as a bar, with six bar stools, four around the circular countertop, under the palapa, and two on the non-cooking side of the grill. There's a refrigerator built into the faux rock base of the island and a couple of stainless-steel doors under the grill. It even has a stereo with outdoor speakers and lights.

"So what do you think?" Ken asks while he waits for me to complete my inspection.

I contemplate telling him that it reminds me of a neon-painted jet ski, but instead I say, "Wow. It's really something."

Ken presses his hands to the barbeque island's bar proudly.

"I know what you're thinking, Mr. Attorney," he says, leaning into the bar.

"What am I thinking?" I ask.

Ken reaches over the bar and presses the power on the stereo and a Jimmy Buffet tune begins to belch out.

"Yes, the palm fronds on the palapa are fire retardant," Ken says.

"Jesus, Ken. Are you wearing a Tommy Bahama shirt?"

"You're just jealous," he says, brushing off my attack.

"So how much for one of these monstrosities," I ask.

"This one right here will cost you 7 grand. It's smallish, but it's got all the bells and whistles. You sell one for full price, and you make—" he looks up as he calculates the commission, "$560. Eight percent commission on the base. Anything over the base, you get twenty percent."

"Wait, why would anybody pay more than the base price?" I ask, skeptically.

"Because you are going to convince them to," Ken responds glee-fully. His eyes brighten. He chuckles and makes little huffing noises as his head and stomach bounce. He looks as if he just discovered gold alchemy.

I ponder this for a second. Ken holds his pose, anticipating an exu-berant response from me.

"So wait a second," I say. "I sell it for 7 grand, and I make $560 but I sell it for 8 grand, and... I make $760?"

"That's right, Counselor!" Ken is so excited he can barely contain himself. He reaches down and turns up Jimmy Buffet.

I flash my plastic laminated badge to a bored security worker and walk past the line of people waiting to get into the home show. In the massive bathroom, I wash my hands and stare at myself in the mirror. I look dif-ferent than when I got out of prison. I'm fatter, and I've been trying to grow into my new, more artsy self. I've even begun writing a little. My hair is down to my shoulders, and I've grown a full beard that glistens in the light. It's red, blonde, and brown with several threads of grey that I attribute to my days of incarceration. I wear navy blue Vans shoes and a pair of khakis with white paint stains from painting a wall that a commercial director suddenly decided should be stark white instead of off-white.

I stare at myself in the mirror. Before I go out there, I have to admit to myself why I'm so scared. It's not the job. Yes, I'm a little nervous, but what's really bothering me is my name. I don't want people to know my name. I guess I'm ashamed of my own name. When I flashed my badge at the security guard on the way in, adrenaline shot through me. I half expected him to stop me. I imagined him hustling after me. "Excuse me, sir, yes. Please, come with me. You are on the list, and we can't let you in here. It's company policy. You'll have to leave." And when Ken excitedly gave me my new business cards, I had to pretend that read-ing my own name didn't terrify me. "Joseph Naus, Sales Consultant, Paradise BBQ Islands." I immediately played through a scenario where a customer searched my name on the internet. I see an angry man with his wife and child in tow. "You've got a fucking child molester working for you! What do you think the Better Business Bureau is going to think about that! There are children here!"

There it is, I think to myself. It's my fear. I see it. It's real. The thing I'm afraid of is real. These scenarios are possible. Fine. All I can do is live one day at a time. I whisper my version of the Third Step prayer into the mirror, ignoring the stare of the old man washing his hands next to me. "I'm in your hands, God. Tell me what to fucking do, and I'll do it. Amen."

Ken introduces me to Bob, Ned and Brian. We shake hands. Brian is the manager. He runs the shop where they build the barbeque islands. Ned and Bob are salesmen straight out of Central Casting. Ken tells Bob to show me the ropes, and tells him I've never sold before. Bob rolls his eyes and shakes his head. He doesn't even try to mask it. Clearly they've had words about my presence here.

Ned pipes in, "He's on his own Ken. I told you. I'm here to sell—" Ned breaks off and walks toward an approaching couple and says, "How you folks doing today?"

Bob asks Ken, "Do I get half newbies commission?" and before Ken or I can respond, he says, "I'm just kidding. I'll show him the deal, but you can't teach 25 years of sales experience in an hour."

Ken begins talking with Brian about a barbeque island that was sup-posed to be displayed but isn't here. Ned is driving hard on a young couple that looks like they have money. "Are we here to buy or are we here to look?" he asks them.

Bob takes me aside to one of the six islands on the far end of our open sales floor.

"Look bro," Bob says. "We are pulling down a few grand a show. Everyone wants to work here. I got friends that've been selling hot tubs since the '80s, and Ken brings you in, lookin' like Grizzly Adams? What's the story?" Bob snorts and wipes at his nose as if he's pretending he just did a line of coke. The face of his gold Rolex is blurry from my angle, a telltale sign that it's fake.

"Oh you know, Ken and I have been friends for a while—" I answer, before Bob interrupts me.

"Yeah, yeah, yeah. Same vague B.S. Ken told me. What? Are you in the C.I.A. or something? Whatever, I'm going to find out."

"Dude, there's nothing to find out. He's just a friend."

"Bullshit," Bob says.

I don't know why, but I like Bob. I just do. He's so purely who he is.

He lays it all out, rapid fire. "This is a home show. You got Friday, Saturday, and Sunday. They walk, you lose. Chance of them coming back—one in a fuckin' hundred. If they walk, you let them know they just walked out of the deal of a lifetime. You start the price high so you've got room to cut, but not too high. We salesman have an agreement. We don't ever go below what'll net us five percent commission."

He hands me the cost list for each island with the commissions written on the back of his business card in tiny writing and says, "Copy it. Memorize it."

Bob stands uncomfortably close to me. I can smell the cigarette smoke on his clothes and the alcohol beneath the mints. "Now you listen to me," he says. "Listen to me, man. You size them up. Some looky-loo motherfucker will have you talking your ass off for hours, stringing you along, sinking that hook in you deeper and deeper. Meanwhile, Ned over there is making kills, your kills and his kills, too. Got it?"

"Fuck Bob, this is some real *Glengarry Glenn Ross* shit right here," I joke.

"Whatever, man. If you don't want to listen, fine," he says and stares at me, with a touch of hurt in his eyes.

"Sorry, Bob... I was just—" Bob interrupts me with a machine-gun burst of laughter.

"See what I just did? I manipulated you! I controlled you. See? That's what you gotta fuckin' do with your god damn customers."

A couple with a stroller walks up to the barbeque island behind us. The man lifts the hood of the grill and looks at his wife. She shakes her head. Bob elbows me. A rush of energy shoots through me like a blast of cold air.

"Can I help you with something?" I ask, smiling dopily, like I don't know what to do with my face.

"No, just looking," the man says. He smiles at me guardedly, shuts the lid and leaves.

I walk back to Bob. He's laughing at me and imitates me in a whiny voice, "Can I help you?"

He says it three more times and laughs harder following each one. I wait.

"You done mocking me?" I ask.

"There is nothing worse that you can possibly say than 'Can I help you?' Everyone knows that 'Can I help you?' is the thing salespeople say to which everyone responds, 'Just looking.' Don't give them the option. Say something that forces them to engage or to be rude. Most people will engage."

The home show is filling up. Bob and I look over at the giant double-sided monster barbeque island with a tree-sized palapa, the biggest one on the floor. Ned stands with a short man he greeted 10 minutes ago, writing up a contract while his tall wife talks on her cell phone excitedly. The thought of making a sale like Ned just did thrills me and yet seems more than implausible.

"Fucking Ned. He's a pit bull," Bob says. "He's always top sales, probably top salesman in the whole industry. He's been in prison three times, all for driving drunk, fucking deuces. He's got deuces in three different states. Can't get a license in California ever again."

"How do you know?" I ask.

"He told me. Ask him. Fucker is proud of it. We always drink on show nights. He's got more stories than you got taint hair."

Bob approaches a fat man wearing Bermuda shorts and sporting one of those thick gold bracelets that's designed to look like gold nuggets.

Bob opens with, "So where in your backyard are you thinking this might fit best?"

The man looks up. He's got earbuds on under his hat. He pulls them out. Bob repeats his question.

"I rent an apartment, actually," the man answers and then asks Bob if barbeque islands run off natural gas or propane. Bob points him to Ned and tells him that Ned is the expert and to direct all questions to Ned.

Quite impressed with himself, Bob turns to me. "You ask that mother fucker, 'What can I help you with?' and he's asking you all these questions, come to find out, hours later, mother fucker doesn't even own a home!" Bob laughs and snorts and does his post-coke snorting move again. "What, you gonna put this in your fucking apartment's living room?" He laughs some more.

At least there's some laughs here, I think. There's no laughing in P.A. Nation. Of course, P.A.s get paid as long as they show up. I could stand here all weekend and not make a dime. The real thought of that possibility momentarily wobbles me.

Ned walks over waving the contract with one hand and smacking it with the back of the other. It makes a little pop sound each time he does it. The smell of over-buttered popcorn wafts through into our open sales booth. "C'mon boys," Ned chides. "Time to get closing. Doors opened 30 minutes ago and ole Ned's already got a deal."

"That was a fuckin' gift," Bob says and waves Ned off. "You didn't close them. They closed themselves. Lucky bastard."

Ned walks back to the other side of the booth.

Bob yells after him, "Hey Ned, show Joseph how you can pull your gold chain through one nostril and out the other."

Ned flips Bob off without turning around. Brian sees Ned giving Bob the bird and admonishes him lightly.

There are tons of people milling around. They weave in and out of our booth. I talk to a few, try to spot the ones that might actually buy. I use Bob's tip and ask people whether they have room in their backyard now or whether they'll have to clear something out to make room. This works well. They don't even have to answer. I can tell just by the look on their faces. I get one couple talking. They are Hispanic and have two adorable boys. She's got a huge diamond ring, and I can tell they are new money. He's a mortgage broker. He's dangling his Cadillac SUV key around. Their baby's stroller is even top dollar. It looks like it was designed in Sweden, all sleek and clever, like an Olympic bobsled. Thirty minutes later, and all their questions having been asked and answered, they've picked out the barbeque island of their dreams, and it's just a matter of Mr. Santa Cruz pulling out his wallet.

"So," I say, nervously, feeling like I could blow this with one wrong word, and probably will. "It looks like we've got it all worked out. Do you have any more questions or—" I let it hang, hoping that Mr. Santa Cruz will say he's going to buy. But he looks at Mrs. Santa Cruz, and she nods her head, and he tells me they are going to talk it over. They walk off. Bob walks over to me with his head down like a baseball manager about to yank a pitcher that just gave up consecutive home runs. Apparently, he was eavesdropping the whole time.

"Don't like to feel uncomfortable, huh Joe?" he says, jabbing at me with his finger. He imitates me, "Do you have any more questions?"

"My name is Joseph, not Joe," I say.

"Oh I'm sorry Joseph. Joseph doesn't know shit about sales. Joseph just threw away $600."

"Okay, fine. I'm here to learn," I say in surrender. "What should I have done, Bob?"

"I'm glad you asked, Joseph. Listen carefully. You," he says emphatically, and taps on my chest, "You... You have to be willing to be more uncomfortable than the customer. You answered all their fucking questions, you were nice to them, you worked out a fair price. You did your fucking part. Now you look them in the eye and you say, 'How do you want to pay for this today? Cash, check or credit card?' You do the most honest thing you can do. You ask for the fucking money." Bob pokes me with two fingers. "It's the hardest part of the job. You look them in the eye, and you ask for the money, and then you shut up and stare them right in their eyes. You make them decide."

"Okay," I say, defensively.

"You just let them off the hook. You didn't make them choose."

"Alrighty," I concede. "Makes sense."

"You don't let them walk without some serious pain. They need to think they just walked away from the best deal they're ever going to get."

Macy, me and her son, William, are in an LAX hotel ballroom. There are hundreds of people milling about. Me being here falls under the category of not exercising "contempt prior to investigation" despite some serious contempt. This is fucking weird. There are a bunch of New Agers and hippies milling around. They are here to get a hug from some Indian woman named Amma. Macy and William are waiting in line, a line that snakes around the ballroom, a line that takes hours, literally hours, to get through. At the end of the line, where a speaker might speak if this were an insurance industry convention, there is a squat stage full of pillows, and it's decorated in the colors and fabrics of India, reds and yellows and purples, silk and cotton and tassels. The word "maharaja" comes to my mind. So far, no one has asked me for any money, and they even have vegan Indian food for only a few bucks. There are a few booths on the outer edges of the packed convention floor. They sell incense and candles and New Age books with titles like *This Thing Called You* and *Enlightenment for All,* naturally dyed saris, sleek water bottles with stylized Buddha logos and various New Age-branded paraphernalia.

Macy sits cross-legged on the floor, as does everyone in line except for a few old or disabled people who have chairs. William plays his Nintendo Game Boy. He's got big hair like his mom. He's so precious. Sometimes it's hard for me to be around him. I don't know how to act. I want to pick him up and squeeze him like he's a big stuffed koala bear, but it's like he's made of porcelain. I think I'm going to say something or do something stupid and break him. I just don't want to fuck up. I just want to make sure, no matter what happens with Macy and me, that my existence in his life is good, and I don't know if that's possible.

Macy peers calmly over the room. William sits between us. She looks at me and smiles softly. I smile back. I'm happy, or maybe I'm at peace. Whatever this feeling is, it's enriching. She's let me into her beautiful little life and her beautiful little family. I just want to be a good man. She's still with me, even after I told her I was a two-strike felon, a registered sex offender, because she knows I am down. I am down to do whatever it takes to turn my life around. I am down with the 12 Steps. I am down for family. I am down for wholesome. I am down for God, whatever that is. I am down for her and William. I am even down for some New Age hippie shit if it's for the good of this little family.

The line scoots along slowly, slowly. It'll be at least a couple more hours. Macy says she's fine to wait, and I get up and go to the kitchen and volunteer. This is what 12-Steppers are taught to do when they go to parties and events: start helping. So I do. None of the volunteers say anything to me, they just nod and point until I find myself where I belong, at the helm of a commercial dishwashing sink, just like the one at Pasadena Recovery Center. I slide on thick plastic yellow rubber gloves and I scrape the food remnants off cafeteria-style burnt orange plastic plates into a giant garbage can. Then I use the powerful sprayer to rinse the plates, and I stack the dishes into the tub. Another volunteer steps in silently, and washes the dishes I rinse. We get in a rhythm, not a word spoken, and I find myself in a state of euphoric flow. The sound of the kitchen mixes with the ambient noise of the masses of quiet people coming and going down the hall and in and out of the ballroom floor. The smell of jasmine rice, hummus, naan bread, cauliflower, and yellow curry accents the harsh smell of dishwashing soap, which clouds up into my nostrils with the hot water's steam. This goes on for nearly an hour, and when I finally catch up with the now-diminishing flow of dirty dishes, I tie up the black plastic trash bags and heave them out to the dumpsters in the alley of the hotel. A few New Agers, one of Amma's Indian staffers and a couple of hotel employees gather together and smoke cigarettes near the dumpster.

I switch out with Macy so she can go eat. William is asleep with his head on a pillow. Seeing him here now sleeping in this giant room and observing how his parents treat him like he is the most precious thing on the planet, I cannot help but compare his childhood to mine. At his age, I was wandering the streets by myself, navigating invites for car rides from creepy men who sometimes followed me after I politely declined, and trotted or pedaled my bike away as fast as I could. I think of William, like I was, hungry, figuring out how he's going to eat. I shudder. I shouldn't even think these thoughts. I don't want him to ever experience anything like that. And he never will. William's father Leo and Macy wouldn't let him miss a dentist appointment let alone go hungry. Leo and Macy are united in that they would do anything and everything to protect William. So would I. I ponder the question that I've always wanted to pose to my parents: "How could you?" My brain knows the answer: addiction; but my heart isn't fully ready to forgive yet.

William groans and turns skyward. "Can we leave now?" he asks me.

I feel tears arise and I push them down hard. "We'll be hugging Amma soon," I say and wink at William.

He rolls his eyes at me, sits up and turns on his Game Boy.

Macy returns.

Over the last four-plus hours we have scooted the distance of a par-three golf hole, and the snaking line is finally at its end. There she is, this magic woman. A chubby, cherubic Indian woman in a pinkish-orange sari sits upon a large flat decorative square pillow. There are handlers all around her. She sits there, famously, all day long, giving hug after hug. Her handlers rub baby powder on her left cheek, I presume to avoid a rash. I can see her hugging now. She's only 20 feet in front of us, everyone squished up together in front of her sitting on the floor, like we are at a gigantic slumber party.

William puts his Game Boy in Macy's purse, and Macy tousles his hair. I can tell he's excited. We all look at each other, all about to embark on this spiritual ritual.

There are only four people ahead of us. We are corralled tightly by Amma's handlers.

A woman handler whispers to us, "You want to go all together, your beautiful family?"

"Yes, yes," Macy says.

I look into Macy's giant brown saucer eyes. We could be a family. She could become my wife. He could become my son. It's a fantasy I rarely indulge, but today it seems possible, maybe even plausible.

We are up! We are jammed up against Amma. My pulse pounds. She's magnificent! She smells of baby powder and incense and candle wax. She pulls us in to her, tighter than I expected. She is thick and wonderfully strong. My mouth gasps air into my throat. My head is pulled into a bushel of hair, Macy's, William's and Amma's thick dense hair. Now I'm pressed against Amma's neck. My doubts vanish. Love pulses through me. She is real. This is real. It's pulsing through us. Oh my God! I tremble, and tears bubble up and fill my eyes and drip down. Amma says something. I don't know if her words are in English or Hindi, and I cannot repeat what she says. But I can feel her energy. It's powerful and undeniable.

Amma lets go of us. I feel as if I was pulled out of baptismal waters into new air. We are whisked away and helped off the stage toward the exit. I'm shaky. I didn't expect to be moved like this. I've never felt bliss like this. Macy is beaming and even William is wide-eyed. I place my arm around her. She's holding William's hand. He's swinging her hand. Macy giggles lightly and bites her lower lip and looks at me, anticipating my reaction.

"Oh my God. That was so intense!" I nearly yell as we walk through the hotel lobby. A few people grin knowingly.

"Right? Isn't she amazing?" Macy asks.

On the way home, I'm buzzing, wondering what exactly just happened. Was it the build-up? Was it the anticipation? Was it because of all the people? Or did that lady, Amma—did she really just hug me and infuse me with pure energy, love vibrations, like a modern shaman? I don't believe in hippie New Age bullshit, but whatever that was, it was real.

I'm running late to my meeting at Café Tropical, or "The Trop" as we call it. I curse myself for being late. I'm never late anymore. Punctuality is one of my new things, but not today. I had to squeeze in one more cigarette. It's starting to get dark earlier. It's the golden hour. Everything is lit vibrantly. As I trot across Sunset, I see the door is closed to the meeting room. Everyone is already inside because the meeting has already started. There is only one person outside. It's a homeless guy, crouched on a step in an enclave next to the meeting room door. Homeless people, most of whom are addicts too, often hang out here before and after meetings. We 12-Steppers are a great crowd to solicit for cigs and a little cash.

This man's form is familiar. I can't see his face, just the silhouette of a cigarette burning in his mouth. The man swaps the cigarette for a swig of something from a paper bag, I presume a tallboy. This could be me, I think to myself, but I wouldn't hang out here. I'd be too prideful to show my face. I just couldn't do it. I'm a few strides away when the man's silhouette materializes. Jesus Christ. It's Paddy! He looks horrible. His hair is overgrown and mangy, and he's bearded. Before, he always looked like he came straight from the barber. His face is darkly tan and dirty; grease fills his crow's feet. He's a decade older than when I last saw him a few weeks ago. But his eyes are as blue as ever, just now they're glazed and groggy.

"Can I get a dollar," Paddy says without looking. He holds out a paper cup.

"Paddy, dude, it's me. What the... fuck?"

He lurches a bit and rises unsteadily.

"Oh man, eh, uh dude," he says, slurring. "Joseph, man. How are you?"

I'm embarrassed for us both. I'm shocked.

"I'm just going to the meeting."

"Oh yeah, yeah man," he says. Paddy's eyes blink slowly, and he takes a puff of his cigarette, which has burned down to the filter and is mostly ash. His head descends as his eyes close. "Okay, man. Joseph, man... dude."

"I'll talk to you when the meeting is over," I say.

"Okay," he says and jerks back up and holds out his cup. "Can I get a couple bucks?"

I pull out a $5 bill. I think of the story in the Big Book about a sober guy giving a guy who relapsed some money and the sober guy feeling good about it, but when he considered it, he realized it was about his own ego, and that he should have given the money to his home AA group instead. It was some classic Bill Wilson shit, a parable for the unquestioning dullards. Why do I have such a vitriolic opinion about this?, I wonder. I don't know, but it is virtually certain, if my personal history is at all prescient, that I will later realize I am completely wrong.

Of course, at Trop meetings, 12-Step contrarianism is uproariously ap-
plauded, due to a certain punk rock pedagogy, always, of course, qualified at share's end by a somber and snarling "but this motherfucking
program is saving my life."

I open the door. I get lucky, and there is a seat next to Trenton. Upon
seeing him, I recall that I saw his bike outside locked to a signpost. The
room is nearly full, and it's musty with the sharp residue of the strong
detergent regularly applied to the bare concrete floor. A woman with a
raspy voice is reading Chapter Five, "How It Works."

I lean over to Trenton and whisper. "Did you fucking see Paddy outside? What the fuck, dude?"

"Yeah dude," Trenton whispers. He shrugs and shakes his head
simultaneously.

Through the entire meeting, all I can think is, What am I going to
do? Should I take him back to his sober living house? Should I take him
to my apartment? I guess he can sleep on the couch.

The woman who hosted the party Macy and I first spoke at, who
wears a tiny '50s retro hat that for some reason reminds me of Truman
Capote, is talking about praying so she can deal with her fucked-up boss
where she works at a rehab for teenagers. I hear the muted sound of the
toilet flushing and then the sink running.

I think of the Big Book where Bill Wilson writes about an alcoholic
committing suicide in his home, and that another alcoholic, I think I
recall, lit his and his wife Lois's couch on fire. For some reason this
reminds me of the famous line from the Big Book, "We are not a glum
lot." Well, Paddy sure was looking glum. I decide I'll take Paddy home
and get him cleaned up. He can sleep on my futon. I don't have a door
to my bedroom. It's 10 feet away from the futon, so I'll be able to keep
an eye on him. I'll just tell him he has to be out during the day when I'm
not home. At least he won't be sleeping on the streets at night. I can feed
him. But what if he doesn't want to stop drinking? I'm not Bill Wilson.
Bill Wilson didn't have the kind of problems I have. Whatever, it's the

best I can do. Even if he drinks, I'll let him spend the night on my futon as long as he doesn't drink in or near my apartment. And I'll put a time limit on it. He can't stay at my place forever, and the nights I stay at Macy's, he'll have to find somewhere else to stay.

Someone reads the final reading of the meeting, which ends with everyone chanting, "… contempt prior to investigation—Herbert Spencer." Someone says "Dee Snyder" instead of Herbert Spencer, and it gets a few chuckles. We all hold hands, pray out, and everyone starts to file out of the stuffy packed room. I'm waiting for people to clear while telling Trenton about my decision to let Paddy stay at my apartment. He responds by raising his eyebrows. "What else am I supposed to do, dude?" I protest. "I can't just leave him out there, fucking homeless. That's Paddy. He's our friend."

"I don't know, man. He's just pretty fucked up. I don't think that he's just drinking."

Everyone huddles up on the sidewalk, lighting cigarettes, talking in little groups. I look for Paddy in the enclave, but he's not there. I look in the café, and around to the bus stop and down the little alley in back behind the Silverlake Lounge. I trot to my car and drive around, up and down Sunset and the nearest side street, trolling slowly. I cringe when I realize that my search for Paddy feels like when I used to cruise for prostitutes, that if a cop saw me, he might pull me over. The idea of it is unfathomable now.

I park on Silver Lake Boulevard near the Sunset bridge and peer into the makeshift homeless pods erected in the areas between the bridge's pillars and sandwiched between the boulevard and the sidewalk. This, I think to myself, is where Anthony Kiedis was talking about in that song about shooting dope under the bridge. These are children's forts gone terribly wrong: filthy, shabby boxes; shopping carts; sleeping bags; plastic junk; tennis shoes; a glass coffee pot; a cracked blender, junk of all sorts, bound together. I pull back flaps and stick my head around boxes in my attempt to find Paddy. Most of the residents aren't home, but one is. I can only make out the general form of a woman. She mumbles something aggressively at me and rolls to her hip and straightens herself up as if to threaten to get up and chase me. I move quickly enough to appease her. My eyes sting from the exhaust from Silver Lake Boulevard, the shit, and the piss. I drive a couple more loops around the area, but no Paddy.

Here I am, out here, smoking in the dark again. Thinking and smoking.

The truth is, it wasn't that hard to quit the sex stuff and the drinking. Sure, I had my days. I almost relapsed a couple times, but I used the stress I was under to justify it. I was in so much pain. I thought about how it felt good and how I wanted to feel good again, just to replace the pain. I still drool like Pavlov's dogs over the thought of a Jack and Coke on ice. I didn't ever want to quit. Why would I quit something that made me feel so fucking good? I never tried to quit. But I never craved it all day. I never dropped to my knees to beg God to get me through the day sober. I just drank whenever I could. It didn't have to be every day. The sex stuff was different. It'd sneak up on me. But once I hit my bottom, found myself in handcuffs again, I stopped. I had a relapse, but it was a one-off during a time I was under debilitating stress. And the porn, it took a while; there was a relapse here and there, but it ultimately just faded away. Masturbation just took a little more imagination. I no longer had stockpiles of elaborate porn memories to draw on. I had to reset my sexuality. I joked to myself that after years of prostitutes, porn, and drunken one-nighters, my orgasm tolerance was so high, I needed two prostitutes, a car battery, and a set of jumper cables to get off. I had to stop thinking of sex with my partner as a performance. I'm still learning to let go and be present with myself and Macy. Sometimes it's scary. Sometimes it's uncomfortable. Sometimes I can't do it, and I check out into fantasy. "Intimacy," now that's the magic word. Macy reads me excerpts of David Schnarch and Pia Mellody. She knows all about this shit. I don't always give her the satisfaction of full agreement with her opinions on the subject, but I get it. I'm on the road to full recovery. I'm becoming more, as the learned-ones like to say, "fully integrated" all the time.

I see the tips of fireworks flashing and fading away over Dodger Stadium. I light another cigarette and sink back into my thoughts.

Cigarettes are different. These own me. I've wanted to quit for so long. When I was in Sober Living and took those anti-depressants, Wellbutrin, and they made me not feel my cigarettes, not feel the nicotine high, I panicked. I smoked through it, though. I beat those pills. I got my nicotine high back. Alcohol and sex, they were never like this. I'm a slave to nicotine. I'm in love with these things. I tried to do what I did with the sex stuff. I went to a few of the 12-Step meetings for sex addicts, but I didn't like them much, so I made a deal with myself that I didn't have to go if I remained abstinent using my regular 12-Step meetings. It worked. I stayed abstinent. Some people ask me how I have sex with my girlfriend—do I get triggered? How do I handle it as a sex addict? Those people have no idea. They don't get it at all.

Two young couples are walking on the curb, chatting. The one with the '70s throwback, feathered hair and bell-bottom jeans, she has a felt Dodger blanket draped over her shoulders. She's the only one of the four that notices me, sitting here in the dark, under my umbrella, the conspicuously unlit porch light, smoking. Her car is facing steeply downhill and inches from the car below. She struggles to pull her car off the curb, gassing it without success, but finally does so with a chirp of the tires. She and her friends drive away, and it's quiet again. I light another cigarette.

Cigarettes had me in a chokehold from whatever day it was that it stopped being a choice, a decade ago. I went over 100 days without smoking while in Twin Towers and Chino prison. After a while, I didn't even think about smoking, probably because it was an impossibility.

But then when I got out, the very day I got out, they popped into my head and did a little pirouette, peppering dopamine all over my nucleus accumbens, and I was instantly back to a pack-a-day habit. I've never looked back. I've tried to quit a few times. I can't last a day. Not even close. I don't smoke cigarettes. Cigarettes smoke me.

Black Cat jumps on the chair across the little wood table. I stopped feeding him after he last bit me, either because I didn't feed him the right way or because I stopped petting him for a moment to change the television channel, I forget which.

"Black Cat, bad ass," I say softly. I go inside and pour a saucer full of cheap cat food from a box with a precocious animated cat on it that I got at the liquor store. Black Cat wraps his tail around my ankle and purrs as loud as a small motorcycle engine. I set the cat food down on the step in front of my door. Before I've even taken a second drag off my newly lit cigarette, Black Cat has gobbled his food and darted off.

I tried the cross-addiction technique that I used for the sex stuff with the cigarettes. I prayed a little. I don't think I really wanted it that bad. I don't know if I was ready. It makes me mad. I quit alcohol and sex addiction; I survived prison and jail; I lost my Bar license; I'm a registered sex offender. Despite all the damage, I'm forging a new life, doing the best I can, and yet the truth is, I'm killing myself with cigarettes. I can feel the heaviness in my lungs, my stripped throat, and even my occasionally-blipping heart.

"Fuck!" I yell, loud enough for my landlord to hear if she were home. I stare at the orange and grey tip of my lit cigarette. I take another drag. "Fuck," I whisper.

I've killed a whole pack, out here thinking. I'm exhausted. I drag myself inside and lay on the futon, kick off my shoes, and unburden my body of consciousness. I'll deal with tomorrow, tomorrow.

FOURTEEN

I'm on my way to the LAPD Skid Row station to register. Happy Birthday.

I drive down Sunset like I'm taking my driver's license exam, and the DMV examiner is sitting in my passenger seat. I've got my hands at 10 and two, staying far behind the car in front of me. I signal and look at all three mirrors before changing lanes. Just like the last two years, I've steadily declined into a mood that becomes a flared depression leading up to the day I have to register. I fantasize about the myriad ways I can end up not complying with Penal Code Section 290. Failure to register is a felony.

A car sideswipes me. I'm in the hospital. I can't speak. Keri stands over me. She says, "Is there anything you need from me?" I struggle, but I can't say the words. If I could, I'd say, "Please let the police know I'm in the hospital, that I was on my way to register. Please!" Or, I'm working on a movie. The set is on the American River. We are shooting white water rafting scenes. I'm scheduled to be back days before I have to register, but something goes wrong, maybe an avalanche. We can't get back to base camp. Everyone is stuck. Or maybe I just plain forget. I have calendaring notices everywhere—in my phone, on my computer calendar, on my wall calendar, a stickie on my refrigerator. "Register!" But I wake up and realize it's the middle of February, and I haven't registered. I just forgot. These dreams, daydreams, fantasies, they always end the same way. Police pound on my door. They pound on my door so hard and so loud it rattles the whole building. I freeze in terror. They pound and yell. "Mr. Naus. It's the police. Open the door!" I open it. They spin me around and ratchet handcuffs on my wrists. They force me into a police cruiser. The whole nightmare starts over. I'm back in Twin Towers, back in front of a judge. The D.A. smiles at me like a coyote. She hates me so much, is so thrilled to have me back in her sights. "I'm not done with you yet, Mr. Naus. I'm not done with you by a long shot."

It's just like the last time I registered, but this time, I have to park on the curb. I feed quarters and dimes into the meter. There are sidewalk tents and dark homeless men crisscrossing the street. They are not of this world. A bony woman walks toward me switching her hips violently and holding a cigarette underhanded with her elbow raised high. She stops talking to no one and asks me for a cigarette, then some change, then asks if I want a blowjob, baby. She has scabs on her face and an open, yellow-centered abscess on her neck. I hand her my excess meter change, careful not to touch her.

I come early to get it over with. It's 7 a.m. sharp, but it's still packed with the homeless and soon-to-be homeless. I wait. I stand against the wall, next to the bench of homeless men. I lean against the defunct payphone next to the bathroom door with the askew sign that reads "Out of Order." The cop takes my photo and my fingerprints. I feel no judgment from him. He's apparently seen too many of us to have much energy left for an overtly expressed opinion. I'm just another widget in his factory job, and I'm grateful for it.

He has been gone for an awfully long time. I try to keep myself calm by pretending I'm at the DMV. But every minute that ticks off that big black and white wall clock increases my anxiety. I just need to hold it together and wait for the cop to come back and give me my completed registration form and my driver's license. C'mon, just let me go. This isn't the DMV. This is a place of danger. Don't lie to yourself. "Mr. Naus, can you come with me?" That's what he'll say. Something is wrong. "We show that you are out of compliance. Out of compliance, Mr. Naus. Non-compliant!" He will shout like a Nazi soldier checking papers. "Back to the shit with you, Mr. Naus. Back to hell's labyrinth. You might not get out this time, Mr. Naus, you know, three strikes and all. Put your hands behind your back, Mr. Naus."

"Mr. Naus," the police officer says.

"Yes," I reply, trying to mask my impatience.

He looks down at my registration form as I walk toward the counter. He doesn't say anything.

"Do you still have the same car?"

"Yes," I say quickly.

"Is it here?" he asks, suspiciously. He's seeing if he can tease out a lie.

"Yes," I answer.

"It's parked out front?" he asks.

"It's parked on the street, half-block down."

"What street?"

"The one that way," I say, pointing. "What's that, east, right?" I say, a little frustrated and confused. I didn't know my map skills were going to be tested.

"You don't know where you are parked?"

"I think it's Maple, or Wall. No, it's Wall. I'm south a half block on Wall on the east side of the street at a meter," I say, picking up confidence as I go. Fuck this guy. I've got nothing to hide.

The officer picks up the sign-in clipboard and calls the next name on the list. He hands me my driver's license and registration form. I thank him perfunctorily and race-walk out of the station. A man is stooped against a retaining wall at the base of the steps that lead down to the sidewalk. He sits on dirty cardboard and extends his arm out for change. He holds his hand as if he's holding a cup, but his hand is empty. He mumbles. I slide my sunglasses on so no one can see my tears, and the morning sun is a fine alibi. I shake all over and I'm sobbing so hard that I'm more bouncing than walking.

I lock myself in my car and take deep breaths. I close my eyes and focus on my breathing. I repeat the Serenity Prayer several times aloud.

I call my sponsor and leave a message, and in the middle of the message, my chest starts bouncing again.

"Lack of acceptance is the source of all pain," I say aloud, quoting some coffee table spiritual book Macy has in the magazine rack by her toilet. It's Buddha or Jesus, one of those guys.

I think, what if I can't accept something? What if it's completely unacceptable? What if you are the victim of a horrible situation? How will I ever recover from this? This is for life. I've been permanently labeled a registered sex offender. How will I ever be okay with this?

I wait for my sponsor to call back. He doesn't. He has a job. I call Macy. I apologize for calling. I tell her where I am, that I'm devastated. I'm regretting having called her while I'm telling her why I called. I'm thinking she's going to break up with me. She's got enough problems without having me around. She can do better than a broken man.

"You are a child of God," Macy says.

Macy is unyieldingly committed to her spiritual beliefs. She is not half-stepping. She has no less belief that God exists than that her shoes exist.

She tells me I am loved, that I have friends that love me, that God loves me, that God wouldn't bring me this far just to drop me off. She tells me that I know the truth about myself. That I am a good, sober man that is of service to myself and others. She says these things with absolute resoluteness, and I believe her.

She tells me she loves me. I tell her I love her. I tell her I love her because I do.

Our call ends. I start my car and head back to my apartment. She's off to work, and I've got cigarettes to smoke.

I'm at the Los Angeles Country Fair, at the Paradise BBQ Island booth. I'm here to sell islands. Beside our booth is the bungee jump ride, so there is a 200-foot high crane towering over our tent. Over and over, all day long, it slowly tows a steel cage up to its tip. The steel cage opens and usually, a teenage girl jumps out, followed by her shrill screams. She stretches the bungee cord to its limit, and she rebounds up and down, each time with a reenergized scream. All the while, Justin Timberlake's modulated voice pumps out of the bungee ride speakers at spectacular volume. Justin is bringing sexy back. He's bringing sexy back over and over and over... It's seemingly the only song on the carny playlist.

Ned leans into a woman, the identified decision-maker of the couple he's been pitching for 20 minutes. She holds her ground, but is uncomfortable with the turn of the conversation. Her husband lifts up the heavy grill plates from under the barbeque's stainless-steel hood and bounces them in his hands to feel their weightiness.

"Darlene," Ned says and pauses until he's got her waiting for his next words. "Do you agree that these are the best barbeque islands at the fair?"

She fattens her upper lip and shimmies her head and shoulders a bit, looks over at her husband and back at Ned and gives him a full nod, "Yes."

"Of course you do. This is the biggest show in California. We've got every vendor in the business here. You've seen them all, and you came back to Paradise BBQ Islands."

Ned pauses. He looks to Darlene and to her husband. He's establishing, as Bob taught me, "buy-in." They both nod in agreement.

"Why are we the best?" Ned asks.

Darlene considers, looks to her husband, and then reiterates some of what Ned spent 20 minutes driving home. "Your burners are definitely the best. No question. And the frames, aluminum welded. Y'all are the only ones that got those."

Ned spins the bezel on the face of his Rolex, his real Rolex. He always does this when he thinks he's about to close a deal. He gets up and grabs a contract. He slaps it down on the jade-green, marbled island countertop.

"These are the best islands. You want one," Ned pauses to build up the tension. "So the only question I have for you, Darlene and Richard, is this: If I can get you a great price on this island, are you going to buy it today?"

This is the moment it all leads up to. You qualify the customer. You lay the foundation. You get passive buy-in, then active buy-in, if you can, and then you bring it home. You ask for the money, and you keep your damn mouth shut. They used different adjectives and cuss words, but Bob and Ned both told me the same thing. Keep your mouth shut, and stare at the customer in the eyes and wait for the answer. No matter how long it takes, no matter how uncomfortable you feel, keep your mouth shut.

After a few seconds of facial hemming and hawing, Darlene answers, "Well, we aren't sure. I mean, we like it, really, but—"

"I understand, it's a lot of money," Ned interrupts. "But you will never get a better price. All that competition, that spells, deals." Ned waves his hands outwardly and contemptuously. "This is how I make a living. Now I've spent a half-hour with you all, and I did so because I believed you were serious customers that wanted to put one of these beauties in your backyard. Was I right or wrong? Please just tell me."

"Ned we—" Darlene's husband starts to say but is interrupted by Darlene.

"You get us a deal, and we'll buy," Darlene says, defiantly. "But it has to be a real deal."

Ned stabs his hand out to Darlene. "I promise, you are going to walk out of here with a deal and with a barbeque island that is going to make you happy for years."

Ned shakes hands with them both. Fifteen minutes later, after a mock back-and-forth with our manager, Brian, where Ned pretends to twist Brian's arm into selling below market, he's sold them a stock island with two downgrades at $500 above our standard price, netting himself a cool $800 commission.

I hadn't sold a single island through two home shows. That was six excruciating days of pitching barbeque islands for 10 hours a day without one single deal. I was making zero dollars per hour. Macy showed up at my second home show and brought me lunch. Bob's opinion of me immediately changed. Now he was desperately curious. Macy kept telling me to stick it out. And then I finally sold one, a small one, and I only made a $300 commission. But then, at a show in Las Vegas, I sold three, and at Phoenix I came in with the highest total commission of the five salesmen we had on the floor. Bob and Ned say it always happens, beginner's luck. I'm not in complete disagreement. When I sold shoes at Harris', I was the top seller of all the departments for the first two weeks, but after that I never cracked the top five. However, this time I've got 12-Step wisdom on my side. The first and foremost is humility. I know I have no chance of beating Bob and Ned and the other lifetime slicksters Ken brings in at a game they've been playing for decades, so I decide to learn from them but do what the 12-Steppers say: Take what I like and leave the rest. I like the emotional-based techniques: "You have to be willing to be more uncomfortable than the customer," and "Look 'em in the eye, ask for the money, and shut up." I don't like the lying. I'm not good at it, and I'm not going to lie. There's no reason to. We really do have the best barbeque islands. Yes, barbeque islands are ridiculous, but these are the best ridiculous barbeque islands. Ken built them. He's an engineer and worked in manufacturing at a Fortune 500 company for 20 years. Most of our competitors don't have the know-how Ken has. I also like the "buy-in" concept. It's reminiscent of trial techniques. Get a hostile witness to repeat a fact that supports your theory of the case. That's Trial Advocacy 101. I don't like the "let me ask my manager" game. It's bullshit and everyone knows it, and even if they don't, I'm not doing it.

When I was practicing law, I used to do this technique I called "walk 'em." It started before the client ever saw me. On real estate litigation cases, where I felt that I truly was talented, I'd only take appointments if the client paid a consultation fee equal to my full hourly rate. It forced the client to take it seriously and value my time. Sometimes they'd show up without the money, and I'd have my secretary walk them out and reschedule. Other times, I'd sit with them at the conference room table and listen to them, but quickly get to my hourly rate and the retainer they needed to come up with. If they balked at all, I began to "walk 'em." I'd tell them there were a ton of young hungry attorneys out there that'd take their case for cheaper than I would. I'd casually note these other attorneys didn't have the real estate litigation experience I had but, I'd say, "Who knows! Maybe it isn't necessary with your case." I'd usher them out the door as fast as I could. It felt so damn good, freeing and indulgently arrogant. Often, they'd return with the money.

It's been an hour since Ned closed his deal, and I have a live one. Justin was singing about being sexy again, and the screams from the bungee jump kept coming, as fast as they could lift teenagers up and down that crane line. I can smell the kettle corn. Ned and Brian munch while pretending they aren't watching me try to close this deal. I had to cut off Bob, who was far behind me but making a beeline straight for the couple heading into our tent. They had all the trappings of the nouveau riche-via-mortgage equity set. Her: fake tits, high-end hair extensions, giant diamond earrings and a Gucci bag big enough to double as a bowling ball bag. Him: pushing a fancy stroller, True Religion jeans and matching distressed shirt with a gothic cross, and a key ring clipped to his jeans with a big fat Mercedes hideaway car key. As hungry for sales as I was, I had to try out my walk 'em technique.

"Hello, I'm Joseph. I'm a dreaded salesman," I say.

She chuckles. He smirks and says, "Yeah, we've met a few."

"Well not like me," I retort.

They look at me, surprised, but confirming, at least by sight that I'm being honest. I'm wearing threadbare Levi's, worn black Vans slip-ons, and I have a long, thick beard and long hair. I'm wearing the Paradise BBQ Islands t-shirt instead of the collared oxford like the other salesmen.

"You sure don't look like the others," the man laughs and looks over at his wife for confirmation.

"Are you going to put one of these next to your pool?" I ask.

"Pool is under construction," he says proudly.

This makes me doubtful of the wisdom of my technique, at least in this situation, but I've already closed a sale, so I'm all in.

"Have you looked at other island companies?" I ask.

"We walked by one, but this is the first we stopped at."

"Well, you've got it backwards," I say. I pull out a map of the fairgrounds. I draw a circle with a marker around the area where all the islands are. "Okay, you should start here at BBQ's Galore. You'll get the hard sell there, and they have some nice-looking stuff, but it's cheap. But if that's what you want, you know... Open the door on any island and you'll see they're built with steel studs." I look at them. "You know what those are right?"

"Yeah, of course," the husband responds.

I open the door below the grill on the island we are standing by. "See that?"

He hands off the stroller to his wife and crouches down and says, "Yeah."

"Welded aluminum, right?" I ask rhetorically. "These are outside all the time, but that doesn't rust. Steel studs break down, right? It doesn't matter when you are a building a house because they are inside the walls in a house. No rust to worry about. But these are outside, right? You get the picture."

He nods as if I let him in on a little secret.

"So anyway, if you are serious about getting an island, go look at all the others. Normally, I'd tell you we are the best, but we are a little more expensive. But not at this show. We lower our prices so we can do volume, so it's a win-win. Anyway, here's my card, just ask for me when you get back looking at the other islands and I'll show you these."

I point them at the booth about 50 yards away, and tell them, yeah start right over there. A little confused, they begin to walk in the direction of our top competitor.

"Oh, I'm sorry. I'm Joseph. I didn't get your names."

They shake my hand and give me their names.

"Oh yeah, and no one else will tell you this, but I work on commission, so I'd appreciate it if you'd come back and at least let me show you what I have. As you can tell, I'm not a high-pressure guy..."

I walk back to Bob and Brian, under the palapa where they're posted up.

"What the fuck was that?" Bob asks. Brian shushes Bob, because Ned is talking to a customer within earshot.

"Sometimes you got to let them go, so they'll come back to you," I say to Bob.

"Look Joseph," Brian says. "You can't be sending customers off to our competitors."

"They'll be back, and they will buy an island from me. I guarantee it. You just make sure one of these sharks," I say, indicating Bob, "doesn't jump in and try to steal my sale. That's Mr. and Mrs. Hernandez—my sale."

"Never let them walk!" Bob says through gritted teeth.

It occurs to me rather suddenly that I may have just thrown away my rent; that my walk 'em technique may be flawed; that the Hernandez's will probably find an island they like elsewhere and get some clever explanation as to why steel studs are actually better than welded aluminum. It's not true, but I've heard Bob and Ned convince people water isn't wet.

I'm deciding whether to defend my technique to Bob when I see Macy walking toward our booth. She's driven all the way out to Pomona, 30 miles, to come see me. She's in a state of wonderment, gazing around, all wide-eyed, like a kid's first time at the beach. She has a cone of kettle corn and is munching away. Bob and Brian, who met her at the Los Angeles Convention Center when she came to visit me on my first of six shut-out days, regard her with great curiosity. It's not just that she's striking and elegant or that she wears thrift store clothes that she's hastily altered with a pair of scissors that look remarkably fashionable. It's not even the way she disarmed Bob by simply repeating his name with a calculated and warm smile after he made a sarcastic comment about her hair the first time they met. They probably don't know it, but I think they want to know about her energy.

I trot over and hug and kiss Macy.

"I haven't sold one yet today, but I'm keeping the faith," I report.

"Oh my God, this place is amazing," she says.

"Macy," Bob says. "Have you come to rescue Joseph?"

"Bob, it is very nice to see you," Macy responds with wry formality. "And you too, Brian, Ned."

"I meant to ask you last time," Bob says. "How'd you and Joseph meet?"

"Oh Bob, so many questions," Macy says and then turns to me. "Can I take you for a quick bite to eat?"

"Joseph won't answer any of my questions, either," Bob says to everyone and no one specifically. "Ken won't tell me. Just some guy dressed like he's homeless or a roadie suddenly shows up and is part of the team. Nobody knows anything. But I'm going to find out."

"Bob," I say. "There is nothing to find out."

Truth is, I enjoy keeping Bob in the dark. At some point, I'm sure I'll tell him part of the truth, but for now it's a fun distraction. Luckily, he's old school—doesn't even own a computer—or he'd just punch my name into the internet and all would be revealed.

Macy and I eat corn dogs. She has to be back in Hollywood at the station writing TV news in a couple hours. I'm happy, just listening to her talk, the way she thinks of the LA County Fair in Pomona as an exotic little adventure—so Macy. She tells me about all the things and people she's observed, the cute little Asian baby that she held while waiting in line. She's that type of person. She can meet a family in line and end up holding their baby. She tells me about the tilt-a-whirl ride, the plant exhibits, even the parking lot. She can make any place fun. I listen and smile, but I never stop thinking about the Hernandezes. Rent is coming due, and this is the last show for the month. I was expecting a big number. Why did I do that? I don't say anything about my walk 'em experiment to Macy. She'd just say, "God's got you" or something like that. I try to stay positive. It doesn't come naturally to me.

We walk back to the booth and find Bob talking to the Hernandezes.

"They just got here, waiting for you," Bob tells me.

Mr. Hernandez says, "You were right about those steel studs."

I hug Macy goodbye. I'm ecstatic. An hour later, the Hernandezes buy the biggest double-sided island we sell, with custom Viking grill, Subzero refrigerator, an extra searing grill and an upgraded stereo. I make an $800 commission, and I don't even have to lie or play any psych games. And then, just as I am preparing to end my day, a customer I spoke with yesterday comes in and buys a floor model, and I make a $400 commission. I walk to my car as if I'm filled with helium, light and giddy. I call Macy at her desk at the newsroom and tell her the good news. She says something about God.

FIFTEEN

It's early Sunday morning. Macy drives like she's playing *Pole Position*. We pass Mohammed's Auto Repair on La Cienega. I think of telling Macy about Momo, but I decide not to. We pass a sign for Baldwin Hills, aka the Black Beverly Hills. I remember driving to Baldwin Hills from Riverside when I was a lawyer at Thomas & Coleman. I was picking up my client, a wiry, tough, old black man, a wealthy landlord. He was being sued for wrongful death. A couple that rented a trashy apartment from him died of carbon monoxide asphyxiation. It was a meritless case. The gas leaked while they slept because they'd been using the wall-mounted gas heater's pilot light as a torch lighter to smoke crack. The crime scene photo is a permanent stain on my brain. They lie dead and naked on a bare queen mattress, splayed out as if they fell asleep after sex. On the man's side of the bed, there is a liter bottle of Jack Daniels tipped over onto the dirty taupe carpet; on the woman's side, a yellow-stained glass pipe, as if it dropped from her hand to the carpet as she fell asleep one last time. As I sit here now in the passenger seat of Macy's SUV, I can see myself reading the investigation report and staring at the haunting photo, sitting behind my wooden desk, there in my glass-walled corner office, wearing a suit and tie, my secretary, Rosie, gawking at the photo over my shoulder. I'm sure I'd thought I had absolutely nothing in common with these depraved dead people.

To me, we are running late. To Macy, we are right on time. She gets everywhere right when the action starts; any earlier, and she considers it wasted time. The parking lot is full, but she pulls all the way to the front. She assumes we'll find a spot. I presume we won't. She wedges her SUV into a non-parking spot, or at best, a marginal one, which I presume will result in her car being towed and she presumes is just fine. As we trot hand-in-hand to our destination, I consider whether I should explain that she'd be much happier employing my method of showing up early everywhere and securing the best possible parking spot as a matter of course, not luck. We walk past a loading dock and enter a large building. At the end of a hallway, a smiling older woman with grey hair and a colorful dress beckons for us to hurry. We jog toward her. She hands us each a brightly colored program and opens the door. We are in the Agape International Spiritual Center, Agape for short. The lights are dim, the ceiling is vaulted and open. It's a converted light-industrial building that has been fashioned into a church sanctuary. There are hundreds of chairs, rows upon rows.

We walk across the exterior wall, past large colorful portraits of Martin Luther King Jr., Mahatma Gandhi, the Dalai Lama, Amma, and the man who leads this place, Reverend Michael Beckwith, piously posing. I roll my eyes. We walk down an aisle down the right half of the sanctuary and find seats about 20 rows in.

The stage is raised several feet. It's 100 feet wide, decorated with bright flowing cloth and stage lighting. Behind the stage, raised even higher, are several rows for a choir. Stage left and back, enclosed behind plexiglass, is a band with guitarists, a keyboardist and a drummer. A black grand piano sits stage left below the band, facing center stage. Reverend Beckwith's wife *wo*-mans the piano with great exuberance and power. The place is rocking.

We sit down, and I follow Macy's lead and I don't stand, even though nearly everyone else is standing and clapping raucously. I love this about her. She's not being defiant. Macy isn't standing up because she has decided not to, completely independent of everyone around her. She's a rare species, a pure neutral, but is often viewed as obtuse. She's even neutral to others' opinions of her and will say, and actually mean, "Others' opinions of me are none of my business." It's an Al-anon thing.

The choir is belting out a rendition of Stevie Wonder's *Higher Ground*. They are all dressed in flowing robes and loose clothes in solid, vibrant colors. They dance in place and sing into one of several microphones hanging down from the ceiling. Macy rises, and so do I. She sways rhythmically and claps her hands with such ease and grace. For me, this clapping while swaying to the music is uncomfortably close to public dancing. I'm relieved when the song ends and everyone sits. Now I'm in my natural state of nonparticipation—the bemused, judgmental observer. A woman from the choir begins to sing a gospel song. She performs vocal acrobatics, a la Whitney Houston. I enjoy it more than a bee sting but less than an ant bite. The more she gesticulates with her voice, the more people cheer. I refuse to join. Instead, I peer around and categorize the congregants. There are people straight out of a deep-south Baptist church. There are the West-siders, looking casually wealthy in jeans that cost more than a decent watch. There are the New Agers, with their wooden meditation bead necklaces and docile smiles. And then, to my disgust, there are a few congregants dressed as if they came straight from the gym.

After five minutes of wailing followed by a baffling minute-long standing ovation, a man makes announcements about the goings-on of the church. He looks like Martin Short and is annoying and yet funny, much like Martin Short. Perhaps he is Martin Short. Whoever he is, by the end of his spiel of spiritual puns, a riddle wherein he rhymes "meditation" with "levitation," and one short of one-too-many exaggerated double-takes, I decide I am a fan and cheer for him the way everyone else cheered for the Whitney Houston-like vocal acrobat.

Finally, Reverend Beckwith takes the stage. I recognize him from the movie *The Secret*. He's a short black guy with dreads. He wears a collarless black suit and a head-microphone. The congregation's anticipation and excitement is definitive. He owns the place. He pauses and stands with the toes of his shoes hanging off the stage, his eyes closed, chin tilted up. He remains silent for several beats. Then he begins. He says, "God is good, yes?" and then "Life is good, yes?" and the congregation shouts back, "Yes!" Reverend Beckwith speaks rapid-fire. I try to keep up. He doesn't spoon-feed us. Then he says, "If anyone is here for the first time, please stand up."

I turn to Macy and shake my head no. She does not oppose me, thank goodness. The people that stand are faced by the entire congregation. They hold their hands out to them. Reverend Beckwith says things like, "We know who you really are" and then something about us newcomers being the "spiritual likeness of God." There is a couple next to Macy and me, standing, dealing with this whole newcomer thing. All the people in the congregation turn toward the couple with their hands out, as if showering them with magical invisible rays, while repeating Reverend Beckwith's words. The woman of the newcomer couple is absorbing it all. She smiles, her big white teeth plugged into an electrical outlet. Her man is nervously smiling, his eyes bouncing from one enthusiastic congregant to the next.

Everyone sits, and Reverend Beckwith speaks for a half hour, seemingly without taking a breath. The words just flow. He's funny, he's smart, he's fast. He mentions Jesus of Nazareth, Buddha, Gandhi, Krishna, and quotes from African proverbs. He says our purpose is to become more of who we are, so that we can exalt our God-presence. I don't know what this means, but there is no question he believes it absolutely.

Then he says, "It is done unto you as you believe it to be true."

This verse I recognize. It has always poked me.

I can't recall exactly when, but I'm sure I first heard it in church as a kid. I last heard it from that whacky little film, *What the Bleep Do We Know!?*, about a deaf woman in Portland, Oregon who has a spiritual awakening. Keri had a copy of it. We watched it right after I got out of Chino prison. I thought it was full of illogical overextensions of scientific principles to spiritual concepts, but it also left me with a feeling that there was some truth to it, something that might help me.

"It is done unto you as you believe it to be true." It's one of those phrases I can't get out of my head, like certain laws I memorized for the Bar exam and can still recite verbatim. But it's more than that, because this verse challenges me. Every time I hear it, I think, "It's true. Just because I don't act on it, doesn't mean it isn't true." It's a natural law, just like gravity. I keep thinking that I recreate the same situations. I keep attracting different versions of the same problems. I know this is true, and I know that my thoughts shape my reality. How could they not?

At the end of the sermon, Reverend Beckwith and his wife sing on the stage and everyone in the congregation holds hands. At the end of the song, we all raise our hands up in the air and hold them there. Reverend Beckwith prays aloud. And then he says, "And so it is!" and everyone says it back to him. It has a nice ring to it, I think to myself. "And so it is."

We walk outside. I feel shaken, in a good way, like after coming off Space Mountain at Disneyland. There are people outside waiting to get into the next service. There are tents set up with people selling books, hippy clothes, crystals, food, and there are tables set up for Agape-related organizations—one for bereavement, one for prisoners.

Macy jockeys us out of the bustling parking lot without hurting too many feelings. I inquire about Agape and Reverend Beckwith. She tells me about the wiki on Science of Mind and Ernest Holmes, the founder of the movement. She says she has a couple books I can read.

Since my arrest four years ago, it seems like I experience more I-can't-believe-this-is-fucking-happening happenings than happenings I can believe are happening. And here's another one. Macy and I agreed to meet with Leo and his therapist. Leo is William's father and Macy's ex-husband, not the last ex-husband, but the previous one. The baby daddy. The situation we are here to discuss is me, the registered sex offender.

Karen Grisham is Leo and Molly's therapist. Molly is Leo's new wife. She has an 8-year-old son from a previous marriage, and Macy sometimes babysits him, so Molly has skin in the game besides just William. Leo says Molly wanted to be here today, but she couldn't get the time off from work. Leo is not a good liar, and I don't believe for a second that Molly wanted to be here. She's probably afraid of what might come up. Nevertheless, Leo says Molly wants to meet with me over lunch. I just smile at Leo, say, "Okay" and nod in agreement. Leo looks at Karen, and she nods in approval, I presume because the lunch with Molly, given Molly's absence today, was Karen's idea. I'm not looking forward to it, but whatever they need me to do to feel comfortable, I'll do.

We are in a small room with a low ceiling. Macy and I sit together on one side of a sectional couch, and Leo sits on the other side. The couch is too low and the cushions too deep, so we are all sitting with our asses on the edge. I wonder if this is by design. A pant-suited Karen sits in a wood-framed leather chair behind a low circular table. It's as if we've been relegated to an attic where the unused furniture is shoved in the corner.

Karen loosely reads from an outline of introductory remarks the way a car salesman summarizes the small print on a bad lease. She drones her way down the list of topics, occasionally going off-script to give an example. As she discusses payment terms, non-disclosure, confidentiality, medical emergencies, etcetera, I remind myself why I'm here. I was so grateful that Macy didn't break up with me after I told her I was a registered sex offender that I agreed to this. I love Macy, and I love William. I would never intentionally hurt them. I know the truth, and so does Macy. I was in a blackout the night I was arrested. I wasn't going to commit a rape. And now I'm committed to 12-Step recovery and my new life.

"Well, I appreciate that you are all here. I know this is not pleasant, but it shows your true commitment to the welfare of the children involved ..." Karen begins.

When Macy said she needed to tell Leo about my status, I envisioned Macy and I sitting in Macy's living room with Leo. I'd tell him the facts of what happened the night of my arrest. I'd show him the police report, the transcript of my sentencing hearing, and all my letters of support. I didn't expect that he'd be happy about the situation, but I did expect he'd come away understanding that I wasn't a threat to William or his stepson. And maybe, after some time, he'd come to appreciate me.

"We don't have a lot of time," Karen says. "So let me give you my opinion right up front, and then we can discuss it further."

Karen pauses like a kindergarten teacher, so we can all get ready to listen intently, and I can feel a shift in Macy's mood as she leans in toward Karen and glances across me to Leo with suspicion and curiosity. Leo's eyes are flat. He knows what's coming.

"We are not here to second-guess a judicial determination that resulted in Joseph pleading guilty to rape, but rath—"

"Excuse me, Ms. Grisham," I interrupt. "Not rape. I pled no-contest to Assault with Intent to Commit Rape. The victim was a man, so—"

"Yes, Joseph. I apologize for that, but that's not the point. The point is, you are a registered sex offender, and it's my opinion that you shouldn't have contact with William or—"

"Wait," Macy says abruptly. "Are you suggesting that we shouldn't even consider the actual facts of Joseph's conviction or his recovery?"

I squeeze my abdominal muscles tightly to suppress my anxiety. This is just like my bail hearing—one woman defending me and one condemning me. I feel powerless, again.

"It's not about that Macy," Leo says.

"What is it about?" I ask.

"Joseph, Macy, it's about the children," Karen says, lowering her voice and speaking slowly. "William has already been through so much."

Macy's chest rises and falls. We both know where Karen is going with this—Macy's Bad Decisions. Bad Decision Number One: Macy divorced Leo when William was a toddler and broke up their family for no good reason, other than realizing she wasn't in love with Leo. Bad Decision Number Two: Macy ignored all the bright red flags and married an adulterer who cheated on her, before, after, and likely, during their wedding. Macy and William left the adulterer, and William is still devastated. Bad Decision Number Three: Me, Joseph W. Naus. Shacking up with a registered sex offender.

Macy remains silent with steadfast eyes. Karen thinks that she has defeated Macy, but Karen hasn't said anything that Macy doesn't know. Of the three decisions, Macy only regrets marrying the adulterer. That one still stings a little. I put my arm around Macy and look to Karen and then Leo. I want to say, "You have no idea how big this woman's God is," but I don't. They wouldn't understand what I mean.

Thinking she's rendered Macy speechless, or maybe just unable to withstand the silence, Karen refocuses on me. "Joseph, these are very serious charges, and you pled guilty. You admitted your guilt."

I nod and say, "Yes, that's true." With this admission, my anxiety wanes and my serenity rises. It's not that I don't care how this meeting goes, but I now fully realize I have little control of it. We are not here to discuss anything. We are here so Leo can have Karen tell us that I shouldn't be around William. It's that simple.

Karen continues. "Again, I'm not here to make a determination of your guilt or innocence or your fitness to care for William. Quite frankly, the judicial system has already done so."

I suppress a chuckle. The little extra jab at the end was more than I expected. "I understand your opinion," I respond, exemplifying the concept of non-confrontational.

"Joseph," Karen continues, her script somewhat rushed, given that I'm not putting up a fight. "I have to accept the facts I'm given. Whether Macy wants you in her life or not is obviously her decision, but whether you play a role in William's life is another matter. I don't think it's what's best for William."

I ignore Karen and make my case, calmly, directly to Leo. I repeat everything that Macy has already told him, but I think that maybe if he sees me say it and he can look in my eyes, he'll see the truth. If not, I think, that's alright, too.

We all stand. I look to Macy, and we both look to Leo, more confused than anything else, as if asking, "Was that what you wanted?" Leo isn't indignant or angry. He's just plain sad. I wonder if it would be weird if I gave Leo a hug

"Joseph, I hope you understand," Karen says. She extends her hand out carefully, as if she's not sure whether I'll shake it or break it.

I shake Karen's hand perfunctorily, and I give her a Buddha smile. I'm not even angry at her. She's just doing what she thinks she should do. I actually feel a mild sense of joy. Some of it is because this ordeal is over, but mostly it's because I'm using my 12-Step tools. Looking at the situation from other people's perspectives. I can see everyone's role and the pain they are enduring, especially Leo. Here he is, sitting across from his first wife and the mother of his child who left him. And now, she's dating a registered sex offender who is going to be spending time with his son. He seems like a quintessentially nice guy. I wish we could just be friends, but I understand we all have a role here, and my role is to be the identified problem. Fair enough.

I sit on the couch in Macy's apartment paging through *Dwell* magazine when Macy comes up the stairs from putting William to bed and asks, "Joseph, do you want to join us?" Given the intensity of our meeting with William's father and Karen, Macy's request surprises me. But I'm thrilled and a little nervous. I walk across the squeaky floor, very carefully, as if how quiet I can be is somehow connected to how well I'll perform in this all-important, precious ritual. Macy takes my hand, and I follow her downstairs.

Macy and I sit cross-legged in William's little bunk bed enclave off Macy's downstairs bedroom. The lighting is warm. A single bulb encased in a clever Ikea configuration lights the room perfectly. William leans against the bunk bed. It's all kid in here: the multi-colored comforter, the little plastic and wooden toys, the glow-in-the-dark five-point stars stuck to the low ceiling.

William is a child, an 8-year-old. I don't know exactly how to be around him. I've never been around kids. I just want to carry him around piggy-back and put him down occasionally so he can pick out bright colored candy and packs of Yu-Gi-Oh! cards. Sometimes we play video games, and he beats me, and I try not to say or do anything stupid in front of him. Macy and Leo treat him as if he's the most precious thing in the world. He is their first priority. It's astounding. I wonder what that must be like. He, of course, knows nothing else. This is his life. William attends a private school that Macy can't afford where kids are so important, their parents ruthlessly compete to get them enrolled.

Macy and William negotiate over which bedtime story to read. One has something to do with a turtle, the other a ninja. They are not related in any way. I lean against the wall. I'm trying to act normal, like this isn't a big deal, but I feel like I've wandered into a Japanese tea ceremony and am standing on tatami with dirty work boots, boorishly guzzling the tea.

William wears pajama bottoms that aren't quite long enough. They stop at his calves, and his little tan feet protrude out from the pant legs. His feet are heart-achingly cute, like a baby's, just bigger.

"Mawwm!" William says, his final word in the minor debate over which bedtime story to read.

"Okay, fine, Munchkin," Macy says.

I feel dizzy with wholesomeness. I think: If I start crying, it'll be really weird.

Macy begins reading. Her voice is radio-quality, low and yet sweet, unencumbered, and she pronounces each word with elegance. Each syllable is given its full due. I take in every moment. I look at William. He catches me and bugs his eyes playfully as if to say, "What are you looking at?"

After several pages, Macy announces that reading time is over. William protests. Macy says she's read enough.

"Joseph," William says. "Will you read?"

Macy doesn't seem to mind William's circumvention and looks to me. My mouth releases. My jaw bones are hot glue sticks. I want to stay in this moment forever.

"Yes, yeah, of course," I say with feigned casualness.

I read as best I can. I read slowly, and with great enthusiasm. All the while, my innards puddle. I read the final sentence. "The End."

William hops into the lower bunk bed, and Macy pushes his moppy hair back, kisses him on the forehead and says, "Good night, Munchkin. I love you."

"I love you too, mom. Good night. Good night Joseph."

I twist the lamp light switch. The room is illuminated by glow-in-the-dark stars.

"Good night, William," I say.

Café Tropical again. This time it's for cigarettes: 12 Steps for smokers, how absolutely pathetic. What a defeated group we are.

A guy I recognize from another 12-Step group reads aloud: "We tried not smoking in front of other people, only when outside, or only smoking during a certain time of day. We tried countless self-help books, psychiatrists, doctors and hypnotherapists. We could quit smoking for a day, a week, sometimes longer, but we couldn't stay quit. Nothing worked, and we became deeply demoralized."

Exactly. "Deeply demoralized." I've got a cargo ship of problems. I've got all the fucking problems. Now I've even got this thing when I breathe, like there's something deep in my throat, wet and rattling, blocking my airway. Now I regularly get painful swollen glands in my neck, and I quit smoking just until the pain subsides and I absolutely have to have a cigarette, and then the swollen glands return even worse than before. After being in great shape when I got out of Chino prison, I'm now 30 pounds heavier and rarely run or work out. What's worse is that these cigarettes control me. I want them more than I want anything. I need them more than I need anything.

I sit in the back of the room on a dirty couch. There a couple dozen people. They share with great specificity about how they smoked, much more so than other 12-Step programs. They are decidedly gleeful. A woman shares how she used to throw her cigarettes in the trash and then dig them out a couple hours later. Check, I've done that. She said she used to soak her cigarettes in water, throw them away, but then would dig them out and dry them out by microwaving them. Genius, I think to myself. I've soaked them but never thought to try and dry them out. A man shares about smoking after a dentist appointment, smoking through the pain. Damn, I forgot about that. After I got my wisdom teeth extracted, the dental assistant told me not to smoke for two days because if I did, I'd get dry socket. I asked her why she told me that, as if I didn't smoke. She looked at me and tilted her head like a mom responding to a lying child, like, "Are you kidding me?" And I'd thought, of course she knows I smoke. My mouth is probably a wreck. I lasted 11 hours. I smoked, and sure enough, I got dry socket, and sure enough, it was as painful as she said it was going to be.

There's this funny guy I'd met in the 12-Step rooms. He used to be a comedian. He's hilarious. He's here sharing and looking right at me, probably because I was the only one to take a chip as a newcomer. And he says the three things that really helped him quit were: one, if you have a problem and smoke, now you have two problems; two, if you have a craving, it'll pass in seven to 10 minutes whether you smoke or not; and three, my personal favorite, if you debate, you lose.

I rub my black nicotine 12-Stepper, 10-minute chip between my thumb and forefinger. It's a poker chip that has "10 Minutes" inscribed on it in gold-colored ink. I love that. That's how hard it is to quit. Ten minutes is an accomplishment. They have 24-hour chips, one week, 30 days, 60 days, 90 days. I quit for 111 days while I was incarcerated. He's right about the debating. It wasn't hard at all. I knew smoking wasn't a possibility, so I didn't even think about it. But I hadn't quit, I'd just stopped. I smoked a whole pack the very day I got out. And every time I've tried to quit, I rarely last a day.

Nearly everybody in the meeting shakes my hand and introduces themselves to me after the meeting. I'm invited to go to fellowship, which, like in other 12-Step groups, is when some members of the group go out to eat together after the meeting, to hang out and talk. I love Thai food, and the thought of Chicken Pad Thai makes me realize how hungry I am, but I kindly reject the offer and lie and say I have to be somewhere. I take a copy of the meeting's phone list. The funny guy circles his name on it and tells me to call him before I smoke. He emphasizes "before." I tell him I'll call him.

7-Eleven is further down Sunset than Mae Ploy, the Thai restaurant they go to for fellowship, so I'm not worried about any of them seeing me. I purchase a large coffee, a new lighter, BIC red, of course, and a pack of Marlboro Red 100's. I go back to my apartment, sit outside in the dark, smoke, and let my thoughts swirl chaotically: my love for Macy and William, the Law of Attraction, Amma the hugger, that preacher guy, Reverend Beckwith at Agape and the spiritual glow of his piano-playing wife, Rickie. I think about Keri and whether she is going to convince the district attorney to "Change the Numbers" and save me from a life of hiding in the shadows. I think about how little work I am getting in commercials and films and how the barbeque islands sales are going well enough to keep me afloat, barely, but that it isn't something that's going to last forever. After several minutes, my thoughts funnel into one single question, "What the hell am I going to do with my life now?"

I take a deep drag off my cigarette and a long sip of coffee and think how grateful I am to be quitting smoking.

"You are not a victim," Macy says. She stands behind her kitchen counter and taps the air with a soup ladle to emphasize "not" and "victim."

I stand and walk to the window, overlooking the 5 Freeway and Atwater Village. My nostrils flare in anger, as I repeat, sarcastically, "You are not a victim." I'm so mad I could pick this fucking couch up and toss it through this window 300 yards into traffic.

"You know what … fuck that," I say with as much acid as I can produce. I am angry at her, and I want her to know it.

"You think you're a victim that—" Macy says before I interrupt her.

I shout, "Those motherfuckers ruined me! I don't deserve this. I was in a blackout. Even the fucking judge said he didn't think I did it. Those fucking evil motherfuckers took away my livelihood, labeled me a sex offender for the rest of my life, Macy, the rest of my fucking life!"

"You don't think your behaviors led to this?"

"They used me, Macy. I was in a blackout. I had no idea what I was doing. I would never do that sober. They knew, they fucking knew I didn't have the intent to commit rape. That's fucking ridiculous. People just don't suddenly become rapists. They used me to feed their fucking prosecution stats—"

"I'm not saying it's fair," Macy says. She's twisting her face as if to stop from crying. She looks desperate, as if failing to convince me that I'm not a victim will have dire results. "I'm saying you brought it upon yourself. You created this for yourself."

I want so desperately not to escalate this, but I feel rage in every part of my body.

I yell loud enough for this to be a domestic disturbance. "I am a victim! That's exactly what I fucking am!"

Macy doesn't respond. She stares at me, arms crossed, with those big brown eyes. I love her, but I only know it by memory, because all I can feel is anger.

"Is this that law of attraction bullshit? I willed this to happen, right Macy? It's all my fault. I decided, yeah, I think I'll become a disbarred lawyer. I'll just throw away my entire career that I fought for. And you know what?" I say, viciously and sarcastically. "Why don't I go to prison for a bit, for something I didn't fucking do, and you know what? Fuck it. Let's go all the way. I'll be a two-strike felon and a registered fucking sex offender. For-fucking-ever!"

Macy cries. The pain in her face should make me feel horrible guilt, but I feel justified, like I'm finishing off a weak opponent in the ring, one that talked trash during the weigh-in.

"Do you know how cruel that is, Macy? To tell me I deserve this, to tell me I deserve to have my life permanently ruined for something I didn't even do?"

I stand here and watch her cry convulsively. She's trying to help me. Why am I doing this? She loves me, and I'm hurting her. She believes with all her heart that "it is done unto you as you believe it to be true," so for her to hear me say that I am a victim, that I am permanently damaged, shakes the foundation of our relationship. She's willing to be with me if I have abandoned myself to God like she has. She wants me to believe that I can overcome anything if I believe and trust in God, but right now, I can't believe it. I can't even fake it. I'm not ready. This is my truth. I believe I'm ruined.

I dash out the door. I have to. Macy follows me. I know there is nothing crueler than walking out on her after I promised I wouldn't anymore. I am, once again, the abandoner. She follows me out hysterically, toting my ugly green plastic laundry basket. She's yelling at me with so much pain in her voice. She throws my laundry basket over the stair railing down the hillside and shouts something about how ugly it is.

I drive home and shout at myself. I don't care if anyone sees me. Let them think I'm crazy. I am fucking crazy. Macy's right. I've gotten everything that deep down I believe I deserve.

At 7-Eleven, the man behind the counter tells me that they are out of hard packs. This is ridiculous. Fuck this. I'm going to another store. This is unacceptable. I was going to quit today, but it'll have to wait until tomorrow.

───────────

SIXTEEN

Keri wants to wait a while before she sets the hearing to try to Change the Numbers. She wants to let some time pass, make sure the judge and the D.A. know I'm not going to relapse, show them what a good boy I've been. I should do some research on it, put my legal knowledge to work for me, but I can't. Every time I start digging into the law about sex registration, I find myself incapacitated on the couch, making deals with myself just to get up to get something to eat. I smoke, nap, watch TV and repeat until meeting time. I memorize episodes of *Scrubs* and tear up during the ending sequence, usually a montage, where I am taught simple and compassionate lessons of life.

My cell phone rings and Trenton's name and number appear on the screen. Finally, he calls me back. Good, I can remind Trenton to write me a letter to Judge Von Silkman for when Keri files my motion to Change the Numbers.

"Hey man, thanks for calling me back so fucking promptly."

There is a long pause.

"Trenton?" I say.

"Uh, it's me, Hannah."

It's Trenton's wife. It's one of those calls I get from time to time. Trenton is out. He hasn't come home in days. He's not taking his psych meds. He calls Hannah every day but won't come home. He's manic. He's bipolar. He's relapsed big time on prescription drugs. She doesn't know if he's on meth or drinking, probably both, but she's sure he's on prescription drugs. I tell her I'm sorry. I give her the softball Al-Anon pitch, which is, take care of yourself first. This always reminds me of a stewardess explaining how to put on the flimsy little oxygen mask before helping someone else. Hannah cries, and I can't understand what she's saying, so I just wait. I tell her I'll keep calling him, that if he calls her, make him promise to call me. Trenton and Hannah lived in Boston before moving out here, and she never learned to drive. She's a librarian and looks and acts the part. I offer to give her a ride. It's selfish, of course. I'm completely convinced that I have found the automotive fountain of youth for 12-Steppers: Use your car for 12-Step service, and it'll never break down. She declines my offer and says she's used to taking the bus.

After a Dr. Cox-centered episode of *Scrubs* and fast-forwarding through an hour of Tiger Woods dominating some tournament in Florida, Trenton calls me.

"Hannah says you demanded I call you." He sounds more exhausted than high.

"Dude. What the fuck?" I say, as if it's somehow odd that a drug addict is taking drugs.

"Don't worry. I'm off work. They don't even know. I'm going to quit right before I have to go back and teach."

"Seriously? That's your plan."

Trenton explains how he was living with a prescription drug dealer he met on craigslist; it went surprisingly well. He was using his computer skills to help his drug dealer not get caught in exchange for free pills. Rent, Trenton explained, was not part of the deal. It was just easier for him to live with his drug dealer.

I'm astonished, and I'm astonished that I'm astonished. I never seem to get used to people relapsing, especially when they are my friends. I have so many things to say, I can't choose. It's like not being able to order at one of those restaurants with the eight-page menus.

"Well, what about Hannah?" I ask.

He doesn't answer. I hear video-game noise. He's shooting something.

"Hello!" I yell.

"Dude, yes," he says, and now I think he's high and tired. Of course he is. "I'm going to need to borrow some money."

"You know I don't have any money. You're the one with the job. And by the way, this is fucked up. You're not just fucking up your life. You've got a wife, Hannah, remember? And I was going to ask you to write me a letter, and I was kind of looking forward to playing golf at Rosy again, too."

"Dude, it's all good. I just had to move out of Armen's apartment, and I'm in a motel on Alvarado, not far from you. I just need some cash."

"Your craigslist drug dealer's name is Armen?"

"Yep."

"Okay, fine, Trenton. Come and get it. You are close. You know where I live. Come on over."

"That I can't do," he says and fires off a few more rounds. I hear video game deaths. "I uh, I can't come over, Joseph. I'll talk to you later—"

"Trenton!"

He hangs up.

I'm running late to my meeting. I'll call Hannah later and see if she can tell me which motel Trenton is in. Maybe I'll call my sponsor for advice. I'm not quite sure how to handle this, and things could get weird, so I should probably bring Clarence and Paul with me if I visit Trenton. Given his condition, it's best to treat any visit like a formal Twelfth-Step service call, straight out of the Big Book. I was hoping that the next time we were all together, we'd be at Rosy playing golf, not trying to talk Trenton out of destroying his life at The Crack Pipe Inn.

I find a miracle parking spot in front of Café Tropical. Some 12-Steppers say God gets them parking spots. I try to not to judge these people, but I'm not always successful. I find a seat right by the speaker. The energy in the room is low. It's as if the lights have been dimmed. This is usually a raucous meeting, but people are subdued. It reminds me of the days when I worked at Thomas & Coleman after 9/11. Oddly, there was a refreshing unity to it, kind of like Christmas, but instead of family and shopping and time off work, people were thinking of terrorism, death, and American flags waving in slow-mo.

Chapter Five of the Alcoholics Anonymous text is long, and people sometimes speed through it, but today, at this meeting, it's read slowly. "... Their chances are less than average. There are those, too, who suffer from grave emotional and mental disorders ...".

I think of Trenton sitting in a motel room. The only light is from the edge of the black-out curtains and the glow of his video game. He's probably been playing it for hours, only breaking to snort or pop pills. Or maybe he did score meth, and he's snorting it or shooting it or smoking it. I've heard you can do just about anything with that shit. Trenton is bipolar, so when he's off his meds, he acts bizarrely. It's hereditary; I remember he told me that. His dad was same way.

The introductory part of the meeting is over, and now I'm listening to the leader share. He says, we are not a glum lot, a phrase from the Big Book, but if anyone doubts the seriousness of this disease, we need only think of our friend who was sitting in these rooms, sober just several weeks ago. Oh fuck, I think. My mind races with who he could be talking about. I bet it's that black guy with the dreads who was a drummer in a punk band. He's always relapsing and then when he comes back, nobody gives him the hard, real deal, 12-Step treatment because he's Silver Lake royalty. Fuck, I should have just broken through his enabling and adoring fans and told his pretty ass that he's going to die if he doesn't start working the steps and taking this shit seriously. But I didn't, because I was intimidated. He's so popular. I have a resentment. I hate that they treat him differently just because he was in a famous punk band. I'm supposed to be of service, not just to those I like. What an egoic and asinine way for me to think. I look around, and sure enough, he's not here, and he's been here consistently the last several weeks; he raises his hand as a newcomer every week because he can't stay clean. Those are always the ones that get swallowed up first.

The speaker clears his throat and begins. "Before I go into my pitch of 'What it was like, what happened and what it's like now,' I just want to, uhm, you know, like, acknowledge this tragedy."

I cringe when the speaker misquotes this section of the Big Book, as nearly all of them do. It's not 'what **it** was like'. It's 'what **we** were like,' which, when converted to the singular, is 'what **I** was like.' It's not a grammar issue. It goes to the very crux of the Program: It's an inside job. If I thought this Program was about what **it** was like and what **it** is like now instead of what **I** was like and what **I'm** like now, I would think this Program doesn't work very damn well, because **it** was pretty good for me and **it** is pretty shitty for me now. I had a good career and money and a girlfriend, so **it** was pretty good. However, *I*, the inside of me, was a fucking suicidal disaster, a raging addict with no solution, and now I'm getting better despite my shitty exterior life.

That's why it's so hard for people to get sober before they hit a material bottom. They may be in enough discomfort to come into the Rooms and check things out, maybe get their boss or their significant-other off their back, but until they are staring down jails, institutions or death, it's hard to see that **I** is the problem and not **It**. I should have had the courage to bypass Punk Rock Star's fan-friends and whichever woman he was ensnared with that day, and offer my help, tell him the truth about his predicament, that he was going to die if he didn't start participating in the Program instead of being an observer.

"He was a regular at this meeting," the speaker continues. "He was a good guy. But we have to know that it's not unusual that he's dead. What's unusual is that we are all still alive ..."

No shit, right. That's some truth. God knows I could be dead. My drunk-driving accident, and then breaking into someone's home in a blackout. People have died doing far less. Trenton could die. It's possible. He probably won't. This isn't the first time he's relapsed. Dude is Teflon. He'll be teaching again, cracking Clarence and Paul up on the golf course again, just like last time.

The room is dead silent, except for one young woman who is crying, and the people making a fuss over her, getting her tissues. I think of what they say in Al-anon: Don't give them a tissue, let them cry.

"Yeah, we are the lucky ones. We are the ones who got the gift of sobriety," the speaker says. "So anyway, God bless Paddy. May he rest in peace. He was a good dude. So, what it was like..."

He said Paddy. He did. He said Paddy. It wasn't Punk Rock Star. Paddy's the one who died.

I feel light. I feel as if I must breathe carefully. The tube that takes in air from my mouth down to the bottom of my lungs is cast in the most delicate glass. The muscles in my face feel so heavy. I recall Paddy's face. Those bright blue eyes against that tough, tanned, Irish-thick skin, his beard like high-grit sandpaper. That knowing grin. Fuck! God dammit, Paddy, you bastard! I rock in my seat. I'm terribly self-conscious. I don't want to attract attention to myself and away from the speaker. Paddy, that was a fucking stupid thing to do. I have to leave. I wait for a little break. The speaker says, "So, what happened," signifying Part II of his pitch, and I get up. I mouth "sorry" to the speaker and point to my watch, idiotically, manically, ridiculously. I climb all over people to get through the packed room and out the door.

Back at my apartment, I smoke and drink coffee on the porch. I've developed a painful sty in the inner-edge of my left lower eyelid from blowing smoke out of the left corner of my mouth, so I'm trying to blow my smoke out to the right, and it feels equal parts awkward and irritating. I talk to myself, quietly, so my landlord won't hear me.

"You idiot, Paddy! I didn't even know you that well."

I think of him in my car telling me the story of his beautiful ex-girlfriend. She's South American. He smiled when he thought of her.

"You can't fucking fight if you're dead, fucking Paddy. That's Rule Number One! How you going to get back to flipping houses if you're dead, you dumbass?"

I smoke more. I drink coffee more. I cry a little. I think of what it must've been like to just give up and say "fuck it" like Paddy did. I've been close. Paddy couldn't get it together. He couldn't get a job. I don't know how hard he tried. He'd been living miserably in that sober living/halfway house for a long time.

Is that what it's going to be like for you, Joseph? Are you going to keep your chin up, whistling in the dark, like an idiot, pretending everything is alright, even though you know goddamn well you are as fucked as fucked gets? You ain't ever getting a real job. C'mon. This barbeque island bullshit is going to end, and you haven't worked a commercial in a month.

I think of Bill. Bill Fucking W. What's Bill got to do with me? That's olden-time shit, back when the cops gave you a ride home if you were driving drunk. Bill W. was about to relapse, and his dumb ass was flipping through the phonebook in an old phone booth outside a bar looking for an alcoholic to help. Can you imagine if I opened up the Los Angeles area phone book and started calling hospitals asking if they had any alcoholics that needed help? Or worse, if they had any sex-addicted alcoholics? Lawyers?

I laugh aloud and think, AA Number Three, he was a lawyer. There's that drawing on the wall at Pathfinders in Atwater Village where all they have is constant 12-Step meetings. It's a picture of a young Bill W. and Dr. Bob sitting on a hospital bed talking to AA Number Three, who is hospitalized again after a spree. Of course, unlike me, AA Number Three wasn't handcuffed to the hospital bed about to be charged with six felonies.

I smoke until my throat is raspy, my cough is raw, and my sty is pulsing against my left contact lens. I sit in my apartment watching Tiger Woods on DVR. He wears his signature red polo while closing in on another win. The phone rings and I pause the DVR. It freezes on Tiger proudly holding his follow-through at the top of his swing. I'm tempted to ignore the phone. I want to see how close Tiger sticks it, but I see it's Trenton's number.

"Joseph," Hannah says, letting out a breath. "He's home." She sounds terribly relieved. "He's going into detox tomorrow morning. He's asleep now."

"Oh my God, that's great," I tell her.

She thanks me, and I thank her. I tell her we'll go visit him, since I know it'll be hard for her to get to the detox facility by bus. It's out in an industrial area in San Fernando Valley. I've dropped guys off there before and I went there once to speak on an AA Hospitals & Institutions panel.

I press play on the DVR, unfreezing Tiger Woods. He poses with his hands high near his left ear, holding his club perpendicular to his spine and intersecting the back of his neck. The camera follows Tiger's golf ball through the air against a blue sky and wispy white clouds, and then another camera picks the ball up right before it lands on the green. The ball lands a pace past the flag and spins in place and then rips back several feet like a yo-yo on a string. It comes to rests a couple feet short of the hole.

The announcer says Tiger is in "complete control of his game," and the color commentator makes a forced reference to Tiger's recently deceased father.

I drive down Franklin to pick up Hannah, to take her to see Trenton. Traffic is backed up. I consider calling Macy. She'd have some insider's way to get to Trenton's in half the time it's going to take me. I don't mind. It'll give me time to think, to unwind all these new thoughts that are just short of complete. It's that feeling I used to get in math class where I'd almost understand. I can feel it. I'm on the other side. I just need to apply a little brain to it.

I've been thinking about *Palsgraf.*

Palsgraf is about foreseeability. Is it foreseeable that a blackout drunk who has a history of running and jumping and climbing over fences and into empty buildings in blackouts, who is also a sex addict that frequented massage parlors, would climb into a massage parlor in the middle of the night in a fugue state? Probably not. But it is totally foreseeable that he'd do something crazy. It's kind of like those premise liability cases I recall from law school. A guy has a pallet of dynamite stored out in the open on his property. He catches some kids playing on his property and chases them off, so he's on notice that kids can come on his property. Then later, the kids are climbing over the fence, like a scene from *Stand by Me.* They're all running around, playing, having a good ole time, and one kid trips on the pallet of dynamite and tears his knee up real bad, but the dynamite doesn't explode. The kid's parents sue the owner under a premise liability theory. The owner's lawyer argues, "Okay fine, it'd be one thing if the dynamite exploded. Even though the kid was trespassing, we can't have a situation where some kid is fucking around and climbs a fence and gets his leg blown off, but this kid just tripped. He could have tripped on anything. The point is, the danger of the dynamite is that it might explode, not that somebody is going to trip on it, right?" Then the kid's lawyer says, "But here's the thing, the owner was negligent in having the dynamite lying around in the first place, so who cares how exactly the kid got injured?"

Huh, I don't recall who won.

Hannah is waiting in front of her and Trenton's condo, which is in this strange spot scrunched up between Beechwood Canyon, the 101 Freeway and Hollywood. It has that weird Hollywood feel, like around every corner, there is some would-be star from Ohio that is now homeless on meth who vacillates between mischievous and murderous. Maybe he'll ask you for some change, or maybe he'll just stab you. German tourists don't see Hollywood that way. They're always walking around Mann's Chinese Theater and the Hollywood Wax Museum wearing fanny packs, smiling. I don't get it at all.

"Do you know how to get there?" Hannah asks as she slips into my car. She's so petite that the seat belt rides up close to her neck.

"I wrote down directions," I respond, and tap the yellow sticky note I've affixed to my dash.

I feed her a small dose of 12-Step hope, and she's polite but quiet. We talk a little about her shitty job as a librarian/research assistant for a large law firm, where she is paid a tenth of the amount of most lawyers. I recall that she graduated from law school, and I consider unraveling my chain of thoughts regarding the evil of big firms, which would be involuntarily laced with braggadocio regarding my experience in and against big law firms, but instead I turn up the radio and remain quiet. While reveling in the actual physical joy of deciding to keep my mouth shut, acting on my decision, and thus avoiding the post-talking heartburn of self-disgust, I wonder if Hannah is anxious about seeing Trenton. Of course she is.

Hannah and I wait in the cafeteria of the detox facility. It has that institutional smell, like a too-used dish sponge. The cafeteria is empty but for a janitor in a navy-blue uniform, mopping the floor with a large, white-dreaded mop and a yellow bucket on wheels with a strainer for the mop and a red drawing of a stick figure mid-fall, a warning that strikes me as particularly apropos. I think of pointing it out to Hannah, making my little clever joke—ha, ha, but again, I'm somehow able to shut-the-fuck-up, a newly emerging skill. Trenton walks out from somewhere behind us. He looks beaten and embarrassed and is surprisingly plump. Hannah hugs him and I follow. He sits across from us.

"So, here we are," he says, always the jokester. He still looks full of life, and I just want to hug him again and tell him I miss him and his big Jew-fro, and tell him he fucked up but we'll let him come back to "the A and A." That's our little inside joke. I told him my grandpa calls Alcoholics Anonymous "the A and A," and he thought that was hilarious.

I chuckle, but not too much. Hannah doesn't react at all, as if she didn't even hear Trenton, even though he's sitting across from her, and it's so quiet I can hear the slight squeak of wheels turning on the mop bucket. This should be awkward, but it's not for me. I've been where he is. It feels familiar. I know how this works.

Trenton responds to Hannah's non-response by becoming serious and he thanks me for coming and then he lays out a synopsis of where he's been and when he crossed the line and couldn't stop. He tells us about living with his craigslist drug dealer, the motel, and about a short stint riding his bike aimlessly. He isn't too specific about the drugs. Hannah just wants to know about the next step. Trenton explains the where, how and what of the rehab he's going to check into tomorrow after this detox visit is over, how they wouldn't let him in without any clean time, so that's why he came here first. I offer to pick him up and take him to the rehab, but he declines and explains that he has to pack, and we discuss some possibility of Hannah packing for him and then giving me his suitcase because she has to go to work in the morning.

Trenton apologizes to her sincerely. They've been through this many times before, before I knew Trenton, mostly when they lived in Boston. She's the Lois W. and he's the Bill W. I excuse myself to give them some privacy. I walk around the table and give Trenton a big hug and handshake, tell him I can't wait for him to go golfing with me because he's the only one of our foursome that's worse than me.

"Alright, dude," Trenton says.

"I'll see you soon, dude. One day at a time, okay? Okay, fucker?"

Trenton walks back to his wife, and I walk to the waiting room.

I sit and notice how good I feel. The Big Book says, I think I recall, something like, there is nothing that will insure against a relapse more than service to another alcoholic.

Macy and I sit with a couple dozen others in a large circle of chairs in the Agape Spiritual Center's sanctuary. Without the Sunday service stage lighting, crowd, energy, ushers, and sounds, it's strange to be here. It's like being in the dugout of any empty baseball stadium. The energy lingers.

"I'm so excited," Macy says to me as she pages through a syllabus while everyone settles into their seats and scopes the room.

"It's like the first day of school," I respond. "I guess it is the first day of school."

This is another last-house-on-the-block for me. I'm out of answers. The Anonymous programs and their 12 Steps have saved my life, but as they say, I need a bigger God. Whatever that means is just whatever to me. I'm running out of options. Macy seems like she's got something, and it seems to be working for her and William. She's not quite as fucked as I am, but still pretty fucked up, or at least she was. Now it looks like she may become a Hollywood writer. But she's not out of the woods yet. I guess that's why she's here with me. Twelve-steppers are instructed to just say yes. So I said yes to this. I said yes to this New Age crap, which Reverend Beckwith refers to as New Thought Wisdom. I'm not here for crystals or learning how to chant while sitting on Tibetan-monk-made pillows. I'm here for results, practical results.

The lady teaching our class welcomes us and then gives introductory remarks. Then each of us introduces ourselves. We are a rainbow of people, all so positive, but under the surface, this is no different than 12-Step meetings. No one comes here because things are going so damn well in their life. The difference here is that most people aren't saying it, but I can see it in the tick of the smile of the overly-skinny, obviously-rich white woman. She screams recent-divorce. And the young man, he's just graduated from USC with a degree in—and then someone coughs. He doesn't exactly say it, but it's obvious, he's one of the new middle-class poor. He bought into the idea that if he graduated from a good school, he'd get a good job and pay off his well-over-six-figure student loan sooner than his death.

"I'm Joseph, and I'm—" I say and pause, just for a beat, realizing how close I was to saying I'm an addict. "I'm here to learn more about the principles behind the teaching I've heard at Agape."

Oh, that's good, Joseph, I think to myself. Real good. You could have said, I'm here because I'm fucking desperate, more desperate than you could possibly imagine. You have no idea how crazy I am, how desperate I am, how fucked I am. So I'm here for some of that magic my girl Macy seems to have. She says she got it here, and I want me some.

Macy introduces herself. She's smiling and smart and says something clever, but not intentionally so. I didn't hear it. I was too busy scanning the men, seeing which ones are interested in her, the ones making too much eye contact, nodding their heads too much. There are a couple of them, which makes me feel good. I'm certainly not beyond being validated by other men's desire for my girlfriend. I've got that going for me, at least.

Dr. Cheryl Ward is our teacher over these next few weeks. She's a lawyer. She was the dean of a regional law school. Dr. Ward's voice is soothing. She explains stage two and three of spiritual growth. Stage one is the law. It can be directed by feelings, which are energy. You lift feelings through gratitude and appreciation. We create feelings through visioning, prayer, and affirmation. God is within us. We are always creating something.

Okay, that's what I want to talk about. That part where my thoughts create my reality.

Dr. Ward says we choose our thoughts and thus our feelings.

Good enough. I get that. I know my thoughts affect my feelings. I can think of dead babies and be sad, or I can think of live babies and be happy.

Now about the third stage of consciousness.

In this stage of the universe, the presence of God works through you. We become aware that we are one with God, and God is in us. This consciousness is often referred to as being in the zone.

Dr. Ward tells us we will be selecting a single, very specific thing that we want from this class. She doesn't use the dreaded M-word—manifest—but that is what she means. Good, good. That's what I'm here for. If this shit works, let's be specific about it. I'm not here to learn how to smile.

My doubting subconscious works on me: But you, Joseph, you have to do what she tells you. She's telling you that you have to believe. You have to believe before it'll work. That's how this shit works. This manifesting shit, that's how it works. Do you have it in you?

At the break, Macy and I walk outside and mingle with the other students. Macy talks to a woman we both know from 12-Step meetings.

"What's your thing?" the woman asks Macy. She has marionette-mouth frown lines, so a smile bucks her nature. But she's smiling now and excited to hear Macy's answer.

Macy knows what she's here for, so when she *hmms*, I know she's not contemplating what she has decided she wants to manifest, but rather whether to tell this woman.

"I know mine. I want a good job that pays well," I blurt out to my own surprise.

"It's important to be specific about what you want," the woman says. She appears slightly irritated that I've interjected and her perma-frown resets.

"So I should say ... I want a job doing something I'm good at, and I want to make a certain dollar amount? Why wouldn't I say I want to make a million dollars a year?" I ask.

Macy and I both look at the woman anxiously. It's literally and metaphorically the million-dollar question. Now I recall, this woman was an executive at an accounting firm and was recently laid off after years of service. She told me this before a 12-Step meeting after I was rambling on about my opinion regarding all these scumbag mortgage brokers—some I used to represent—selling mortgages that people couldn't possibly afford once the five-year-no-interest loan was up. She had replied, "You have no idea how bad things are." It shook me. She was on the inside of big-business finance, and she was one of those reserved types, never saying things that she isn't completely convinced of.

"That's a good question," she says, "and I know the answer."

What the—who talks like that? I recall an E.F. Hutton commercial, and then decide that I'm all ears. She just seems so confident. I press my face forward.

She speaks as if into a microphone. "You can affirm a job that pays a million per year, but this is like any other muscle. It takes exercising to grow. Most people aren't able to envision something that is so great, and the most important thing is to believe in your affirmation. That's where all the power is. If I've never made over 50,000, it's going to be hard for me to believe I'm going to make a million. I don't know what your number is, but whatever it is, you have to believe it. You have to act like it's already done."

Macy and I look to each other as if doing so was choreographed for a television audience. We raise our eyebrows. We both know what we just heard. The Real Shit.

A student announces that class is back on. We all take our seats.

Dr. Ward speaks. I feel energized. I believe this woman. I can do this.

"My cell phone's blowin' up," I say, rap-style to Macy. She appreciates my rap references. I think of her standing on her coffee table dancing to a Tupac song. I love the way she dances to rap. It's so funny. She infuses everything with lightness.

My phone sounds.

"Who's calling?" she asks, just after turning down Biggie, who was playing on my knock-off iPod-to-car-cassette-player.

"Dang, girl," I respond. "Why you gotta kill Biggie Smalls?"

We idle at a traffic light waiting to take a left on Slauson. I turn to her, and she rolls her big brown eyes, sticks her tongue out half-way and smiles at me. I kiss her on the cheek playfully. We are both in post-Agape, anti-gravity moods.

I report the calls I received since we were in class. "A few calls from Trenton, one from Clarence, and one from Peter. Trenton probably needs a ride to rehab. I'll call him when we get home," I tell Macy.

"Did you like anything you heard today?" Macy asks.

We drive north on La Cienega past the dozen or so pumpjacks that smoothly fuck the earth for its oil.

"I liked it all," I profess.

I don't have to look at Macy to know she's pleased. She is only with me because I'm willing to go deeper. She has a theory about me. She thinks I'm like her. She thinks I'm completely willing to live a spiritual life like she does, and sometimes she's even right. I'm not there yet, not like her. She is living from the inside-out. When she says she's handing it over to God, she's not fucking around.

"You know that part about making every part of your life your ministry?" I ask.

"Yes," Macy responds.

We pass a strip mall sign that reads "Tokyo Massage." It has a red and blue neon sign in the window that proclaims it is open. A collage of my past creepiness flashes through my mind and a wave of ick follows. I let it pass and re-enter the post-Agape energy.

"That ministry stuff made me think of Parker's Sporting Goods when I was a teenager," I tell Macy. "I worked there for three years during high school. I loved it so much. I didn't know it, but it was like a ministry for me. I walked in there smiling, so grateful to have a job. I showed up early. I did the work nobody else would do, and I didn't care that other people didn't work as hard. I learned everything about every department. And the weird thing was how I was with the customers. It didn't matter whether they were being dicks or not, I didn't change. I was polite and helpful, sincerely. I didn't do that passive-aggressive bullshit when a customer got mad."

Macy imitates a nasally salesgirl. "I'm sorry sir, but if you don't have a receipt, I can't help you. I know I sold you that yesterday, but no receipt, no return. Sorry."

"I never did that shit. It was like nothing could make me unhappy. They loved me there. Everyone else stole from that place and I never did. I got raises, but I was still barely making more than minimum wage, and that was fine. I figured there were guys working their butts off at McDonald's making less than me."

"And?" Macy asks impatiently. I can tell I'm about to get a "don't bury the lead," Macy's favorite line.

"Well, two things happened. First, they hired one of the owner's nephews. Dude was absolutely worthless, a total dick, and he showed me his paystub, and they were paying him twice what they were paying me. I was so mad. I just said 'fuck it' and started doing what everyone else did. I stole some stuff and justified it, and I didn't really care. I was still nice to customers, but I didn't do any extra work or really put any care into it. It was all downhill after that."

"And?" Macy prods.

"Jesus, Macy. What am I, on the clock here? I gotta get this out in under 60 seconds like one of your TV-news blurbs? Waterskiing squirrels delight Fourth of July crowd!"

Macy turns my knock-off iPod back up in joking defiance. A lesser Dandy Warhols song plays. I begin to speak, and she blasts it on mock-accident, and then turns it back down.

"Okay, okay. I'll get to the point," I say. "The barbeque islands, right? I've just got to be of service. It's my little ministry. In a sea of asshole salesman, I'll be the good guy. Fuck the sales. I'm tired of being in fear about not selling any. My first priority is just being kind to the customer, like I'm in a 12-Step meeting and the customer is a newcomer. I'll just tell the customer the truth and help them pick out a barbeque island if they want one. From now on, I'm going to approach my job the 12-Step way. I do the footwork. God handles the results."

It's dark. Macy and I are taking one of our walks down her street. We walk west toward Los Feliz. We aren't holding hands. Macy has this thing about how I don't walk in sync with her when we hold hands. There's fresh rain on the ground and on the leaves and trees. There is a long smooth wall enclosing the convent that used to be a mansion owned by an industrialist. He owned a tire company or radio station or both. I forget. He's dead, he was Catholic, so the convent and its nuns are here. Macy and I talk about what we like about each home we see and what we don't. I like to think about how nearly every one of these homes is connected to a movie or television show. I like to think of a computer map with a bird's eye view with little thought bubbles connected to each home. And in the thought bubble is an icon of the movie or show. Macy talks about buying a home. It's her dream. I can't dream that big, not yet at least, but I don't tell her that. I do tell her that the home prices are absurd, that they're the equivalent of the P/E ratio of tech stocks in the early 2000s. Last week, we went to an open house on this street. It was a slick little two bedroom, and it was priced just short of one million dollars. I decide not to repeat my theory about the house of cards that is the mortgage industry and about the real estate agents I represented. It's all just humble brag. I can't stand hearing myself spit out these anecdotes with no purpose other than making me look smart or trying to prove how horrible the world is.

We silently wind through a cute little neighborhood on the border between Silver Lake and Los Feliz. Macy comments on the raised and lit brushed-steel address numbers and their stylish font on a small apartment building. We head back up Macy's street. It's poorly lit and narrow and only part of it has a sidewalk. The occasional white, yellow or orange house light or dim street light causes the asphalt road to twinkle. I decide not to tell Macy how they always wet the street for car commercials or in movies when they want the scene to look particularly beautiful. I'm sure I've told her this before. I'm sure she already knew. She was married to a director, after all. I'm running out of clever things to say.

The moon peeks out between the thin clouds and lights up a little patch of soggy overgrown grass, puddles and mud. And there, just sitting there, as if he was waiting for us to find him, is a giant toad. This isn't a city toad. This is a fairy-tale toad that's big enough to stare down a cat. We stop and gawk. I'm in slack-jawed awe.

"It's huge. Look at it," I whisper, as if I might scare it away.

"It's enormous," Macy responds.

I think clearly and precisely, as if reading off a ticker tape running across my mind's eye: "I'll never forget this moment," standing here on this romantic wet street, staring at this fairy-tale creature. I almost expect it to say something.

A car's headlights arc around the corner and head toward us. I take Macy's hand, and we cross the street and wait. The car passes. We cross back, and the fairy-tale toad is gone. Macy is lit up by the moon and she's gliding along, euphorically. Something is happening to her. It's more than optimism. Whatever it is, I want some, too.

We make love, and I'm not sleepy, but Macy likes us to go to sleep together, so I just lie here in bed and think.

SEVENTEEN

I awake with a gasp, as if someone has shaken me violently. Macy rolls over and groggily asks if I'm alright. I whisper, "I'm fine, go back to sleep," and I kiss her billowy lips. Our lips stick together and separate like two glazed donuts being pulled apart. She rolls back onto her side, and her breathing settles into a long, slow cadence.

I feel energetic. My mind is alert. It's dark and cool, and I can smell the freshly washed sheets. An urgency overwhelms me. I was dreaming of something, something very important. I rise from Macy's bed and sit in a chair facing the large window and peer out into the night sky. Light freeway traffic, accentuated by the intermittent grinding downshift of a tractor trailer, plays like ambient music.

I stare into the nightscape. What was I dreaming that has me feeling so alert and as if I'm on the verge of something? I must remember.

Palsgraf, that's what it was. I was dreaming about *Palsgraf.* It's a landmark legal decision all law students study in law school that has to do with foreseeability. I was dreaming of the lady, the plaintiff, Ms. Palsgraf, and for some reason, she's wearing a hoop skirt. It's in the 1920s or '30s and in New York or maybe New Jersey. I'm not sure if my memory is exactly consistent with the facts of the case, but I do recall them generally. Ms. Palsgraf was on a platform waiting for the train. And then there were men running to catch a train, one of them an employee of the train company. He's wearing one of those silly little hats. The other man is a would-be passenger, and he's carrying a package. He drops his package while the employee helps him jump to board the train. The package explodes, causing a huge old-timey scale on the platform where Ms. Palsgraf is standing to fall on her, and in my dream, she is surrounded by a team of modern-day paramedics. As I sit here now, I recall from the facts of the case I read in law school that the package that was dropped by the passenger was full of fireworks. In my dream, I was transported from the scene of *Palsgraf* to a podium at Pepperdine Law's large lecture hall, where I was explaining to Macy the legal issues involved in *Palsgraf* and why the decision was wrong, but I'm dancing around some of my explanations of the reasoning behind the majority opinion versus the dissenting opinion, because I don't know the case as well as I should, and I'm exasperated, and Macy knows I don't know. She's the only one in the audience.

I stand and take a deep breath and stare out the window. I can see the dark outline of the Griffith Park mountains. Macy stirs. I sit back down.

The issue in *Palsgraf* wasn't whether the train station employee was negligent in trying to help the passenger get on the train while it was moving. I think that much was conceded. That is to say, the train company employee definitely had a duty of care, and in taking the dangerous action of trying to get a passenger carrying a package onto a moving train, the employee violated that duty, or, as the legal term goes, he "breached" that duty. The issue, rather, was did that duty of care extend to Ms. Palsgraf? While it was foreseeable that the guy running to board the moving train might have been injured by the employee trying to help him, it wasn't foreseeable that his package of fireworks would set off a chain reaction that led to Ms. Palsgraf's injury.

The majority decision was authored by Judge Cardozo—who later became a Supreme Court Justice—and the minority opinion by Judge Andrews. I had to know that for the California Bar exam. So Ms. Palsgraf lost her case. The Court ruled that it wasn't foreseeable that she would be injured by the train employee's breach of his duty of care. His duty of care didn't extend to an unforeseeable injury—or something like that. I never agreed with Cardozo. I agreed with Judge Andrews. If I recall correctly, Andrews opined that a breach of a duty of care extends to any injury it might cause within some level of proximity to the originating wrongful act, hence the concept of "proximate cause" as one of the five elements of a negligence cause of action.

"Joseph?" Macy says, her voice quiet and hoarse, as she feels my absence in her bed.

"I'm right here, baby. Go back to sleep."

Macy mumbles something and turns over, away from me, and I return to my thoughts.

My memory of the rationale of *Palsgraf* gets a little foggy regarding how proximate cause relates to foreseeability. But so what? Why am I dreaming of *Palsgraf*? It has to do with foreseeability.

In my dream I was frustrated trying to explain *Palsgraf* to Macy. She doesn't say anything. She just sits there in the middle of the giant classroom listening to me.

Macy's belief in me was rocked when we had our big fight, the one where I professed my victimhood and she pleaded with me not to. She's rebounded since then, mostly, I presume, because we are going to the Agape Fundamentals Class together, but I'm still on shaky ground. It's coming back to me right now. I can feel the nerves in my shoulders and sickness in my stomach—like when I medicate my depression by eating an entire deep dish pizza from Masa of Echo Park and chase it with a pint of Ben & Jerry's New York Super Fudge Chunk ice cream—thinking of how I droned on and on with such passion to convince Macy that I'd been wrongly treated by life itself, that I was the unluckiest man on earth. I recoil at the memory of me saying, "If it happened any other way that night, I'd still be a lawyer! If somebody would have come out of their apartment while I pounded on the door of the massage parlor, if the window had been locked, if he wasn't home, if I'd have realized which window was which ... if anything happened any other way!"

Macy turns in her sleep and groans. It startles me. It's as if she has joined me in reliving the memory of me pleading my victim case to her during our big fight. I freeze. I feel as if I've been caught doing something wrong.

Macy settles, and I relax and return to my thoughts. That fateful night when my life changed forever, was what happened foreseeable? Was it foreseeable that I would do what I did? Of course not! But maybe, like Judge Andrew's response to Judge Cardozo in *Palsgraf*, I'm not asking the right question. It's not that it was foreseeable that I'd cause the harm I caused in the way I caused it, but it was certainly foreseeable that I'd cause some type of harm. In fact, it was more than foreseeable, it was predictable.

More and more frequently, I became crazed when I drank to blackout, and more and more frequently, I drank until I blacked out. I even used to say that I was an athletic blackout drinker. There was the time I ran a mile at top-speed, wearing a suit and wingtips, after smoking two packs of cigarettes and drinking a half-dozen vodka and Red Bulls and limped for two days. There was the night I climbed over the fence into the Venice canals and explored an empty house that was for sale, stole a canoe from its dock and paddled around until I tipped it and fell into the salt water, again wearing a full suit and tie. I recall walking down Pacific Avenue as the sun rose. My shoes squished with every step, and water dripped from my suit. I carried a large plastic oar that I had somehow managed to bring back with me over the security fence. I was bleeding badly from a cut on my arm. Then there was the time I was in a bar's parking lot after last call, not ready to call it quits. I used a baby palm tree as a punching bag and kicked it until my shin and the tree were nearly destroyed. Thankfully, the owner of the bar, a client of mine, came out and convinced me to stop. I did, and I ran over two miles to my high-school best friend's family home at 3 a.m. and woke his mom, who hadn't seen me in years. I was hysterical. She was terrified, and she called the police. And then, of course, there was my drunk-driving accident. I had never driven after drinking before, and yet I did that night.

I rolled my car off the freeway at 85 m.p.h. It's a miracle I didn't kill myself and my passenger.

But this is nothing new. I've done the twelve steps. I understand that my disaster was more than foreseeable. In fact, I came to believe I was truly an alcoholic when in rehab I realized that while I didn't get in trouble every time I drank, every time I got in trouble it was because I was drunk. So why am I having these dreams about *Palsgraf?* What is my subconscious trying to tell me?

I run my fingers through my hair as if to pull the answer out of my scalp. On the nightstand next to Macy's bed is a copy of Ernest Holmes's little book, *This Thing Called You.*

And then it pops into my brain.

"It is done unto you as you believe it to be true."

Since I was released from jail nearly three years ago, I've heard this so many times from so many sources. I stayed with Keri, my ex-girl-friend and criminal defense lawyer, for a couple weeks right when I got out of Chino prison. She had a copy of a weird movie, *What the Bleep Do We Know!?* It was about this deaf woman, and the whole point of it was that her thoughts and her attitude affected what happened to her. It was corny and pseudo-scientific, but there was something that spoke to me. Then there was *The Secret.* It was even cornier and was downright false-science. Reverend Beckwith of Agape was one of the many talking heads woven into it. It was a weird little movie, too. It was about the Law of Attraction and seemed to be wildly overreaching. I recall a scene where a boy wants a bike, and suddenly he gets a bike, and it seemed like it was all based on some magical wishful thinking; some other guy talks about how he got a mansion with wishful thinking. But just like in *What the Bleep Do We Know!?*, there was this kernel of invaluable truth in *The Secret* that seemed to always come back to that saying: "It is done unto you as you believe it to be true."

I reach over to the nightstand and pick up *This Thing Called You.* Macy gave it to me after we made up after our big fight. I'd tried to read it, but it wasn't sinking in. One thing Ernest Holmes wrote that I did understand is that everything starts from the inside. Like an acorn to an oak tree, everything on the outside is a result of the inside, the unseen. That's how I understood it, at least. The idea spoke to me. It wasn't as if I was deciding whether the statement was true, it was as if the undeniable truth of it had been revealed to me. It reminded me of something that Reverend Beckwith said on stage a couple Sundays ago. I envision him with his little dreads and his head-microphone. He said that no one invented the Number One. One was always One, and it was One before we started calling it One, and it'll be One forever.

The muted grinding sound of a trucker's downshift on the freeway, *waaaahhhh*, is followed by a collage of memories. Each memory elicits the same feeling: deep shame and self-loathing. My step-mother catching me masturbating to a porn mag I found on the sidewalk when I was 14 years old; dropping off a prostitute in silence on Market Street after she fellated me in the back seat of my car; the countless times I slinked away like a beaten dog after another "last time" leaving a massage parlor; so many times waking still-drunk and buzzing from nicotine after a night—sometimes two—of binge drinking and smoking when I'd sworn to myself with absolute conviction I would never do it again, and then coming down so hard I felt like I had the flu for three days, only to do it again; and recently, seeing the faces of Aunt Suzie, Uncle Billy, Grandpa and my mom at Christmas, none of them having a clue what to say to me after I'd dropped a nuclear bomb on my life.

My heart pounds. "No, I don't need to go through this again," I mouth to myself, looking over my shoulder to make sure my sniffling and tear-fighting hasn't woken Macy.

"I've paid the price, and I'm in recovery. I don't do any of that anymore. I've forgiven myself, or, at least, tried. Why am I bringing up all this painful stuff now?"

I stare through the window and into the black sky for quite a long time, letting the question linger in my consciousness, and then, quite suddenly, the answer slaps me hard. "Oh my God," I gulp, and I sweat while the truth I feel is translated into words that fill my mind: *What happened that night, the night of my implosion, was absolutely perfect. It couldn't have happened any other way. I created a masterpiece. I manifested on the outside exactly what I was on the inside. Inside of me was 20 years of shame, 20 years of doing things that disgusted me, 20 years of promising myself, with every cell in my body, that this was going to be the last time. And every time I broke the promise to myself, I loathed myself more and more until all that was left of my self-esteem was a condom-thin mask. Twenty years of powerful, wordless messages, sent from my consciousness to the deepest parts of my soul, festered within me: You are a disgusting creep. You can't control yourself. You are worthless. You don't deserve anything.*

My stomach squeals with rising acid. Tears fill my eyes, tip my eyelashes, roll down my cheeks and drip onto my t-shirt.

Oh Jesus, now I know the truth. I did this to me. I'm not a victim. *My subconscious conspired with my soul to create the perfect event in order to save my life.* It had to be drastic, and it had to reveal my truth. And it had to involve every aspect of what was killing me in the exact way it was doing so: one part wild "athletic" blackout alcoholism; one part secretive, self-loathing sex addiction; and finally, one part, closeted, uncontrolled, binge-smoking.

"How perfect, how elegant to create a scenario where the world sees me the way I saw myself, even though I didn't commit the crime I was convicted of," I say under breath and tears. "Of course I've become a registered sex offender. It matches my insides exactly."

I stare through the window, dabbing my eyes with my t-shirt and squeezing my knees into my chest. Finally, I understand. It's graceful and precise. One incident, the whole thing lasted less than 15 minutes, involving everything that was killing me, and an outward expression of all my darkest feelings and secrets. And, the effect was as concise and perfect as a simple math equation. One plus one equals two. The end result was my crucible: Choose a spiritual life and live, or don't and die.

I take a few moments to breathe and gather myself, and I carefully crawl back into bed. Macy stirs but doesn't wake. I lie on my back and close my eyes. I feel a deep sense of relief and relaxation, and I think to myself, "Yes, it was done unto me exactly as I believed it to be true."

EIGHTEEN

I'm on my way to the Alameda County Fair to sell barbeque islands for a week. I drive up the 5 Freeway toward San Francisco, north up the gut of California through the Central Valley. The warm peaceful feeling I had when Macy and I drove home from Dr. Ward's class at Agape has been replaced with acute anxiety. All I can think about is that I have to register as a sex offender in Alameda, or, at least, my reading of Penal Code Section 290 seems to require me to. I asked Keri if I was correct, and she said she wasn't sure. When I told my probation officer, Maya, about my short trip to Alameda, and that I thought I might need to register, she sighed as if I was being too much of a stickler for the rules. I told her, "Yes, I think I have to register the same as if I'm moving," and "Yes, I know, you're right, Maya, it's absurd. You're telling me?" Then, I called Central LAPD at Skid Row, and an officer with a deep voice said, "Wait, you're only going for a week, right? What section of the statute do you think requires you to re-register? ... Oh ... I see. Well, alrighty." He sighed as if I was too exhausting for him to endure, and he told me to fax him a letter "or whatever," as if he was doing me a grand favor. I hung up and dialed the Alameda County Sheriff to make an appointment. I was connected to another officer who had the talent of expressing exhaustion, irritation and bemusement with few words. "What? An appointment? Why? ... The statute? ... Okay, fine. C'mon in if you have to."

My calls to LAPD and the Alameda County Sheriff's Department took all of 10 minutes, but I am exhausted. I lay down on the couch, still thinking about whether I should even register in Alameda at all. It seems like I'm calling unnecessary attention to myself. Nobody seems to care or even know what Penal Code 290 actually requires. I close my eyes and fade into a daydream. I see myself lying on a hotel room bed after a long day of work selling barbeque islands in Alameda. My shoes are still on the floor, and I am watching a *Six Feet Under* rerun on HBO. I jump from the sound of pounding on my hotel door. "Police! Open the door!" I get up to open the door, but they barge in, yelling, handguns drawn. They wear green windbreakers with "Sheriff" screen-printed in yellow block letters.

I open my eyes from my daydream. All doubt as to whether I should register in Alameda is eradicated from my mind.

I set my car on cruise control at 79 miles per hour. Endless perfect rows of nut and fruit trees bend in my peripheral vision. I'm listening to one of the cassettes that Macy gave me. It's an Agape Sunday Service. Reverend Beckwith is speaking, but I can't focus and I can't follow what he's saying. So I turn my car stereo off. My old car's air-conditioner blasts cool air. I feel anxious about registering in Alameda. I'm afraid I'm going to get caught in some administrative trap, and I'll be right back in their control. I try to shut my brain down, but I give in to the fear. I recall a deputy sheriff at Twin Towers Jail in Los Angeles. It was right after I'd been to court for my sentencing hearing, and the judge ordered my release. I was going to be free. I was overjoyed, and when I went back to Twin Towers, I presumed to be immediately processed for release, I'd forgotten myself. I acted as if I was in normal society. I was surprised when deputies took me back to my pod instead of Processing. I asked the deputy sheriff in the control booth at my pod when exactly I'd be released. I was midsentence explaining that the judge had ordered my release, and that bringing me back here must be a mistake, when he cut me off, saying, "Shut—the fuck—up!" with such viciousness that I gasped in response. When I looked at his face and saw his icy stare and clenched jaw, I knew that if I said one single syllable in defiance of his order, he'd have pulverized me. It took them two days to release me, and I didn't say another word.

I pull off the freeway and buy gas, cigarettes and a Coke. I drive down a frontage road and find a reasonably good smoking spot under a dying tree in a derelict strip mall's parking lot. I sit on a curb and smoke several cigarettes, chasing them with warm Coke. The Coke sticks to my teeth. I get in the car, start the engine, turn on the air-conditioning and call Keri.

"What's up, homey?" she asks.

"Hey, what's up?" I respond.

"You alright?" she asks.

Keri can always tell if I'm not alright. For nearly 20 years, in various intervals, she's endured being my lover, girlfriend, teammate, criminal defense lawyer, and confidante, but we've always remained friends, even when we didn't talk much. And Keri is always Keri. Unlike me, she's developed a self that she's not hell-bent on changing.

"Not really, Keri," I say. "When are we going to get that hearing going on trying to Change the Numbers?"

"I think we need to wait at least several more months. Maybe your D.A. will get promoted or get a better job," Keri says, I think, half-joking.

"She seems to like her job—quite a fucking lot, Keri."

"I gotta go," Keri responds.

"No, Keri. I—I gotta go."

"Later Holmes," she says and hangs up.

I drive and think. Fuck it. Do the footwork and leave the rest up to God. That's the reality, whether I like it or not. These cops don't give a damn about me. Do what they say, and then go sell a truckload of barbeque islands.

I think of Macy, and then I think of William. My heart warms, and my nerves recede. I tell myself, everything is alright. You aren't going to Alameda to sell barbeque islands. You are going to Alameda to be of service to everyone you come in contact with, even the assholes you work with.

I drive straight to the Alameda County Sheriff's office. Besides the hour wait, registering is painless and uneventful.

The Alameda County Fair is slow but fine. It's like I'm back at Parker's Sporting Goods when I was a teenager, just having fun. I'm not trying to sell anybody anything. I'm just answering questions and talking to people. I know whatever is supposed to happen will happen. I'm going to be alright. The fear that I'm not going to be able to pay my rent pops up often, but I ignore it or tell it to go away. Sometimes the fear and anxiety get so bad that I can feel it buzzing in my shoulders and radiating down my arms. I fight it off by repeating one of four of my favorite 12-Step axioms over and over.

God is my employer.

One moment at a time.

Chop wood, carry water.

Do your part, and let God take care of the rest.

I'm still processing the grand revelation I had a few nights ago sitting in Macy's bedroom while she slept. When I think of how it came to me, it's like trying to remember a bizarre dream. I'd dreamt and then woken up alarmed, with the subjects of my dreams still dancing in my mind. I dreamt and then thought about the *Palsgraf* case, the concept of "foreseeability," and that saying that keeps coming up, "It is done unto you as you believe it to be true." I've since searched it on the internet, and according to the Apostle Matthew, it's straight out of Jesus The Christ's mouth. Somehow, that night, all of those thoughts led me to an undeniable truth, one I believe so completely that I could pass a hundred lie detector tests: My subconscious conspired with my soul to manifest a scenario that forced me to face the truth about myself. Bizarre as the night of my arrest was, it was as perfect as a circle, and it couldn't have happened any other way. I am not a victim. I am a creator. It hurts to admit that I created all this pain for myself and for others, but there is great freedom and power in it, too. While in my active addictions, I lied to myself and acted against my own principles. I depleted my soul, and it led to a hell because I believed I was deserving of hell. So then now, in Recovery through the 12 Steps, I am true to myself, and I act in accordance with my principles, principles based in love and integrity, and thus if I believe I am deserving of a heaven it can lead me nowhere else. Spiritual laws work the same as physical laws. This law of belief acts the same as the law of gravity. It does not judge, it simply works. Innocent babies or mass murderers fall off a cliff just the same. It—whatever it is—is done unto me as I believe it to be true.

Standing in the Paradise BBQ Islands booth under a pop-up tent, the only one of the three of us not with a customer, I think to myself, this is all fine and good, but right now, I need to make some money. My landlord does not accept spiritual truisms in lieu of cash. I think of Dr. Ward urging us, her Agape students, to believe in what we want so much that we believe it has already happened. I try, but I have to accept the truth. I'm not there yet. I'd like to believe that I'm going to sell a dozen barbeque islands and make $10,000, but I simply don't believe. But what I do believe is that everything is going to be alright today. I'm not sure exactly how it's going to happen, but if I just do my job and be of service to everyone I meet, everything will work out, one day at a time.

I meet a nice old couple. I pretend my grandpa is thinking of buying a barbeque island, and I'm casually talking to him about it. I tell the couple that if they buy an island, they have to cover it, and these cheap umbrellas we sell simply won't do. I tell them they have to run a gas line to their barbeque island—don't believe you are going to be happy lugging propane tanks around. The whole point of these things is to have an outdoor kitchen. I tell them that if they don't have water and electricity, they are going to want to run those, too. I ask them if there is sufficient access to move the barbeque island into their backyard. If not, they'll have to rent a crane, and cranes are expensive, and a lot of salesmen will tell you it costs 400 bucks, but that's the lowest possible estimate, and it'll probably be at least twice that much. Grandpa and grandma raise their eyebrows and nod. I say, "I bet nobody told you this stuff, huh?" Grandpa and grandma thank me, and then they walk away, and I feel good.

"You walked another customer, huh?" Bob chides. "How's that workin' out for ya?"

And then Macy visits our booth. She loves a road trip. It doesn't really matter where. We did a home show in Bakersfield, and she came with me, and she acted like we were in Barcelona. And now she's aglow with this adventure. I take a break, and we go look at the Angora bunnies. I tell her they remind me of William. And for a string of moments, walking around the fair with Macy, who drove all the way here to be with me, my fear and anxiety evaporate. I dare to dream of living with her and William in a cozy little home as a happy, wholesome family, that maybe my life will become more than just a shocking cautionary tale.

Macy goes to the hotel, and I go back to work. The old nice couple returns and buys a barbeque island that I know they are going to love. They want to upgrade to a Viking grill, but I tell them to stick to the standard one and save $1,000, but they really want the Viking, so I sell it to them. Then a young couple comes in, and they don't jibe with me at all. They want the hard sell. I'm just confusing them with all my real talk, and my full beard and Vans and non-chino pants. The man even says, "What kind of salesman are you? Are you an artist or something?" And I laugh, because to me, that is a great compliment, but he isn't joking and doesn't appreciate my laughter. And then the fear rises up in me, a direct transfer from his angry eyes. If he knew I was a registered sex offender, he'd probably call security or want to talk to the manager and ask why he'd hired a dangerous felon. Then it occurs to me that I'm not going to make enough money. I've only sold one island. I got lucky. Just give the angry man what he wants, Joseph. Be a dickhead salesman.

Bob smokes a cigarette and stands across the path from our booth, hawking my interaction with the displeased couple.

"Bob!" I shout across the path. "Can you help me out?"

There is another unoccupied salesman in the booth I could have gone to, and, by his own admission, Bob is an absolute snake, but he was kind enough to teach me some of his salesman's tricks when I was first hired. He fumbles to put out his cigarette, surprised at my request.

"These two nice people are really interested in this beauty-of-an-island, but I have to go. We haven't discussed prices yet. I just showed them all the good stuff about the construction—"

"Nice to meet you folks," Bob says and then wedges himself between them and me, with his back to them so they can't see him and mouths to me, "What the fuck?"

"These are serious buyers, right?" I say to them over Bob's shoulder.

"We certainly are," the angry man responds. "But we need someone who is serious about doing a deal. Your company isn't the only one—"

With great pleasure, I nonchalantly walk away while the angry man is mid-sentence. I go to the food court and buy a half-vanilla, half-chocolate frozen yogurt swirl in a chocolate-dipped sugar cone, which smells like graham crackers and divinity. I saunter around the fairgrounds admiring the flower exhibits, licking my cone like a little kid, while I repeat to myself, "You are going to be alright ... you are going to be alright." I return to our booth, and Bob tells me he sold them the most expensive model on the floor and that he's not sharing his commission with me, and he lists several reasons why. Despite his intense desire to engage in this potential argument, I simply congratulate him on his sale and think of the axiom I heard in Al-anon, "It takes two to fight." Bob scrunches his forehead and struggles to let out a "thank you," which is laced with heavy reservation, as if he knows it's a trap but can't figure out why.

The fair winds down. I'm in the parking lot, trying to recall where I parked. My clothes smell of kettle corn, and I'm hoping Macy is hungry, because I'm craving barbequed ribs and macaroni and cheese. My cell phone rings. I presume it's Macy. It's not Macy, it's Trenton. "Dude! Nice of you to call," I say sarcastically. "How's rehab?"

There is no response.

"Hello, hello, Trenton, dude?" I say, thinking we must have a bad connection. I hold my phone in front of my face to see if I have full reception bars. I do.

A woman's voice cracks and spaces my two-syllable name into three. "Jo-se-ph,"

"Uh, yeah?"

I hear crying and then suddenly realize who it is. It's Trenton's wife, of course. I think better of speaking and wait for her. She probably called me from his cell phone because she didn't have my number. Although I'm quite sure I gave it to her when I dropped her off at their condo after we visited Trenton in detox.

"I'm sorry. I'm calling you, and I can't even speak," she says, sniffling between words and jerky inhalations.

She's probably calling me because she's fed up with Trenton's relapses. It must create absolute havoc in her life. She seems so sweet and loyal. I don't know what to tell her other than go to Al-anon, which I already told her.

"It's alright to cry," I tell her. "Don't worry about it. Are you alright?"

"Trenton is dead."

The oxygen evaporates from my cells, starting in my chest and expanding out to each extremity. My throat tightens. My nerves rise up, in my forearms, my cheeks, my ears, my neck, down to my stomach. My feet tingle.

"I'm so sorry." I choke the words out and then I start crying.

We talk between sniffles and wiping of tears. Trenton never made it to rehab. He insisted on coming home first, and then he decided not to go. She came home from work. He was sitting in a chair folded over his laptop. She could tell right away. Then she confirmed her instincts. He wasn't moving. He wasn't breathing. He was surely dead. She mentions a service at Trenton's aunt's home. She wants me to have his golf gear. I ask if she needs anything. She says she'll call me if she does.

My brain blares: Okay. Alright. Okay. Alright. Okay. There it is. Uh-huh. You got that? You feel that? There it is, brother. She just said Trenton is dead. So, Trenton is probably dead.

I stumble around dazed until I find my car. I sit in my car. I dry my tears on my kettle corn-scented shirt. I start the engine. I drive, and I talk to myself. That's how these things go. I used to think there'd be a lot more to it, but there isn't. Things get practical real quick. Not long ago, Macy and I were at Trenton and Hannah's home watching the Super Bowl, eating spinach dip, talking 12 Steps.

This is not my first 12-Stepper friend to die. There have been quite a few, but never one that I considered a close friend. There was Michael. I dropped him off at his girlfriend's apartment, and he died that night. He had a big Catholic funeral, because his parents had money and his brother is a rock star. His brother stole that show, too. And then there was Dallas, the gentle artist. He hung himself by the railroad tracks, that's what I was told. And of course, Paddy. I liked Paddy.

In rehab, they ought to do what they do at some law schools on the first day of class: "Look to your left, look to your right. One of these people isn't going to make it." Actually, probably neither of them will make it. The dead pile up. Is addiction a disease? I don't know, but it sure does kill a lot of people. "Jails, institutions and death," that's what they say. I'm two for three, and now Trenton is three for three.

Back home in Echo Park, I stand near my bed and stare at my naked self in my flimsy full-length mirror. It's as if I've been given new eyes to see myself. My teeth are uneven and nicotine-yellowed. My eyelids are asymmetrical, my left lid more closed than my right. My hips are wider my shoulders. I'm bloated. I think of what is taught at Agape and .sper to myself, "As within, so without."

I move closer to the mirror. I peel the clear nicotine patch off my right shoulder, then off my left. I admire the skin debris-spotted underside of the patches. I move my attention to a blackhead on my right clavicle that's been with me since I was 19 years old. Beth, my first girlfriend, used to beg me to let her milk it. She'd squirm with delight, as the pus curled out like frosting from a pastry chef's icing bag. I press into each side of it with my index fingernails. It stings just a little, and the puss peels out. It'll be refilled within a couple weeks. I've been hiding addictions, fighting addictions, denying addictions, and hating myself for it for 20 years. My mind and soul have been affected, and my body has, too. Of course it has. I've grown around my addictions like a shrub hopelessly entwined with a barbed wire fence.

I step back, and with my new eyes, I see my entire stature as if through a security camera's lens. I'm literally crooked! There has always been this thing I couldn't quite figure out, about how I appear, especially when I see photos of myself. And now it's so obvious. My chin points down, and I push my head out, like I'm imitating E.T. I turn to look at myself in profile. It's even more drastic. But I'm not even trying. It's become my natural stance. I used to see photos of myself, and there was always something wrong. A collage of them run through my mind. I throw on jeans and t-shirt, and I pull out a photo album and a manila envelope stuffed with old photos and take them out to the patio. I smoke and look at photo after photo. There's my class photo at Pepperdine Law, the one of me at a golf tournament at Thomas & Coleman, the photos of me competing in moot court, family photos at Christmas and birthdays. It seems to have started when I was about 18. In each one, I've got my head awkwardly pushed forward and right, with my nose down, and back rounded like a question mark that's about to fall away from its sentence.

I take a last drag of my cigarette and drop the butt into the 16-ounce water bottle I've been using as an ashtray. The cigarette butts have overtaken the yellow-orange water—the same color as my teeth—so this cigarette isn't extinguished by the water, and instead burns a perfect little hole through the clear plastic, from the inside out.

I run inside and stand in the mirror, armed with my new discovery. It's so obvious now. Look at you, Joseph! I try to stand up straight, let that proverbial string pull me up from the crown of my head with my chin held parallel to the floor. It strains my neck and the base of my head like I'm pulling against taut wire. I stand against a doorway and try to put my shoulder blades and the back of my head against the back of the door with my heels flush against the door. I'm so irrevocably contorted that I can't even stand with proper posture when I try.

I laugh out loud and say, "Jesus Christ, Joseph. You are so broken that you literally can't stand up straight."

I look at myself in the mirror again. As with my *Palsgraf* revelation, the truth hurts, but it also feels good to know it. For once, I see what I actually look like. "It's alright," I try to assure myself, feeling untethered by yet another scary self-discovery. "It's just another defect to put on my Sixth Step. I don't have to fix anything today."

Macy and I sit in padded fold-up chairs, in a circle, along with a couple dozen of our fellow students listening to Dr. Ward. It's the final class. I repeat in my head, "I'm all in." I am. I've been doing everything Dr. Ward told us to do. I've been visioning, praying, and meditating. I've been trying to—wait, not trying—trying isn't doing. I've been choosing not to run with negative thoughts. I had a little slip when I was driving up to Alameda thinking about registering and a couple other times, but hell, I'm dealing with this head of mine all day long, every day. There's no rest. Even when I sleep, I dream about how broke I am or about being in jail or prison or dealing with cops trying to arrest me.

Dr. Ward says you don't need to know how it's going to happen, just believe that it will. Twelve-steppers say something similar, but I have a hard time with that, so I just envision a trail toward my desire. I can feel it. Not completely, but I can feel some of that lightness that Macy has. Macy can genuinely say, "I know it's going to happen for me!" but the best I can do right now is significantly less self-assured. "There's no reason to believe some good shit can't start happening for me, right?"

Macy drives us back to her place in Silver Lake.

"I've got two amazing prospects going," I say to Macy. "So I'll just say yes to them both, right?"

I go on to explain that I've got the barbeque islands and the commercials. With the barbeque islands, I have a huge idea. I've asked Ken to finance a barbeque island store. I'll run it and pay him back with the profits, plus interest, and for his trouble, he'll retain a percentage of the business. There is a ton of money in the San Fernando Valley, and the only competition is BBQs Galore, and they don't specialize in the big barbeque islands. So that's plan number one. Plan number two, which I'll do simultaneously with plan number one, is commercial Locations work. I'll keep following up with Tyrone. He digs me. He's the Locations guy who hired me to take photos that one time, when I was paid $600 for a couple hours work. Eventually, I'll get in the union.

"What union are Locations people in?" Macy asks.

"Hmm," I consider. "I don't know—I think it's called the 'Let's Get Joseph Some Medical Insurance and Pay Him a Living Wage Union.'"

Macy loves these ideas. I think she just wants to see me hustle like her. She believes—and tells me all the time—that if you put the energy in, you'll get results, maybe not as you planned, but God always delivers.

Keri calls. I send it to voicemail. Macy isn't that comfortable with my ex being one of my best friends. She has this once-you've-had-sex-with-them thing, which I kind of agree with, with the only exception being

Keri. Keri is like my sister now, except for that whole part of having had sex with her. I guess Keri is not really like my sister.

"So do you want to go with me to scout retail spaces for my barbeque island store?" I ask Macy.

She agrees, and we head off to the San Fernando Valley, digital camera in tow. We stop at several locations I've already mapped out. I need at least a couple thousand square feet of commercial space, completely open, with large access doors so we can easily move the islands in and out. Ken already has a shop in Anaheim, so I have an idea of what one might look like.

I'm energized. I'm all in. This is what I've been waiting for—an insurgence of energy. I'm doing it all. Why wallow in pain when I can get out and try? I've always known this. Why's it so hard to get started? It doesn't matter now. I'm going to my regular daily 12-Step meetings, and I'm the treasurer of one; I'm attending Al-anon and Agape; I'm meditating, praying, I'm making the calls to Tyrone, the Locations guy and others, trying to get commercial work. I'm sending Ken emails full of photos of different retail spaces with budgets and floor plans and business proposals. Maybe I'm not quite where Macy is, as far as believing that wonderful things are going to happen to me, but I can at least try my best and say, "Fuck it—why not me?" I can at least be neutral on positivity, and the more action I take, the more success seems like a possibility. Isn't that part of the deal? If I believe, won't I be taking action consistent with that belief?

Keri calls again, and I remember that I forgot to call her back. I sure hope it's something positive regarding the hearing to Change the Numbers.

"Homey, why didn't you call me back?" Keri asks.

"Sorry, I was too busy to pick up and then I forgot. What's up?"

"Well, you remember my mom works for Rancho Rebar?"

"Yeah, I remember going there with you to pick something up. Charming little place with a steel mill and everything, right?"

"No, that's not their steel mill. That's not a part—" Keri interrupts herself out of apparent frustration with being sidetracked. "Anyway, it was bought out by a big company, a Fortune 500 company out of Texas. Not the steel mill, Rancho Rebar. It's called CIW now. CIW Rancho Rebar."

"So there's a steel mill and then Rancho Rebar, and they were bought out by CIW? Okay ... yeah, this is really interesting, Keri."

"The mill has nothing to do with it! Jeez Louise, homey."

"Okay. Then what does it have something to do with?"

"They need a contract manager, and my mom thought of you, so I called you. I'm emailing you the application."

It takes me a nanosecond to process the absurdity of this suggestion. I think Keri feels guilty for not insisting I get help back when I got in my drunk driving accident, and now she's trying to help get my life in order, which is wonderful, but this is just a waste of time.

"Keri, I love your mom, but isn't she a secretary over there? Not exactly a lot of pull with management."

"She's been working there for ... since she was in diapers ... and ... what is your problem?" Keri says, frustrated.

"Keri, c'mon. I'm a disbarred lawyer, two-strike felon and registered sex offender. Your mom, I presume, knows all these facts. You think a Fortune 500 company is going to hire me to do their contracts? That's kinda LOL, right?"

"Actually, no, my mom doesn't know. You are familiar with the attorney-client privilege, or did they flush your brain of all legal knowledge when they disbarred you?"

"Oh, you're a funny girl, Keri."

"Look homey, just apply. It won't hurt you. I emailed it to your stupid email address, addiction commerce..."

"It's addictive content," I correct her.

"Yeah, whatever," she snipes back.

We hang up, and I check my email. It's one of those forwarded from a forwarded email and has too many attachments to deal with on first glance.

Another call comes in, this one from Trenton's cellphone number again. I'm getting a call from a dead person. There are too many dead addicts in my cellphone, and the list is growing.

"It's Hannah," she says.

I feel a pinch of anger in my jaw. I want to say, "Yeah I kind of figured it was you, not Trenton," but that's probably not the right thing to say to a freshly anointed widow. Instead I just say, "Hello, Hannah." She sounds frantic. She tells me she's cleaning out their condo and wants me to take Trenton's golf gear. I think of arguing that maybe she should just donate it, but I don't. I want his golf bag. For some reason, I really want it.

Trenton's funeral has barely passed. It was weird. What the hell is anyone supposed to say? We stood around a swimming pool. There were only a few of us 12-Steppers, but Trenton's family knew who we were. They were nice, but I think they thought we failed. They wanted to say, "Nice try, maybe next time. Oh wait…There won't be a next time." Or maybe they were thinking that I was next. Paul, who had sponsored Trenton, wasn't there. I walked around angry about that, circling the swimming pool with my plastic cup of carbonated apple juice. Paul said he didn't go to "dead-addict funerals" anymore. That's what he called them, "dead-addict funerals." I kept repeating that in my mind, "dead-addict funerals." I thought of it when Trenton's aunt was talking to me, telling me a story about Trenton's childhood, before she started crying and excused herself. I fantasized about driving over to Paul's apartment, snapping all his golf clubs, and throwing his Vespa scooter through his front window.

I'm sitting on a sea green leather couch in Kamella's tiny office, waiting for her to return for our therapy session. This is my third session with Kamella. She's Macy's therapist, has been for many years. Macy speaks of her as if she is the Oracle from *The Matrix* and she does look quite similar. I'm not convinced that therapy works, but, at Macy's insistence, I'm willing to try.

Kamella enters the room and smiles warmly and widely. "How are you, Joseph?"

"I'm fine," I say, as I recall the discussion wherein I agreed to do therapy with Kamella, and I asked Macy why I needed to go to therapy, and she said, "Are you serious?"

"Okay," Kamella starts, "Well I want to pick up right where we left off ..."

Kamella attempts to hypnotize me again. It hasn't worked yet, although it was very relaxing the first two times she tried. I close my eyes. I listen to her slow soothing voice instructing me to breathe deeply and slowly. "Envision a place of beauty and comfort," she says. The last two times she tried to hypnotize me, I made up an imaginary place, but this time, I choose the Episcopalian Church in Pasadena. After my arrest but before going to jail, when Will and I still had our law office in Pasadena, and I'd been in such anguish I couldn't take it anymore, I'd walk to the Episcopalian Church, sit in the pews, and meditate and pray. It was just like a Catholic Church, dark and quiet, high ceilings and stained glass. I listen to Kamella's voice, and I feel as if I'm falling asleep. I'm not going to fight it like I did the first two times I came here. I didn't want to embarrass Kamella. But this time I'm not going to fight it. I'm paying for this. If I fall asleep, I fall asleep. Kamella will just have to deal with the fact that she can't hypnotize me. I stop my internal dialogue and listen to Kamella's voice fade. "Go there ... you are there," she says.

I awaken. I'm not sure how long I've been asleep. I open my eyes. I'm not on Kamella's couch.

"There you are as an 8-year-old boy, sitting there. Picture him. See him," Kamella instructs.

I'm in the Episcopalian Church. I see me as an 8-year-old boy. It's me at the time when my mom and I lived in the Alley in Riverside, the scariest time of my life.

"See him," Kamella instructs. "He is there."

I do, I do. He's me. He's sitting there in the front pew of this empty, cavernous church. His feet don't reach the floor. His skin is so pure and eyes so blue and his hair is the brightest blonde. He's pretending he's not scared. His hands are pressed against the pew seat, arms locked at the elbows, pushing his chest out. His bare feet dangle nervously.

Kamella's slow voice: "Go to him slowly and sit with him."

I walk toward him. I'm barefoot too, and the carpet is a deep red, and it feels velvety against my feet. As I get closer, I see that he is shaking with fear.

My chest riles like heated popcorn kernels.

"See him. Really see him," Kamella instructs.

I see him. He's so scared. I know why he's so scared. I cry in slow motion.

"Tell him that you are here now," Kamella instructs.

I see myself over his shoulder, and then I see a close up of my own self, as if in a mirror, but there is no mirror. We look so different. What happened to us?

"I'm here now," I say to my 8-year-old self, and my tears do not interfere, they only intermingle.

"Tell him that you are here to take care of him now," Kamella instructs.

"I'm here to take care of you now," I repeat, and the sentiment is mine, completely.

My stomach rumbles up into my throat, and I squeeze my face tightly. My eyes and nose run. I feel the need to flee.

"Look at him," Kamella says, "and tell him that you will take care of him, that you will never leave him again."

I see him. He tilts his head as I contemplate the words. I see me. I see him seeing me. He's attentive, waiting for me. I'm frozen. I stay silent. He looks back behind the pews nervously. They go on forever, like an endless stadium, and fade into darkness. There is a noise and shadows emerge, revealing something coming toward us.

I open my eyes. I see Kamella. I cry. I'm embarrassed and confused. I want to dart out of her office.

"You weren't able to stay with him?" Kamella asks.

"No. I couldn't," I respond, breathlessly. I look through the lenses of her eyeglasses and into Kamella's eyes, then at her mouth, looking for a crimp, a twist, a twitch of the lips, a nod, something. Tell me something. Tell me how disappointed you are in me. But she gives me nothing.

"Are you alright?" Hannah asks.

My mind is running so hard, I'm hardly aware that I'm here standing at the security gate of my dead friend's condo.

"Oh, oh, yeah, sorry, just thinking a lot. I just came from therapy," I respond.

"Yeah, I've been thinking a lot, too," she says almost dreamily.

I can't imagine how she feels. I follow Hannah upstairs. There are boxes and piles of stuff everywhere. She tells me she's selling the condo, quitting her job and moving back to Boston; she says it with finality and urgency. She's doesn't seem meek anymore.

Hannah drags out Trenton's black golf bag and bumps an office chair, which swivels ominously. I wonder if that's the chair in which she found Trenton hunched over dead. I shake this thought and ask her if she needs help moving. She declines dismissively, as if the idea is absurd. She is eager for me to leave, for her to leave. I hug her. I tell her to call if she needs anything. I know intuitively that I will never see or hear from her again.

At home, I dig through Trenton's golf bag. There is a white leather golf glove hardened from sweat into the shape of a claw. There is a large Ziploc plastic freezer bag full of, I count, 22 refurbished premium golf balls, the kind professionals use. How perfectly Trenton. I remember him excitedly telling me about bidding for these balls on an internet auction site, and how he scored them for less than the price of one new sleeve of balls. I play with cheap balls, I think, because I know I'm going to hit most of them in the trees or out-of-bounds within a couple holes, but Trenton, even worse at golf than I am, has figured out a way to play with expensive balls and save money, because he is internet-savvy. He was internet-savvy. Trenton is now past-tense, and I'm present-tense. These were Trenton's premium golf balls, and now they are mine. It's just a transfer. Hannah will transfer their condo via a grant deed from Trenton and Hannah, as husband and wife, to solely Hannah, a single woman, and then from Hannah to whoever buys it. It's just a simple transfer of property.

I'm in the back room of the Café Tropical, where all the 12-Step meetings are held. I can smell the cigarette smoke on the woman sitting next to me. She appears to have transformed from the cigarettes-keeps-me-thin variety of smoker to the cigarettes-makes-me-look-sick variety of smoker. People are taking chips for lengths of "smo-briety." They say that: "smobriety." I like it. The dying deserve this word. I can take a "newcomer" chip or a "10-minute" chip, but that's all I qualify for. A couple days ago, I had over 24 hours without a cigarette, but now I don't.

"Anyone for 24 hours?" a man standing at the head of the room asks excitedly.

The woman next to me rises sluggishly. The people with clean-time in the room hoot and holler and cheer for her. She goes up to the front of the room, gets a hug from the chip-person, and says her name, Cindy. She says she's a smoking addict. The entire room responds uproariously, "Hi Cindy!" She holds up her little black poker chip and comes back and sits down, pulls out a keychain with several other 24-hour chips she's received, several in this room that I recall, and rattles them to show me. I smile. She raises her eyebrows in solidarity with the other person in the room, me, who can't seem to get any time off cigarettes. She's got more humility than I do. I don't even take newcomer or 10-minute chips anymore. I can't bear having people see me relapse over and over. Of course, that's the very attitude that will keep me smoking. I know this. How can I admit my powerlessness over it and let God—"the power that Is," as I now identify my God—remove cigarettes from my life if I'm not humble enough to go up there and take a chip? I've heard nearly everyone in this room, even the ones with a decade off cigarettes, talk about how many times they tried to quit. I'm not special.

A woman shares about her divorce. She shares about this every week. What a nightmare. Her husband sounds like a real prick. I bet he's in some other meeting sharing and some other person like me is thinking that his wife sounds like a real cunt. I tune her out. Less than a week ago, I went to Agape's addiction recovery meeting. The woman who led the meeting, an Agape Practitioner, is a 12-Stepper, too. I told her I can't quit. She prayed in this way they do at Agape—fast and furious, like they are claiming something, like they are saying, "This is mine!" She hugged me afterward, and it was like an Amma hug. I felt wrapped in love. She squeezed me and enveloped me, like I was a baby. I felt energized and relaxed at the same time. Macy and I left, and as I walked out, I thought I'd never smoke again. The Agape Practitioner healed me. I got four days off cigarettes, and then I was sitting at home watching a recorded *Scrubs* episode, and I didn't fast-forward through the end of the recordings and delete it like I normally do; I just let it run while I went to the bathroom, because I needed to pee. The television defaulted to the channel it'd been on, and the daytime news was on, and I could hear a news reporter interviewing a woman about a new California sex offender law that was going to be on the ballot. It would prevent registered sex offenders from living within 1,000 yards of a school or park. I flushed the toilet and rushed in, and sure enough, I heard right. I thought, "If that passes, I'll have to move, I'm most definitely within 1,000 yards of a school and a park." I was banging a pack of Marlboro Red 100's against my left palm within 10 minutes. I smoked that whole pack thinking about that law. The effects of that woman's Agape super-hug couldn't withstand the onslaught of fear.

"If you have a problem, and you smoke over it, now you've got two problems," a man says. He delivers it with a zesty mixture of cheekiness and sincerity. I'm sure he's an actor or comedian. He's one of those guys who couldn't stop being funny if he tried. He goes on. "And for you newcomers ... and this one really helped me in the beginning ... 'If you debate, you lose'. Think about that one. ... I'm Tom A., and I'm a smoking addict, and that's all I got."

I've heard Tom A. repeat those axioms many times, but this time, one caught me like a right cross to the jaw and the other a right hook to the kidney. He couldn't be more right. That's what happens to me every time. I debate whether to have a cigarette, and maybe I win a couple times, but eventually the cigarette wins. It always wins in the end.

The meeting ends. I feel frantic. I shoulder up to Tom A.

"I just realized something. You are right about the debate thing and the cravings passing whether you smoke or not, but here's the thing." I speak rapidly. "I don't want to quit smoking if I'm going to spend the rest of my life craving cigarettes. What a horrible way to live. I'd rather die young."

"Well," Tom A. begins. He smiles at me with his sitcom-close-up quality smile and pauses as if to slow me down. If I weren't so manic, I'd probably start laughing, but I don't. He adjusts his glasses and stretches his nose and clears his throat. He seems to be relishing this opportunity to speak to someone so interested in what he's got to say, or maybe this is some comedic technique. It's working. I'm rapt.

"I got good news for you, Joseph," he says, then pulls the toothpick from the corner of his mouth. "If you stop debating and don't smoke—no matter what—and you do the steps in this program, and you keep coming to these meetings, the obsession will leave. I promise. The only time I think about smoking is when I'm here. If I'm wrong, I'll refund your misery."

I pull in to the 7-Eleven parking lot and debate whether to buy a pack. "You debate, you lose," I say to myself aloud. "Tom's right. Once I join the debate, I've already lost."

I get home with my pack of cigarettes and my large coffee. I set them on my coffee table and I begin to yell at them. "You win! No more of this. I'm not getting in the ring with you anymore. You win! You own me! I'll smoke forever or not, whatever you want. I'm not going to live like this."

I sit on my futon couch, panting and flush. I catch my breath. I stare at the cellophane-wrapped red and white pack of cigarettes. Its shape, its logo, its font, its weight, its dimensions, it's all more familiar to me than my own body. I stare and do as the 12-Steppers say, I play the tape through: Yes, I'll be one of those alcoholics like Bill Wilson who dies from smoking. Fine. You win. You killed my grandma, and I'm sure you'll kill my mom and my grandpa, too. Have at it, Marlboro-boy. What's good for Bill Wilson is good enough for me. That clever bastard invented Alcoholics Anonymous, and he couldn't even quit smoking. How the hell can I? But here's the thing, Marlboro-boy. We are going to that Smoker's meeting every fucking Friday for the rest of our lives, and we are taking a newcomer chip and a ten-minute chip every single time. You like that, asshole? You and me, Marlboro-boy, every Friday. Maybe I'll start wearing you rolled up in my shirtsleeve like Patrick Swayze did in *The Outsiders*. That'd be cool, right? You'd like that, huh?

I go outside and smoke five cigarettes end to end. I have that familiar sickness in my stomach, and it makes me drowsy. I begin to throw the rest of the pack away, but then laugh and think of how absurd that is. I'll never throw away another pack. Big Tobacco owns me. I give up. You win. No more fighting. I leave the pack right in the middle of the table for the next time I decide to fuck my mouth for cancer.

NINETEEN

"The caramel popcorn was exceptional," Macy says. We alight from the dark underground hall of one of the many subterranean theaters at movie Mecca, The Arclight Hollywood.

"That's your review?" I prod.

"It was too violent and too long," she responds.

Our two-hour vacation from reality is coming to an end. I feel the comforting warmth in my chest seep out like air from a leaking tire. Macy and I walk hand-in-hand down the hall along the red carpet with its geometrical shapes, past the well-lit black-and-white photography exhibit and the smell of hot buttered popcorn. I don't want to go back to the world. I can feel the fear spread through me. I tamp it down and gather my thoughts.

"It wasn't *Goodfellas*," I say. "And it wasn't even *Casino*, although it felt like it was longer than both combined."

Despite Macy's trick right knee and her chunky heels, we decide to take the stairway instead of the escalator up to The Arclight's grand domed lobby. We follow another happy couple up the stairs, and just before the lobby's ceiling comes in to view, I see it. It's impossible not to. It's the woman's ass. The woman is just in front of us, and her wardrobe choices—black pleated short skirt, white Brazilian-cut panties, and high-heeled boots—enable this moment of voyeurism. It's an ass from the pages of *Maxim*, one that has yet to suffer the indignities of gravity or a missed Spin class. This moment is happening in slow motion. I'm shot through with the excitement of this unexpected visual treat, which is immediately overridden by a panic that I'll be caught looking at this woman's ass, and that I'll be punished. I can't imagine it's illegal for a registered sex offender to look at a woman's ass that has been thrust upon him, but certainly not turning away in a timely fashion is at least a violation of my probation. I look away just as I realize how ridiculous this thought is, and I turn toward Macy. Macy is in her own state of panic. She is looking at me, and it's quite obvious she did not approve of how long it took me to turn away from the stunning ass.

"Macy," I start my defense. "C'mon, how could I not look at that?"

Macy drives, and we fight. We fight all the way across Hollywood, down Franklin Avenue through Beachwood Canyon, past the Upright Citizen Brigade Theater, La Poubelle Restaurant, and the Scientology Celebrity Centre. My compassion wanes and my temper rises.

"Any heterosexual male would have looked at that woman's ass! It was right in our faces!" I shout at Macy.

We are behind a line of several cars at a stoplight. Macy grips the steering wheel at 10 and 2. Her knuckles fade to white. She turns to me. "It's not that you looked. It's your energy!"

I can feel a case of the fuck-its coming. I bite my tongue. I know where this is coming from. This is Macy's kryptonite. This is about her, not about me. She's co-dependent. She's the daughter of a pimp who repeatedly left, abandoning her for crime, drugs, and ass. She just got out of a marriage where her husband was cheating on her the whole time. And she's scared that I'm an untreated sex addict who is white-knuckling my addiction. She's scared that she has picked another man who is going to betray her.

Macy tells me she wants me to go to 12-Step meetings for sex addicts.

I contemplate her request. My first thought is, "Damn, girl, you already got me going to therapy!" But then I think, it can't hurt. I already go to 12-Step meetings. Maybe it'll chill Macy out. Maybe there won't be tension between us whenever we are within view of another attractive woman. Maybe she's right. Maybe my energy isn't right.

"Fine," I say.

"Fine what?" Macy responds.

"I'll go to the sex addict meetings. I don't think I need to, but if it'll make you happy, I'll try it out."

Macy is surprised. She thanks me, and she turns up the radio, and we listen to '80s pop music while we drive down Los Feliz Boulevard past grand estate homes. I think of the line from one of the AA books, something like, "None of us wants to be so lustful as to rape." It always makes me wince, probably because there is a certain basic logic to it. It's like Trickle Down Economics. It seems somewhat logical until you actually start "thin-slicing" it, as Macy would say. I wonder if people think that about me—that I was a sex addict that decided to commit a rape because I was desperate for my fix and couldn't get it any other way. I think that's insane, not because I accept the oversimplified pop psychology theory that rapes are crimes of only violence and control and not lust, but because I know myself and how my addiction worked. Rape simply wasn't part of the equation.

Here I am in some church hall in the Mid-Wilshire neighborhood on Sunday morning with a large group of men. They serve bagels, lox and cream cheese. I'm very hungry, but there is something about eating cold fish and dairy at a sex addicts' meeting that doesn't sit well with me, so I eat a plain bagel.

The meeting is just like an AA meeting, but instead of talking about drinking, they talk about "acting out" sexually. Most of the men in here are gay, and many of their sex escapades are much more drastic than mine were.

"I just kept going back," a thin, handsome young man says with no more emotion than if he was talking about eating a bag of chips. "By the end of the night, I'd been with eight men."

A man behind me whispers to his friend, "Oh Lord—enough al-fuck-ing-ready, Twink." To which the friend whispers back, "I know, right? *Hellooo*, didn't you share the same fucking story last meeting?"

I want to see what the men whispering behind me look like, but I don't turn around. I continue listening to the shares. They are strangely refreshing.

I thought sleeping with two women in one night in Mazatlán or having sex with two massage parlor prostitutes at the same time was shocking, but these gay dudes talk about having sex with multiple partners in one night like it's pedestrian. They talk about "acting out" like it's a drug, and they were just scoring their drug. Each fellatio, coitus, porn-session, all just different types of drugs. It's exactly how I was. These men's stories are different than mine only in quantity because being a gay sex addict is like being a child millionaire in a candy store.

"I'd go back to the dance floor and within a couple songs, I've got another one following me back to the bathroom ..." the man continues.

I tune Twink out, and a collage of images strobes through my mind's eye. A dark hotel in Mazatlán, Las Vegas, drunk in Tijuana, cruising in my car for prostitutes in Hollywood, Riverside, San Bernardino, and Oceanside. I'm disgusted by these memories of myself.

Two days later and I'm at a different type of sex addicts meeting. We are in a small room. Nude-colored metal fold-up chairs line the perimeter of the room. There are 10 of us. A shaky-voiced woman reads a preamble, which indicates that this brand of 12-Step sex-addiction meeting is a combination of sex addicts and love addicts. With the exception of one gay man who identifies as a love addict, the women are love addicts, and the men are sex addicts. It's like a meeting of lions and antelope, if the antelopes were addicted to being mauled and were secretly more vicious and conniving than the lions. The antelope women talk about their emotions.

"I needed him. I needed him," Lisa, the secretary of the meeting, repeats with great intensity. "No, that's a lie! I needed him to want me. That's my disease."

Lisa's eyes flicker and dart as she speaks. She reminds me of when my grandma would suddenly turn against my grandpa and say, "Don't fucking touch me!" My grandma would shout that in a crowded restaurant, her eyes aflame with hate. Lisa is dressed as if each item was selected for a different occasion: black pointy heels, frayed bell-bottom jeans, and a vintage iron-on t-shirt with an orange tabby kitten that on anyone else, I would presume was purchased secondhand and ironically.

I want out of here. It's too small a group to get up and leave without making a scene, so I endure the remainder of Lisa's share, describing how she couldn't stop going back to the boyfriend who cheated on her, and, if my metaphor decoder is working, occasionally beat her. And then there's the woman who declares she was in three different relationships with three different married men concurrently, and that she has now progressed to only one married man. And then a man describes his recent relapse involving an ex-girlfriend and porn, and Lisa reminds him, "We share in a general way." And yet he keeps referencing specific porn sites and racy internet search terms, and Lisa is aghast, and I strongly consider leaving, but I also want to see how this ends. This man has apparently just come here from the gym, and the scalp below his thinning sheen of hair glistens, reminding me of the slimy, translucent edges of lox.

The sweaty man continues, "And she walks in on me during the part where the guy is just about to blow his—"

Lisa, horrified by what the sweaty man is about to reveal, is rescued by a man who sits to her left. He admonishes, "That's too many times, Jerry. You need to wrap up now, please."

I take the opportunity and bolt to the door. There is no graceful or quiet way to do it. I noisily slide a chair aside and nearly trip on my way out. Once out in the sunlight, I sense that someone is following me, as often happens in 12-Step meetings. A newcomer can't handle the pain or whatever, and maybe needs some help, so a well-intentioned 12-Stepper follows them out to make sure they're alright, maybe give them some advice. I don't want to be a part of that, so I keep my head down and move quickly. Once through the parking lot, I accelerate to a full jog down the sidewalk, wishing I was at the meeting with my gay fellows over at the giant church on Wilshire. I'll stick with the gay guys, I think. They get me. "Acting out" sexually for me equals addiction, just like alcoholics drink alcohol and junkies shoot dope and crack-heads smoke crack. It's really that simple.

Last night something shifted. I got on my knees at the side of my bed in the dark and prayed. I went through all my standard prayers—the Lord's Prayer, the Serenity Prayer, the Third Step Prayer—and then I thought of all the people I always pray for, the list must be 50 names long now, and it always ends with the same person. I always end with Deputy District Attorney Carmen D. Villa, always. It has been years now. Even in my prayers, I could only see the red that a bull sees when I thought of her. I have an entire victim's diatribe about her: how she used me to further her career; how she refused to offer me a non-sex-offense plea deal even knowing that I'm not a rapist; that she knew I didn't intend to commit a rape that night. I've tried, while praying, to argue my way around that. "Oh, she was just doing her job." Or, "Maybe someone she loves has been raped, so her trauma made her believe that I was guilty." I reasoned that I, too, became blind to facts when advocating for my clients when I was an attorney, so I shouldn't blame her. But these are judgments, and I don't believe any of them are true. I believe she violated her duty to seek justice in my case. I believe she knowingly used the overwhelming power of the State of California to force me into accepting a sex offender plea bargain.

But isn't this the point? Anyone can forgive the innocent.

Last night, for the first time in over four years of praying for her, I said her name, without the colorful epithets, and I felt something new. I thought that she has children, and I saw her playing with her children. That was it, just a vision during my usual prayer. She was just a woman playing with her children. I said, "God bless you, D.A. Carmen D. Villa." I saw her face clearly, and she was joyous. And my burning resentment disappeared.

I wake, still thinking about how my resentment against Deputy District Attorney Carmen D. Villa was miraculously lifted.

And then I realize it.

Oh my God. I don't think I smoked last night!

I fumble with my glasses and take the four steps to get from sitting on my bed to looking out the barred front window onto my smoking patio. There they are. I run back into the bedroom and pull on a pair of pants and walk outside and sit next to my cigarette pack. Morning dew has formed little droplets that sit atop the cellophane wrapper. I pick up the pack and swipe off the moisture, which sends a tiny sheet of water onto my jeans. I count the cigarettes. Fifteen. I'm surprised that it adds up, but yes, that's right. I smoked five cigarettes the day before yesterday. Wow. I set the pack down. I don't know what to do with it. I can't just leave it here. I'll smoke them. I have to do something.

I have a thought I've never had before. I'll call someone from the smoker's 12-Step meeting phone list. I think that I'll be bothering them. It's morning. They're at work. It's absurd. What's the matter with you?

But they said to call. If they didn't really mean it, they shouldn't have a fucking phone list. They don't mean it. Nobody ever calls.

I call.

"Oh, hey, it's Joseph from the Friday meeting at Café Tropical. I'm sorry—"

"Nothing to be sorry about. How are you?" a man responds, full of pep, and with nonchalance, as if we talk every day.

"I just uh, just ... well," I say, stumbling and then regrouping. "Okay, so I woke up and realized I actually didn't smoke, or at least I didn't think I had, and I was right, and then I went out to see, and there are my cigarettes. I still have 15 sitting there. You know?"

"Okay. Good. You didn't smoke for 24 hours. That's great. Hold on, Joseph," the voice says, and I hear a woman's voice and a car door shut.

"Go ahead," the voice says as a car's ignition alarm dings in the background.

"I'm sorry. You must be driving—"

"Don't worry about it. This is huge! Getting 24 hours off nicotine is fucking huge."

"Thanks, man," I say, glad for his recognition. "So what should I do with the cigarettes?"

"As you know," he says, "throwing them away isn't the key to quitting, right? We've all thrown a pack away and sworn we'd never smoke again. We just dig 'em out of the trash or, you know, buy another pack! It's not like heroin. We don't have to score from a dealer. Actually, it is like heroin, but anyway ..." He laughs heartily. I can hear the woman chuckle in the background.

"So ...," I say.

"So, look. Throw them away, but just know you stop smoking one day at a time, and the only reason you are throwing them away is because—" A car's horn blows and he says "Oh shit!" and then laughs.

A few moments pass while the phone sounds as if it's being juggled, and then I'm on speakerphone.

"People drive like fucking idiots!" he shouts. "Okay Joseph, don't smoke no matter what, right?"

"Right," I concur.

"And call me before, not after, you smoke."

He hangs up.

I'm waiting for Ken to get back to me on my business proposal for the barbeque island store. This has to be the thing. It's perfect. I can be my own boss. No one can fire me because of my criminal record. I can use my legal knowledge for the business side and my newly acquired sales techniques. We'll build a reputation as an honest store, the only one of its kind. Who knows? Maybe I'll open up another and another. People love these outdoor kitchens. Why not? Why not believe that I can do this?

I open my email to see if Ken has responded yet. I think better of sending another email. He's busy. He'll let me know. What's next? I check my phone to see if I have a text message from Tyrone about a commercial Locations gig. I sent him a text a few days ago. "I'm ready to go when you need me," it read. He responded, "K." Okay, what's next? I scroll down my email inbox. There is the contract manager job-thing Keri sent me. Whatever's in front of me, I'll do it, if for no other reason than to put the energy out there in the world that I'm ready to start working. And, it'll be funny to tweak my résumé around. I ought to put a red flag watermark on the page, because that's what it is. All roads lead to hell. Oh, you went to Pepperdine Law, but you don't practice law? Why not? Oh, you used to practice law but you don't anymore. Why not? Hey, what's with this nearly three-year gap of unemployment? And why'd you go from owning your own law firm to working as a grunt on commercial film shoots and selling barbeque islands? What the hell is a barbeque island?

I prepare a résumé. But at the bottom, in the section where people typically add things like, "CPR Certified" or "Volunteer at Glendale Senior Center," I write: "In 2005, I pled no-contest to a felony assault I committed while in an alcohol-induced blackout on the night of July 26, 2003. As a result, I lost my California Bar license. I've been clean and sober since July 2003, and I am active in 12-Step recovery." I prepare a nice little cover letter email and attach my résumé. I hover the arrow-shaped cursor over the "send" button, as if daring myself to click it, but I don't. What's wrong? It's almost as if I believe applying for this job is a crime.

TWENTY

I drive up Hillhurst Avenue past the dream homes that lead into Griffith Park. I don't have enough money for a bucket of range balls, let alone green fees to play nine holes of golf. It's been two weeks since my last commercial gig, and the home show I was relying on to pay my rent was canceled.

I pull into Roosevelt Golf Course's parking lot. It's the middle of the week, I can practice here for free. There are two giant putting greens, which are alternately closed, and there is a driving "range" that is one part abandoned carnival booth and one part derelict batting cage. I've never seen anyone else use it. There are six hitting stations, three on each side of a squatty broken kiosk, where, many years ago, tokens were inserted and balls dispensed. Each station has a thick, square, green mat atop concrete. The deeply worn mats face a half-dome of tattered black double-netting. The hitting cage is designed so that golf balls hit the net about 15 feet in front of the hitting stations and then roll back down a slope into a catch basin. But now the green outdoor carpeting and the wood slats that once guided the returning balls are so tattered and weather-damaged that most golf balls get caught in little pockets of dirt, weeds and carpet tears.

I walk over to the driving cage and set down my golf bag. I get the feeling that the old man in the starter's booth is going to holler at me over the loudspeaker, "What are you doing? That thing's been off-limits for 10 years!"

The air is damp, and it's overcast. I open my golf bag's long side pocket and pull out Trenton's gallon bag of refurbished premium golf balls all labeled "Titleist ProV1." One ball looks like it's never been hit. It's dimpled white surface shines like wet glue. All the other balls are marked "1" or "2," but this is the only one marked "3." I write Trenton's initials, "TP," on it with my blue Sharpie, and I put the ball back in my golf bag. "Much better than ashes," I mutter to myself.

I begin to slash, cut and flub balls into the net with my seven-iron. After several swings that clang off of every part of my golf club except the center of the clubface, I finally hit the sweet spot. It sends a warmth of goodness up my arms and through my body. I try to repeat the swing. I want that feeling again. I pull back and let it rip. I shank the ball off the hosel, the part of the club that connects the shaft to the head. The ball fires dead right into a portion of the netting that is for safety, not golf.

"God fucking damnit!" I yell.

I'm shocked and embarrassed by my own lack of self-control. My cussing feels involuntary, like a sneeze. I peer over my shoulder to see if anyone on the putting green is gawking at my outburst, but there is no one there because it's closed, and the putting green that's open is 40 yards away, far enough away that my outburst was probably muffled enough to be mistaken for the cry of a typically frustrated duffer. I sit cross-legged on the dirty golf mat and rub a golf ball between my right fingers and thumb. The ball has black markings from the dirty net, and its pristine whiteness of just minutes ago is now dull and grey. I spit on the corner of my golf towel and scrub the ball vigorously. I'm able to revive it somewhat, but I know it'll never be the same.

My phone rings. I dig into the upper pocket of my golf bag and accidentally press the button to answer the call before I see who it is.

"Hello, this is Joseph," I answer.

"Joseph, it's Ken."

"Howdy, Ken."

"What do you mean, hello this is Joseph? I called your cellphone. You can fucking see my name—"

"I accidentally pressed the button when I went to grab the phone, from my, uh ..." I stop myself, deciding not to say golf bag. It'll send the wrong message. I continue, "Anyway, Ken. Jesus, you really care how I answer the fucking phone?"

Ken laughs.

I'm so relieved to hear from Ken, a friendly voice. We can finally work out the details on opening my barbeque island store.

"I've got some good news and some bad news," Ken announces, and apparently isn't going to give me the customary choice of order. "We got a show in Tucson next week. Should be solid. I need you to close hard on this one, just like the last one."

"Of course. I'm top sales and have been for the last half-dozen shows. This one will be no different," I say, half-jokingly, half-cocksure, but still more cocksure than I feel, and also realizing Ken doesn't really care who sells his barbeque islands as long as someone does.

"So, what's the bad news?"

There is a pause and then Ken says bluntly, "Joseph, I can't go forward with the store."

I feel like I'm alone in an elevator, free-falling because someone just cut the cables. I know there is nothing I can do, but I can't help but try.

"Ken. I've put in a ton of time on this fuckin' deal, man. I have all these good spots. The Valley is the logical next step for us. The terms make sense. C'mon, Ken, you know you can trust me, and you know I can sell. It's just—"

"It's not that, Joseph," Ken interrupts. "It's just cash flow right now. I've got so much sunk into the maquiladora, and the home shows aren't what they used to be. The home equity loans are drying up. We used to sell 20 islands a show. Now we are lucky to do 10."

"Okay fine, Ken. I get it. Then just co-sign on a business loan, and we'll go that route. No *problemo*."

Silence.

"Ken, please!"

"Yeah," Ken says, distractedly. "Look, Joseph. I trust you. You are a, uh, you know, pretty good salesman, and you were an even better lawyer, but I'm not going to go into this retail shop with you … in this environment, when you don't have any skin in the game."

I contemplate arguing, but I realize it's futile. The AA phrase "restraint of pen and tongue" crosses my consciousness. "Okay, fine," I say as politely as I physically can. "I'll see you in Tucson."

I stand up. I feel drained and dizzy. The sun has broken through the clouds, and its rays bake my fear. I nudge a ball into place with the toe of my seven-iron. I swing, and I strike the mat several inches behind the ball. The ball trundles three-quarters up the slope, maybe 10 feet, rolls back down, catches a chunk of ripped outdoor carpet that forms a little ramp, pops over the collection gully and lands on the mat back at my feet.

My anger rapidly melts into a physically heavy depression, and it takes a Herculean effort to collect my now-filthy golf balls and lug Trenton's golf bag back to the car. It must weigh 200 pounds. Driving down the hill, my cell phone rings again. I pull over to answer it in front of a white, two-story Spanish-style home with a massive dormant rose garden.

"Howdy, Tyrone," I answer, masking my surliness with sunshine. "I'm glad to hear from you. How are you?"

"I'm fine Joseph."

"Is everything alright?" I ask impatiently. I can't stand to wait for even a second longer. I need him to tell me we have a solid gig; that I'm going to work Locations with him for 600 bucks a day; that I'll get to use those hours toward getting into the Union. This is what I need to hear right now.

"Uh, look. Joseph. I can't use you. You keep calling and everything. I appreciate you trying. I mean, you know, uh … You keep trying, but I'm having a hard time getting, you know, any work, and so when I need someone, I'm usually obligated to go union ..."

"But if that's—you know..." I pause, so as not to burn a bridge that may be burned anyway. "I just mean, why didn't you tell me that from the beginning? I mean, c'mon, nobody is going to work harder than me, Tyrone."

"For someone inexperienced, you did good work," he concedes. "Look man, I did you a favor. And most guys wouldn't even be calling you. They'd just ignore you. You know how the biz is."

"Okay, I appreciate it Tyrone, but why never. It sounds like you are saying, never. Is that right?"

"Joseph. Look, you know I didn't know about everything, you know ... about your, uh, past. You know, it's a bit of a risk working with you. I mean you know, right? You used to be a lawyer, for God's sake ..."

There is silence. It's as if he's waiting for me to say something, but I can't. I'm stuck. This is too much. My mind is spinning.

"Man, Joseph. Look, I'm sorry about this. Hey man, I've got another call coming in. So I gotta let you go." Tyrone hangs up. I hold my phone out and stare at it. After several seconds, the face of my phone returns to its home screen as if nothing happened.

Macy and I park on a street in a posh neighborhood just north of Santa Monica. Only the home's pale roof is visible above a very serious wall. We are buzzed in through a security gate. A woman opens the front door. She is Hollywood royalty. Her face reads melancholy despite a smile that stretches across her giant actress head. She seems severely fragile.

"Macy, how are you?" She hugs Macy for a purposefully long time.

"This is Joseph," Macy introduces me.

I shake her hand and try not to act starstruck. Macy and I follow her into her home through a crowded living room with stained oak furniture and a tall, perfectly-shaped Christmas tree with pale pink and green ornaments. There are familiar shiny trophies on the mantle. I recognize the Grammy, and I think one is an Oscar or an Emmy.

We walk past a Hispanic woman who is tidying up, and into a living room that is open to a kitchen. It's all immaculate yet comfortable. The backyard is filled by a carpet of green grass and a spectacularly blue rectangular pool.

"Hey Macy," a man says. He looks like the male version of Macy. Macy says he's a rock star, but I've never heard of him.

Macy hugs him familiarly. He says William is playing in Casey's room. Macy asks for him to show us the new digs, and he says there is nothing worth seeing except the pool house. We follow him out. It's a fabulous thing. The walls open up so that it flows into the backyard. It's part recording studio, part high-dollar tree-house.

He takes us to Casey's suite-sized bedroom. Casey is William's best friend. There are several kids in the room. Casey has a full-sized pinball machine, and William is playing it while another boy leans on it, following the action. Casey sits on his bed and strums a guitar.

I break into a sweat as it suddenly dawns on me that I'm in a room with the children of Hollywood elite. It would not be good for anyone, especially William and Macy, if they found out that I was a registered sex offender.

A man walks in and greets his son. His son bemoans that it's time to leave the sleepover. The man is so famous that he probably can't walk around in public outside of Malibu without being chased by paparazzi.

"Nice to meet you, Joseph," I hear him say, in an English accent, above the chatter of my brain.

I'm thinking that I should assure him that I am not affected by his fame, which is a lie, and that, more importantly, I should make a preemptive strike and explain to him that I am not a threat to his son or any of the other children in this room.

"Is this one yours?" he asks.

"No, no," I profess. "William is Macy's son. I'm Macy's boyfriend."

"He's adorable," he says.

We leave before anyone discovers me.

Macy drives and speaks into the rear-view mirror, trying to get William to tell her something, anything, about his sleepover. I stare out the window into the middle distance. My heart feels heavy. I ponder our visit. Something is wrong. It occurs to me that for the first time ever, Macy didn't introduce me as her boyfriend. I can feel her pulling away. I want to blame it on her. I want to say to her, "Oh, now that you are having success, you aren't really feeling me, huh?" I want to remind her that I loved her when she was still a broke, single mom, failing out of her job as a local news copywriter, fresh off her third divorce. In one of our more memorable arguments, I told Macy that she might just consider that maybe I've had something to do with her success. Maybe being with someone who believes you are a super-talent even when the world doesn't see it yet was that extra push she needed to make it. She took this as me taking credit for her success, and it made her mad as a hornet. I've always given her credit for guiding me in my spiritual life. She took me to Agape and Amma. She opened up my mind to a whole world of artistry and a belief in something greater. When I felt like giving up, she told me that I had to do what she does: "Whatever it takes!" And I've followed her guidance, even when I didn't want to, as with therapy and sex addict 12-Step meetings. I guess I just want some credit, too.

I could blame her pulling away on the real danger that comes with dating a registered sex offender. It's explosive. There is no question that if people found out it could harm William and Macy. I do believe that Macy fears this. She tells me that it's no one's business, but I know what she really fears. She fears my fear. She believes what is taught at Agape. Fear is just a prayer for the worst to happen. My insistence that the reality of being a registered sex offender is harsh and scary is a promise that it will be harsh and scary. I understand this intellectually, and I'd like to change my thinking, but I'm not there yet.

As much as I'd like to blame Macy, the truth is, I'm not sure we belong together. I suppress this feeling. I tell myself that the "in love" feeling always wanes. I tell myself that relationships are hard work, not fairy tales. I tell myself that my addictions have affected me emotionally and sexually, that I just need more time in recovery. I tell myself that I'm committed, and it doesn't matter how I feel now. That's not how relationships work. But it doesn't matter. That still, small voice comes through. It says, "Maybe you are more of a fan of Macy than her lover." "Maybe you needed each other when you were both fresh off of life crises, and now it's time to move on."

We are almost at William's dad's house. William is playing his Game Boy. Macy turns down the radio.

"Are you alright?" she asks.

"I'm fine," I respond, "Just daydreaming."

I think to myself: Fuck all that nonsense. I've talked my way out of every relationship I've ever been in. I'm not giving up on this one. Whatever the problem, we'll work it out. I'm not giving up.

We arrive at William's dad's house to pick up William's backpack for school. I offer to stay in the car, so as not to cause any waves. Macy surprises me and says I should come up. I think, it must be a bit of rebellion on her part, a "fuck you" to Leo for the painful therapy session we endured with him and Karen Grisham. Leo and Molly are both home, and they both pretend they aren't shocked to see me. They both awkwardly blurt pleasantries. I've nothing to hide. But I was wrong about what I said to Leo in therapy, and I want to tell him so. I want to say, "I can't say that your son is better off with me in his life. You and Karen Grisham may be right. I may be a danger to him, just not directly."

"Hi Leo," I say dryly. "How are you?"

I stand in the living room. It's in a state of mid-remodel that makes me feel uneasy. They are installing the usual stainless-steel kitchen appliances, opening the kitchen to the living room, and adding a pale wood floor.

Their dog, a Rhodesian Ridgeback mutt mix, growls and then barks at me. I kneel down and beckon to the dog. Dogs love me, because I love them. This is a fact that I know with absolute conviction. And yet, their dog moves in closer and bares its teeth.

Leo says to the dog, "Daisy, no!" and then to me, "Oh, it must be the beard," which makes me feel even worse, because he's trying to find an excuse for me, but I know what everyone is thinking: Dogs are perfect judges of character. Everyone knows that. This confirms my unfitness to be around William.

"I don't know," I say, truly confused. "That's weird. Maybe you're right, must be the beard."

I'm shaken by this canine betrayal. I recall being a kid and at my aunt's house, it was just me and her. Uncle Billy wasn't there, and this creepy salesman came to the door. Ranger, my favorite dog, a big black Labrador, a dog that loved everyone, he lost his doggy mind, baring his teeth like a rabid wolf. We could barely hold him back. Ranger practically burst through the door. And I could see it in that salesman's eyes that he'd been discovered. That's always been my proof that dogs just know.

I bend down again for another try. "C'mere Daisy, c'mon ..." Daisy bares her teeth and growls even more viciously. For a moment I think Daisy might even attack me. Molly must think so, too, because she grabs Daisy by the collar and walks her into the bedroom. This is so damn awkward.

"I guess I'm the creepy guy," I say and immediately regret it.

Leo responds kindly, "Oh, it's the beard. Don't worry about it."

"C'mon, William," Macy says, breaking the awkwardness. "We're going to Game Stop to get you some Yu-Gi-Oh! cards."

The three of us drive down the hill. William is excited to go to Game Stop. I'm happy to be leaving but still shaken, and Macy, I'm convinced, is thinking about breaking up with me.

A 909 number appears on my cell phone. I don't answer it. 909 is the Inland Empire. There is nothing in the Inland Empire for me, save a few old friends that I'm not prepared to talk with right now. We do not regret the past nor wish to shut the door on it, sayeth the Big Book. Well, I'm making an exception for the I.E. I've had plenty enough of that shit. I'm never going back.

I listen to the voicemail.

"Hello, this message is for Mr. Naus. This is Connie from CIW Rancho Rebar. We'd like to set up an interview with you for the position you applied for ..."

I forgot. Rancho is in the I.E. Rancho is about as I.E. as I.E. gets. I don't understand why she's calling me. This is probably one of those corporate compliance things where they have to interview a certain number of people before they can award a job to an insider. In fact, I remember going to an employment law seminar when I was a lawyer and hearing that discussed. Fuck that. I'm not driving 60 miles out to the I.E. to fulfill someone's corporate compliance regulations.

I call her back immediately and leave a message. "Hello, this message is for Connie. I received your call, and I appreciate uh ... I just don't want to waste anyone's time. Did you review my résumé? I just want to make sure you understand that I am a disbarred lawyer and have a felony conviction for an assault I committed during a ... uh, blackout. Call me back if you are still interested. Otherwise, I'll assume you didn't have a chance to review my résumé before you called. Thanks."

———————

TWENTY-ONE

The entryway to the Rancho Cucamonga Bass Pro Shops is bigger than many of the stores in the outdoor mall that it shares a parking lot with. Its logo is posted everywhere. The logo is of a bass frozen in time, at the apex of its signature move, an above-water aerial that resembles a twisted boomerang. I recall several years ago, sitting in a dentist's lobby, staring at a wall-mounted television, anxiously waiting for my dentist to dispense my physical and fiscal pain. On the screen was a goateed man in a magnificently appointed, flat-keeled bass fishing boat, sitting in a stern-mounted chair, angling while wearing what appeared to be the top half of a NASCAR driver's uniform.

There is no one around in this Bass Pro Shop entryway, as the store has just opened, so I get right up on the Bass logo and examine the fish carefully. Yes, it has a dead eye, I confirm, a tiny dead fish eye. Despite its athleticism and beautiful markings, it has clearly conceded defeat.

A sign next to the logo reads "180,000 Square Feet!" My barbeque island store was going to be around 5,000 square feet.

"May I help you?" asks a woman sporting a khaki vest with a bass logo.

I continue reading a sign on an easel, taking this opportunity to confirm its outrageous claims.

"You have entire boats in here?"

"Yes, we do. Would you—"

"You guys have a fishing, uh like, aquarium, in here?"

"We do," the lady says, her voice indicating her resignation at waiting-out my astonishment, as I read each item of the advertisement.

"A shooting range?"

"Yep."

"A restaurant?"

"Yes, sir."

"Bows ... I can shoot bows, like bows and arrows?"

Her face twists as she realizes this is more of a skit to me than a genuine interaction. I consider apologizing and explaining that giant retail stores, massive casinos, malls, freeways wider than four lanes each way, and anything else that exemplifies the multiplier effect, alter my mood into something I might describe as a laymen's imitation of low-spectrum autism. Some might even call it a minor fetish.

"Is there something specific I can help you with, sir?"

"Oh no, sorry. It's just a little overwhelming—right? I mean, look at this place."

I wander about the giant woodsy themed retail monstrosity. I might be the only customer in the whole store. It's 9:15 a.m. on a Tuesday. I left Los Angeles at 8:00 a.m. for my 10:15 a.m. interview at CIW Rancho Rebar. It's a 50-mile drive, so I left early. Traffic is always a wildcard in Southern California, and showing up late to an interview, even a ridiculous interview like this, is a death knell.

I walk across the parking lot to the Victoria Gardens outdoor mall. I don't see any gardens, but there are dozens of meticulously maintained chain retail shops and restaurants. There is a little choo-choo train that winds through the mall. I have more time to kill, so I go into the mega bookstore. I peruse the shelves and pull books down randomly. I hold a beautiful navy blue hardback up to my nose and take a deep whiff of its new paper. A clerk sees me and smiles knowingly. She understands. I return her smile and open the book, careful not to crack the spine. The font is subtle, and the precision of the printed word on the page is immaculate. Books remind me of my mom. When I was a kid, she always had a book going, no matter how bad things were, maybe because of how bad things were. One of the first books I remember reading was *Flowers in the Attic*. I'd been transported to another world, far more than when watching a movie or a television show. When I was a teenager, I'd dreamt of writing a novel. That was before all my free time and energy was spent on prostitutes, alcohol, and cigarettes.

I pull into the parking lot of CIW Rancho Rebar. The building is no-frills. Beyond the office building and a large sliding gate is a giant metal roof, supported by square metal beams. Underneath it are men in helmets and welding masks, and men driving forklifts between various industrial contraptions, all somehow related to the one thing that this place exists for, rebar.

I announce myself to the receptionist and wait in a chair of pure utilitarian quality. Minutes later, a man appears.

"I'm Ted Wilkinson, regional manager," Ted says, all smiles. He's my height, and trim, in his late 50s, and commercial-handsome. He's pretty much exactly what I expected. Nothing to dislike—everything from his hair to his shoes is standard issue.

I follow Ted down a narrow hallway. The old tile is lit by fluorescent lights set into the low drop-ceiling. There are rooms on the left and right. We pass a sad break room. It's decorated with corporate-compliance posters about minimum wage and sexual harassment, a wall-mounted fire-extinguisher, and a large three-burner coffee maker with one orange-rimmed and one brown-rimmed glass pot. A woman looks curiously at me. We pass a conference room with a framed poster on the wall that reads "Team Work" and has a photo of a group of skydivers holding hands mid-air, forming a symmetrical cluster. Ted's office is devoid of personality besides several golfing trophies. I stare at them.

"Kelly says you are a scratch golfer, did I hear that right?" Ted asks.

I sit down across the desk from him.

"She must've misunderstood. I'm a hack golfer, not a scratch golfer. I'm not even quite sure what scratch means."

Ted chuckles.

I hope I'm not here because Ted thought he was bringing in a ringer for corporate golf outings.

"Oh, well, I guess I got that one wrong. A, uh, scratch golfer is someone who has an index of zero," Ted explains, and continues to explain, presumably because of the blank look on my face, "It means, basically that a golfer with a zero ... okay. So, a zero shoots par a lot of the time."

"Oh," I say. "The idea of shooting par on a real golf course is something I can only dream of."

"Yeah, well, I've been playing all my life and I've never done it—come close, though," Ted says, seemingly reminiscing for a moment.

Ted explains that he runs the entire west coast of the company. There are several shops like this, and they have thousands of employees, mostly union ironworkers who install rebar on high rises, many in downtown Los Angeles, including the Staples Center, and parking structures and anything with concrete.

I still don't exactly get what rebar is, and since I don't really think I have any chance of getting this job and drove all the way out here and will probably never get that Bass Pro Shops fish logo out of my head, I figure, what the hell, just ask.

"I'm a bit embarrassed, Ted," I say. "You know, when I was a lawyer, I really did my best to be prepared .... Anyway, what exactly is rebar?"

Ted laughs. I like him.

"Oh, it's reinforcing bar. Anytime you see concrete in a building, a freeway bridge, a parking structure, there is rebar underneath. It's laid down ... Here," Ted spins his computer monitor around and shows me a photo of a large worksite with men frozen in time lying rebar down atop the bottom of freshly excavated earth. A crane boom is visible, and from it hangs a bundle of rebar.

"Oh, okay, okay. I get it. I remember inspecting a home being built before the foundation was poured when I was an attorney, and I was doing a lot of real estate litigation, and I wanted to learn the basic process of how the plumbing goes in and such, and they had rebar laid out."

"You got it," Ted says and spins his laptop back around. "So, you used to be a lawyer. What do you know about contracts?"

"Well, I'm aware of the basic structure of deals in construction: owner, architect, general contractor, subs. I know construction liens and generally how bidding works, on a theoretical level, at least. I've represented several big and small contractors, mostly fencing and general contractors, never concrete or rebar, obviously. Actually, my dad owned a fencing company. He didn't do public bids, but I learned something about the practicality of construction contracting. But as far as contracts go, I imagine the big money issues, outside of trade-specific scope issues, are about the usual suspects: ADR, attorney's fees, choice of venue, insurance, and of course, the biggie, indemnification—"

I stop speaking when I see Ted's eyes light up at the word "indemnification." I can tell he is dying to tell me something.

"Indemnification—that's a million-dollar word," Ted says with gravy dripping off every syllable. He goes on to tell me a rather typical litigation story of how CIW Rancho Rebar had been the rebar contractor on a freeway bridge on the 210 Freeway, and how the architects blew the design, and how it had nothing to do with rebar and yet CIW got dragged into the case for over a year and had to pay several hundred thousand dollars to settle it, just to get out of it and stop racking up attorney's fees.

"I shouldn't have said that," Ted says.

"What?" I ask.

"Several hundred thousand," he says and exaggeratedly looks around his office as if searching for spies. He says, hushed, leaning forward toward me. "It was a confidential settlement."

I laugh, cautiously. I'm not sure how much he's joking. But then, apparently, completely, because he joins in with me.

"Let me guess," I say. I'm doubling down on the informality of the moment to show off my knowledge. "Rancho Rebar, since it's now owned by a big Fortune 500 publicly traded company is self-insured to five, no 10 ... 10 million?"

Ted smiles and pumps his thumb skyward to indicate more.

"Twenty mil?" I ask.

"Bingo," Ted responds.

"And I imagine," I continue, feeling as if I'm really on a roll here, "that given the nature of trade subcontracting, you have an attorney that Rancho Rebar has used forever and you don't use the insurer's attorney until you reach the limit of the self-insured amount. And they usually just hire him if he's willing to accept the hourly they'll impose on him. And you use Donald Stripe, right?"

Ted is shocked. "How did you know that?"

"Well, I just did a Westlaw search and saw his name come up as representing Rancho Rebar, and I know him from a couple different cases. Solid attorney. He wrote a little book on mechanic's liens, I think I still have it, a little orange book."

"Very impressive, Joseph. You are obviously well qualified, actually, over-qualified ... obviously," he laughs nervously, and picks up my résumé. "But about this...situation referenced at the end, here."

"Yeah ..." I say and take a deep breath. "Well, it's like I wrote on the résumé—"

"I have to apologize. Connie, from HR, mentioned something about this trouble you had, but I'm just now reading the specifics here."

"Oh," I say a little too disappointedly. For a moment I let myself believe I had a chance at this job, but now I know I'm here because Ted didn't do his homework. "I had a very serious DUI, back when I worked at Thomas & Coleman," I tell Ted.

"T&C? Great firm," Ted says.

"Yeah ... well. I left T&C, and unfortunately, I didn't quit drinking. I thought I had a driving problem, not a drinking problem. So, I moved and got a better job at a firm in Santa Monica. They don't exist anymore, but they were an offshoot of O'Melveny and Myers."

The world seems to pause for a moment. Everything seems surreal. Telling this story—it doesn't seem like it really could be happening. Here I am in this office, in another situation I wouldn't have ever thought possible.

I continue. "My DUI case settled. I was very lucky. So, I left that firm because I was drinking so much and just, uh … things were getting worse, and I joined up with a friend from law school who needed a partner. You know, despite the DUI, I was still a commodity, at least in my head."

I pause for laughter, but Ted doesn't laugh. He's intently listening.

"Anyway, I keep drinking and one night I black out again, but this time, really bad stuff happens. I got in a fight with someone and got arrested and ended up in jail and they charged me with a host of crimes, but I ended up pleading guilty to a felony assault."

"Oh, wow," Ted says. He seems engrossed in my story.

"Yeah, I went to rehab and then sober living, and I had to do a short stint in jail and also did what's called a 90-day evaluation."

"That's quite a story. I'm sorry."

"Oh, thanks. It seems like a nightmare that happened but didn't happen … I guess I should add, I'm sober. I haven't had a drink since that night—"

"That night, when, uh, was that?" Ted asks, looking for the answer on my résumé.

"July 26, 2003."

Ted stays quiet, so I go on.

"Yeah, well, I was just saying that, you know, I go to 12-Step meetings and help other people get sober, too. That's part of the deal."

"Huh …" Ted says, more as a noise than a question. "I've got a few employees around here who you might need to talk to."

"Gladly," I say.

Ted's phone intercom sounds. He picks up the receiver. "Just a minute," he says and hangs up. "Well, it's been a pleasure to meet you, Joseph. I've got several other candidates to interview, one waiting right now, in fact."

"I appreciate you seeing me, Ted. Can I ask you a favor though?"

"Sure."

"Whether I get hired or not, I'd like to see the yard, see what you guys do here. Is that possible?"

Ted smiles and nods his head as if I just scored the winning run. I laugh in my head and think, I'd probably get this job if I wasn't a two-strike felon, registered sex offender, disbarred lawyer!

Ted passes me off to the general manager of this location, Erik, a stout guy who used to work in the field "placing bar," as he called it. Erik shows me around the yard for a couple minutes and then passes me off to one of the workers, who clearly isn't used to giving tours. He shows me giant racks of rebar and bending machines. We wear hard hats and little yellow earplugs that I rip out of a sealed plastic baggie. A man works a shearer, cutting rebar into various lengths from 10 to 20 feet. We walk out from under the covered concrete pad where all the machines reside and onto the dirt. It must be 10 acres. There are men building cages and piles, which, I'm told, are the steel bones of the circular and square pillars that support freeway bridges and high-rise foundations. This reminds me of my dad. He'd love this.

Hector hands me a piece of rebar. It's heavy and thick. It has ridges across it, I speculate, so the concrete will bond to it. The piece I'm holding is raw and has a dusting of surface-rust on it. It dawns on me where I've seen rebar before. It's always in post-apocalyptic movies, jutting out of deteriorating buildings. And right before I went into Chino prison, I read an article in *The New York Times* that some of the inmates in a recent riot at Chino prison were able to rip pieces of rebar out of the walls because the buildings were so derelict. I can't recall whether the prison guard that was murdered during the riot was impaled with rebar, but that's the image I had after reading the article, scared out of my mind.

I go back inside the office and rack my hard hat and pocket my earplugs. I'll keep the earplugs as a souvenir of the time I ventured back out to the I.E. and visited the land of giants: giant bass fishing store, giant book store, and the giant business where they supply the rebar for all the giant concrete structures in Southern California. What a bizarre place.

A man with a British accent stands upon a tiny stage. He wears a microphone on his head; the tip of it hovers around his mouth, like an obstinate fly.

"It's amazing! It's the most amazing thing you'll ever see in your entire life!" the man says, and then looks down upon the crowd of less than a dozen onlookers that have cautiously gathered, their exit plans at the ready. He spots a bemused couple.

"Pardon me, lovely couple. I've lied to you. This is a great knife, but it is certainly not the most amazing thing you'll ever see. Are you from Tucson?"

Our barbeque island sales booth is more cramped than usual. We only have room for four islands, not six, and, even with only three salesmen, we are bumping into one another. The crowd is brisk, but that's because this is a free show, and it's over 110 degrees outside of the Tucson Convention Center, and I think most of these people are here to escape the heat and get some free home show swag.

The man selling the knives slices through a tomato and says "Amazing, right?" to a new bemused couple. They shake their heads in agreement. "What is so amazing about cutting a tomato?" he asks.

The woman looks at her man and makes a silly face.

"I jest, ma'am. This is what's amazing." He places his finger on the wood cutting board and then looks to them. "Are you ready?" he says. The woman, clearly the spokesperson for her couple, makes another silly surprised look, making an "O" of her mouth.

"You were going to let me cut my finger off, weren't you?" he says, emphasizing his Britishness.

Bob leans against the island between me and the knife salesman, intentionally blocking my view.

"There is no chance you are selling an island today," Bob admonishes me. "Even I might not sell one, in this shitshow of a home show."

"Get out of my way, Bob. Dude's going to cut that Pepsi can in half with that paring knife."

Bob snickers in response but doesn't move.

"I see you finally cut your hippie hair and beard. Macy finally tell you enough is enough?"

"She liked it, actually. I'm—"

Bob interrupts me to speak to Ned, who has decided to join our conversation. He's looking more coke-wired than usual.

"Ned. You on something?" Bob asks, then taps his right nostril with his right index finger, the universal cocaine gesture.

"This isn't a fucking home show," Ned says. "Ken flies us out here for this shit. There isn't a buyer in the bunch." Ned walks off to attack an unfortunate man who just entered our booth.

Bob redirects himself toward me. He's particularly slinky today. "We are going to get wasted tonight. That hotel bar is waiting for us. I might even get out of this bullshit show early. You in?"

"Of course I'm not in, Bob. What the fuck is the matter with you?"

"Oh, I forgot, you're sober," Bob says, pretending he doesn't recall. "What exactly is your story again? You're in AA. You used to be a lawyer. You've got this hip girlfriend. Now you are working this dead-end job."

"I'm a superhero, Bob. We've already discussed this," I say dismissively. "I'm going to go get some frozen yogurt. Make sure Ned doesn't maul that guy."

As I walk off into the packed walkway, Bob yells, "I'm going to figure out your story, Joseph."

Bob isn't that much older than me, although he could pass for 60. It's amazing that he doesn't think to simply search my name on the internet.

"Sir," the British knife salesman calls out to me. "Do you want to see something amazing?" he says as he places his finger down on the chopping block.

I spin toward him, pinching the Paradise BBQ Islands home show badge hanging from a cord around my neck.

"Half my customers are fellow salesmen," he quips. "We all need knives."

After the show, I shower and eat alone at our surprisingly nice hotel. Welcome to The Overlook Hotel, I think. I'm alone at my table, and I'm alone in the restaurant. They don't even have a waiter. The bartender takes my order. I've been up and down the elevators, through the lobby and have seen only a handful of guests. I theorize: Financially, just being open, this hotel is losing gobs of money. It's only open in the hopes, the expectation, perhaps, that things will change, that they'll get better. But at this rate, it's all net loss.

Downtown Tucson at night is quiet and hot. The businesses that are open feel reluctantly so. I walk past a closed pawn shop. There is a used Husqvarna chainsaw in the window, ominously lit by the street light. Further down the eerily empty sidewalk is a diner, and a young woman peers out at me as she locks the door from inside. She wears a pink '50s dress, has blue-black dyed hair, pulled back and bobby-pinned to a pink paper hat, and sports sleeves of colorful tattoos on each arm. She's intentionally ironic, but I'm not sure the diner is.

I pull out my cigarettes, think of how people in 12-Step meetings joke that it's not a relapse if it's in another country. Does that apply to another state? I light up. I'm not fond of walking and smoking, but there is no place to stop. If I sat on the curb, and smoked, I'm absolutely certain a police car would show up and arrest me. This is not a place to stop. I must find a place to smoke.

I walk back toward the hotel and pass a government building of several stories—a building of poured concrete that is lifted on tapered beams so that beneath the entire footprint of the building is shaded space. This is, I ponder, how cities like this are. The old downtowns of Riverside, Fresno, and San Bernardino come to mind. Once commerce moves on to newer areas, the government comes in and rents out the old beaten edifices. The Federal Prosecutor, Immigration, Worker's Comp Courts, IRS or State Tax Boards and the like have no need to impress customers.

I find a low planter wall to lean against and smoke and smoke. A security car slowly drives by. I blow puffs of smoke into the night air. I grind my foot into the cigarette butts I've left, trying to destroy the evidence. I'm sure a police car will arrive soon, so I head back to the hotel. There is a group of adobe-style, squatty buildings that reek of a forced municipal revitalization project. I follow the noise and energy of people and come around a building, and there are a few dozen people watching a movie that's being projected on a wall. Some sit on blankets and some on fold-up chairs. I watch the driving scene of an old noir detective film. No one sees me. I walk back to the hotel and find a perfect smoking spot: on the sidewall of a recessed loading dock. I think about a knife that can cut through a Pepsi can, how I belong back in Los Angeles, and that Tucson does not disagree.

I sleep well, but I wake to aching lungs and swollen lymph nodes from smoking a pack and a half last night, exacerbated by the hotel's air conditioner. I'm at the booth just before 10 a.m., and I'm the only one. Yesterday's shoppers are today's buyers, and I make two quick sales, the only sales that have been made by any of us, as yesterday was a complete shutout. After an hour, Bob shows up. Ned follows an hour later.

Bob slithers over to me and sits at a bar stool and leans heavily on a barbeque island's chalky travertine bar. He nurses a coffee and groans.

"Ned did a little drinking last night," Bob says and swivels his head around toward Ned, who is struggling to unseal a large bottle of aspirin. "Isn't that right, Ned?"

Ned ignores him.

"Good night to do it, though ... a shut out—I fucking told you," Bob says and smirks. "You are going to need to find a new job, Kemosabe."

"Lots of people but very few buyers ..." I say. I'm enjoying withholding the fact that I made two sales while Bob and Ned were sleeping off their hangovers, but it's a guilty pleasure as I am cognizant that somewhere in my new 12-Step/Science of Mind-driven life philosophy, there are clear instructions against being a smug prick.

"What is this!" Ned shouts. He marches toward Bob and me aggressively, holding out two pink legal-sized pages, shaking them at arm's length, like rattles. He stops in front of us. His eyes menacingly move from me to the pink pages and back again.

"Those, Ned, are contracts for barbeque islands I sold this morning," I say, bubbling with glee.

"Did you get a down payment? Twenty percent," Ned bellows. "It has to be twenty percent. Did you?"

"Of course I did, Ned," I reply casually.

"This is fucking absurd!" Ned yells loud enough for the growing crowd of aisle dwellers to take notice. Ned marches back to his post across the booth under the sagging palapa of our largest island. He mutters to himself.

Bob glares at me and snickers. "You little fucker. Fuck me. You lucky fucking bastard."

"That's me, Bob. Lucky Joseph. I'm going to grab some coffee," I say and begin to walk away, and then dramatically turn back. "Bob, please do me a favor. If any of my customers return, please call my cell phone or ... you know what? Just entertain them until I get back."

Bob flips me off.

I drive through an old neighborhood in Downey, an industrial city several miles east of downtown L.A. I've designed and sketched an absurd monstrosity of a barbeque island per the request of a potential customer that I met at a home show. I've abandoned the idea of "deal-or-done" that is the old-school, high-pressure sales philosophy of Bob and Ned, and decided that if I can't sell a customer a barbeque island at a show, I'll collect his or her email and follow up later. This has led to nine sales, 10 if I close today, and now I sell nearly as many islands as Bob and Ned combined. This is much more my style. I send the potential customers emails with pictures of islands, and little tidbits of information, and links to other websites, and I get to know them a little. No pressure. It's funny, while price is always the issue at home shows, it rarely even comes up when I sell an island this way. The customer just wants what they want, and I give it to them.

Most of the homes in this neighborhood are small homes built in the late '50s, just like the one my mom grew up in. I remember visiting grandpa and grandma's house when they were selling it in 1990, after having owned it for 40 years. I was in college and hadn't been there for over a decade, because family gatherings had been moved to Aunt Suzie and Uncle Billy's house, a much larger house that allowed Uncle Billy to move freely in his electric wheelchair. As I remember grandpa's house from my childhood, it seemed like a big house. My mom and I had exclusively lived in apartment rentals, so everything seemed big. But it was more than that. When I walked in, so many years later, now a foot taller, I felt like Gulliver in Lilliput. There is a photo of me standing in the front yard with my mom and grandma and grandpa on the day they moved. My head barely clears the porch roof. When I walked inside, I was shocked at how tiny the house was. It couldn't have been more than

800 square feet. There were two bedrooms, but the bedrooms weren't much bigger than a king bed. It was as if I'd been in a different reality for all those years.

I spot the 1542 address number and find parking. My customer's address is 1544. I walk toward it, and it comes into view between a row of 40-foot-tall, skinny, Italian Cypress trees on its neighbor's border. It's new, two stories, and sparkling white. The old home was apparently demolished and replaced, unlike its neighbors, who only sport conspicuous new cars, reminiscent of new-money lottery winners, spruced up lawns and new roofs, the result of refis from being inducted into the rapidly expanding California home equity millionaires' club. There is a white fountain in the front yard, a bright white Neptune with water drizzling out of his pitchfork. Neptune is surrounded by impossibly green St. Augustine grass, that, at first glance, I mistake for artificial. A row of yellow, red and white roses fence the driveway from the yard, crowding the Greek god and his little pool into an off-Broadway stage set of a classic mansion's front yard. In the driveway is a mammoth black Hummer SUV with a blinding amount of chrome, including rims the diameter of a backyard fire pit.

I press the backlit doorbell, hear the sound from inside—a muted chimes version of the dant-dant-dant-daann from Beethoven's Fifth Symphony—and I note that the giant brass knocker of Neptune's head on the front door is for display only. The eight-foot-high door opens and a woman, I presume my customer's wife, answers.

"Hi," she says, breathing hard.

"Hello, I'm Joseph, about the barbeque island ..."

She says, "Okay," breathlessly. She turns inward and yells "Honey, barbeque island guy!"

She's wearing a sweaty white sports bra that must have the tensile strength of a schooner's mast rigging in order to withstand the force of her silicone medicine balls. Her nipples look like half rolls of nickels. I look away.

"Bring him in!" a man's voice sounds out.

The smell of bacon frying wafts over me as I walk into the entryway.

"I'm in the middle of a goddamn workout!" she yells.

"Jesus Christ, Mandi!" the voice responds.

Mandi rolls her eyes, and I follow her past the living room, where an absurdly large television has a frozen image of a woman holding little pink dumbbells in front of her face, her mouth mid-word, eyes encouraging, as if she's screaming, "You can do it. C'mon!"

I follow Mandi down a hallway, and she opens double doors and walks away.

My customer is posing behind a glossy dark wood desk. On a matching credenza behind him are three large flat-screen monitors, edge to edge, displaying colorful charts atop black backgrounds.

"I work from home. I was selling home mortgages; still do—a little— but now mostly day trading," he says and nods me over.

I step around the desk and stand precariously, as there is no place for me to be in this space. He doesn't seem to care. It's as if he's reading lines from a script.

"It's all right here on these screens ..." he says and looks for me to fill in my name for him. I oblige.

"Joseph, that's right. It's all right here, Joseph. I made over a quarter million last year alone, most from refis, but a lot right here. I'm mostly in high-tech. That's where the future is. Three years ago, my wife and I were working, and barely bringin' in 60 grand between the two of us. Then I took a chance and got into the refi biz."

"Wow. Impressive," I say, trying not to sound sarcastic.

"Well, let's get to this," he says, getting up and leading me through his bacon-scented house and out to the backyard.

It actually is impressive, I think, correcting myself. Just because I think he's boorish and has horrible taste doesn't mean all this wealth isn't impressive.

His backyard is long and narrow. The island he's asked me to design is about half the entire width of it. It'll intersect the yard. It's a terrible idea, the equivalent of putting a hot tub in an apartment's living room.

"Are you sure you want it this big? You understand we'll have to bring it in on a crane in several pieces. This will be the largest island I've ever seen, and I've seen hundreds."

He's not dissuaded. In fact, he seems to think the bigger, the better. I add three feet to it. It's a 52-foot long granite counter with a stucco base, colored bright white to match the house, a bar along the entire length. It has three table-rounds, one in the middle, and one on each end, where full-sized palapas will be installed. Each end will have its own waterproof outdoor television mounted on the palapa's poles under the palm fronds. It'll have a full Blaupunkt stereo system with Bose speakers, a 54-inch gas Viking grill with meat searer, a specialized separate barbeque station for charcoal and mesquite grilling, a Viking warming drawer, a Sub-Zero outdoor refrigerator, a full-sized stainless-steel sink, and three stove-top burners. Surprisingly, I am able to talk him out of the Viking burners, saving him $3,000. The entire island is just over $30,000.

Mandi walks out to the backyard. She's freshly showered, with wet hair and sporting bejeweled and intentionally distressed jeans, high heels and a tight V-neck t-shirt with an Ed Hardy sailor tattoo design.

"Honey ... thirty G's for this thing," Sal says proudly to Mandi with expectation in his voice, as if he's trying to bait her into a fight.

She doesn't take the bait, but rolls her eyes, her fake eyelashes looking like tarantula legs, and says, "No offense, barbeque guy, but I don't even want the fuckin' thing."

I expect this is going to be a deal killer, and I'm almost okay with it. I'm absolutely broke, but I won't see any commission money from this until long after my rent is due, and I can't see past that impending deadline anyway. Also, Ken is going to go nuts when he hears all the components he's going to have to buy at top dollar from Viking. My ambivalence feels good.

I look to Mandi and shrug. I reply with something that belies my thought of supposedly not caring about this sale: "I understand. That's a lot of money. It'll be the most outrageous and expensive barbeque island I've ever seen, let alone sold."

At this, as I predict, Sal expands with pride, like a puffer fish. He laughs, almost maniacally and quotes me with bravado. "The most outrageous and expensive barbeque island ever!"

"I'm going to the store," Mandi says.

"I'm buying it," Sal responds, with spite.

"Whatever," Mandi says and walks back into the house.

"Normally, Sal," I say, "we'd only require 10 percent down, but this is like a construction project. Just the components alone are going to cost a lot. I'm going to need 50 percent," I continue to play. I can't help myself. "I don't expect you to be able to write a check for 15 grand—who can do that? It's not like your Bill ... uh, what's his name from the big computer company?"

"Bill Gates, Microsoft," Sal says, indignantly, as if he can't believe I don't know who Bill Gates is.

"Yeah, the computer guy," I reply.

Sal changes his demeanor and suddenly mellows. He doesn't say a word for a few moments while he pulls on his chin hair as if he's an actor on set and the movie director just told him to do something that makes him look like a wise man thinking. I play along and stay quiet.

"You know what?" Sal says. "I want a beer. You want one?"

I decline, and he disappears into his house, which from the back is so plain compared to the front that it looks like the back side of a Hollywood studio lot set. I sit in the sun, breathe deep and take in the smell of fresh-cut grass, and I try to pretend I don't desperately want to close this deal. Breathe. This is going to happen.

Sal comes back with a dark, frothy beer in a pint glass, the head perfect, like a vanilla ice cream cone. I sincerely expected him to be carrying a checkbook. Oh well. Sal takes a sip and holds an "ahhh" for a little too long for my comfort, wipes his mouth, and sets the glass down on the table. He pulls out a check and pops it between pinched fingers. I hand him a pen. He writes, "15,000.00" in the number box as if he's just signed the Declaration of Independence. He winks at me and says, "Who do I make this out to?"

I drive home with the windows down. The wind must be blowing the right way because I can smell the ocean, even stuck in traffic on the 60 Freeway. I think I actually like Sal. He's completely who he is, with the new money and all the tacky shit. Why not spend some money? Why not build a ridiculously large house that takes up the whole lot? He'll probably make that money back off one barbeque party full of equity millionaires just waiting to refi and pull some of that money out. Hell, he'll probably refer me a bunch of customers who want absurd barbeque islands, too.

I feel good, because Sal just bought me some time. If my worst-case scenario becomes reality, and it sure as hell looks like it will, I can tell my landlord that the money is on the way. I can even show her the contract. I've never been late on my rent in my entire adult life, but I can't see how it's not going to happen this time. Even if I start working on a commercial tomorrow, I won't get paid before my rent is due.

I've never asked my dad or mom for money in my life. My grandpa has given me money quite a few times. If it wasn't for him, I'd probably still be in jail or prison. He even co-signed my student loans—my student loans, which are somehow government-backed and yet carry higher interest rates than a home mortgage, almost as high as a car note. Between interest and penalties, I probably owe more now than I did the day I graduated law school, and I've been paying on them—granted, inconsistently—for 10 years. They are so overwhelming, I can't even open the bills anymore. When they call, I say to them, I actually say to them:

"I am a two-strike felon. I'm a registered sex offender. I'm on proba-tion, and I'm a disbarred lawyer. I'm barely staving off homelessness." To their credit and training, they don't react at all. They just stick to the script and offer me the same deferment programs I've already exhaust-ed. Then they agree to put me on a list where they'll only call weekly, instead of daily. I thank them, knowing I'll redo the whole thing—about a 15-minute process—the next week, when a new collector calls. I'm starting to feel somewhat more emboldened since my grandpa remind-ed me that I've probably already paid back the entire principal of the original loan. So while I may not be holding up my side of the contract I signed, I haven't cheated them out of their principal. I think Sallie Mae and its lobbyists are going to be alright until, if, I ever get back on my feet. Student loans are on a long list of things that depress me, and there is nothing that cures depression more than smoking, at least for the first 20 seconds or so.

At home, I smoke in the dark. I stare into the cigarette tip's ember, the color of flowing lava. Oh, my old friend, can I ever leave you? Are you all I have left? In the dark, smoking, I can feel alright. I feel a small relief at my financial stay of execution. I miss Macy, too. Something has shifted. We are still together, but it's not the same. The universal set of our Venn diagram, once nearly an eclipse, is spreading apart.

I hear the ring of my phone, and the usual dread pumps through me. Then I see the 909 number, and I'm excited and terrified at once. It's ridiculous for me to think I've got a chance at this job, no matter how well the interview with Ted went. But I'm proud of myself for doing what Macy and my sponsor suggested: Chop wood, carry water, leave the rest up to God.

"Hello, this is Connie from the Human Resources Department at CIW Rancho Rebar."

"Yeah, hello, Connie. Thanks for calling," I say. I have my television on mute, and I'm watching a golf tournament I've recorded. On the screen is a down-the-line rearview of Tiger Wood's golf swing in slow motion. Lines are being drawn on the screen by Peter Kostis, highlighting Tiger's impeccable swing plane.

"Well, Joseph. I just wanted to call to inform you that we've decided to offer you the position."

My jaw goes limp, my chest bounces and a tear squeezes out of each eye. I hold the phone away from my mouth so Connie can't hear my reaction. I begin laughing and crying, and my nose runs.

"Hold on one second, please ... just one second, Connie," I say, and I place the phone down and run to the bathroom and yank off several sheets of toilet paper. I blow my nose and then splash water on my face. I look at myself in the mirror. I look at me being happy. I have a real smile on my face—a deep, real smile. I rush back to the phone and nearly fall traversing the three steps down from my bedroom.

"Sorry to keep you waiting. I just had to, uh, sneeze and blow my nose," I say and immediately regret my over-share.

"That's quite alright. So, I presume you are interested and will be taking the position?"

"I, uh .... I'm definitely. I guess, I would uh ..."

"You'd probably like to know the package details."

"Yes, can you tell me?"

I look over at the television, and there is a commercial for erection pills on. A man who is fit and dapper and is playing mid-50s but could pass for an early-greying 30-something gropes his sexy female counterpart.

"The position starts at $76,000, with medical, dental, 401k with matching contributions, stock option plan, and discretionary bonuses. It's a management-level position."

I feel dizzy and giddy. The man and woman on my television are now in separate outdoor claw-footed bathtubs.

"Wow, I uh..."

"Our benefits are absolutely top-notch," Connie explains. "You might not consider this, but the way our stock continues to climb, the stock option can add a good 25 percent to your salary, and bonuses aren't far behind, although you will not be eligible coming in this late in the year."

On my muted television, a fidgety Irish man is preparing to hit his approach shot from the middle of a perfect green fairway. The idea of negotiating with Connie pops into my head and is immediately assassinated. I gather myself. Fear grabs me, shakes me, and reminds me that I can still blow this. I need to accept this gift now!

"I'm excited to learn about the business and get to work. When do I start?"

"Well, it'll take about two weeks to clear everything and get you started. I'll email you over the authorization forms."

"Oh ... okay," I say, surprised at how long it's going to take. I'm already doing the math on how long it'll be before I get my first paycheck. God knows I need it.

"Same email address, right?" Connie asks.

"Yes ... uh, can I ask, authorization for what?"

"Oh, just a standard credit check and criminal background check," Connie says nonchalantly.

Fuck.

A television replay shows the flight of a golf ball sailing through a blue sky, streaking perfectly in line with the flag, but instead of landing on the green and rolling toward the hole, it catches the greenside bunker and plunges deeply into the sand. Tough break.

I thought a real dream was coming true. For a second, I actually believed this could happen. Why am I being tortured? My mind scatters at great speed with a dozen ideas in a dozen different directions, and out of the chaos I'm compelled to try something, and for some reason, I'm compelled to do it now. Now! It's the only chance I have.

"Connie, I'm so excited about this position," I say, my heartbeat quickening so drastically my voice throttles. I try to modulate it back to normal.

"But, uh, I have one issue, and I'll just let you know, and maybe you can think of a way to solve it."

Empower the customer to help you, I think to myself. Humble yourself and let them be the hero.

"Well, if I can, Joseph—" Connie responds cautiously.

"See, I've been in the entertainment production field for a couple years, and in that business it's all about getting your foot in the door and being ready for opportunity. I've got several jobs lined up, and if I cancel them, and then something goes wrong, and CIW doesn't end up hiring me, I've basically ruined my career—all the work I've done to get to where I am will be lost because you can't say 'no' in the production biz."

"I see ... well. I'm sure you have nothing to worry about. You already disclosed your ... uh ... issues—"

"Exactly!" I interrupt to capitalize on her point. "I've already disclosed that I have a DUI conviction and a violent felony assault conviction that I committed in an alcoholic blackout, so that's what's going to show up on that background check. And as far as a credit check, my credit is a nightmare. I lost everything, and I'm trying to get back on my feet."

Connie is silent for a long time. I think of Bob's sale's advice: Ask for the money and shut up.

"Well, I don't know what to say," Connie responds. "I mean, I understand you have to let your employers know so that they can replace you, but we have corporate rules."

"I completely understand ... You know what Connie, let me just ask you for what I want. I want an offer in writing that I can accept and be secure in. I know it's a lot to ask, but, Connie ... I need to make sure I'm covered. Changing careers like this is a big deal, and I just want to make sure I'm covered. And again, I've already disclosed that I'm a convicted felon and a disbarred attorney and recovered alcoholic."

Connie is silent for the time it takes Ernie Els to stroke a 40-foot putt 50 feet.

"I'll have to get back to you, Mr. Naus," Connie says, rather coldly.

"Okay. Thank you. I'll wait for your call."

The line goes dead. I pick up my television's remote control and press the mute button to restore its sound. I don't know what else to do. Vijay Singh hits a towering draw nearly 300 yards down the fairway. That's what I need, a perfect shot. I gave it my all. I know that I've got no chance at the job if they find out I'm a registered sex offender.

PART III

The Spirit (Cause)

TWENTY-TWO

I can't stop thinking about the job offer. I can't stop going over scenarios. I'm in the middle of a transaction at the drug store, buying things I can't afford on a credit card I've been paying the minimum monthly payment on for years—cat food for Black Cat and toothpaste. The cashier, a teenage girl, chomps gum aggressively and asks me, "Do you need a bag?" as if the words are audible Ambien. I don't respond, and after several beats, she rolls her heavily-mascaraed eyes to signify her impatience at my non-responsiveness. I'm mentally clicking through scenarios of how my job offer might play out like I used to click through internet porn clips.

"Uh, yes. I do need a bag," I finally respond.

The teenage clerk hands me my bag and drones, as if allergic to fully enunciating consonants, "Thank you for shopping at Rite Aid."

I sit in my car in the parking lot. I face Sunset Boulevard. It's dark, and it's quiet in my car, but outside is a lively world. Pedestrians exit a long bus with an accordion middle that seconds as a billboard for an animated movie featuring a silly monster. The bus pulls away clearing my eye line to the traffic on Sunset. It's fall, and it's getting darker earlier, and the holidays are coming. I love the holidays. Macy doesn't share my opinion of the holidays, but some of my zealousness rubbed off on her last year. We even went to the mall with William, and I felt an old joy. Things are just better during the holidays. There is something to look forward to, even if it's just some time off from work or school, and it permeates everything and everyone. Right after Halloween, I can feel it coming with the Santa Ana winds. Last year, Macy and I took William trick-or-treating in a popular neighborhood in Silver Lake. William is normally reserved, but he was skipping with joy, just bouncing from house to house. I felt warm. I felt wholesome. I'm feeling some of that now, thinking of how it might feel to have a real job again. I'll be able to buy William a Christmas present. And I'll be able to take Macy out to dinner.

Just as I'm about to start my car and head to a meeting in Atwater Village, Macy calls. I excitedly tell her of my possible good news, my conversation with Connie from CIW. Macy politely cuts me off. Another bus pulls up, this one shorter, this one with a career college advertisement featuring a smiling young Hispanic woman in a white lab coat.

"We can't keep doing this ... I can't keep doing this," Macy says softly.

I feel the gravity and finality in her voice. I let it sink in. She's serious. For just a second, I contemplate saying okay and hanging up. That is exactly what the old Joseph would do.

There is a long silence.

"Joseph?" Macy says.

The old Joseph knows exactly what to do. Freeze the blood in my heart; ruthlessly cut her out of it; move on; never look back. "Yeah, I'm still here," I say softly into my phone.

"Are you going to say something?"

Just hang up, Joseph. Cut her out. No, I can't do that. I'm not that person anymore.

"Macy, I love you. I've done everything you've asked of me," I implore.

"It shouldn't be this hard, Joseph. I just can't keep this up with—" Macy says, her voice steady and low.

"Don't you love me?" I ask.

"Of course I do," she responds, her voice cracking.

I break into a full sob.

"Nobody knows you like I do," I say. "Nobody laughs with you like I do ... I believe in you!"

I try to stop crying, but I can't.

"Joseph, I know that, and I love you, but I need someone who—"

I know what she's about to say. She going to say the truth. She needs a lover, not a fan. She needs someone who doesn't just love her but who is in love with her. And I know she's right, and I can't bear to hear it. I begin yelling, attacking her. I feel ashamed before I even start, but I can't stop. "I was there for you when you weren't successful. Now you've got a big-time Hollywood writing job and things are good, and you are just going to be done with me. After all this time, I'm too much of a liability now! I knew you were a star before anyone else did. You think that doesn't matter—that I'm not part of your success! You're just going to abandon me now that you've made it!"

"You know it's not that—" Macy says, keeping her cool.

"Fuck it isn't Macy!"

I hang up on her, and I hate myself for it. I turn my phone off. I sit in my car and stare out the windshield at passing cars and busses for a long time.

I go back into Rite Aid to buy a pack of cigarettes.

"Marlboro Red 100's in a box please," I say to the same teenage cashier who sold me the cat food and toothpaste. I begin to cry again.

The cashier swipes the cigarette pack across a scanner.

"I guess today isn't the day to quit after all," I say, sniffling.

She looks up at me, seemingly confused about why I'm speaking to her. And then I can see in her face that she recalls that I was in here just a few minutes ago, and then she registers that I'm red-faced and tearful, and a panic invades her face.

"Yeah, uh, I guess not," she replies and burps a nervous laugh. Her lower lip relaxes and her eyes widen. "Here's some matches?" she says as if answering the question, "How do I respond to a tearful man at my cash register?" and hands me two packs. With a rattle from an automated change dispenser, several coins tumble down a metal slide into a basin.

"Don't forget your change, and I'm uhm... sorry," she says. "Try to have a good night." She smiles at me, genuinely, softly.

I sit on my porch and open my brand-new pack of cigarettes. Six months of smobriety gone. I smoke, drink coffee and recall memories of my times with Macy and William. Macy and I at Agape, Macy sitting across from me eating fries on our first date, her precocious smile, her dancing on her living room coffee table to Prince, us holding hands and walking under the dim yellow street lights, she and I reading a bedtime story to William and tucking him into bed. It's five cigarettes worth of memories.

I go into my apartment, and I open my email account to see if there is anything from CIW, as I've been doing with OCD-level regularity since my conversation with Connie. She'll probably call, not email, but that doesn't keep me from checking constantly. And there it is, that high-lighted line at the top of my inbox! The email even has an attachment. I hover over it with my cursor, but I can't click it. I just can't. I know exactly what it says. She would have called if it was good news. She's doing me and her a favor and letting me down in a way that offers me some privacy. I can't open it. I can't take another disappointment.

I should call my sponsor. I should whip out the Big Book. I should read *Twelve Steps and Twelve Traditions*. I should call a newcomer. I should pray and meditate. I should go to a meeting. I know what to do. I'm in dangerous territory here. But I can't leave, and I can't pick up the phone, and I can't pick up the Big Book—not even to take three minutes to read pages 86 and 87, the two-page "quick guide" within the 164-page instruction manual for how addicts might live sober each day. All I can do is sit outside in the dark and suck on a Marlboro Red 100 and drink coffee. The smoke evaporates into the vapor and sound from Sunset Boulevard and the occasional muted roar from Dodger Stadium. Black Cat jumps on the chair across from me and cautiously places his front paws on the small wood patio table. I go inside and pour some dry cat food from a cardboard box into a saucer and bring it out to him. The porcelain saucer scrapes on the concrete until Black Cat has it pinned against the single stair below my front door. I wonder exactly what that email says. Maybe it says, "You can go to all the Agape classes you want, but that isn't going to change the fact that registered sex offenders don't get hired for good jobs."

I run inside and click on the email. It reads only, "Please see enclosed."

I slam my laptop shut so hard that I wonder if it'll fire up the next time I open it.

I trot out the door and jump in my car. I call my sponsor on speakerphone. It rings and rings and then goes to voicemail. Thank God he doesn't pick up. I pop in a cassette tape of a Reverend Michael Beckwith sermon. Reverend Beckwith calls out to his congregation, "God is good, always, yes?" The congregation calls back, "Yes!" My new sponsor, Francisco, calls back. I turn down the stereo so that Reverend Beckwith is whispering, and I listen to the phone ring. It's the default Apple ringtone, which is less unpleasant than most ringtones, but it still makes my nerves rumble just under my skin.

Francisco's advice is very practical: Chop wood, carry water; one day at a time; use all the tools in your toolbox: pray, meditate, exercise, call an addict with less time than you and ask him how he's doing, go to a meeting, and don't isolate! But this time, I want something more, something that'll do more than just get me through it, I want to transcend it, "Rocket to the fourth dimension," as I recall hearing in so many meetings, although I'm not sure if I read it in the Big Book. Macy always says, "go deeper" and "lean into it." I love that about her, and now that the loss of her is another one of my identified problems, I find myself using her advice even more. Yes, Macy, that's right, "go deeper," and "lean in."

I open my eyes, ending my meditation. It's 7:00 a.m. I'm seated in the back of the Agape sanctuary. This is the Early Bird Service. Ever since

Reverend Beckwith appeared in the movie *The Secret* and started hanging out with Oprah, Agape has grown so much that we have three services on Sunday. How Reverend Beckwith and his wife Rickie do three services in a row with such tremendous energy is truly a marvel.

This is where Macy and I usually sat, occasionally with William. But now, for the first time, I'm here alone. The sanctuary is half full. One benefit of being alone is that I can stay until the end of the service. Macy always insisted we leave early, and it irked me, especially when Reverend Beckwith specifically requested that no one leave early so as not to disturb the service. It's not that I think she doesn't care about others, I explained to her during one of our last arguments, it's that she's taken on a kind of free-market, libertarian interpretation of Science of Mind, something akin to Al-Anon codependency recovery gone awry, where one who used to abandon their own needs and wants for others now goes much too far in the other direction. It's very easy to misinterpret Macy's behavior as plain selfishness, and many of our mutual acquaintances do so. I always defend her.

Rickie sits behind the piano and sings out that God is good, always. Everyone stands, encasing me, and I remain seated in my chair and in my mind, reminiscing about Macy.

The first time I came to Agape, I put my arm over the chair around Macy's shoulders and the metal bar atop the chair dug into the area between my bicep and tricep so much that my arm ached for days after, just like when that cop at Twin Towers handcuffed my wrists so tight that it cut off the circulation to my right hand, and I couldn't feel the top of my right hand for weeks after. I'd used it as a reminder that pain doesn't hurt, that there was much more pain to come, that'd there'd always be pain. Don't run from it, feel it. That's what it's there for.

I've strategically seated myself so as to be far enough away from anyone else that I won't have to participate in the face-to-face-with-a-stranger affirmations. These affirmations, I've convinced myself, are Reverend Beckwith's way of making us feel uncomfortable, to make us participants and not just observers in his lessons, and if discomfort is his goal, God knows it works. Sitting face to face with a stranger and staring them in the eyes for several minutes and saying things like, "I see the beauty in you!" and "I'm going with God, and I'm taking you with me!" makes me want to run out of the sanctuary screaming all the way to my car.

Rickie sits at the piano on stage and sings my favorite Agape hymnal, and the words appear on the large screens on both sides of the stage. At the end of the song, I open my watery eyes, and a woman is sitting right next to me. Damn, I'm going to have to do the affirmations with her.

Reverend Beckwith is on fire today. It's one of those sermons that is so intense that I feel it more than I learn it, but I do make a conscious effort to memorize the basic theme: If you think it can't be done, you are right, and if you think it can be done, you are right, too. Normally, I'd be building my wall of intellectual counter-arguments, but today I just try and listen without judgment. What is the harm of believing something wonderful about my life and life in general instead of believing in a brutal world? It was only a couple months ago that I sat in this very room with Macy at the Fundamentals Agape class with a feeling in my heart that warmed me to the bone, and I believed that I was choosing to move out of hell and into heaven, and that if I believed it to be true, it would be. And now, there is doubt and darkness swirling in me. I'm in this sanctuary, the place where I've come closest to believing in something beyond what my mind can conjure, listening to a man preach and his wife play piano and sing, both patently possessed of the spirit, telling me that life can be beautiful if I only let it. But right now, I know deep down that the totality of my beliefs is a preponderance of fear.

Reverend Beckwith talks about Nelson Mandela sitting in a cell in South Africa for over 25 years, that he never lost faith, that upon his release, he forgave his captors. Reverend Beckwith speaks of Jesus who knew the truth about life. The Rev is shot-gunning now, the way he does. He's in the zone, and I am with him, and we are all with him in the congregation, riveted, feelin' it, and now I'm in a full lather, so much so that I break out of my reserved self and shout out, Pentecostal-style, "Amen Rev!"

Reverend Beckwith instructs us to turn to the person next to us and look them in the eye. It's time for the affirmations.

I turn to her and she to me, and I look at her, and I fully commit. I will not concede to the awkwardness and deflate the power. I lean into it. Do it right, I tell myself. She has brown eyes. That's all I see. Smile slightly and breathe through your nose.

"Repeat after me," Reverend Beckwith instructs.

"You are one with God."

The entire congregation repeats this, and I say it to the lady and she to me.

"I see beauty in you!" Reverend Beckwith continues.

"I see love in you!"

"I see divine inspiration in you!"

"You are one-of-a-kind wonderful!"

I hold on, but my ego is pulling out all the stops to disrupt me. I ignore my embarrassment, my inner critic.

Reverend Beckwith states the final affirmation, and we all clap uproariously and hug our affirmation partners.

Back home, feeling a little hope, I open the attachment to Connie's email.

"Dear Joseph,

We are pleased to offer you the position of Contract Manager at CIW Rancho Rebar. This offer will expire on this coming Wednesday. ..."

A smile starts right between my ribs and migrates and grows until it reaches my mouth and eyes. A buzz of energy rounds my shoulders. I giggle and close my eyes.

"My God!" I shout aloud.

I read and re-read the letter. It's clear as day. Connie did what I asked. She wrote an unconditional offer letter. It cannot be revoked without damages once I accept it and detrimentally rely upon it, my lawyer mind determines. I try to stop it, but I can't. Your lawyer mind didn't get you this job, Joseph. Your spiritual practice got you this job. Don't blow it by lawyering it. Your lawyer mind said you couldn't get this job. Your lawyer mind said it was impossible, literally impossible. And yet here we are.

I can't not do the only thing I know to do. Maybe my lawyer mind can just seal the deal.

I immediately begin drafting a letter.

"Dear Connie,

Thank you for your unconditional offer of employment. I accept. I have notified my now-previous employers of my career change and have canceled all upcoming committed work.

I am very excited, and I am very grateful for this opportunity and look forward to becoming a part of the CIW Rancho Rebar Team.

Sincerely,

Joseph W. Naus."

It's exaggerated, but there is some truth to my claim of canceling all upcoming committed work. I will let Ken know that I can't go to any traveling shows or work on Fridays, but the reality is that the home show circuit gravy train is reaching its final stop. And I will have to give Macy's friend a heads-up at AFI that I can't manage the Arclight theater for the film festival. As far as commercials go, I wouldn't be surprised if I never got another call for a P.A. gig again, and my dream of getting into the Locations part of the commercial biz is as dead as Trenton and Paddy.

Wow. This is huge. I'll be able to pay all my bills. I won't be constantly worrying about how I'm going to pay my rent. I can start paying my student loans and my credit cards and my back taxes and maybe even save some money. I'll have medical insurance again. I've never had medical insurance in my whole life except when I worked at Thomas & Coleman and VSB, a total of five of my 37 years on the planet. When I was a kid, I never went to the doctor. We couldn't afford it, and when we did it was the clinic, and that was just to get the shots I had to get for school. I never had a routine medical exam until I had to get one for my California State kickboxing license when I was 19.

I'm going to be in an office around people. I'm good at that. I'm good at being at a desk and pushing paper. I can't imagine what it's going to be like to have all the tools of sobriety at my disposal in the workplace. No bridge-burning. No sleeping with co-workers. No binge working and then showing up late—always being the hero or the zero and nothing in between. I'm going to be steady and solid like the guys I always envied at Thomas & Coleman. I won't blow my entire reputation in one night by acting like a fool drunk at a company party or coming to work visibly hung-over. This is truly a gift from God. I don't quite believe it yet.

I want to tell someone, but I don't want to jinx it. But who do I want to tell? My mom, my sponsor, Keri, yes, I want to tell them all, but that's not it. Of course, I want to tell Macy. That hurts. If we were still together, this would mean so much to her. I could finally take her out without stressing over money, and we'd be so much more at ease, at least I would. Maybe we could have moved in together.

While it is true that Keri and her mom, Kelly are the cause-in-fact of me getting this career job, and I will always be grateful to them, Macy is the spiritual proximate cause. She kept telling me that the only thing holding me back was myself; that if I believed, it would happen, no matter what my history was. God would find a way. She was the one that introduced me to Agape, and gave me a living example of how to "go deeper" and "lean in." And now there is no us. I'll tell her, and she'll be happy for me. She'll even think of how, had it happened earlier, it might have changed things between us, stabilized us, but in the end, she'll easily move on. It's one of her gifts. We have that in common.

I remember the first time she drove in my car. We'd barely just met. My breathalyzer went off. It was horribly embarrassing. I had to pull over to make sure I performed the sequence of blows correctly. Red-faced, I explained it to her. She said she thought it was great. She said it was a constant reminder of the consequence of addiction and the importance of the 12 Steps. Classic Macy. She's so all about the lemonade that she can't even see the lemons.

I sit in Kamella's office. I wonder if she knows Macy and I broke up. If she does, she certainly isn't going to let me know. I think Macy has had at least one session with Kamella since our break up. It doesn't matter. It's just more pain to pile on top of the mess Kamella is helping me discover and discard.

"That's wonderful, Joseph," Kamella says upon learning of my new job.

I look at her eyes carefully as I tell her that Macy and I broke up. Her eyes dart away toward the door as she responds quickly, "Oh, I'm so sorry."

I guess she's not a good poker player.

"We can talk about that if you like later, but I'd like to get back to where we were." She leans closer to me with her elbows on her knees and her chin cupped in her hands, full therapist style. "Let's get you through this today, Joseph, okay?"

"Okay," I say.

"You need to tell him that you are here now, and that you are going to take care of him. Tell him you'll never abandon him again. Do you understand?"

"Yes," I say solemnly.

"Go deeper, lean in," I think to myself. I close my eyes and ready myself to go deep.

I think maybe I can be hypnotized if I believe I can be hypnotized. It takes several minutes for Kamella to guide me back to the Episcopalian church.

Everything is black and white. I can see my own hands atop my knees as if I'm in a first-person video game. I'm in the interior of the church—all gold leaf and dark wood, organ pipes and Jesus in stained glass. It's empty. It's just us, me and 8-year-old me. I feel calm.

Little Joseph sits in front of me—rosy cheeks, big dimples, little bleach-white teeth. Little Joseph is wearing a Hang Ten horizontal striped t-shirt in earthy colors, my favorite. There aren't that many photos of me from when I was kid, but I remember that t-shirt from a yellowing Polaroid of my mom and me. It was when my mom attended Riverside Community College. I have no memory of it being taken. I just know it was before we moved to the Alley, before methadone, before the break-ins, before she quit on life, before things got scary.

Little Joseph's face is tight. He's scared. He's sitting on the pew in front of me, dangling his feet. This time, he has little cowboy boots on, the ones from the photo when I was four, or maybe five years old, and grandpa is helping me open a birthday present and mom is in the background nodding off.

"Tell him, Joseph," Kamella instructs.

I'm in between worlds. I know that I'm here on this couch in Kamella's office. And yet the church is becoming more and more real. Details become more vivid, colors fill in. Cloud-bounced rays of sunlight ignite the stained-glass windows high above.

It's in my chest again, that tight feeling, the one I get before the tears.

"Hello, little man," I say.

He's looking down at his feet, dangling them right and left, right and left.

Kneeling at his feet, I dip my head low, so I can look at his face.

"I came here to tell you something very important," I say.

Little Joseph raises his chin, and he stops swinging his feet. He presses his palms into the pew's seat cushion. His eyes are so big and blue, and his skin is as smooth as the surface of a puddle of paint.

"I'm here now, okay? I'm here," I whisper.

He nods and begins to crack a smile, but then his smile turns and his chin begins to quiver with fear as if he's about to cry.

"No, no, no. It's alright. It's alright," I say softly. "All that stuff is behind us. I'm going to take care of you from now on. No matter what happens, I won't leave you. I'll never leave you again."

He stares into me. He's listening.

"I'm going to take care of you. I promise. I'm so sorry I left you."

We stand up. I take his hand. His hand is soft and tiny and fits into the palm of my hand like a silver dollar. We walk up the aisle together toward the backlit double doors that lead out the church and into the world.

I wake just before noon to pee and smoke. I feel as if my will to live has been downgraded, and all my cells are transmogrifying into fat cells. My organs and brain need barely function. Not unlike a screensaver, the only purpose of my physical movements is to keep me just active enough to stave off *rigor mortis*. I'm not depressed. I'm safe. I haven't felt like this since my living nightmare started five years ago. I've felt good from time to time, joyous even, but there has always been a real big Boogey man right around the corner. What do I fear? The same thing I've always feared. Poverty, real poverty. I live in a capitalist society. That is the ultimate fear. Homelessness, destitution, these are real possibilities for me. Sure, I could couch surf with friends for a while, but there'd come a point where I'd stop imposing my problems on them, and I'd leave. It's real. And now, for the foreseeable future, I have a plan that will keep my bills paid and give me a roof to sleep under. All I have to do is be a good worker, play the game, and I get to survive. I used to want more. Now, I'm just lucky to survive.

I eat donuts, ice cream, drink coffee with toxic vanilla creamer in little blue containers, and I smoke. Oh how I smoke! "How could I have ever left you?" I think to my little buddies. "I love you so much!" I sleep, and I nap, and I watch reruns of *Scrubs*. I try not to think of Macy and William or the last five years. Then I smoke and nap some more and grub-out on sugar-infused cakes, donuts and cookies, dip French fries in ketchup, and eat street-truck burritos with more coffee, and then watch reruns of *Six Feet Under* and then more *Scrubs*. I do still have to go to my meetings. I go to ones where I don't know many people, and I sit in the back and speak to no-one, needing to get back to my apartment to smoke and eat and nap and watch television. I'm going to do this until I start my new job, my new life. Until then I'm hunkering down in my cave and applying all my remaining pain-reduction devices.

I've been waking up later and later, deep into the day, even later than when I drank. My phone's ringtone wakes me. It's just before noon. It's that horrible ringtone that portends an audible attack. I don't get calls, I get shots. Actually, I think, most of the bad-news-callers have completed their attacks, so I do get the occasional friendly call. Lately I've been getting calls from friends in the Program wondering where I am. They leave sincere messages. That's probably who called this time. Maybe, I'll listen to the voicemail and call back. I'll tell them the truth. I'm hunkered down, deep, deep, but I'm still clean, sober and abstinent and still alive. I'm starting a new job, and my life is going to change dramatically. I'm very lucky.

I decide to be a good 12-Stepper and listen to the voicemail instead of deleting it.

"Joseph, uh, this is Connie with CIW Rancho Rebar. I need you to call me back right away." Connie sounds panicked.

I go outside and have a cup of coffee and four cigarettes and then sit at my desk, gather my wits and call Connie back.

"Joseph," Connie says, exasperated. "Uh, hold on."

Light rock on-hold music plays. It continues for several minutes. I pretend to myself that I'm not sure why she's calling. Truth is, my gut knows exactly what's up, but I just can't quite accept it.

I hear Connie's voice. "Okay ... uh, let's see. Okay, I think we've got it. Joseph, you there?" Connie says.

"Yes. I'm here."

"Okay, I've got ... uh... I'm here and Ted and Erik, who you met, obviously, west coast regional manager and local operations manager."

"Actually, they're calling it, California operations now," Erik says.

"Oh, oh, okay," Connie says, nervously. "California operations manager."

"I was just trying to add some, you know, uh, levity," Erik replies.

"Okay, alright, uhm. You are on speakerphone," Connie says, and she sounds hyper-nervous, almost shrill.

"Look Joseph, uh, this is Ted. So, we are calling you because we got your criminal background check back."

"Okay," I respond.

"Yeah, so uh, this is far beyond what we were anticipating. I mean, I remember you telling me about your story and the DUI and a drunken fight. Uh, you know, we understood you are a disbarred lawyer—"

"Let me just jump in here," Erik says. "I'm just going to say it, I mean ask, Joseph. Are you a registered sex offender? I mean, it says here—" I hear Erik's voice rise as he apparently gets closer to the speakerphone. I hear the wrangling of papers. "Yes, here. Assault with Intent to Commit Rape."

"Yes," I answer, "That is correct. But let me just—"

"No, let me first say," Erik interrupts me tersely. "I'm one hundred percent sure you didn't say anything about rape. We have women working here, Joseph. I'm in charge of the safety of our employees."

"Joseph," Ted interjects. "We aren't saying you are going to rape someone, but this is a large business. We have to take precautions, and the bottom line is that you didn't disclose this. So, we are going to have to—"

"Ted, Erik, Connie, I'm sorry to interrupt, but just please hear me for a second—" I nearly yell.

"There is nothing else to say," Erik interrupts me back, aggressively. "We have it in black and white."

"Just, uh, let him speak, Erik. We can hear him out," Ted says.

I take the opportunity and jump in hard. "Erik, I'd feel exactly the way you do. Let me say this. One, I did disclose what happened. It's right there on the résumé, felony assault, but—"

Connie and Erik both start talking loudly in response, but I can't understand what either is saying.

"Hear me out, please, hear me out!" I shout over them. "That's not the issue. I want an opportunity to bring in some documents from my court case, to explain exactly what happened. I assure you that you will be confident that I'm safe and sane and ... uh, like I said, sober."

They mutter indecipherably.

"Please," I interject. "Just give me the opportunity to explain myself. Just meet with me, please. Ted, Erik, Connie, will you at least grant me that? Please?"

Ted takes the lead. He is much calmer than Connie and Erik. "That's fine, Joseph. Why don't you come in tomorrow after lunch."

I hang up and stare at the phone. I'm sweating and panting.

Back to war. I mobilize. I spend the next several hours gathering papers. I create four separate three-ring binders. I create a cover page that reads, "Joseph W. Naus, Supplemental Information re: Felony Conviction, CONFIDENTIAL, The recipient of this information—Ted Wilkinson, West Coast Regional Manager, Erik Holm, Operations Manager, Connie Devine, Human Resources Manager, agrees to return this document to its author and to not disseminate or reproduce any of the documents or information contained herein without the express written consent of Joseph W. Naus." I create a table of contents and list all the documents by page number. I buy tabs, so each page is easily accessible, just like when I used to submit motions with exhibits to court. This document is more than the contents contained in it; it, in itself, is a sales tool. I'm showing them that I can put together something persuasive and professional. The first documents are excerpts from the judge at my sentencing hearing. Then I include excerpts of the police report, all the relevant information, not just that which is helpful to me. Next are letters of support from lawyers, Keri, Will, and a judge. Next are letters for the Lawyer's Assistance Program, then letters of support from friends and family. I create labels for each three-ring binder, including the recipient's name. I put them all into my old briefcase, which, for some reason I haven't thrown away. It's the same one I used to take to court.

I write an outline for my pitch. I revise it. I go to a 12-Step meeting, but all I can think about is the meeting with Ted, Erik and Connie, and exactly what I'm going to say to them, how I'm going to control the meeting and yet still show deference. When I get home, I can't sleep. I just lay awake and rehearse my lines.

We meet in Ted's office. I was hoping we'd be in the conference room, so I could maneuver it such that they are all in the position of an audience, or a small jury. Also, Erik is running late. This is not going per plan! I have to keep my cool.

"Thank you for meeting with me. I'm very grateful for your time," I say and hand out the binders to Ted and Connie. Then Erik walks in.

"Sorry, I'm late," Erik says to Ted.

I greet Erik and hand him his binder. He reluctantly shakes my hand. His eyes skirt away as I look him directly in the eyes. I'll have to focus on winning him over. I'm quite certain he's lobbied Ted against me. My internet research revealed he's not from the business side, but the construction side. He played football, ran a small rebar company in Hawaii, has young kids. He's exactly who I'd expect to be particularly cautious of a registered sex offender. Ted, on the other hand, is older. He's from the business side. He has grown kids. He seems a bit more nuanced. He's quasi-lawyer, like many businessmen. Connie, I'm not quite sure why she's here. Her position is only as a facilitator, but I can't underestimate her influence. Oftentimes, like a judge's court clerk, it's those who control the ministerial tasks that are powerful in peculiar but real ways. Connie is married to a semi-pro senior golfer, she's big into horses, they have grown kids. Demographically, she'd be of the right wing, hang 'em high crowd, but she doesn't seem phased by the fact that I'm a registered sex offender. She may be like the young black republican on a jury, bucking the stereotype.

"Thank you all for giving me this time," I re-start for Erik's benefit. "Is it alright if I just show you what I brought and speak for just a couple minutes?"

Erik adjusts himself in his chair as if he's about to say something, but Ted looks at him, and Erik turns his attention to the binder instead. I notice today how big Erik is. He's over six feet and looks like he could bench press as much as he decides to.

"Go ahead Joseph," Ted says. "We have a staff meeting in 30—well, now 25 minutes—but the floor is yours."

I stand up behind Connie's chair, forcing her to move toward Erik and Ted, to form my jury.

It's go time.

"I was a reasonably successful lawyer," I say. "As you know, I've worked at a couple highly regarded law firms, including one that has represented Rancho Rebar, in the past, before CIW bought it out. Several years later, my friend and I from Pepperdine formed our own law firm, and we were doing well. The problem was that I was drinking, heavily, to the point where I was blacking out. I'd already had a very serious DUI, and thank God, no one was seriously hurt. I should have known better—"

Erik fades away, seemingly more concerned about his Blackberry, which he has sitting in his lap so that he can read messages covertly.

"Erik," I say to get his attention, "You've been in the construction business for a long time. I'm sure you've seen the ravages of alcohol."

Erik sparks up, looks to Ted and then back at me and nods, apparently glad to be included.

"But most guys, once they get in some trouble, they stop right?" I ask rhetorically, "But not me. I kept drinking and things kept getting worse, and I was doing some other bad things. I won't go into the details in mixed company."

This bit of male chauvinism plays well with Erik and Ted and, surprisingly, even with Connie.

"On the night of July 26, 2003, literally a day after I was supposed to start classes for my DUI—and Ted, you'll like this, I was supposed to meet my law partner and client for a round of golf early in the morning—"

Ted smiles softly and then makes a fake surprised face. I return a wry smile and continue.

"I didn't make that meeting, and I didn't get to play golf. What I did was drink a dozen Jack and Cokes at a bar, black out and go to a massage parlor that I'd been to in the past. I somehow went to an ATM to get money out to pay for it—I don't remember any of it—and I went to the massage parlor and knocked on the door, I was all loud and drunk and I woke a bunch of people up at the motel that was connected to it—"

I've got everyone's attention now. Even Erik is leaning into his giant quadriceps.

"Getting no answer, I went around to the back and crawled in the window. But it turns out it wasn't the massage parlor, it was an adjoining motel room. It was dark, and I walked in on some poor guy who was dead asleep—"

"Wow," Ted half-says, half-mouths, shaking his head.

"Yeah, wow, right?" I repeat back. "So the guy wakes up, we fight. I put him in a chokehold. He breaks free. We both run out of the room, and he and his buddy trap me on a lawn across the street, and they beat the hell out of me. The emergency doctor had to put in 10 staples to close my scalp."

They are all rapt. I pause. I look at Connie. She's visibly uncomfortable, like a mom accidentally watching a movie's sex scene with her teenage boy.

"That was the end of my life as I knew it. The district attorney charged me with attempted murder, because I put the guy in a chokehold, something I learned from my kickboxing days. It was terrible. I broke into some guy's house in the middle of the night and fought with him. Just terrible … I was humiliated and embarrassed."

I look to Erik and say, "I'm still embarrassed." His eyes soften just a tad, and he uncrosses his arms.

"So," I continue. "I go to jail and then alcohol rehab for four months. I fight the criminal case for two years. I would have just pled guilty if they'd charged me with drunkenness, assault or breaking and entering, but the D.A. changed the attempted murder to something even worse, a sex crime. She claimed that my intent on entering the apartment was to commit a rape."

From the pinched look on their faces, my three-person jury are all wincing internally. I hope it's because they are contemplating what it would be like to be me, and not because they think I'm a psycho.

"Look," I say with a tone of deep sincerity, "I deserved to be punished for what I did that night, whether I was in an alcoholic blackout or not, but do I deserve to be a registered sex offender? No, it was absurd. You know how the system works, though. They force you to gamble with your life. Had I gone to trial and lost, I'd have done 20 years. So, they offered me 90 days in prison, but I had to plead guilty to assault with intent to commit rape."

"And now you are a registered sex offender," Erik says. I can't quite read his tone, but it seems dead square between sympathetic and accusatory.

"Exactly, Erik," I respond, hoping I'm not overdoing the "say-their-name" technique.

Now for the line I rehearsed. It's risky, but I think it'll land.

"People ask me, 'If you are innocent, why didn't you go to trial?' It's a great question. The answer isn't just about the risk of losing at trial and doing 20 years. Obviously, there is that, but there is the issue of who I am. I'd be in downtown Los Angeles. The jury pool is going to be highly diverse. And here I am, a six-foot-four, white male attorney, who breaks into somebody's apartment in the middle of the night. It'd be the reverse of the OJ Simpson trial. They wouldn't care if I had the intent to commit a rape or not, they'd want to punish me. To a jury like that, I'm the opposite of sympathetic."

Ted and Erik are both big, privileged white boys. I'd bet my life—although that's not the high stakes it used to be—that they are both law-and-order conservatives, both making six figures, both defensive about their place of privilege. I've always benefited from my white-maleness; I don't deny the reality of it; and, I'm trying to make it work for me again.

I walk them through a few key entries in the three-ring notebooks, particularly the judge's statements indicating he didn't believe I had the intent to commit a sex crime. I also read my victim's testimony where he admits that I didn't say or do anything sexual to him.

I delicately mention having quit my other jobs in reliance on CIW Rancho Rebar's unconditional offer. I know this company is big enough to fight me, and if push comes to shove, I wouldn't sue them anyway. I just want my mini-jury here to know that I used my negotiation skills and knowledge of the law as best I could to lock them in to making me an unconditional offer. Ted is smart enough to make the connection, to recognize that this type of thinking will make me a valuable asset to the company.

I remind them of my qualifications and my sincere excitement to work for them. I remind them that I've been sober since the night of the incident, nearly five years ago, and that I regularly attend 12-Step meetings. I thank them for the opportunity, and I tell them that if they hire me, I promise to be an outstanding employee. Then I slap my binder closed.

Chop wood, carry water. Leave the results up to God.

I shake Ted and then Connie's hands. They are equally flat. They are seemingly finished with me and already thinking about their next meeting.

"Thank you, Joseph," Ted says. "We'll consider this information, and we'll let you know."

I shake Erik's meaty hand last. I look right at him. He has aqua blue eyes, just like Jimmy, my Chino prison cellmate, and unlikely protector.

Fifty miles and 90 minutes later, I'm back at my apartment. I smoke and drink coffee and replay the meeting in my head over and over.

I go to a 12-Step meeting, meet with my sponsor and tell him what happened. Francisco says, "You did the footwork, now God is going to handle the rest. Pray for the willingness to accept the outcome either way." Francisco has a traditional God. I don't, but I agree with him when he says, "It's God's will." That is exactly what I believe. I tell anyone who will listen, "I know exactly what God's will is for me: It's whatever happens. How could it be anything else?"

I want this job. I need this job. I go home and read over my notes and the outline from my Agape Foundations class. My notes read, "What I want: I want a job where I can use my skills and make good money. 'Good money' is crossed out, and I've added at least $80,000." I even initialed my amendment as if it was a legal document. Another section of my notes, which is written in unusually nice cursive, barely recognizable as mine, reads "Good employment = you go to be of service, not only to make money. Your employment belongs to God, not you. Your employment is a ministry."

It's true. When I started thinking of my job selling barbeque islands as being of service to the customers—whether they bought a barbeque island or not—it changed everything. I started enjoying the work. It relieved the pressure. I started laughing with the customers and even with Bob and Ned. And then I started selling more than anyone else, without struggle.

I rush home. I do believe in energy, I think to myself. My thoughts affect my reality. This is definitely no time for my cynicism. I lock my door. I sweep up my faux wood floor and roll up the throw rug. I mop. I push the coffee table away and clear space. I create a little ceremony space like Macy and I did for New Year's Eve. It was the best New Year's Eve ever, just her and I hanging out and doing our little self-made ceremony.

I drop a throw-pillow on the ground and make a circle of tea candles, light them, and shut off all the lights. I get out the Big Book and the *Twelves Steps and Twelve Traditions* and a journal. I pray and I meditate. I read the story about the Native American pilot who got sober and got his pilot's license back after many years. I write in the journal. I imagine myself working at CIW Rancho Rebar. Imagine me, working sober, with all my tools of sobriety, at something I'm good at. I'll be a blessing there. I'll be of service. Am I crazy? Is this just me doing something to feel better? Does it matter? It does. Why not? Why wouldn't I sit on the floor and read passages from AA literature and pray and meditate about something that I want, that'll be a blessing for me and for others? God, I sound so corny. Who cares? Remember where my best thinking got me before I got sober: Chino prison. What else should I do? Smoke cigarettes, watch TV, and obsess? No, this feels right. Whatever happens, this feels right.

I'm mid-meditation, somewhere in my mind's world between where Kamella took me our last hypnosis session and the vague dark shadows created by staring at my inner eye, when I hear Black Cat meow. He keeps meowing. He knows I'm home. I saw him lying on the warm hood of my car when I took out the trash while readying for this ceremony. He was curled up tightly like cats do, with his chin on his back paw. But now he won't stop meowing, so I let him in, and pour him a bowl of cat kibble and set it between two candles on the floor. He eats loudly and noses the dish around until it pushes into my leg, then he curls up in my lap. He purrs, and I meditate. I'm like some New Age witch, I think. I open my eyes and pet Black Cat. After several minutes, I stop petting him, and he bites me in retaliation. And then he uncoils and walks to the door and meows incessantly. I open the door, and he shoots across the street and disappears into the night.

I sit and smoke in the dark, and all the fear rushes back in, noisily, like water filling up the basin of a washing machine: I'm not going to be able to pay the rent if I don't get a job. Ken was my ace, but the barbeque island business is drying up quickly. I've got no career in commercials. I've got nothing. I observe these thoughts and smile and commit to another 20-minute meditation. I'll sit here with my back hurting and my ass throbbing, meditating, until I choose to stop thinking these horrible thoughts. I can't stop them. I need to replace them. I recall Revered Beckwith leading a meditation at Agape and instructing the congregation: Think of a time in your life when things were good and you were filled with joy. Bring that experience into your present consciousness. Really feel it. Breathe into the joy, the warmth, the light.

TWENTY-THREE

Joseph walked up the last mile of the three-mile trek, a steep hill up Perris Boulevard and down Jaclyn Avenue. He usually enjoyed walking down Jaclyn Avenue, past all the ranch-style homes, recalling which ones were decorated elaborately for Halloween, but this time he felt sick to his stomach. When he started on the long walk from the apartment, he was determined, but the closer he got, the more doubt crept in. Joseph stopped in front of Uncle Billy and Aunt Suzie's home. He stared at their front door and gathered his nerves. Through a lightly curtained window, Joseph saw the familiar silhouette of Uncle Billy whizzing down the hall in his electric wheelchair followed closely by Ranger, their black Labrador. Joseph rang the doorbell, and immediately heard the *ca-click* sound of Uncle Billy's electric chair changing directions. But it was Aunt Suzie who answered the door.

"Hi Auntie Suzie," Joseph said, his voice shaky.

She knew right away that something was wrong, and moments later, Joseph found himself sitting in a chair at their dining room table, Aunt Suzie and Uncle Billy waiting to hear what he had to say. He felt like a fool. He wasn't supposed to be doing this. He was breaking all the unspoken and unwritten rules of his family. He felt as if he were about to jump off a cliff. He swallowed hard and suppressed a wave of white-hot emotions rising up into his throat.

"Can I stay with you guys for a little while?"

Aunt Suzie looked surprised and relieved and scared all at once, and Uncle Billy was happily reserved, as usual. Joseph told them what they seemed to already know: Things were really bad at home and getting worse. He blamed it all on Carlos, barely even mentioning his mom, but he still felt as if he were betraying her. He thought about how mortified Marie would be when she found out. He knew in his bones he shouldn't be causing a hassle. He shouldn't be making a big deal out of this. That's probably, Joseph thought, what Auntie Suzie and Uncle Billy will tell him. They'll just pretend he didn't ask them if he could stay. Joseph figured they'd just feed him lunch, let him play with Ranger for a while, and then send him home. And he'd make sure to make them promise not to tell Marie or Grandpa what he'd said, because he hadn't meant it. It wasn't a big deal. He'd been wrong to cause a hassle.

"Of course you can," Aunt Suzie said.

And that was that. For the first several days, he felt as if he were in a dream. He felt guilty for leaving Marie behind. He thought maybe he should ask Aunt Suzie and Uncle Billy if his mom could come live with them, too, but he knew that wasn't possible. When Aunt Suzie called Marie to tell her he was going to live with them, Joseph felt sick to his stomach, because he knew he'd have to talk to his mom and hear the stress in her voice. But when Aunt Suzie gave the phone to him, Marie didn't say anything about Joseph leaving. She was upset, and he could hear her smoking hard, but she just asked him if he was alright, and she told Joseph that she loved him. Joseph squeezed his face and fought back the tears and responded as he'd responded nearly every day for his entire life, "I love you, too, Mom." He'd wanted to tell her he was sorry that he'd betrayed her, that he would come back for her when he had some money. But he didn't say anything. He just handed the phone back to Aunt Suzie.

That night, Aunt Suzie made frozen pepperoni pizza and salad with Italian dressing, and Joseph slept in the guest room with the statuettes of Charlie Chaplin and W.C. Fields and framed watercolor paintings of camels and Bilbo Baggins. When Joseph woke in the morning, he was surprised that he hadn't been transported back to his room in the apartment. When he came home from school for the first few days, he wondered if Aunt Suzie and Uncle Billy would ask him why he'd come to their house. Hadn't he gotten the message that it was time to go home? On the bus ride home, Joseph rehearsed his response for when this inevitably happened: I'm sorry to bother you guys, it's just that I left my toothbrush in the bathroom.

Aunt Suzie and Uncle Billy's house was the biggest Joseph had ever been in. It had three bedrooms, two bathrooms, and a garage with an electric garage door opener that Uncle Billy could activate by pressing a button in his van. They even had a swimming pool. Aunt Suzie had her own car, too, a fancy green Buick Skyhawk. They had their own laundry machines in the garage, and they didn't require quarters. They even had a machine that did the dishes for them. Their refrigerator was huge, and it always had food in it. Aunt Suzie and Uncle Billy, and now Joseph, ate breakfast, lunch and dinner every day. In the living room, they had a big-screen television that folded open, and sometimes they watched the scary movies that Aunt Suzie liked, or they all played *Utopia* or *Alpine Skiing* on their Intellivision video game console.

As each day passed, Joseph became less suspicious that this was all a dream. Aunt Suzie and Uncle Billy acted as if they were his new parents, and this was his new home, and so, he thought, maybe it is. The guest room became his room. He was given his own key to the house. He had chores. He had a bed time. He took the bus to school with all the rich kids that also lived on Snob Hill. Aunt Suzie gave him lunch money every day.

Aunt Suzie was cool and stylish. She painted watercolors of animals and stuff from movies, like Boris Karloff as Dr. Frankenstein's monster, the *Jaws* movie poster and scenes from the animated *Lord of the Rings* movie. She'd gone to nursing school, too. She was thin and had long blonde hair, and she was always tan from laying out by the pool. Aunt Suzie was so popular in high school that there was a full-page photo of her in the yearbook. Marie had showed Joseph the photo of Aunt Suzie smiling, sitting in the shade of a tree. Uncle Billy went to high school with Marie and Aunt Suzie. He was a star baseball player, and according to Marie, all the girls swooned over him. He'd set a batting average record in Connie Mack League, and he might have become a professional baseball player had he not broken his spine in a freak diving accident while in Guam on his way to serve in Vietnam. Uncle Billy couldn't use his legs and was confined to a wheelchair for the rest of his life, but he acted as if he was the only one in the world who didn't know it. He was always busy, and he always had a smile on his face. Uncle Billy could do anything everyone else could do. He just had to try harder, and sometimes he needed a little help—as with the special equipment that was installed in his van so he could drive, or the lift that lowered him into the pool. Uncle Billy could even do things that other people couldn't do. He had a computer that looked like a tiny white television, and he was going to college to learn computer programming.

These were his new parents. Joseph had never been taken care of like Aunt Suzie and Uncle Billy took care of him. It was as if they thought Joseph's problems were now their own. If Joseph was hungry, Aunt Suzie fed him. If his clothes were dirty, Aunt Suzie washed them. If he needed money for a school field trip, Uncle Billy gave him money. One time when it was raining outside, Aunt Suzie got up early and drove Joseph to school, so he didn't have to walk to the bus stop in the rain. He didn't even ask her. She just did it.

Aunt Suzie and Uncle Billy gave Joseph a floor. He'd never had a floor before. He didn't even know he'd been free-floating all this time, but now he had something to press off of, something to land on, something to limit his fall. He was born again. The fear that had been his very breath had been replaced with confidence, excitement and joy. Joseph was determined to make the best of his new life. He wasn't going to let himself or Aunt Suzie and Uncle Billy down.

He started getting up before school, when it was frigid out, and peeling off the pool cover and swimming laps. He started doing his homework every night while Uncle Billy was working on his computer. Joseph went from getting an F in Pre-Algebra to having the highest score in the class. He wanted to be able to run the mile in five minutes like his friend Andy did, and so he started running. Aunt Suzie took him clothes shopping and bought him rad new clothes from Miller's Outpost, and she bought him a t-shirt that had a screen print silhouette of a runner on it, and read, "Nike. THERE IS NO FINISH LINE," just like the shirt Andy had. Joseph wanted to talk to girls like his friend Scott did, and so he did that, too. And it wasn't nearly as hard as when he'd tried before, because he felt like he didn't have anything to hide from them; that there wasn't any reason they wouldn't like him. He even entered the school talent show, and he and his friend Kevin did an *Amos 'n' Andy* skit, and when Joseph was backstage, he'd exchanged ass-grabs with the finest girl in school.

And, on what was probably the best day of his life, he had a sleepover at Aunt Suzie and Uncle Billy's house—his house—with all his friends. Aunt Suzie loved scary movies—was even the president of the Boris Karloff fan club when she was a teenager—and she let Joseph and his friends watch *Evil Dead* and *Night of the Living Dead.* Uncle Billy ordered a giant pepperoni pizza from Lorenzos. All night, Joseph glowed like a *Star Wars* toy lightsaber. Now, he was just as good as his friends. At eighth grade graduation, Aunt Suzie bought him a dress shirt and a thin light blue tie like the one Richard Gere wore in *American Gigolo.* Aunt Suzie took photos of Joseph and his friends with the heavy black camera she used to take photos of the animals that were the subjects of her watercolor paintings.

That summer, just before Joseph was to enter high school, Aunt Suzie got a call from Joseph's dad. At dinner that night, Aunt Suzie and Uncle Billy told Joseph that he was going to live with his dad. A couple days later, a young woman, not much older than Joseph, pulled into the driveway in an old red pickup truck. She was Joseph's dad's girlfriend, sent to rescue Joseph from paradise. Joseph didn't cause a hassle. He packed his suitcase and pretended everything was fine. He knew Aunt Suzie and Uncle Billy hadn't signed up to be his parents, and he was grateful that he'd experienced what it was like to live as a prince. He fought back the tears. He thanked them. He told them he loved them. And then he left.

TWENTY-FOUR

I sit in Connie's tiny office. Her desk is stacked with piles of papers and files atop files. She walks in, sits, and starts moving piles. She looks older, more stressed and fragile, than when I saw her last week.

"Things have been crazy busy around here," she says without looking at me. "Ugh, where is your file?"

I don't respond, just smile. She keeps searching. She sighs and becomes genuinely upset.

"This is craziness! Files everywhere!"

She dashes out of her office. I look out over her printer, through the leaves of a small plant Connie has apparently neglected. The parking lot is filled with cars, many shiny Ford and Chevy trucks. The top brass here drives high-end trucks, not BMWs and Mercedes. Out beyond the parking lot are men in yellow hardhats involved in a modern dance with a towering rebar cage, the bones of a soon-to-be concrete pillar.

"Here it is," Connie says as she drops into her seat with such force that her chair rolls back until the wheels strike the file cabinet that holds the printer and the dying plant.

Connie looks like the stressed-out employee in a commercial for something stressed-out employees need, maybe a pain reliever or a vacation. If it weren't for the physical symptoms—the bloodshot eyes, the depressed posture—I'd think she's being melodramatic, as if trying to prove to her boss that she needs an assistant or a raise or both.

She talks and talks as if she has no entry point into our conversation and thinks rambling will lead us to the door of the subject, and it does.

I finally understand why I am here and what she's trying to convey, but it's as if her office is bugged, and she's betting that if she's overwhelmingly convoluted, eventually, the spies will stop listening. It's a bizarre shift from what I'd seen of her and CIW Rancho Rebar in general on my previous visits. She reveals, one little piece at a time, what she needs to tell me, but never directly. She does say, however, after quite a while, "We are in a rather difficult situation." I listen hard after that, but then she floats around some more, and within a few moments she's talking about horses. Connie loves horses, but it's not that she's revealing a hobby of hers to get to know me a bit. I hypothesize that she is, oh-so-cryptically, telling me how much better horses are than people.

The facts slowly come, and they are magnificent. Rancho Rebar was recently purchased by CIW, hence the clever new name, CIW Rancho Rebar. Rancho Rebar is a very profitable company, and so CIW, based in Dallas, has been slow to enforce its corporate policies. The top brass—not particularly familiar with the construction side of the rebar business, since most of CIW's business in other parts of the country consists of manufacturing and selling rebar, not bidding jobs and actually being a part of the construction of high-rises and freeway bridges as Rancho Rebar has done for decades—has largely left Rancho Rebar alone. More than once, Connie says, "As long as we keep making money, Dallas leaves us alone," but then she drifts again and refers generally to the stack of papers, which she says are killing her because now the CIW Corporate Headquarters Human Resources office, "HR," in Dallas is requiring her to do twice what she used to.

"People around here just don't understand. They don't see it. They don't know how much more I have to do," Connie says as if in therapy.

Finally, atop all of Connie's fragmented background talk, it finally comes out: CIW Rancho Rebar sent me my unconditional offer letter without Dallas's blessing. She says it's "no big deal" with a slight tremor in her voice, and then repeats her safe words: "As long as we keep making money, Dallas will leave us alone."

Connie continues, "But then, Dallas does require background checks and, well, you know … your hiring has become, you know, a situation…"

So there it is. I'm a "situation."

"And, of course, we'd prefer you didn't reveal any particulars about your background," Connie offers, and punctuates her thought forcefully. "To anyone."

So, I think, no "Congratulations, you're hired!" Rather, just a "Well, you're here now, so just keep it on the down-low, will ya?"

I reassure Connie. "I've been through this before in my last job. I won't say anything, but obviously, given my position, my education is going to come up, which is going to prompt that I went to law school, which is going to prompt whether I practice law …"

I explain that what I plan on doing is to say nothing, but if pushed, it's best to reveal enough to satisfy the inquisitor by offering that "I used to practice law, but I got in trouble because of drinking. I got a bad DUI and luckily no one was hurt, but I lost my Bar license." With that explanation, even if they look me up on the State Bar website, they'll just see that I used to be a lawyer and "resigned with charges pending."

My plan seems to please Connie greatly, and she hands me an employment package with a stack of papers to review and sign. I'm hired! She looks at the clock, declares an upcoming conference call with Dallas, explains that I am the subject of this conference call, and then rushes me out.

I find myself in a cubicle, still struck by the fact of my hire and the oddity of it all. I read through the employment papers Connie gave me. Ted stops by and beckons me into his office. I offer him my "policy position on Joseph's background" which seems to visibly relieve him and precludes the necessity of him repeating, or even acknowledging, for that matter, what I learned from Connie. The phrase "plausible deniability" comes to mind. Ted congratulates me with a hardy handshake. Erik stops by and shakes my hand and slaps me on the back. It's as if they've already purged my criminal background check results from their minds. If only I could do the same.

I spend the rest of the day reading through the packet of employment papers. This is a real job. The benefits are gold standard. I'll have health insurance in 30 days. Imagine that. Health insurance! They even have a free life insurance plan that pays out a couple hundred thousand dollars of benefits. If I kill myself, I'll make it look like an accident. I fill out the form and name William as the beneficiary. Just because Macy broke up with me and I won't be in his life anymore doesn't mean I can't give him something. I'm pretty sure his mom is going to be wealthy pretty soon, but if not, and I happen to die soon, college is on me, William.

I drive home. It's a 50-mile trip. It takes 40 minutes to drive the first 45 miles and 20 minutes to drive the last five miles, through the intersecting freeways that frame downtown Los Angeles. But I don't care because I'm giddy. I feel joy. I feel safe. I can pay my bills! I have a real job. Halle-fucking-lujah!

A week later and the day before my official first day at CIW Rancho Rebar, I meet Erik in downtown Los Angeles a couple miles from my apartment at the job site of a mostly-built, modern condominium highrise called Evo. He hands me a yellow hard hat with a CIW logo on it. His hard hat is much cooler than mine; it's dark brown, looks like woven Kevlar and has a bunch of Local 416 Union Ironworker stickers on it. We take the construction elevator, a steel cage attached to the side of the structure, to the top floor, 23 stories up. There are men in hard hats like Erik's unloading a bundle of rebar dangling from a crane arm. The foreman sees Erik, sparks up, and rushes over. Erik introduces me as the new Contract Manager. The foreman, an old cowboy, takes off his right-hand glove and squeezes my hand in his. His grip is a testament to hard physical labor.

The foreman's darkly weathered face creases with concern as he hangs on Erik's every word. As if this is expected, Erik doesn't react. Erik asks the foreman how things are going. I can't hear the response over the traffic noise from below and a grinding noise that sounds intermittently, but I make out "crane-time bullshit." Erik nods with fraternal understanding.

"Okay," Erik says, "I'm just here to show our new Contract Manager around. You can get back to work."

"Alright boss," the foreman says and rushes back to his men. With renewed hustle, the men carry sticks of rebar, which bow over their shoulders, from the bundle lowered by the crane. It strikes me that unlike with office workers, there is no underlying apology for the fact that the foreman is Erik's subordinate. They both accept this fact without reservation and with absolute clarity.

Erik and I walk toward the western edge of the tower. The view is epic. The Staples Center and the Los Angeles Convention Center are several blocks west. These giant structures are framed by Figueroa Avenue and the 10 and 110 Freeways, which, from here, look like veins under a microscope, with blood cells flowing to and fro.

Erik walks nonchalantly toward the edge of the building. I watch him carefully and trail behind. I keep following. Erik stops, standing within a foot of the edge. There is no guardrail, no safety net. He's a foot from a death fall. The nerves in my knees conspire against me, and I feel a sickness swell in my stomach. I keep walking toward Erik. I stop five feet from the edge.

Don't look down, I tell myself. Just look at Erik.

Erik beckons me closer. I shuffle toward him with little baby steps. My legs are just a big mess of firing nerves. My knees have vanished.

"Staples Center, that was us," Erik says and points. "Nokia Theater, LA Live, that's us. Rancho Rebar placed the rebar for half the buildings in downtown, and right now it's exploding down here. Sometimes we have a half dozen projects going at once in downtown alone. In Southern California right now, including San Diego, we have hundreds of union ironworkers working for us. It's extremely hard work, and they make good money."

"Who's in charge of them?" I ask, spreading my toes within my shoes and trying to press my feet deep into the floor for ultimate stability. I'm not moving a step closer to that edge.

"They answer to their foreman, who answers to the field manager, who answers to me. I answer to Ted. Ted answers to the CEO of the whole company. CIW has dozens of locations all over the country and even some international. Right now, there isn't a single CIW entity that makes more money than we do. Hell, that probably even includes the mill in Seguin in West Texas, but maybe not."

"So they kind of leave us alone as long as we make money?" I parrot Connie.

Erik's mouth lands somewhere between a smile and a smirk. His strikingly aqua blue eyes glint. I'm not sure what to make of that, whether he's the manager that wants his boss to leave him alone, or whether he's making the connection between my hiring and CIW's corporate headquarters' hands-off policy.

A helicopter chops above us, weirdly close. Erik yells over it. "I got to get back to the office."

I'm exceptionally grateful to regain the normal nerve density in my legs as we walk away from the ledge. We take the construction elevator back down the side of the building, which is as thrilling as a roller coaster, and alight back onto Grand Avenue. Erik tells me to keep my hard hat, says there have been guys working at CIW for years that have never been to a building site. I reply, "Wow, really?" I think he's starting to like me, and that makes me exceptionally happy.

I wake up the next morning and decide to take the Metrolink to work. As Rancho Rebar is part of the construction business, office start time is 7 a.m., so in order to get there on time, I have to be out my door by 5 a.m. I ride my bike down Sunset a couple miles to Union Station. It's mostly downhill. The street is empty. It's dark, and the cold air rushes over my face. There are mostly busses on the road. The exterior of Union Station is old Spanish style, like a mission building. The large train depot's exterior has smooth white walls topped by red clay tiles. There is a large archway and a clock tower of the same Spanish design. Towering palm trees, lit up by spotlights at their bases, stand sentry as if announcing Southern California. I walk my bike through the grand building, admiring its cathedral-height ceiling and deep, dark, waffled wood beams, towering windows and an intricate geometric marble floor, like some complicated game board for giants. I make my way past rows of built-in chunky wood and black leather chairs.

There are people, the go-getters, the hard-workers, walking briskly in the cool air toward their train or bus. And I am one of them. I've officially reentered society. I'm a salaryman again, and I couldn't be happier. There is no place in my precarious existence for my entrepreneurial spirit. I was a makeshift canoe taking on water, but now I've been rescued by an ocean liner.

The Metrolink train is brand new—nothing like the piss-scented busses that make their way down Sunset Boulevard into downtown Los Angeles. It's nearly empty. I roll my bike next to my seat and admire the views only available by this train. I have my coffee in a sealed cup. It's barely 5:30 a.m. The sun is just now revealing itself, and yet I'm filled with zeal. Is there anyone on their way to work who is more purely joyous and alive than I am right now? Me, Joseph W. Naus, plucked out of destitution, to rejoin the happy ranks of corporate America!

We funnel past the old train yard and concrete river basin, which is decorated with giant swaths of colorful graffiti, some, chintzy adolescent tags, others, massive intricate works of art. Then we run parallel to the freeway, passing cars. My view into the old East Los Angeles neighborhoods feels voyeuristic. At each stop, people load onto the train, and by the time we reach Rancho Cucamonga, 75 minutes later, the sun is up, and the train has nearly emptied again. I roll my bike out and ride the remaining couple miles.

I pedal my way through the mostly empty streets. Enormous concrete tilt-up buildings populate giant industrial parks. Tractor trailers are more common than sedans on these roads. The streets are as wide as freeways. Everything is clean and kept, white concrete and fresh parking lots and pleasantly curving sidewalks neatly adorned with trees and bushes, efficiently fed by drip lines. After 15 minutes of brisk pedaling, I arrive at CIW Rancho Rebar at 7 a.m., right on time.

I walk through the side door and make my way past the detailer's bays. This is where mostly Filipino men take concrete plan-drawings and add in the rebar according to building specifications. There are a couple dozen drafting desks. They are filled with giant rolls of building plans. Some of the men draft by hand and some work on computers using specialized black-screened CAD programs. There is a separate windowed room where an enormous copy machine continually spits out construction plan drawings the size of Oriental rugs.

I'm in a window office facing the street. It's as generic as possible, but it's comfortable. Within a few minutes, Larry walks in. I met Larry briefly when I was first hired. If there was a company photo, Larry would be the one that looked like he was cut and pasted into the photo. He's just over six feet. He has bright white hair, bowlishly cut. He wears silky khaki trousers and a geometry enthusiast's version of a Hawaiian print shirt.

"Welcome to my credit department," Larry says. He watches my reaction carefully through his square gold-rimmed glasses.

"Credit department," I repeat, registering confusion.

"Oh Lordy, I was afraid of this," Larry says. "Ted just hires you and doesn't say a word about lil' ole me." Terry has a southern twang to his voice, a lot of lilt, and I'm not sure if he's gay, but if he's not, he's sure doing a good imitation of a stereotypical gay man.

"Well, no matter," he continues. "It's like this, my department handles all the credit, all the collections, and I'm in charge of the contracts. The reason you were hired was to help me."

Larry begins coughing, and I wait for him to finish, but he doesn't stop, and for a moment, I think maybe I should do something, like maybe administer the Heimlich, but he finally stops.

"Oh-kay," I respond cheerfully.

"When you get settled, come into my office," Larry says and disappears into his office right next door.

I really have nothing to do but follow the instructions on how to set up my company email, and finish looking over the hefty packet of employment papers, including the CIW Employee Manual. This interaction has thrown me for a loop. Larry's name was barely even mentioned when I was hired. Ted and Connie made it clear that I was hired to handle the legal side of the contracts, to make sure all the company policies are complied with.

As I page through a ream of employment documents, I start to think about my Contracts class at Pepperdine Law. I loved Contracts. It was logical. My professor, a sweet old Southerner, would yell, "I accepts!" whenever he taught us about the basic elements of a contract: offer and acceptance. The most important thing I learned in Contracts was barely a footnote on my professor's syllabus: the Contract of Adhesion. A Contract of Adhesion is a contract where a large corporation screws an individual because it has the power to do so, like with a mortgage, a gym membership, a credit card agreement, a car loan, a bank account agreement, or a student loan agreement.

I stare into the computer monitor and watch the CIW logo screensaver slowly float around and bounce off the edges of the monitor. The thought of my ever-increasing student loan debt turns my stomach. I imagine sending a letter to Sallie Mae telling them I'd like them to eliminate my loan interest, that I shouldn't be charged interest on a government-backed loan for an education that increased my earnings, which leads to me paying more taxes to the same government; and furthermore, I imagine writing, I know that Sallie Mae bribed Congress to privatize student loans so they could turn me into a human profit center.

I walk back into Larry's office. He has his desk phone handset pinched between his ear and shoulder. He's leaning back in his desk chair, rocking, with his right foot atop his left thigh, his immaculately spotless loafer hanging off his heel. He's scratching his foot with the end of the recessed tip of his pen. He waves me to sit in a chair next to his desk. I do so. Larry reeks of cigarette smoke. He rolls his eyes at whoever is on the other end of the phone for my benefit and begins to wrap up his conversation.

"Will do, Dick. I've got the young man sitting in my office right now. I'm sure it'll work out. They're just doing what they've always done ... You know, it always has to be their way. I'm just a second-class citizen ..."

Larry sits up, readying to end the phone call. His grin reveals he's relishing the fact I'm hearing what I'm hearing.

"Well, I do appreciate that Dick. You've always been there for me ... okay ... alrighty, you give that sweet thing of yours a peck for me ... okay."

Larry hangs up the phone and focuses on me.

"So that was Dick. We go way back. He's in Seguin in Texas. He basically runs this company. Let's say Ted is here," Larry says and holds up his right hand flat, palm down, chest high. "Then, Dick is here," he says and raises his left hand as high as he can.

"Oh," I say, trying to match Larry's enthusiasm and mask my disbelief.

"Yeah, that's right, Sweetie," Larry says. "Sometimes they forget about that 'round here."

I try to process that he just called me "Sweetie" and decide to pretend I didn't hear him.

Larry slides his loafer back on, stands up and walks over to a wall of flesh-colored file cabinets, head-high and stretching all the way across the room. He slides open a cabinet drawer and leans against another. He hands me a file. It has three pieces of paper in it. I follow along as Larry explains.

"Every single general contractor that we bid, whether we get the job or not, has to have a credit file. Each file has a Dun & Bradstreet credit report, no more than a year old, and a credit form. The form is an application for credit that is submitted to me by the sales department. If I approve it, I write in the total amount of credit allowed. It's net 30, which means the customer has to pay all billings within 30 days, or they are in violation of their credit terms, which means they'll be sent to collections."

I hand the file back to Larry, and he slides it back into the cabinet and slides the cabinet closed with added drama, as if he's exhausted and shutting the drawer has taken his last bit of energy.

"So, here are the contracts," he says, opening another file cabinet. "These are all the contracts for all the jobs that we've had since I've been here, in this 'wonderful' place—jeez, what? Seven years now—seven 'glorious' years. My lord." Larry says "wonderful" and "glorious" with as much accentuated femininity as I imagine is possible. He even puts his hands on his hips. It's as if he's imitating Rip Taylor. I suppress my surprise and chuckle uncomfortably. "What the hell?" loops in my mind like a siren.

"I understand you're a lawyer, and you probably know a lot about contracts, a lot more than me, even though I've been doing this for over 20 years ..."

Larry waits for a response from me, I suspect, some deference. I give him none.

"Well, we just follow the protocol and do a simple addendum to the contract," Larry says and begins to shuffle through a tray labeled "inbox" on his desk.

"Addendum?" I inquire.

"Addendum," Larry repeats and hands me one.

I look it over. "You mean … uh, these big general contractors let you amend their contracts with this?" I say, more incredulously than I probably should.

"I been doing this a long time, Kiddo," He says, but then he looks at my face, which is clearly signaling my displeasure at being called kiddo. "Sorry 'bout that. It's just how I talk."

"No problem," I say, with a stoic face. "Just Joseph is fine."

"Well, anyway, Joseph, that addendum right there. That's how I've been handling contracts since I got here, and it's working out just fine. In fact, no offense, but I don't really need any help."

"Just so you know, Larry, I'm not a lawyer. I went to law school, but I'm not licensed to practice law, and I didn't get hired in the capacity of a lawyer. I'm just a contract manager."

"Right, of course," Larry says, chuckling dramatically, as if for a camera I can't see. "Here we go," he says and hands me a thick contract. "Just look at the back page."

Larry's phone rings. "I need to take this. You can take that back to your office."

In my office, I can hear him talking. He's talking to Dick again. About me. I can't hear everything, but he says something about "the lawyer." He begins to cough when he's listening to Dick, but then he coughs for so long, he's barely able to choke out the words to let Dick know he has to call him back. He coughs for so long I begin to get worried. I go to his open door and ask if he's alright. He waves me off, while he tries to drink water. I go to the break room and get him more. When I return, Maria, the receptionist, is standing outside his office looking concerned. She takes the water from my hand and tells me this happens all the time.

I shut my door to drown out the coughing, which continues intermittently. I review the contract. It's a form contract from one of the largest contractors in California, McCallister Construction. It's for a hospital's parking structure, and the total dollar amount for the rebar placement subcontract is $1.2 million. The scope of the job is mostly incorporated via reference to the original bid documents, so there is no way of knowing anything specific about the job other than the dollar amount and that it's a parking garage. The rest of the 12 pages is legal-ese. All the usual suspects: late penalties, billing protocol, insurance, indemnity, dispute terms regarding arbitration, mediation and attor-ney fees, change order process, and safety issues. It's all one-sided, in favor of the general contractor. It requires that if McCallister is sued for anything having to do with the scope of rebar, CIW will pay for the defense of McCallister and any damages awarded against McCallister, no matter whether CIW did anything wrong or not. I recognize this as a Type One indemnity clause, which basically makes CIW the insurer of McCallister. I'm pretty sure this indemnity clause isn't even legal in California.

I turn to the final page of the boilerplate contract, and, as with nearly all form contracts, it has signature lines for each party to the contract and a date line for each signature. It has the usual language that dictates that nothing outside of the contract shall amend or supersede the con-tract unless it is signed and dated by both parties. The contract is signed by McCallister's Project Manager and dated August 5, 2007. The line for CIW Rancho Rebar is signed by Larry and dated August 1, 2007. Behind that page is a single piece of paper entitled "Addendum." It's stapled to the back of the contract and it has several terms, one for indemnity, one for attorney fees, one for arbitration, one for billing terms, one for insurance, and several others that have to do with rebar. The addendum is dated August 15, 2007 and is signed by Larry. There isn't even a place for anyone else's signature.

The coughing has stopped because Larry has left. He told me that he comes in at 4:30 a.m. and leaves at 3:30 p.m. every day but Sunday.

I go into his office and pull a couple dozen contracts from the file cab-inet. I take them back to my desk. Some are the same as the McCallister contract, with an addendum only signed by Larry. Others are signed by the contractor's project manager but all or most of the terms are crossed out by hand. Some have addendums that aren't signed and aren't even attached. A couple have addendums that don't even have a place for any signature as if Larry got tired of having to deal with the whole "acceptance" part of contract negotiation and decided to amend the contracts unilaterally and magically. I feel like a journalist in a movie that just found the smoking-gun documents. I frantically exchange those contracts for a dozen more. This batch is much the same.

This can't be right. But here it is, over and over. These are multi-million-dollar jobs. It's unbelievable. I try to think of how I could be wrong. This can't be right. It can't be. I must be missing something.

I've been employed here a couple weeks now, and I'm starting to feel comfortable.

I click my computer to sleep, recline my office chair and take in the quiet. There is only a dull, muffled vacuuming from the opposite side of the building. It's just past 6 p.m., and I'm the last CIW Rancho Rebar employee remaining. This is how it felt sometimes when I was a college student, a law clerk, and then a lawyer. I remember how I felt driving home. It felt just like it does now. I feel warm and safe. I'm being a good boy, and good boys deserve to feel warm and safe.

It's dark, and the wind bounces the eucalyptus trees that line the street. I drive through the now-vacated industrial parks into the commuter-filled wide streets of Rancho Cucamonga. Closer to the freeway, the malls, fast-food drive-throughs, and gas stations are filled with working people just wanting to make it home to be with their families.

I'm not about to get on the freeway now. It'll take me two hours to get home. I'll be ensnared in the Inland Empire commuter traffic and the tail end of the Los Angeles commuter traffic. I had put the old golf bag Tito gave me and my clubs, with the rotting rubber grips, in the trunk of my car, just for this situation. I'm going to the golf range at Empire Lakes, just up the street.

I read the multi-digit code off my receipt, punch it into the Kelly green golf ball dispenser, and listen to the satisfying rumble of golf balls feeding into the plastic range bucket. I carry the bucket and my faded navy blue golf bag down to the grass range. The stadium lights cast my shadow in three directions. There's only one other person at the range. She's posted up with a white golf bag that is wider than her and nearly as tall. Her name is stitched across the front pocket below a South Korean flag, and I can only make out the large letters of her surname, "KIM." Out on the range, little flags of various colors blow sideways, under bending poles, and dot the range from red at 80 yards to gold, which is barely visible at around 300 yards. I set up my bag several hitting stations in front of Kim. My baseball hat blows off my head and tumbles toward her. I rush after my hat. From a statuesque posed follow-through position, she whips her iron over her shoulder and pins my hat to the turf. She spins the head of the club and hooks my hat under and lifts it up to me.

"Sorry, sorry," I say, taking the hat from the head of her razor-thin eight-iron.

"Okay. No sorry, okay, good," she says warmly, nodding, bowing slightly and smiling exaggeratedly in a way that I take to mean she doesn't speak English.

"Thank you," I say.

Kim goes back to her swing, but I just stand there. She has two giant buckets of balls, one is nearly empty, and there are four divot lines, three of which are about two-and-a-half feet long and the fourth of which is still in progress. The divots are so geometrically precise in their depth, length and spacing that they look like they were made with a machine. They look like shallow snake graves, about ready for interment. As I stare, Kim uses the tip of the toe of her eight-iron to scoot a ball on to the edge of the backside of her fourth divot line. Realizing that I'm still here and staring, she looks at me and sticks her face out and smiles widely, her eyes bulging, as if to say, "Uh, can I help you?"

I point to the divot lines. "Wow, I've never seen divots like that ... you know, in a perfect line, like that," I say.

She bumps her shoulders in confusion and smiles harder.

"Oh nothing, just divots," I point harder, and say louder. "Divots."

She shakes her head vigorously, and says, "Divots, yes, okay, thank you."

I raise my hand, nod and step back several yards.

Kim places the front edge of her eight-iron just behind the ball. Her body forms around the club's pitch into a posture that is strictly aligned and yet relaxed, as if every part of her is water that has found its level. She takes the club back almost languidly into a position that is pure athletic loading. And while she doesn't ever stop moving during her swing, there is a point at the top of her swing that is neither backswing nor downswing, but a crease in time, and that, it is plain to see, is where the magic resides. With a deep satisfying "thump," the ball explodes off her clubface. Kim poses and watches her ball fly. I turn to do the same, and, it appears she's missed her mark. Her ball flies low and rises. It streaks out a few feet right of her target, the 150-yard white flag. She's overdrawn it, and it continues to turn from right to left and will likely miss the target by at least 10 yards left. But then her ball balloons up, and meets the left-to-right wind, which holds it just above the whipping white flag. The ball drops on the right side of the flag, close enough that I wonder if it went in the hole.

Kim lines up another ball and molds herself gracefully into place. This time, she's aimed far left of the target. With the identical tempo and grace, she swings. The same explosive power, the same satisfying thump sound. But this ball starts 15 yards left of the white flag, streaks low and then balloons. It fades left to right, carried on the wind, and lands about two paces left of the flag, where it joins a few dozen other range balls.

I return to my patch of grass, feeling starry-eyed, feeling as if there is an important question that has been answered, but I don't know what the question is.

I dump my bucket of balls into the low-cut grass. I think of my kickboxing days. With wild-eyed excitement, my instructor, David, held the heavy bag for me, and said, "Don't kick the bag, kick through the bag." The advice immediately improved my power. That's what Kim is over there doing. She's not hitting the golf ball. The ball is just getting in the way of her swing.

I take a flowing practice swing, attempting to implement this idea. Then I take a swing at a ball. I shank it off the hosel, sending a jolt through my arms and up my shoulders. The ball fires hard right, barely above the grass. It dies into the grass 40 yards away.

"Fucking, fuck. Nice start, Joseph," I mumble to myself.

A high-pitched *ting* sounds from behind me. I turn and see Kim posing at the top of her follow through; her driver's big head hovers just above her own. Her golf ball soars out into the night, lands past the 250-yard sign and rolls beyond the light's reach.

I turn back and drag a golf ball into place.

I've always wanted to be great at something, I think to myself, but the truth is, I've barely been good.

There was tennis. I dedicated myself to it maniacally for two years. I became strikingly good for a kid that had picked up a racquet for the first time the summer before his freshman year. I was number one on my mediocre high school varsity team, just good enough to be seeded last at the conference finals, to play the number one seed, who gifted me with the 6-0, 6-1 reality that I was too far behind to ever catch up with serious college tennis-bound players. I'd have needed to start playing about a decade earlier to have any chance.

Ting, the high pitch from Kim's driver rings out over the range.

There was kickboxing. I gave it my all for several years, not with the same intensity as tennis, because I had to work and go to school. But it didn't matter. I didn't have the hand speed to move from solid competitive amateur into the pro ranks. And I became tired of taking concussive kicks and punches to the head.

Ting.

I take a practice swing, line up to my ball, swing, and hit something not unlike a golf shot, just much shorter and lower.

I look back at Kim. She's holstered her driver and is holding a sand wedge and hitting little shots to a flag on a knoll 40 yards out. She exerts no more effort than if she were tossing a balled-up shirt into a laundry bin five feet away. The balls fly high and drop like bean bags.

There was law, of course, or more particularly, trial lawyering. I'd dreamt of building a mock courtroom, outfitted with a jury box and a witness stand, where I'd install video equipment and I would train with other lawyers and prepare for trials. I read books like *The Art of Cross-Examination* and the biographies of Clarence Darrow and Thurgood Marshall. During my years at Cal State, I drove out to county courtrooms in Riverside and San Bernardino. I used to sit and dreamily watch some of the Inland Empire's great trial lawyers in action: Tito Gonzalez, who eventually became my mentor, Don Brown, and the Desert Fox. Then at Pepperdine Law, despite always being either in a bout of depression or manically "turning my life around" one last time, "and this time for real!" I did well in Trial Practice and Evidence and excelled in moot court competitions. But when I became a lawyer, my addictions gradually and then, not-so-gradually, took over my life, and my dream of striving to become a great trial lawyer was nothing more than a fantasy. Now it might be an impossibility.

The thought of my lost career as a trial lawyer washes over me. I feel instantly drowsy, and my temples throb.

Kim quarters past me, lugging her giant white golf bag. I want to say something to her, or at least exchange a knowing nod, but she's facing away and staring into her mobile phone.

I drag another ball into place, recalling the last time I was at a golf range, at Roosevelt, how just making solid contact, no matter how slow I swung, felt good, soothing, even. I do so and make a nice little "click." I feel the ball merge into the face of the iron. I do it again, and again and again and again until I only have one ball left.

I sit cross-legged on the grass. I stare out into the range, thinking about the graceful ease of Kim's golf swing. "Amazing," I say to myself. I look out and imagine the trajectory of her drives, like shooting stars, fading into the night's sky.

I want to know what it's like to be great at something, but even more, for once in my life, I want to know what it's like not to quit.

Several moments go by, and then I say "Golf!" aloud. I exclaim it, as if it's the answer to a riddle I've been pondering for years. "I'm going to master golf or die trying."

I stare out over the range in a state more dazed than meditative. I stand abruptly, and I feel light-headed. I'm so deep in thought that I can barely feel my body. I could just as well be lying in bed as standing in the grass, on this oddly-empty driving range. But this feels right. It feels important. It's as if I discovered a command to myself written by my previous incarnation: "Find something to do and do it to the best of your ability. It will be your teacher. There is only one rule that you must follow: Never quit."

I rake my last golf ball into place, I take a powerful whooshing practice swing, hold my finish position, imitating Kim. I take a deep breath. I visualize Kim's swing and the way her golf balls streaked toward the white flag. I stare at the white flag. In my mind's eye, I see my ball flying just like Kim's. I focus on my ball, and then swing hard. I miss the ball completely.

"Are you fucking kidding me?"

Another Friday night, another Nicotine 12-Step meeting. The people who are off cigs, their faces are lit, they speak of gratitude, how wonderful it is to not be smoking. I had six months, damn near to the day, and then I smoked when Macy broke up with me. Six months! For the first couple weeks, I'd wake up in the morning, and I couldn't believe I didn't smoke the night before. I'd go to bed early just to ensure another day smoke-free. And then, the unbelievable happened. I went a day without even thinking about smoking. That was after I had three months. When Macy broke up with me, I had no defense against the first cigarette. I don't even remember making a decision to smoke. I didn't call anyone from the Smoker's Anonymous phone list. I didn't pray or meditate. I was on autopilot, and I was up to a pack a day within a couple days. Since then, I've quit for a day here and there, and for some reason, I keep coming back to this meeting. There are others like me; they can't quit either. The people with time, some with years smoke-free, they keep telling us newcomers to "just keep coming back" and eventually it'll work, but I've been coming to this room off and on for a couple years, and the most time I've gotten is six months.

Right now, I actually have a full day off cigs, and when the chip person asks if anyone has 24 hours, I raise my hand. Everyone in the room claps as I make my way to the front. They, actually "we," I suppose, love newcomers. Getting 24 hours off cigs is hard. It's a damn miracle. It's a damn miracle for me, no matter how many times I do it. I take my embossed "24 Hours" poker chip and get a hug from the chip person. People are so damn sincere in here. It's refreshing. We are in a solitary war against a fierce opponent, and there is no room for anything but clarity in here. I sit back down and wonder whether I'm going to stop at 7-Eleven on my way home, which, of course, means, yes I am. As we say, "If you debate, you lose."

I eat with people from the group after the meeting at a Thai Restaurant on Sunset, Mae Ploy. Out the window and through the rain,

I can see the giant "Happy Foot/Sad Foot" podiatrist's sign slowly rotating above the street. I sit across from John.

"How are you doing with the smoking?" John asks me.

I consider saying something like, "Fine, you know, it's tough," but I decide to tell him the truth instead. "Honestly, John, I'm wondering if I'm ever going to quit."

Everyone at our table of eight has now stopped talking and are all listening to me.

I continue, "I can't believe I quit all my other addictions, the ones that resulted in me being a felon and losing my career, and yet, it appears I'm going to die of lung cancer or that disease where you basically suffocate to death slowly, what's it called again?"

"COPD," Janice calls out from the opposite end of the table. "It's the most gruesome death."

"COPD, right," I respond.

"Yep," John says, "That's exactly what'll happen. Keep smoking and you'll die a horrible death. So definitely keep coming back, and eventually you'll stop, hopefully before you get cancer or COPD."

Our waitress sets down a large bowl of Pad Thai chicken.

"Oh my God, I love this stuff," John says.

I drive down Sunset Boulevard. I park in the 7-Eleven parking lot, and I just sit in my car. I have nothing left to give. I can't quit. I can't do anything. I'm not going to pray or call anyone. I can't. I can barely keep my eyes open. I feel like I'll pass out if I make even the slightest movement. Through my windshield and through the rain, I see blurry cops in their yellow rain gear, standing outside the 7-Eleven entrance. I'm too tired to be afraid of them. I'm sure my existence in this parking lot is some type of probation or registration violation. Fine, arrest me, but you're going to have to carry me. I can't move.

The craving for nicotine, that little insatiable alien beast, comes to life in my head, in my stomach. It's everywhere, but I'm sorry, little dude, I can't. You win. Do what you will. I can't win. I went to the

Smoker's 12-Step meeting, same meeting I've been going to for literally years now, and yet here I am again, at the dealer's house, 7-Eleven. It's raining, so fuck you. If you want them so god damn bad, you get out of the car. I'm going to sit here. It's getting colder. I don't care. I struggle to put my jacket on, restrained by the confines of my car. The cops leave. It rains harder. The orange and green lights of the 7-Eleven sign blur through the sheets of water that streak down my windshield. I'm going to sleep, and if someone cares, I'm sure they'll let me know, but I'm not moving.

I wake and recall that I dreamt about my time in Chino prison, but it was more like a recording. Nothing happened. I was just there in my cell.

It's still raining. There is a new set of cops loitering, or maybe they are the same ones. I start my car, and I drive carefully down Sunset with the defroster blasting and my windows down a couple inches. I can hear tires peeling away the water from the road.

My office phone rings. It startles me. It's Ted. He sounds anxious, tells me to come into his office as soon as possible.

I sit. He closes the door behind me.

"What's up, Ted. Everything alright?" I ask, probing.

"Look, uh Dick called and he's made me promise to speak to you about not practicing law."

"Practicing law? What?" I say incredulously. "Of course I'm not."

"I know. I know. Larry called Dick and some dust got kicked up at corporate. We'll just let it settle."

I'm riled up enough to feel the heat in my cheeks. I know Ted is on my side. I take a deep breath. I'm powerless over this.

"How's everything else going?" Ted inquires with a genuine smile.

"It's fine," I say and chuckle. "I mean look, I'm grateful to be here, and I'm doing my best, but working 'with' or uh I guess 'for' uh ..."

"Larry," Ted fills in the blank.

"Yeah, Larry. I don't really know what's going on. I thought I was here to handle the contracts, and he's acting like I'm his assistant."

Ted rubs his eyes and sighs. "It's a bit of a transition. Things around here are a little complicated by our relationship with corporate in Dallas. Let's just say Larry is the only one here directly connected to Texas. Sometimes we have to work around him."

I force a smile and nod.

"So are you getting a grasp of how the contracts work?" Ted asks.

I pause, struggling with myself. Ted knows I have something to say, but I am not sure whether to say it.

"Go 'head," he says. "It won't leave this office."

"Okay. Look, I could be wrong, but I've really looked into it, and I'm baffled. I mean, I've never seen anything like it."

I expect Ted to be intrigued, but he's not.

I explain the situation with the contracts, that the addendums Larry does are mostly meaningless.

Ted doesn't need it, but I have to drive my point home.

"So imagine you go to a gym and you sign up for a membership. The contract is the standard boilerplate language, with all the terms favoring the gym. You sign the contract, you take your copy and you go home. When you get home, you type out an amendment to the contract that has terms that conflict with the contract. Let's call it an addendum. It says you can cancel whenever you want without notice, that there is no late fee, that if you get injured, the gym will pay for it ... You get the picture, right?"

Ted nods.

"Maybe you send it to the gym or maybe you don't. It doesn't matter because they just ignore it or call you and tell you you're crazy. Then you staple your addendum, that only you have signed, maybe only you have actually seen—if you get my implication—to the back of the contract. Then you put it in your file cabinet and pretend it's real. That's worst-case example."

"Wow," Ted says and raises his eyebrows as he reclines.

"The difference, of course is that these are contracts for hundreds of thousands of dollars and even millions—"

"Are they all like that?"

"No. Sometimes there is an actual addendum that amends the contract, but it's rare. You can imagine what happens. Larry emails over his little addendum. The contractor's project manager looks at this one-page document that proposes to amend the most important terms of a thirty-page legal document that has been vetted by the contractor's legal team, and she either ignores it, or signs it but crosses everything out but a couple rebar scope terms or, I presume, contacts Larry and tells him to pound sand. Then it looks like Larry usually ignores the situation and keeps the original addendum in the file. Or sometimes, for whatever reason, he does include the mostly crossed-out addendum. Occasionally, usually on small jobs, he gets lucky and some exhausted and unaware project manager signs an addendum, I presume, just to get it off her desk, but that is very rare. Typically, there is no real negotiation going on and none or nearly none of CIW's terms get included in the contract."

"I knew it was bad," Ted interrupts. "But I didn't know it was that bad."

I sit back. I feel nervous about dropping this bombshell.

"Well, this is uh, it's why you are here," Ted laughs and shakes his head and widens his eyes at the absurdity of the situation.

I decide to carry on, get it all out there.

"But that's not what baffles me the most ..." I declare.

Ted's eyes widen.

"The credit thing ..."

Ted's face relaxes, seemingly aware of exactly where I'm going.

"You are a quick learner," he says.

"I mean, it's really kind of uh … amazing right? Larry has files for each and every contractor we do business with. They are two-sided credit files. On one side is a Dun & Bradstreet credit report. Obviously, you know how these jobs are bid. In any event, credit isn't relevant. These jobs aren't based on credit. The contractor gets paid from the owner on billings and progress, you know, the uh, the percentage the job is completed, and once the contractor is paid by the owner, we get paid."

"Yeah, yep, basically—" Ted says, almost bored.

"I guess what I'm getting at is that credit has nothing to do with it. We aren't selling a product to someone. We are builders. It's almost comical, pulling credit reports on some of the largest construction out-fits in the United States as if we are some mom-and-pop lumber store selling two-by-fours."

Ted laughs. "You've really been thinking about these things."

"Well … I just—"

"So did you ask Larry about this?" Ted asks and bites his lower lip in anticipation of my answer, as if it's a comedy skit he's seen before and loves.

"Hell no! What am I going to say? 'Hey Larry, after a couple weeks of being here, I've come to the conclusion that your job is meaningless—'"

Ted laughs and says, "That'd be interesting."

"So am I right?" I ask.

Ted doesn't answer but seems to want to milk some more entertain-ment out of this. He excitedly asks, "So did you ask Gary or Tommy in sales about your theory?"

Gary is Rancho CIW's veteran, star, workhorse salesman. He's one of those guys that can put his head down and work hard and uninter-rupted for 12 hours with seeming ease, and nobody dislikes him because he never says an unkind word about anyone, let alone gossips. Tommy is Gary's boss. With Gary, the question is, "Why isn't he running the sales department or the whole business, for that matter?" With Tommy it's, "How the hell did *this guy* get the job running the sales department?" at least until you realize that under his good ole boy exterior is a cunning politician.

"Not exactly," I say. "I asked Gary, but in a roundabout way."

"And?"

"Gary laughed and said I should mention my observations to you."

Ted laughs heartily and gathers himself. "You see, Larry came from corporate. In Texas, they don't build anything, they only sell rebar from the steel mill. We are the only placer—rebar placer—they've ever had. So Larry came here with the idea that he'd do credit the same way he did in Texas, and that's what he does."

"But it's meaningless!" I say exasperatedly. "I mean, I haven't found one thing that he does yet that does anything for this company. I don't mean in a metaphorical way, I mean, literally."

"Well ..." Ted says contemplatively and with a hint of defensiveness.

I think I may have overstepped my boundaries. I contemplate my firm conviction not to gossip in the workplace. I've made the mistake before, and I know it's poison. But is this gossip?

"Well," Ted repeats after a few seconds. "He handles the mechanic's liens. Are you up to speed on mechanic's liens?"

"Actually, yes. In fact, I bought a book on them to get a refresher."

"Oh?" Ted says.

"I've filed mechanic's liens and sued on them a couple times," I explain. "But I did learn something new. Did you know mechanic's liens are the only specific creditor protection in the California Constitution?"

Ted makes a 'really?' face.

"So, I started pulling the mechanic's liens to see our process. Turns out Larry outsources those to a company in Los Angeles. It's kind of hard to track because they are included in some weird educational package that he buys, so you can't really see them on the invoices."

"Oh ..." Ted says. "I did not know that."

"Yeah, it's quite the racket this little company has. We fill out a form that tells them all the information for the lien, and then they actually prepare the lien and send them out." I shrug. "Why would you do all the work and then pay them? Why not just do it yourself?"

"Good question," Ted responds.

Ted leans backs and sighs. I'm not sure if I'm overwhelming him, and I'm definitely not sure if I'm being strategically sound. I decide to quit now and not tell Ted I've discussed mechanic's liens with Larry, and it's absolutely clear that he has no understanding of how they work.

A loud coughing noise sounds, and we hear a panicky scuttle outside the door. I instinctively leap to my feet and open Ted's door just in time to see Larry dart into his office down the hall. He's still coughing.

I reenter Ted's office, shut the door and sit.

"Larry?" Ted asks.

"Yep," I say.

"He's probably already on the phone to Dallas." Ted rises out of his chair. "Look, I know this is difficult, but I brought you here because I knew there was a problem. I didn't know it was this bad."

"Ted, what do you want me to do? How do I work with him knowing what we just talked about?"

Ted opens the door. "Just take it easy, and ease into it. Change comes slowly around here. But it's pretty obvious who will take over for Larry when he leaves. I mean, just listen."

Larry's cough echoes down the hall. As I walk by his office and glance in, he's red-faced and trying to suppress his cough. I go in my office and search the internet for CPR instructions. Larry is on the phone with Dallas before he stops coughing.

"I've given my life to this company, Dick! They think they can just replace me ..."

TWENTY-FIVE

I can't afford to be a golfer, but I can afford to practice golf.

I dump the bag of golf balls Trenton left me. These are Pro V1s. The damn things cost four bucks apiece and given how many balls I lose when I play on a course, they will double my cost of play, but here, at the net, they aren't likely to get lost.

I review what I'm calling my Official Declaration of Golf:

First, I don't quit golf, no matter what.

Second, I can't do it on my own.

Third, I'm going to be a scratch golfer.

I'm still not sure exactly what it means to be a "scratch golfer." Ted explained to me that it was more complicated than a golfer averaging a score of par. It has something to do with the handicapping system. I do know that a "scratch golfer" is ridiculously, absurdly, unfathomably good at golf. I've never played with anyone who has shot par in their entire life, let alone consistently done so. CIW Rancho Rebar is filled with dedicated golfers, including Ted, who have been playing since they were children, some even members of private country clubs; most haven't even broken 80, and none have shot a par 72.

I rake a ball into place on the hitting mat with my seven-iron. I take the grip I've been practicing in my living room. It feels strange, like trying to write left-handed. I waggle the club to loosen up. This is all straight out of Ben Hogan's little book, *Five Lessons: The Modern Fundamentals of Golf.*

I take my club to the top of my backswing, and I let it rip. The ball clangs off the toe of my club and trundles pathetically into the tattered net. It's a golf swing devoid of power, grace, and patience, devoid of anything reminiscent of athletic movement. From a distance, I imagine it resembles an erect grand mal seizure. Each swing that follows is worse than the one before; the intervals between each ball shorter and shorter; the anger in me rising and rising until it's all I can do not to scream gutturally and throw my club at the starter shack and stomp away. The harder I try to hit the ball, the worse it gets. I'm swinging so hard with so much anger that I realize I might hurt myself, perhaps even stroke out. I sit down in a spot under a tree in the shade and try to cool my temper.

"Why am I so angry? What the hell is the matter with you, Joseph?"

There is a pale old man on the putting green wielding a vintage hickory-shafted putter. He alternates its use between putter and cane. His buddy, a deeply wrinkled man with peanut butter colored freckles dotting his dark skin, misses a short putt in a game the two are playing, and his friend gives him hell for it. They are having fun.

Somewhat inspired, I think about the free beginner's lesson I took a couple months ago. The golf instructor told me to take small swings, to practice hitting the ball on the sweet spot. Partly out of desperation to make one swing that doesn't make me feel physically and emotionally sick, and partly in mockery of myself for having to revert to what seems a child's golf drill, I go back to the hitting bay and pick up my seven-iron. I take the club back so that my hands stay below my right hip, and then I slowly unwind. The club and ball kiss right in the center of the clubface, and there is a nice clean "click" sound as the ball pops in to the air as if off a tiny trampoline. I couldn't have swung much shorter or slower, but it felt so nice. Just so I know this isn't a fluke, I rake another ball onto the mat and repeat my tiny golf swing. Again, there's a delicious little pop.

❖   ❖   ❖

"Larry, I'm just trying to do my job. I don't know how else I could have said it."

I'm in his office, sitting across from him. He's staring at me coldly, and then suddenly his eyes glaze over as if he's in a full dream. I'm real close to asking if he's alright when he finally speaks.

"I know you're sober, you know, Kiddo. I'm in the program, too ... been a long time since I've gone to A & A classes, you know, with how much work I do here."

"Oh, uh ..." I'm struck, scouring my brain for responses. "How'd you know I'm sober?"

"Oh my, my ... child, people talk like schoolgirls 'round here. You'd be surprised what I know." Larry tilts back in his chair and grins as if he's just laid down four aces on a poker table piled with cash.

Does he know my whole story? I'm sure Ted or Erik wouldn't have told him.

"It's true," I reply. "I'm sober, and I don't drink. It's not something I tell people unless it comes up, you know?"

"Of course!" Larry says, and then hushes himself. "Your secrets are safe with me."

I feel nauseous.

"That's, Larry, good to know. Uh ... Is there something—" I say as I contemplate my exit plan.

"We all have our secrets, our issues," Larry declares. "I haven't had it easy. I used to own a collection company. I had a couple dozen collectors working for me. All in a big bullpen. But I ended up working for CIW in Seguin as a collector myself."

I interject, "Really?" and do my damnedest to make it clear that I think he's full of shit. "Why, just out of curiosity?" I ask. "I mean, what made you give up your collection company with uh, what'd you say, dozens of collectors, dozens right, to go to work as a collector yourself?"

I stare at Larry, challengingly.

Larry ignores my sarcasm. "You can keep a secret, right?" Larry speaks softly. He looks left and right, clearly for show, as there is nothing left or right other than office walls, and he doesn't bother to shut the door.

"Larry, I'd prefer not to get pers—"

"Hush child!" Larry whisper-shouts. "It was my son's birthday. It was at one of my two daughters' homes in Texas. They were both with their beaus, near San Antone. You been?"

"No, actually never been to Texas other than flying through."

"Oh dear God, child you got to ... actually," he says, apparently reconsidering. "You ain't missing nothing."

Larry is fully transformed into his natural form, a mixture of stereotypically gay, southern, and catty. I actually like him more this way. At least it's authentic.

I settle in. Larry is enjoying himself, telling this story, going into details. When he talks about the Program, he says "one day of a time" instead of "one day at a time" and looks at me for confirmation, like it's a secret 12-Step phrase. I nod, and repeat it, yep, one day at a time. By the time we get back to the story about his son's birthday, he's divulged that he's been married and divorced from the same woman three times. This is enough to sidetrack my mind. He's obviously gay or pretending to be. I have to refocus. His recounting of his drinking days is pretty obviously for my benefit as he keeps footnoting his story with, "You know how it is, right? You just can't stop, you know?"

After a few more side-bars about his drinkin' days, he gets back to the story.

Larry walks into his son's would-be birthday party and people are gossiping about how Larry's son is too sensitive, and he shouldn't have been snooping around and what's the big deal with the words "homo" and "faggot," I mean, he is one, right? And Larry overhears all this and when everyone sees him and he asks what the hell is going on, they tell him that Larry's son walked in while they were talking and then he ran off, and they hollered for him to come back, but he just drove off. And then Larry walks out of the apartment and looks down over the railing onto the parking lot. "And I just knew it right then," Larry tells me.

"And my son's car is gone..." Larry says. "So I go back home where he lived with me, and I walk in through the front door of the house, and there he is ... hangin'."

I gasp. I'm speechless, but my mind races: Oh Jesus Christ! You got to be kidding me. I don't want to know this. Why the fuck are you telling me this shit! I imagine Larry's son's feet dangling and rotating a little back and forth, like in old Western movies.

"I'm so sorry, Larry. That's just horrible. I'm uh—"

"Well, we've all be through things," he says and pauses, seemingly satisfied with the effect his story has had on me. "So things changed, you know. I ended up ultimately working at CIW, working at a steel mill in the credit department, little ole me. Ain't that a hoot?"

For a couple days now, every time I hear Larry's voice on the phone, even when it's him complaining indirectly about me, or at least, about the situation of me being here, all I can think of is him finding his son, dead and hanged.

Larry has this thing where he says stereotypically gay stuff, like "lil' miss thang," but then in response to any suggestion that he might be gay, he acts as if the idea is insane. He must have guilt about his son, perhaps for never coming out of the closet, or who knows. The result, I guess, is a bundle of weird behavior. Larry has two guys that regularly come into his office after their shifts are done in the shipping department. Both are handsome, strapping guys, one in his twenties, the other in his early forties. Larry lends the young one money pretty regularly. He brags about it to me. Larry's relationship with the other guy goes much deeper. Larry talks about the guy's daughters and tells stories about going to their cheerleading performances, always making note of the fact that he helped pay for uniforms or cheerleading camp.

Larry even bought a ski boat for the guy. Larry tells people they bought it together and gets angry when they ask why he bought the guy a boat, and yet he complains to me about how much he paid for the boat, that he's only seen it once and that it's kept in a trailer at the guy's house that "cost almost as much as the damn boat, can you believe that?"

Larry's livid because Ted has decided that Larry's two friends from the shipping department can no longer visit Larry's office. Our receptionist told a detailer who told me that she overheard Mary tell Suzan that she overheard Ted on the phone telling someone, probably someone at HR in Dallas, that Ted told Larry the visits have to stop because they are becoming a distraction.

But this isn't about him being gay or closeted gay or pretending to be flamboyantly gay or whatever he vacillates between, depending on the day. I don't give a damn who he's attracted to, except that time during my first couple weeks when he creepily put his hand on my shoulder when he was showing me something on the computer and his hand crept down my back until I jerked away and gave him the "I'll kick your ass" stare. It's been several months since that happened. At first, I thought about going to HR, but I didn't. If it were man-on-woman, it'd be a big deal, I guess. I don't know. I'd feel weak going to HR with that, but maybe I should have. Maybe I should have played that card, because the other stuff Larry does is convoluted and nebulous, the kind of behavior that anyone who works with him knows exactly what I'm talking about, but if I tried to explain it to someone else, they'd say, in a questioning tone, with heavy emphasis on the word exactly, "So what exactly did he do wrong?"

I care that Larry plays head games, that he's acting like my boss, that he's running an irrelevant department and getting in the way of me changing it. He needs to leave, take care of his health, take care of his mental health. It's hard to explain how fucked up Larry is. But now at least I know why. That horrific story, it's almost too much to digest.

Every time I think of it, I want to cry. I can't imagine. I guess it's true what they say in Al-Anon, "Hurt people hurt people."

Wait, am I homophobic? Of course I am. "Faggot" was the go-to insult of my adolescence. Only the really bad kids used the word "nigger." That was taboo, but they said "faggot" or "homo" like pronouns. Back then, I used those words, too. I never even thought about it. I don't think anyone did. "Faggots" were "faggots" and "homos" were "homos," and no one wanted to be either. It wasn't debatable, and no one was debating it. Now I live next door to Silver Lake and a couple of miles from West Hollywood. I have gay friends. My new sponsor is gay, and he's one of the kindest people I've ever known. Intellectually, politically, I'm as pro-gay as a rainbow flag. But I grew up in this society as a white heterosexual male, part of the dominant culture, and, as a result, believing that I don't subconsciously think differently about someone who is gay than someone who is straight is no less naïve and offensive than white people claiming they don't see skin color.

Larry aside, my work couldn't be better. Even though I didn't start working until mid-October, Ted cut me in on the annual Christmas bonus. My stock options and matching 401k contributions have kicked in, as well as my health insurance. I haven't had health insurance in 10 years. Hell, I even have a life insurance policy.

CIW, at least the Rancho branch, is overflowing with cash. It's as if Ted and Erik are looking for ways to spend it so they don't have to give it all back to corporate. Ted explained in a manager's meeting that the way it works here is that when CIW buys a smaller company, as they did Rancho Rebar, Rancho Rebar takes on the debt of CIW's acquisition of Rancho Rebar, and pays back the amount CIW paid for it, plus interest, over a number of years. From what I've gleaned from higher-ups and manager meetings, this debt is easily serviced. There are corporate lunches, lavish golf tournaments, and bonuses. Erik, who was a college quarterback, is now getting chunky, so he started a gym program, and everyone at CIW Rancho Rebar now has a free gym membership to 24

Hour Fitness. This works great for me because I can break up my 50-mile commute on the way home and stop at any of the several 24 Hour Fitness gyms between Rancho and Echo Park.

Larry's insanity works for and against me. Of course, I have to deal with him. We still haven't even worked out the minor detail of whether or not he is actually my boss. Ted says, "No, you just work together" although he's never said that in a room that Larry and I both occupy simultaneously. Larry makes his opinion clear: He's my boss. Larry desperately wants me to acknowledge that he is my boss, but I refuse.

Everyone in sales, placement and admin have been dealing with Larry for nearly a decade, so that makes me look like a saint. The salesmen almost fall out of their chairs when I tell them I'll go to a contractor's office and negotiate a contract, that I'll even deal with the rebar specs. I really have very little to do here, so I've been studying rebar specs out of the *Concrete Reinforcing Steel Institute: Manual of Standard Practices* since I got here, so I get the basics.

Ramone, one of the senior detailers, told me the story of Larry going to a contractor meeting for a parking structure job when he first moved from Texas to come work at Rancho Rebar, and when one of the general contractor's project managers in the meeting didn't accept Larry's proposed amendment to the contract, Larry had a fit and walked out of the meeting.

"He had a fit like a baby. He was yelling and ran out of the room. I didn't know what to say. I just stayed in there and finished hammering out the specs," Ramone told me.

"No way," I said.

"Yeah, and he's never gone to another meeting since. That was 10 years ago. The sales guys don't even ask him anymore."

"Wow."

"The crazy part is that we drove together. I was in the meeting for another hour. Larry was just out in the parking lot smoking cigarettes. And when I got back to the car, he acted like nothing happened."

Larry hates golf. Despite recently dedicating myself to the mastery of golf, I completely understand. It's a horrible sport on so many levels. Nearly all of the extra-office activities at CIW Rancho Rebar are centered around golf. They even have a summer league where everyone is allowed to leave early on Friday to go play, although I've learned that since I'm a manager, it's frowned upon for me to go consistently, since managers get to play in corporate tournaments put on by us and our big contractor customers that no one else gets to attend.

There is also a weekly managers' meeting where all the department heads meet and go over statuses. Larry is supposed to go, but he usually doesn't, out of spite about something that happened a few years ago. I attend in his place and report on the status of contracts, and Larry reluctantly gives me the status report on certain collection matters, since he was presented by Ted with the option of either attending the meeting or letting me present the collection report at the meeting. Now, since nobody wants to deal with Larry, most people come to me for anything falling under the credit, collections and contracts umbrella. This infuriates Larry. I appease him: "Larry, I don't know why they come to me for anything other than contracts. I tell them I'm just going to ask you about it, or I tell them to go to you." Other than Gary, who has Teflon skin, no one ever goes to Larry, because they don't want to deal with him.

I try not to consider my job a competition against Larry, but the reality is, little by little, I'm taking over his responsibilities. Ted and Erik are completely on board with this, but it's never formally announced. A few people have asked whether Larry is retiring and I'm replacing him. The idea makes me glow. It'd make my life so much better because I wouldn't have to deal with pretending that things Larry thinks are important are actually important or even actually exist, and I wouldn't have to deal with his constant drama and gossip, some of which I've fallen into myself out of sheer emotional exhaustion; and, even more exciting, I'd make twice what I'm making now, likely more. It'd be buy-a-house money and get-out-of-debt money. And I'd be able to be of real service to CIW instead of playing games to justify the existence of meaningless procedures.

But I also feel bad for Larry. CIW is his life, and there are a few people here who like him. He has an adorable kid, Angel, working for him who annually auditions for *American Idol*. Angel works full-time but has little to do. His job is to wear absurdly tight clothes and listen to Larry gossip in exchange for Larry's continuing defense of Angel's employment from regular attacks from Ted. A week ago, Larry was at the doctor's, and Angel came to me because he had no work. He looked panicked. I had him organize some files. He seemed so thankful. The next day, when Larry found out I'd given Angel work, he was irate. "This isn't your department!" he yelled at me. I told Larry Angel came to me with the nothing to do, so I gave him some work. Larry called Angel into his office and asked him whether he asked me for work. Angel lied. At first I thought he didn't remember. "What!" I said, looking right at Angel. "Angel, no, don't you remember? It was just after eight and you walked into my office ..." Angel was scared. He blinked his eyes and fidgeted. He said nothing, just looked over at Larry, clearly suffering from Larry-induced office-variety Stockholm Syndrome.

Larry told me that his two other office assistants had serious issues when they worked in another department and were about to get fired. He saved them from termination and brought them into his department. To hear him tell it, Larry's department is to CIW Rancho Rebar what AA is to society: "The last house on the block." He also told me that one of his assistants came to blows with another employee. Whether it's true or not, I'm not sure. It's probably an amalgamation of the truth. Sometimes I get locked into his gossip. I'm not beyond it myself, but luckily, I have nothing to offer other than my own sordid history, which I'm not going to talk about. The only other thing I've got to gossip about is Larry himself.

And I don't get in on the real good stuff because I don't arrive at work until 7 a.m. The Gossip Crew's day starts at 5 a.m. with an hour's worth of gossip. They have the place to themselves because everyone else gets to work no earlier than 6 a.m. But sometimes I'll drive to work and get there earlier, just before 6 a.m. and every time, they are in Larry's office laughing and gossiping. I usually walk toward them slowly and listen for a while, but when I reach them, they go silent. "So whaddaya guys talkin' about?" I'll ask, knowingly, with a little grin. "Oh, nothing," they'll say and snicker. Or, the usual, Larry's favorite, "Oh just us ole wives in our morning sewing circle." Sometimes, as I approach down the hallway, I'll even hear them talking about me. It's usually something along the lines of me thinking I know so much more than Larry. "Fair enough," I always think. It's not slander if it's true. Or sometimes it'll be something about my law career or something he heard I told Ted. The weird thing is how engrossed his staff is. I've begun referring to them in my head as The Little Stockholm Syndrome Gang. I envision them wearing black berets, like Patty Hearst, with a rebar-themed logo. After nearly a decade of this gossip-based emotional bonding where, Larry, the most irrelevant and despised manager, leads the outcast admin staff employees, it's become a full, family psycho-drama. And, given that none of them have enough real work to fill half a day, gossip itself has become the subject of their work.

I'm in Larry's office trying to make peace with him. Larry talks about John Davenport— "sweet man but terrible alcoholic, no offense, Kiddo"—an attorney that worked for CIW before going out on his own. Larry claims that his current method of negotiating a construction contract was John's idea, which I doubt very much, unless John is an idiot, but I use this as a segue to talk about the contracts.

"You know Larry," I say. "This method of amending the contracts, you know ... that, uh, you were taught by John, it's not quite right. I'd like to do it a little differently."

Larry stares at me. His face turns red. His eyes flare with anger. I fear Larry will explode at my insolence. I continue, carefully approaching the topic as if I'm critiquing the work of John not Larry. Larry's color returns as he seemingly realizes that I'm giving him a way to save face as long as he doesn't give me any friction about handling the contracts the way I want to. Larry registers shock when I pull out several old contracts and explain to him that many of his addendums are quite literally, meaningless pieces of paper, and that if a legal dispute ever occurred that rose to the level of litigation, the addendums wouldn't even be considered as part of the contract.

I softly ask, "Do you understand what I mean ... how these unsigned or partially signed addendums are, you know ... not effective?"

Larry blurts, "John was an alcoholic. It doesn't surprise me that he steered me in the wrong direction. I'm just surprised he sold Dallas on it. I actually told them ..." Larry trails off. I recognize this technique. He knows that I know he's lying, and he knows that I don't care, so he fades off into an inaudible mumble.

"Really? I didn't know that," I say, playing along, happy with the direction this is going.

"He used to come into my office and cry—boy, he was lower than the bottom of a gopher hole, the ole drunk lawyer. He even spent the night at my house, once. I thought he might kill himself. I guess it's not that surprising he'd make a mistake like this."

"Yeah," I say. "He's just lucky none of this has gotten out. I imagine he'd have been fired on the spot."

I intend this statement to land hard, and from the whiter-than-usual pale of Larry's face, it has.

"Uh, this isn't something Erik or Ted, uh, know about, right?" Larry inquires, almost desperately.

I think to myself: Damn. Ted does know, but I can't tell Larry that. This is how it happens. How can I not lie without starting a war? I play dumb and double down. "Well, of course they do, right? I'm sure this has come up before, hasn't it? I mean all they have to do is look at the contracts. But unless they know the law as well as someone like you does ..."

Through his glasses and into his eyes, I can see the gears of Larry's mind turning. He's doing an impromptu mini risk-assessment of his exposure.

Ted peeks his head into Larry's office and clears his throat. I look at Ted, then back to Larry. Now Larry looks shaken, probably wondering if Ted heard any of our conversation.

"Larry, are you alright?" Ted asks.

Larry fakes a cough and says, "Oh yeah, just had a coughing spell."

"Can I see you in my office?" Ted asks me.

I follow Ted, and he tells me that things have been working out so well and since I've shown such an interest in learning the construction side of the business, they are sending me to *World of Concrete* in Las Vegas. He tells me I can drive or fly and to expense everything. I'm so excited. As much as I'm grateful for this job, getting re-acclimated to sitting in an office chair for eight to 12 hours every day and commuting a hundred miles, five days a week, has been difficult.

When I return to Larry's office, he is yelling about me to Angel. I stand in the doorway. Larry doesn't even attempt to censor himself.

"I've been here nearly 10 years! Do you know how many times I've been invited to *World of Concrete*?" he asks rhetorically. "Zero, that's how many times, Honey Child. All of them are a bunch of pit vipers!" He waves his hands wildly.

Angel looks at me blankly, then back at Larry, as if to ask Larry if he knows I'm here, and whether he should be angry, too.

"Oh, I don't care if he hears me," Larry says, referring to me. "Golden Boy's been here for a couple months, and he's part of the club already." Larry throws up his hands.

"I thought you were too busy to go, Larry," I say, trying to defuse the situation.

Larry seems to appreciate my gesture. It fits right into his narrative. His whole shtick is pretending he's so busy that he has to work long hours and can never take a day off. The joke around the office is that while Larry has never taken a vacation, he has gone back to Texas for his grandma's funeral 10 times. "How many grandmas does he have?" I heard one of the salesmen joke. Of course, nobody cares. Larry could take off a couple months and Ted and Erik would be happy to pay him just to not have him around. Although, I've heard a rumor that Ted got Dallas to agree to pay for most of Larry's salary.

I'm able to wrap up a meeting with a contractor's project manager in Orange County and avoid the infamous "Orange Crush" traffic on my way back into Los Angeles, arriving in time to make it to the Griffith Park Golf Courses just after the twilight rate begins. If the courses aren't crowded, I'll be able to play all 18 holes, and maybe I can check off my first golf scoring goal: break 100. It should be easy. I may have already done it. I've written a final number of less than 100 on my scorecard many times, although I doubt it was ever legitimate. Some of the rules of golf I'd been breaking I didn't even know I was breaking. I thought when I hit a ball off the tee out of bounds that the only penalty was "loss of expensive golf ball." Turns out, the official *Rules of Golf* are much more heavy-handed than that. I'm also pretty sure I thought Mulligans were a real thing. In hindsight, it seems ridiculous that one could simply play another ball off the tee as if the prior horrific shot hadn't even happened. One can't simply rewind time. But I sure do love the idea of a Mulligan. My life is a series of Mulligans.

So now I'm going to get a legitimate 90-something score. I don't care if it's 99 as long as my final score is less than three digits. Breaking 100 is easy. If I alternate bogey—one over par—and double bogey—two over par— on each hole, that's 99. Who can't do that?

I play Harding, the easier and shorter of the two courses. I score a 9 on the first hole, so I'm five-over through one. At this rate, I'll shoot 164. Shell-shocked and demoralized, I walk off the first green and cross Crystal Springs Drive, muttering sarcastically: "Oh, yeah, breaking 100 … this will be easy, Joseph. Good thing you haven't been practicing and reading golf books every damn day for the last fucking three months!"

My anger burns me from the inside out. It's a diet of mild sarcasm peppered with the occasional foul blurt. It's a red hot, ugly anger. It reminds me of my dad, that anger he'd get when he worked on cars. It's dense and violent. I don't like it, but it's definitely me. Each golf hole gets worse and worse, and now it's getting dark and the coyotes are coming out. After my fifth or sixth quadruple bogey, and actually swinging and missing the ball more than once, which I've learned counts as a stroke because of the maniacally cruel *Rules of Golf*, I give up and just crisscross the mostly empty course, playing whichever hole of the two courses, Wilson and Harding, are empty.

I'm not sure that I'll be able to start up again if I stop moving now. It's a good mile to the club house, and my bag feels like it weighs 50 pounds. I have to get across Crystal Springs Drive before the gates are locked by the maintenance crew, and they probably don't know I am here, since I didn't rent a motor cart.

"You think the average man can break 80 do ya, Ben?" I say loud and sarcastically to Ben Hogan.

Ben is not here, and he does not reply.

I think: My grip, my stance, my backswing, my downswing. It all sounds so doable in your little book, Ben. But I can't even hit the damn ball, and I've been practicing constantly. What the hell? "Dig it out of the dirt," isn't that what you say, Ben? I'll dig my own grave at this rate.

"Hey," I hear.

The voice startles me, and I prepare to be embarrassed that someone has heard me talking to myself. I turn to the voice and see a man driving a topless golf cart carrying rakes and shovels instead of golf clubs. He pulls up next to me.

"C'mon, we are closing," he says.

"Okay," I say, trying to read his deeply suntanned face to see whether he heard me talking to myself. All I glean is irritation that he has to deal with me.

"You better grab a seven-iron," he yells back at me as he drives away.

I trot toward the gate, my clubs rattling and clacking against themselves as I bounce. As I reach the gate, he's on his phone and unlocking the padlock so he can lock the gate behind me.

"What was that about a seven-iron?" I ask.

He's listening to whoever is on the other end of the phone, perhaps his wife, I think. He nods down the path where we've come from. I look back into the near-dark golf course, and there are no less than a dozen coyotes trotting out from somewhere, like vampires welcoming the dark. I pull out my seven-iron for the remainder of my walk, another half mile across the other side of the street. On the way back, I spot several more coyotes, their heads hanging down as they run past. A couple consider me. In the foreground of the tall, white-bark, oak trees that line Wilson's Number One hole and Wilson's Number Eighteen hole, proudly stands a full buck with giant antlers amidst several small deer. Numerous coyotes dart around the deer like muggers casing a victim. The buck juts forward at a coyote, and the coyotes retreat. I cross through the little forest. I've been here before, not just to collect errant balls. It's the go-to forest location for commercial shoots. I worked on a car commercial here, I think for Kia. I find a gleaming white premium golf ball. Some fool like me must have hooked it off the tee box.

"What'd you think of this Ben? It's a good omen, right?" I say aloud holding up my little prize ball in my palm as I make my way through the little dark forest in the middle of Los Angeles.

On my drive into work, I usually listen to tapes of Reverend Michael Beckwith's sermons at Agape, but on the way home, I think and talk to myself. I look forward to it, and I cover much ground. By the time I reach my half-way point, where the 57 and 210 Freeways meet, I'm in my own world, long into my conversation. I usually think about the revelation that I've made about the golf swing and how excited I am to go out and fix my swing. But today, I'm thinking about money.

It's kind of bizarre, I am making four times what I was making before CIW, and yet I'm still basically broke. The difference is that now, I'm paying half my take-home pay to service my student loans. Over the last 10 years, I've already paid enough to cover the principle on them, but because of interest and late fees, I owe more than when I started, 10 years ago. I had to use my credit cards to survive over the last few years, so those are maxed out, and I'm paying usury interest just to avoid going into default. I'm also spending several hundred dollars a month on gas. And because I have no kids and don't own a home, and I can't write-off but a fraction of my student loan interest, I am paying a ton in taxes.

But I'm safe. I can pay my bills, and I have a little left over for food, golf and the 12-Step basket. And I'm bullish on CIW stock. I've heard the stories of the people that have worked for Rancho Rebar-now-CIW for 25 years and are now millionaires because they've been buying stock and maxing out their stock options. There's a guy in the shipping department, Randy, he probably makes less than I do, and at lunch he was talking about how he's going to retire in two years. He'll be 63, owns his home and has just over a million in his 401k and CIW stock.

I think of my grandpa. This is what it used to be like in America. You could easily get a blue-collar job, move into the office, if you worked hard, and if you saved your money and put a chunk away consistently in the stock market, you'd be set by the time you retired, easily, if you included your home equity. Hell, it'd almost be hard not to succeed. The New York Stock Exchange historically pays out 10 percent a year, and if you reinvest your dividends and put 10 percent of your gross wages away for 30 years or more—that's the American Dream. Work hard, get married, buy a house, have children, and retire in comfort. That's what the "greatest generation" did—back before all the manufacturing jobs were shipped to second and third-world countries, so the rich here in America wouldn't have to "trickle down" so much of their hard-earned cash to pesky laborers. But for me, it doesn't matter. I'm one of the rare lucky ones. I work at CIW! They can't ship my job to Mexico, China or India. We build bridges and high-rises, right here in America. We are green recyclers, too. We take shitty old rusted cars, melt them down, and produce rebar, the bones of the body of modern society. I won the lottery. I've stumbled on a place where the American Dream is still alive and thriving!

———————

TWENTY-SIX

For the last several months, I've been practicing golf as if it's the only thing I really care about. When I'm not swinging a golf club, I'm thinking or dreaming about swinging a golf club. And it's finally paying off. I broke 100 months ago, even shot a 92, but I haven't broken 90 yet. But I will soon. The last time I played a full round of golf was at the Concrete Institute's Golf Charity Tournament. It's a best-ball tournament, where each player in every foursome drives their ball off the tee, and then the foursome chooses the best drive, and then each player hits the next shot from the drive. I did something so incredible that if I didn't have three witnesses, including Gary, no one would believe it. They were all jumping up and down and hooting like I'd won the U.S. Open. On holes 7 and 9, I hit long straight drives, which our foursome chose as the drives we would use. Then, from 40 yards and 110 yards respectively, I holed out. I had two eagles on par-fours in the stretch of three holes.

Two eagles in three holes! It felt like the time I'd won my first trial, like I'd arrived at a plateau I'd never come down from, only up. But there was doubt, too. Yes, I'd won that jury trial. But I'd already settled with the other defendants for more than the jury verdict, so was it really a victory? I'd shown I could compete with a seasoned trial lawyer. The judge complimented me, said I was rough around the edges but that I definitely had "it." He said the jury listened to me and believed me. It was technically a win, but it wasn't a practical win. The same with my two-eagle golf round. It was an amazing feat, but with a big fat asterisk: * It's a best-ball tournament—it doesn't count.

"C'mon, Joseph," I try to convince myself. "Best-ball tournament or not, anyone who has two eagles in three holes can break 90."

I've been invited to play with the Loose Impediments, an unofficial CIW employees and friends traveling golf club. I have to drive two hours into the hills of deep East San Diego to get here, but it's worth it. Today's the day I break 90. I meet Gary at the driving range, and he introduces me to Steve. I've never met Steve, and I don't like Steve. Steve works at CIW's San Diego branch. His name only comes up when golf is discussed: "Steve could've gone pro." "I once saw Steve carry his drive over 300 yards." "Steve's been playing since he was five years old."

Fuck Steve.

I warm up on the range between Gary and Steve. Gary has been playing for 30 years. The wife of the owners of Rancho Rebar, long before CIW bought it out, paid for his membership to Arrowhead Country Club. This was back when the IRS let businesses expense golf club memberships. Gary's swing is funky but reliable. Gary is odd—he plays golf only for fun. He's never shot par, probably only broken 80 a couple times, and he couldn't care less. I do not relate to Gary.

At the range, I watch Steve expertly hit balls to a red flag 80 yards out. There is no anxiety or doubt in Steve's swing. It's the same flowing motion every time.

I drag several range balls into position and begin to emulate Steve. I aim at the same flag. I take compact, smooth swings, and one after another, I hit high wedge shots that land all around the flag. When Steve moves to a seven-iron, I do the same. I've got nearly a foot and 60 pounds on him, but his seven-iron shots fly 15 yards farther than mine. The difference is even more exaggerated when he starts hitting his driver. His swing is effortless, but the balls launch off his driver like fighter jets taking off from an aircraft carrier.

"How you hittin' em, Gary?" I ask in, what I've come to learn, is the traditional manner.

Gary turns toward me and says, "The usual, short but straight."

"You?" Gary reciprocates.

"I'm looking to break 90 today. The way I'm playing, it should be easy," I say. "Hell, I might break 80." I feel Steve perk up behind me. I might have even heard him chuckle. I wish I hadn't said that. The golf gods reward confidence, but cockiness is brutally punished. I recant. "I shouldn't say that. I'm just saying, I've been practicing a lot, and I'm hoping it pays off today, golf gods willing."

Gary laughs. And Steve, now packing up his bag, chuckles knowingly and says, "Golf gods, indeed."

The Loose Impediments Travelling Golf Club is ready to tee off on the first tee. There are several foursomes gathered in a line of motor carts. My foursome is set to tee off first. I shove my hands in the pockets of my shorts so nobody can see them shaking. My heart flops like a caught fish. I'm stress-sweating through my golf shirt. It's not that I'm nervous to play in front of people. It's that I want so badly for the practice I've put in to pay off.

I'm last to tee-off in our foursome. Everyone's ball is in the fairway. Steve piped one so far, he received half-joking applause, as if this was a PGA tournament. I tee up my ball, nice and high, and I take a practice swing that cuts the air with a loud swoosh.

"Somebody came to play," Gary quips.

I ignore the comment, like Tiger Woods would do, and take another practice swing and hold my finish.

"That's the one," I whisper to myself, feeling imminently confident, looking out over a pond and out to the wide green fairway.

I swing as hard as I can. I hook the ball left into the bushes barely past the ladies' tee-box, 70 yards ahead. I stand frozen in shock. Then a wave of molten anger rolls over me. It takes all my will not to explode.

After several moments, Steve says, "Alrighty, Joseph, No biggie. Tee up another one. People are waiting."

I begin to move, but I don't acknowledge Steve directly. I don't want to reward his cavalier attitude.

I tee up my second ball. I try to overcome the flood of anger. My skin sizzles under the yellow sun. I can't unclench my jaw, lest profanity ring out. I think, "Okay, get it together. It was a freak tee shot. You can still break 90." I take a practice swing, this time not holding the finish because the foursome behind us is grumbling. I can't really hear what they are saying, but they are my co-workers, so I can't tell them to shut the hell up.

I swing as hard as I can. My driver digs into the turf. The ball pops off the crown of my driver and lands in the pond with a *kerplump* sound.

"Fuck!" I yell and immediately regret it.

"Uh, we are going to go ahead and play our balls," Steve says to Gary, because Gary, the driver of our golf cart, is now the keeper of me, the idiot who thought he was going to break 90 today.

Five hellish hours later, I stiffly shake hands with my playing part-ners on the 18th green and walk off the course. Gary asks me if I want to have a drink, and I tell him I have to go, I have a long drive. Scary, a drink, or maybe 10 Jack and Cokes, actually sounds pretty good. The truth is, I don't have to go, but I can't trust myself to be around other people. I can't not say what I'm feeling. And if they know, they won't understand, they'll think I'm crazy, or worse, that I'm an asshole. These are surely both presently true, but they can't understand what it's like to be me, to have this—golf—be the one thing left in my life that I can pour myself into.

Six hours ago, I was driving south, excited and hopeful. Now I'm driving north, shocked and depressed by how horribly I played. It's not fair. What happened? Whatever it was, I'm not giving up. One day I won't be worrying about breaking 90, I'll be trying to break 70. I think of the short doggerel I made up during one of my recent morning commutes. It'll be perfect for my gravestone.

Joseph W. Naus,
Shot par 72,
Not a total loser,
So fuck you.

I'm at the CIW Rancho Rebar retreat in Warm Springs, an old resort with cabins. It's all rock and wood and dusty little trails amongst tall trees. There are two Olympic-sized swimming pools right next to each other, one sulfur water. It smells like rotten eggs, but they say it soothes the skin. There is a complex that was probably some type of community center that is now a series of conference rooms, including the one we'll be having all our corporate meetings in. Across the street is a golf course. We already have tee times for the last day of the long-weekend retreat. One of the gifts of sobriety is using the amenities at hotels and resorts like this one. Gym? Hot tub? Sauna? Free breakfast and coffee? Yes, yes, yes and hell yes. This place even has a hiking trail, so I go running. My new gig has made me fat. I'm up to 225, and the last time I went to buy pants at J.Crew, the saleswoman told me they only carry my size online. I interpreted this as, "We don't want fatties in our store." A 36-inch waist is pushing it, but 38 is where J.Crew draws the line in the fat. I've got hips like Pam Grier. I'm working out, even going to spin classes at the gym a couple times a week, and I usually walk and carry my bag when I golf, but there aren't enough spin classes in North America to compete with CIW Rancho Rebar's donut-filled breakroom and regular Mexican food gastro-attacks that are the go-to stress relievers of me and my fellow employees. Now that I'm not smoking, coffee and food are on constant standby, the last line of defense between me and my feelings.

"This place is nice, right?" I say to Gary.

At this, Gary raises his glass filled with his signature drink, three shots of vodka and a splash of grapefruit juice on ice.

"So, no Larry," Tommy announces, as if reading off a list of topics.

I ignore my better self that is screaming at me to keep my mouth shut, and respond, "Oh no, Larry's coming. At first, he refused, but then when Ted told him I'd be giving the presentation for credit, collections and contracts if he didn't show, Larry said he'd show up only for the last day."

"Fucking Larry," Tommy responds. "He's an asshole."

I feel a guilty charge, knowing I shouldn't be gossiping, but knowing I'm going to anyway. I want more information on Larry's backstory. Gary leaves to get another round of drinks, and I sit with Tommy in the outdoor cabana-themed bar while he drinks on CIW's tab. Tommy and Larry hate each other. Larry famously accused Tommy of calling him a faggot, and there was a big uproar at corporate, but nothing came of it. I don't believe Tommy did it. While Tommy is a truck-driving, tobacco-chewing, self-identified redneck, he's also a savvy corporate climber, and I don't think he'd put his career on the line like that. And Larry lies the way most people breathe. But I could definitely be wrong.

"Yeah, but we should cut him some slack," I say. "You'd probably be fucked up too if you had such a tragedy go down in your life."

"Tragedy?" Tommy asks. "What fucking tragedy?"

"Oh, I shouldn't have brought it up. Forget it. Sorry. I mean, I just figured since you've been working with him for close to 10 years ..."

"No, no. C'mon. What fucking tragedy?" Tommy insists. "Was it that shit about owning a giant collection company and losing it to go work for CIW?"

"Well, kind of," I respond sheepishly.

"Look," Tommy says. "A divorce isn't a tragedy. But maybe don't get married when you're, you know ..." Tommy takes a big swig and looks at me over his glass. "Look, I got nothing against the gays. I don't care if he fucks aliens. Just don't be an asshole."

"Well, uh, divorce isn't what I was talking about," I say, coyly.

"Then what?"

"About his son?" I respond.

Tommy sits up excitedly. "Oh God, yes, please. Do tell. Tell me the story he told you about his son."

"Never mind," I say.

"Stop, just fucking stop," Tommy laughs and pounds his knee. He's a few drinks in and getting saucy.

"Dude, Jesus Christ," I say. "It's like the least funny thing I've ever heard."

Tommy keeps laughing, and I sip on my Coke, waiting to hear why. He finally stops, and dabs tears from his eyes.

"Do you really believe that shit? I mean—you think he told you that in confidence?" Tommy asks rhetorically, and then laughs and takes another drink. "He's told every person in the entire company that story."

Gary returns with two mixed drinks and two bottles of beer.

"You believe this, Gary?" Tommy asks.

"Believe what?" Gary responds.

"Never mind," Tommy says.

"You think he made it up?" I ask.

"I'm going to the head," Gary rises and says, but what he means is that he doesn't want to hear any more.

"He's the smart one," Tommy says, looking over and raising his beer to Gary, as Gary walks away from our gossiping.

"We should probably just drop it," I say.

"Nah, fuck that," Tommy says. He blinks heavily and keeps his eyes closed, trying to recall where we were in the conversation. "Larry was married. A lot of gay guys get married, especially in Texas."

I sit waiting for more, nursing my Coke, while Tommy finishes his drink and starts on another beer. There is a long pause.

"You know he hates you. He's been in my office telling me that you are practicing law without a license, you are trying to take his job, asking for me to help get you fired. Wants me to call Dallas."

Gary returns to the table with Ted, and Tommy and I go mum.

"What are you two jawing about," Ted says and pats me on the shoulder.

"Oh nothing," Tommy says. "Joseph here thinks Tiger Woods is better than Jack Nicklaus was."

"Well then, I better get another drink," Ted says. "This may take a minute."

The next day we go horseback riding on a trail, and I end up with the smallest horse. I can almost touch the ground with my feet. Everyone thinks it's a hoot. There are about a dozen of us, all management of CIW Rancho Rebar, trotting slowly along a trail that ends at a "cowboy breakfast," which is as good as any breakfast I've ever had. The modern cowboys have it all staged for us when we arrive.

There is equipment in the resort's gym older than Jack LaLanne, but I get a good workout anyway. Then, just before sunset, I swim and soak in the sulfur water pool, trying to ignore the putrid smell. I walk around the resort and try to think of something other than Larry and his dead son's dangling feet. There are dirt trails all over the sprawling property, and I go out into the dark, and I can see more stars than I can remember ever seeing before. They are like rebar, I think, always there, I just can't always see them.

Staring up at the stars, I get this feeling. It's happened all my life, especially after my crash-and-burn, it's like I'm in another dimension. I'm there now. It'd be entirely appropriate for Rod Serling to appear from behind one of these scrubby bushes, smoking a cigarette, and say, "Joseph Naus, a wandering mind so lost he's barely sure what's real and what isn't. A man whose tiny world was nearly destroyed by a comet of his own making. A man who now finds himself in ..."

I sit on the dirt, staring up at the stars, vaguely thinking that I dig this state of mind. I come to this mental state sometimes when I play golf by myself, when I drive, and whenever I'm alone, which is the majority of my time. Sometimes I'm alone even when I'm with people.

I follow a moonlit dirt path back to my cabin.

Has anything changed in my life? Yes, of course. There is this spirituality that I'm still wrestling with. There is the agreement I've made with a God, a God I'm still discovering. I recall the deal I made with God while alone in a jail cell waiting to be brought into court for my sentencing hearing. The deal was: If you give me a second chance, and don't send me back to prison, I'll stay clean and help others to do the same. But it's more than just giving up my sex addiction and drinking, and now even giving up cigarettes, it's living spiritually. The only thing I had to change, and have to keep changing, is everything that separates me from God. I don't even know what that means.

The cicadas sing me to sleep, and I sleep the deepest, darkest bear sleep. I dream about Larry and my dad, and I am trying to please them both, running back and forth, dealing with unsolvable problems. I'm so afraid of them both, and I just keep making things worse and worse.

The next day we are in a big woodsy conference room. There is talk that the agenda is more traditional business than past retreats have been. I heard that an open-discussion-slash-team-building exercise that was employed a couple years ago had gone awry. It was an exercise where everyone wrote one good thing and one bad thing about the job that another person does. It got real ugly. The "safe place" turned out to be not so safe. Larry had been bludgeoned so badly that he walked out, which wasn't too surprising, but even some of the other managers had been badly bruised. Not surprisingly, people didn't forget what others had said about them when they got back to the office.

Today's agenda has Ted giving a "State of CIW Rancho Rebar" speech, which I expect to be much back-slapping and cash-counting with a pinch of "we can be even better," thrown in for prudence's sake. Then each department head will give their own short speech with an emphasis on something they are working on to improve the business. Larry's only here because Ted was going to have me give the credit, collection and contracts presentation if Larry didn't show. So now I'm only giving the presentation for the contracts, and Larry is decidedly pissed about that and is conspicuously sitting as far as he can from me.

I'm giddy as hell because my presentation is going to blow everyone's mind. I'm going to introduce an intraweb site on the CIW Corporate website where all contracts from every CIW affiliate in the world will be uploaded. It'll be organized and searchable by date, general contractor, dollar amount, rebar sales-only or placement, among a list of different easily-searchable variables. I'll draft and publish standard "industry best practices" based on our corporate policy. Then every affiliate can look at every contract and see what other affiliates are doing. It'll allow us to leverage our strategic advantage as an international company. As it is now, we have the same customers demanding a certain legal term while in one state, or even in different parts of the same state, while in another state they don't even care about that term, for no other reason than the personality of the customer's project manager. It's a no-brainer, but CIW isn't a dot-com business where they would assume this level of interconnectivity, they are an old-school steel company. I'm drunk with anticipation. I feel like part of the team. And, as a nod to a little inside joke Gary and I have about stupid overused business words, I'm going to use the word "synergy" and hopefully "synergistically" at least twice, if things go well, maybe more.

Looking as if he just witnessed a fatal car crash, Ted rushes in and tells everyone to take their seats. The mood shifts from celebratory to concerned in an instant.

"Sit down," Ted instructs firmly.

Eyebrows raise. The lights go off. We all sit in a half "C" behind linen-covered conference tables with coffee vats, sweating pitchers of iced water, and plates of fruit and Danish. A man appears on the pull-down screen, just his head. It's the CEO of CIW, a man who makes $10 million a year, managing a company that grosses several billion dollars a year. We are one of his crown jewels, one of the most profitable af-filiates in the CIW empire. As a policy, he's loved us enough to leave us alone. Until now.

This Captain of Industry scares us with a barrage of phrases: "auster-ity," "crash," "unprecedented," "bubble," "stock downgrade," "economic downturn," and "mortgage backlash." What scares me is what he doesn't say. He does not hedge. He doesn't say, "Don't panic," or, "We'll get through this." When the lights go back on and the CEO disappears, Ted tells us we are going home early. He says, "Don't spend a penny more. Golf is canceled." All expenses going forward, "I don't care if it's a pencil eraser," must be approved by him. We clear out of the conference room in reverence, and our vehicles caravan out of the resort like a funeral procession.

It's only been a few months since that day, that now-seemingly apoc-alyptic day of my first CIW Manager's Retreat, but everything has changed. It's like 9/11, but the terrorists look just like us. CIW's stock has dropped from $39 to $7. I can't even look at Randy from shipping when I see him in the hall. I try not to literally "take his inventory," as we 12-Steppers say, but I can't help it. Over his 30 years at the company, he'd put his entire savings in company stock. At its peak, his nest egg, a dinosaur egg, was worth $1 million. Now, it's worth $150,000.

The entire office is depressed. People say, "Keep your head down." I swear I must hear that once a day. Or as a friend in college told me they say in Japan, *Deru kugi wa utareru.* The nail that sticks out gets hammered down. It's the new unofficial CIW Rancho Rebar motto. The strange thing is, it's made Larry and I a little closer. We still despise each other, but there is this underlying connection. I first noticed it when Sarah from accounting was in Larry's office and she said her husband's hours were cut and that they might have to sell their Big Bear vacation home. She was near tears. "Can you believe how horrible this is?" she asked rhetorically, her voice cracking. Larry consoled her, and Larry and I linked eyes, and I knew he knew what I was thinking, and vice versa. We were thinking of all the things we'd been through that were so much worse than this. I was thinking about handcuffs and jail cells. I was thinking of police sirens in the Alley where my mom and I lived, the ones on the 91 Freeway next to my upended SUV, and the ones in Santa Monica outside of the massage parlor on the night of my arrest. And I didn't know if Larry was thinking about his son's suicide, or whether he made that up, but I knew that either way, Larry has been through hell, because even if he made it up, no one who isn't deeply damaged would make up a story like that just to get sympathy. Like it or not, I'd thought to myself, Larry and I are bound. We are survivors, like cockroaches in an ice age.

It's Saturday night. I'm back from my regular 12-Step meeting. I'm feeling good. I didn't even give a sideways glance at 7-Eleven as I passed by on Sunset. I'm just grateful to not be smoking, to have a good job, to be sober. I go as long as several hours without thinking about the fact that I'm a registered sex offender, and I'm even hopeful that Keri is going to be successful in Changing the Numbers and getting me off the sex offender registry. I think about Macy from time to time, but I'm so busy that it doesn't last too long. I don't have any creditors calling me because I'm actually paying every one of them, so, for the first time in a long time, I don't have a jolt of anxiety every time the phone rings. Things are good. I'm going to watch a movie and go to bed, get up early and go to the 6:30 a.m. Agape service. I feel wholesome.

The phone rings. It's Macy.

"I'm scared. Can you come over?"

She's moved into her new home. It's way up in the Hollywood Hills. I haven't heard from her in a long time.

"What's the matter?" I ask.

"I keep hearing noises. It's so dark up here. William's at his dad's. We were keeping Daisy, Leo's dog up here, but they wanted her back."

I put Macy on speakerphone and jump into macho, good-guy mode. This is exciting. I get to save the day. As I rush around packing a bag, it occurs to me that she could call Leo or one of a dozen people who live closer to her. She's got friends everywhere, but she's calling me.

I'm already on the road when I call her on speakerphone and tell her I'm on my way. I say, "You know what's going to happen if I come over, right?"

"I know," she says.

I walk in. She's smiling. She looks amazing. The time away allows me to appreciate her beauty more. She's wearing tight expensive jeans and a thin cotton, purple blouse. I hug her and kiss her. I can feel her heat. I walk to the sliding glass door that leads to a balcony that hangs over the little cliff her home is perched upon. The view is out onto a canyon. She's eye-level with the hawks that I'm sure hunt for wild rabbits that live between the parcels of land, some too steep and rocky to build on. It's dark and stormy, and it starts to rain. Macy sits at the grand piano in the corner of her new home. She plays a few notes, the same ones she played for me on her old Rhodes electric piano in her little apartment over three years ago. She dreamt of owning a home for her and William. She'd never owned a home, neither had her mom or dad. It seemed like a pipe dream to me. Nobody I knew owned a home in Los Angeles unless they bought in a shitty area a decade ago or they had help from their rich parents. But here she is, not just in any home, but in this beautiful home on a hill.

"This is what I love the most," she says and beckons me to follow her down the hall.

I already know what she's going to show me because I know what is most important to her. She opens the door to William's room. She's giddy. He has a little desk, a closet, a bunk bed with a new blue comforter. He even has his own television.

"Oh my God, the little muffin has his own room," I declare.

Macy leads me back into the living room. We sit on a couch that is an undeniable masterpiece.

"Isn't it amazing?" she says gleefully in response to my expression of wow.

It's deep and upholstered in dark leather and wood and probably cost more than my car.

She shows me her new BMW, shows me the bathroom she plans to remodel, then the kitchen. There is new art on the walls, including a painting of a standing bear with pink lips, next to the massive black-and-white cowboy piece, seemingly the only thing she kept from her most recent and third ex-husband. I go back to the wall of window. It's raining hard, not Los Angeles-hard, but anywhere hard.

She shows me her bedroom. Her style is on full display. She's no longer confined by budget, and her bohemian-chic mixed with *Dwell* modern and just a pinch of disco, has been fully realized. Big, twin, blown-glass lamps sit atop refurbished, rustic, dark wood end-tables and frame a gigantic puffy bed with a billion-thread duvet sporting a stylized fleur-de-lis design. Candles are lit. The rain pounds the roof, steady and hard.

It's been a long time since we had sex, and it's good. It's smooth and loving. The anxiety that used to exist when we made love is gone. The pressure is off. After, I relax. I see the silhouette of her curves backlit by the flickering candlelight. I peer out the window into the blurry dark, into the Hollywood Hills. We lay wrapped up together, and she fades to sleep. This reminds me of the night when Macy was sleeping at her apartment and I sat looking out the window, and I had my revelation that my seemingly bizarre crash-and-burn was actually perfectly tailored and of my own making; that my internal beliefs were so strong that they became my external reality. I wonder if, for me, having that revelation was the main purpose of our relationship. I wonder what I contributed to Macy. I'd like to think my absolute belief in her talent and power helped her reach her newfound career success.

Just like my mom, I love the rain. Macy has lived in many rainy towns, so it doesn't mean the same thing to her as it does to me, a SoCal native. When it rains, I feel like I need to witness every drop of it. I gently shift Macy's head off my shoulder to her pillow and quietly pull myself out of the bed. I slide a Scandinavian modern chair to the window and watch the rain.

I know this is not my home. Nothing has changed. Macy felt lonely, perhaps even a little scared, all by herself in her dream home, but this is not my home, and she's not my girl anymore.

I wake in the morning, and it's still raining. I decide to let Macy sleep in and leave a note. I quietly gather my clothes and make my way to the bathroom. I look down the hall, and there is water and mud rushing into the entryway. It's coming in through the front door. I throw on my jeans and shirt and open the front door. The rain has subsided into a drizzle. My car is parked on the street, which sits above the walkway that leads to Macy's front door. There is no sidewalk just a raised curb. It's on a downslope, so when I parked, I turned my front wheels away from the curb, as required on a hill. By doing so, I created a little dam where all the mud and water rushing down the curb from the steep street was trapped between my car's wheel and the curb and has since overflowed onto Macy's walkway, apparently, all night long. There are a couple feet of silty mud in her entryway, and it has seeped all the way into the living room. I step out through the front door and my bare feet sink into the silt, past my ankles. With slow slurping steps, I walk down

Macy's entryway sidewalk to see if the mud has run into her garage, under the door. I can see that it has, so I go through the living room to enter the garage from the house. The entire garage is filled with mud, the consistency of cake batter. Macy's new BMW's wheels are a foot deep in it.

I wake Macy, and try to keep her calm, but she isn't calm. She is astonished, and angry and panicked. I don't have to explain what happened. It's obvious. It is, in a word, unbelievable. Had I parked even a foot up the street, or a couple of foot down the street or hadn't turned my wheels, or even if I had turned them but not pinned the tire to the curb, this wouldn't have happened, not a drop of water or speck of mud would have jumped the curb. It simply wouldn't have occurred.

How can I be so unlucky? How can I be so damn unlucky? Why me? It brings me back to the night that changed my life. Why couldn't that guy have woken up before I came in through his window? I'd been pounding on the door to the massage parlor. I woke other people up in the apartment building. If he didn't have the industrial-sized fan going, he would have woken up, too. Why didn't one of the tenants scream at me or call the police? What if I'd gone into the window I'd intended to go into? Anything else but the one God-dammed thing that happened! I know this way of thinking is poison, and it doesn't jibe with my great revelation, but I'm of two minds right now, and my victim-mind has the floor.

Macy is nearly hyperventilating. Her dream home, thanks to me, has been infiltrated with mud, and it's still coming. She blames me. I retaliate lightly. I didn't do anything wrong! You're supposed to turn your wheels to the curb! It's the law. It's just a freak accident. But that's the point. I'm a freak accident. I'm bad luck personified. Macy doesn't deserve this.

"Stop it, Joseph!" I tell myself. I think of Reverend Beckwith. He'd tell me not to say such things about myself. And he's right. I don't believe that about myself, and even if I do, I won't give voice to it. I suppress it.

Somehow, I am able not to fight with Macy. I let her vent, keep my mouth mostly shut, and I get to work. That's what the 12 Steps have taught me. Take the next right action. There is a flathead shovel in the garden, and I scoop mud into a bucket. I worked as hard and as fast as I can for several hours. Macy joins me. It stops raining. We go to the hardware store and rent fans to dry out her oak floor. We even have a couple moments of levity. We clean out the garage, which, luckily, is mostly filled with junk, much from the prior owners of the home, and we clear it all out. We call a hauler to come up the hill and take away all the soppy boxes of junk. Ten hours of working, shoveling and keeping my head down, my back so stiff I can't stand straight, and her home is back to normal.

The way we say goodbye feels permanent—a firm hug, a kiss on her cheek, and the trade of knowing smiles. Hours of hard labor have softened me. My anger and self-pity have been replaced with a sense of deep gratitude. I carefully wind my car down the hill, and I try to put my relationship with Macy into perspective. For me, it will always come back to that first night at her apartment when she sat behind her keyboard and sang that slow, sad, simple song, and I asked her, in awe, "Why aren't you a star?" I didn't know whether the world would recognize her, but I saw Macy's genius, and I believed in her as much as I believe that water is wet and the sun is hot, and I reflected that back to her. I'm not sure that my belief in Macy's genius, or whether being her biggest cheerleader, has anything to do with her success. I'd like to think so, not because I want to take credit, but because I'd like to think she received something from our relationship equally wonderful as what she gave me. She exemplified the life of the Spirit, and she set me on its road. And, despite my circumstances, she saw Good in me. For that I can never repay her. Even if I never see her again, there will always be love for her in my heart, and our sacred connection can never be broken.

TWENTY-SEVEN

My mobile phone alarm sounds. It can't be 4:50 a.m. already. It's dark out, completely dark. It's only Wednesday. 4:50 a.m. Tuesday feels like it was 20 minutes ago. Get up. You are a grinder. You grind. It's what you do. Just go on autopilot. Follow the plan. Bed by 10:00 p.m., up at 4:50 a.m., on the road by 5:20 a.m. I could get on the road sooner, but my eyes won't accept their contact lenses until they've been open for 15 minutes. Every minute past 5:20 a.m. adds five minutes to my commute, every minute past 5:30 a.m. adds 10 minutes to my commute.

5:23 a.m. I'm on the 10 Freeway. It's flowing. I turn on Eckhart Tolle. Aunt Suzie bought me *The Power of Now* on CD last Christmas, and I've been listening to it over and over. This guy sat on a park bench for a year contemplating things, and when he got up he was a spiritual guru. The entire book can be summed up in one short sentence: "Be present." I like it. It aligns with the 12-Step philosophy, "One day at a time." I've listened to each CD so many times on my way to work that I can recite it as it plays, like I used to recite episodes of *Kung Fu* when I was a kid. I can even imitate the voices. The format of the audiobook is question-and-answer. Eckhart sounds like a wise old elf. These two young people ask Eckhart questions they already know the answers to in whispery NPR voices, "But what if I need to think about tomorrow …" I like to imagine outtakes from the recording studio where Eckhart gets angry and shouts at them, "I fucking told you 20 times now, you knuckleheads, stop whining about the past and stop trippin' on the future!" My little mental skit usually gets me laughing at myself, but not today. I'm having a hard time taking Eckhart's advice. I'm not feeling the "power of now" right now. I'm feeling the regret of yesterday, the dread of today, and the fear of tomorrow. I'm wondering how much longer I can keep this commute up. I'm wondering how much more of Larry I can take. I'm grateful for this job, but it's killing me, and I won't even entertain the idea of moving back to the Inland Empire so I don't have to make this drive.

I pull in to the Starbucks in Claremont, half-way to work. I think to myself, this is exactly the time when I need to stay in the moment. If I can control my thoughts I can control my emotions, and if I can control my emotions, I can be happy, right here, right now, just like Eckhart says. What's here in front of you, Joseph? A bagel with cream cheese and a large coffee. Doesn't get much better than that.

A giant orange sun rises up over the freeway. I drive at exactly 74 m.p.h. in the number two lane with a pack of fellow eastbound commuters. Eckhart answers different questions with the same answer. I daydream about swinging my golf club with effortless power like Ben Hogan.

I pull into CIW just before 7:00 a.m. My fellow employees are getting in earlier and earlier. Nobody wants to be the last one in or the first one out, even though there is less and less work to do. *Deru kugi wa utareru.* I walk down the hall where all the detailers sit on stools at their drafting tables. Even the air is heavier now. One of the detailers nods to me, the way you'd nod at a teammate walking off the field at halftime after getting blown out in the first half and about to get a dressing-down from the coach in the locker room.

The weekly managers' meeting is a dim affair. Tommy, the manager of the sales department, tells us what jobs we bid and didn't get, and what jobs we bid and won but had to bid so low that we'll almost certainly lose money. The justification for this that gets bandied around is "feed the factory." It means that we bid jobs at a loss because losing money on a job is better than having to lay everyone off. We have to keep the wheels of CIW's industry moving until the country comes out of this "economic downturn." Randy, amazingly, still able to speak and occasionally smile after losing nearly his entire retirement, gives the shipping department report and covers the operations department report for Erik, who is on a trip to Dallas. More of the same: 20 more ironworkers laid off; one of the biggest jobs we have, a giant parking structure at a hospital, just shut down. Randy says he went there to pick up scrap rebar and there were weeds growing up and around the foundation. I recall the condominium project just down the street from my apartment in Echo Park, across from Chango Café. There are cinderblocks with rebar and weeds rising out of their centers. The weeds overtook the rebar months ago. If it weren't for President Obama's American Recovery and Reinvestment Act, which is funding freeway bridge and overpass jobs, there wouldn't even be a reason for CIW Rancho Rebar to turn on its lights. Every day when I get to the office, I log onto *The New York Times* website to see how many bankers and CEOs from Goldman Sachs, Lehman Brothers, Countrywide, Fannie Mae, Merrill Lynch, Wells Fargo or AIG or maybe some of the politicians-turned-lobbyists or lobbyists-turned-politicians who make a career of taking legal bribes to keep Wall Street running like a deregulated casino are going to suffer public execution, or at least, prison. So far, none, but I'm patient.

There's some good news at our weekly managers' meeting: Ted tells us there is going to be a defibrillator machine installed in the hallway and that we will be trained to use it. People make jokes about using it to jump start the economy, some make the connection that it'll likely be used on the long-coughing Larry.

After the meeting, I sit at my desk, and I listen to Larry in his office next door talk to Angel, about how not-funny it is that the defibrillator was installed right outside his office.

Angel says, like a mother, "Well, you've got to stop smoking."

Larry laughs, and says, "Oh honey child, the sky is falling. Who cares!"

The truth is, he loves this shit. He's surviving. And the worse things get, the more Dallas brass is in the office, taking control of this place, and Larry is their guy. Ted and Erik seem to be receding into the walls of their office more and more every day, unable to do a damn thing about the apparent economic apocalypse that has plagued this business, which, a year ago, was as strong as it'd been in its 50 years.

I sit in my office and take a pause before opening my email to see what austerity measures await me today. I click and watch the emails download one at a time. There is an email from the CEO to everyone. He says he's forfeiting half his salary, and that we'll all get through this, and, like he did, everyone must do their part. I fantasize about ending my career at CIW Rancho Rebar early by clicking "reply all" and drafting a response informing all several thousand CIW employees that, as of last year, only $700,000 of the CEO's $8 million compensation package was in salary, the rest was in stock options, which, by the way, are granted at the lowest rate of the stock price when the CEO elects to take them, so even if the stock rebounds back to half of where it was before the crash, he'll triple his $8 million. And, if you still aren't fully impressed at our leader's generosity, consider that, because of certain tax laws related to stock options, performance-based pay and long-term capital gains, he'll most likely pay a much lower tax rate on his $20 million than you do on your paltry salary. And, since I've mentioned your paltry salary, let's do a little math. Let's generously say that the average salary at CIW is $40,000. Our CEO will make 500 times that in a year in which the corporation he runs will not even turn a profit.

From his office next door, I hear Larry say, "What's he trying to pull with this email, anyway? For Christ's sake, you gotta be kiddin' me. He must think we're dumber than a box o' shit. That shyster has more money than King Solomon himself. I'm not impressed."

"Oh Larry, be nice," I hear Angel say.

I doubt Larry has ever cracked the CIW Annual Report, but I appreciate that we are united in our cynicism.

Then I hear our comptroller, Andy ask, "Larry, did you have any issues with your computer this morning? My password isn't working."

Larry's reply is muffled. Andy bends his neck into my office and repeats his question to me. I shrug. Andy doesn't like me much. He's nearly 10 years my junior, and even so, we are still the youngest managers here. He thinks I'm his competition, but I'm not. CIW put him through school to get his MBA, and the accounting department has a lot more power in CIW than credit and collections, or contracts. Andy doesn't know how lucky I am just to be here. I won't be surprised if he's running this place in a few years.

Andy goes to the next office and asks the same question. Then Connie from HR comes walking down the hall. I hear Andy and her exchange words. Andy raises his voice. Connie lowers hers like an elementary school teacher trying to calm a group of kids by speaking quietly. But it's not working. I stay in my chair, and I hear Larry come out and ask, "What's going on?" Andy heads down the hall, and I hear shouting.

I peek into Larry's office where he and his staff are already gossiping about what is happening.

"Is everything alright?" I ask.

"For us it is," Larry snickers. "I know, I know, it's not funny. I'm sorry, but that's what happens to the hotshots sometimes, right?"

"Larry!" Angel says, mockingly appalled. "You are so bad!"

"So, he's fired?" I ask.

"Yeah, and IT cut off his password before management told him about it. Oops! Little busy-badger hotshot finally got what was comin' to him."

Instead of telling Larry he's an asshole, I keep quiet and turn back around and go into my office. It was as if Larry was saying I was next. He calls me a hotshot all the time, just not when he thinks I'm listening. Andy is competent and thus makes Larry look bad. I'm shocked they would fire Andy. There has been talk that they are going to consolidate some of our operations into corporate. Andy is the first manager to go, but not the first employee. More than once, I've come into the office in the morning, to find an empty bay where a detailer used to sit. I envision them being raptured up through the roof. Nobody says a word about it. The receptionist is gone, several detailers, and now Andy. CIW Rancho Rebar hasn't seen the worst of it. In the last several months, one-third of all CIW employees, thousands of people, have been laid off, mostly field and shop workers, people that actually touch rebar. Private new construction hasn't just slowed, it's stopped.

I keep checking *The New York Times* online for news that Congress is going to pass a law instituting something like a "Mass Economic Fraud Registry," or maybe, I jokingly fantasize, they'll name it after an old widow who lost everything and is now destitute, maybe "Gertrude's List." The list will protect society from further harm from these felonious Wall Street hucksters, fraudulent bankers and greedy mortgage company executives who have devastated so many lives. The U.S. Attorney General will aggressively pursue convictions, forcing most of them to take harsh plea bargains or risk decades in prison. After these criminals are stripped of their professional licenses, drained of all their assets, and finally released from prison, they'll be put on "Gertrude's List" for the remainder of their lives, not as further punishment—they will have already paid their debt to society, and to punish them further would be patently unconstitutional in violation of due process, double jeopardy and cruel and unusual punishment—but to make sure the good people of society know who these criminals are, what they look like, where they and their families live, exactly what crimes they were convicted of, and to make sure it's nearly impossible for them to get and keep good jobs and reenter society. They'll be like Michael Milken, the disgraced '80s junk bond king who, I presume, is still in federal prison or released and living a desperate life of poverty.

❖　❖　❖

I don't think about Macy. I don't think about being a registered sex offender. I don't think about my upcoming Change the Numbers court
hearing that might completely reset my life, get me off Megan's Law
websites, and get me on track to getting my Bar license back. I don't think
about Larry leaving Rancho Rebar—under whatever circumstances God
deems appropriate—and how that would drastically improve my life. I
don't think about the wage garnishment notice I just received from the
IRS, my credit card debt, my massive and growing student loan debt, my
monthly probation fees, or the money I owe the California State Bar,
fees for their investigation of my crime and ultimate summary disbarment. I don't think about which of my coworkers, fellow 12-Steppers,
or neighbors know that I'm a registered sex offender. I don't think about
smoking, either. I don't think about any of these things.

I think about my golf swing. I dream about my golf swing. I journal
about my golf swing. I pray and meditate about my golf swing. When
I'm at work and Larry rambles for a half-hour about a problem he made
up and says, "We have to do something about this!" I nod and daydream
about my golf swing.

I wake up every morning, knowing, knowing with the same absolute
certainty that my lights will turn on when I flip the light switch, that
today is the day I will implement the final piece of the puzzle that will
make my golf swing PGA Tour quality. Every day I can't wait until the
next time I can get to the golf range. It hasn't happened yet, and more
often than not I leave frustrated and disgusted with myself. I often cuss
involuntarily, in violent fits. When my fury subsides, I look around at
anyone unfortunate enough to be within earshot, clench my teeth and
smile apologetically. Then, when I've hit my last ball, I leave, at best
unsatisfied, and, at worst, defeated and on the verge of tears. Then I lug
my golf bag back to my car, sweaty and back-sore.

But I'm like a toddler who falls and cries dramatically and five minutes later is in pure joy, playing and giggling as if nothing happened,
because after I leave the range, driving in my car, before I arrive at my

regular 12-Step meeting, I've already figured out what went wrong, and all my past golfing sins are forgiven and forgotten like so many lost golf balls, and I'm so excited to get back to the golf range that I can barely contain myself.

Today I'm playing Harding at Griffith Park, and I'm going to break 90. It's just me and two Korean men on the tee box. Neither speaks English. They smoke furiously. One throws his cigarette on the tee box and crushes it with his new leather golf shoes. I shoot him a look that says what I feel, "You should be crucified for doing that." I walk over and pick up his cigarette butt with my gloved hand and toss it in the trash. As if in response, they insist I play ahead of them.

After several deep breaths and a positive affirmation of "Don't act like an asshole," I take a bearishly slow swing with my driver and aim far left, anticipating my usual banana slice. I promised myself before this round that no matter how angry I got, I wouldn't say anything negative aloud. For just one shot at a time, I choose not to cuss and act like an asshole. I choose not to express aloud how pathetic it is that after all this practice, I still can't even get the ball in the air consistently.

I score a par on the first hole. One down and seventeen to go.

After suppressing my anger after several bad shots, it becomes much easier, and by the middle of the round, I'm in a state of acceptance. It's not that I'm not upset when I hit a bad shot, just that I've lowered my volume from rage to dissatisfaction. It reminds me of how it felt when I finally decided to quit quitting smoking. The monkey on my back gradually climbed down and lost interest. Two-plus hours later, all I have to do is bogey holes 17 and 18 and I'm going to walk to my car with my first sub-90 round. It's getting dark. My heart pounds, and my hands begin to shake. It takes me several seconds to steady my right hand enough to get the tee in the ground.

I pull my driver, and suddenly feel as if I'm left-handed playing with right-handed clubs. I swing, and I nearly miss the ball. The ball flies 150 yards out, and it's so far right I'm not sure it didn't go over the fence into the street. It's too dark to see.

"Fuck!" I yell aloud, ending my all-time golfing-without-cussing-aloud streak at 16 holes.

I swung so violently that my back is spasming. I gimp along toward the boundary fence. I find my ball buried deep in the grass just inside the fence next to the street. The hole is severely blocked by a tree trunk and low-hanging oak and pepper tree branches.

Take your medicine, Joseph. Just punch the ball back into the fairway, and you'll have 160 to the hole. You can still break 90.

"Go for it, Joseph!" the stupidest part of me says.

I go for it, alright, and I hit it perfectly square into the tree trunk. My ball bounces right back at my head. I duck, and it lands 10 yards behind me. Now I'm too exhausted, too disgusted, and too baffled to be angry. I just do what I should've done in the first place for a double bogey.

I have to par 18, a par-five, to break 90. I take a practice swing, and I say a little prayer to Ben Hogan. "No reason I can't break 90, right Ben?"

After a decent drive, I walk to my ball, pull a five-iron and skull it, sending a jolt of pain through me. My ball flies at knee level and runs up the fairway like a rabid squirrel. The result wouldn't have been better if I had my PGA Tour card. The damn thing travels over 200 yards uphill. My back instantly feels better. The sun has set over the hills. It's officially dark.

I reach my ball, 80 yards from the hole. All I have to do is get this on the green and two-putt.

"Just don't hit it long, Joseph," I say to myself.

I take a smooth practice swing. Then I skull the ball again, and it skates low, through and over the green. It settles in the thick grass just above the top of the green, leaving me 60 feet. I shake my head in disbelief that I was able to do the only thing worse than the worst thing I could think of doing.

It's so dark that I have a hard time finding my ball even though I know where it is. And when I get there, I see that it's even worse than I'd thought. It's come to rest in the center of what could double as an eagle's nest. I've got nothing to lose, so I try a shot I saw Tiger Woods make once, an intentional skull. My ball pops out of the rough and barely makes it onto the green. It rolls and begins to slow to a dead stop, as does my chance at breaking 90. But then it regains speed, rolling end over end, faster, and takes the slope of the green and starts tracking toward the hole. Now I think I might have hit it too hard. I walk after it, watching it lose speed again as it reaches a bump. It nearly stops again. I reach in my pocket to pull out the nickel I use to mark my ball. I'm just waiting for it to come to a complete stop so I can mark it and get this over with. But it never completely stops. It just keeps rolling, ever so slowly, end over end, as if deciding whether to rest or keep going. It feels as if the ball has been rolling for a full minute. "C'mon little ball, roll!" I shout. My ball rolls right to the hole and bounces off the flag stick, leaving me a four-foot putt for par.

I pull the flag, I mark my ball, I set it back down, kneel behind it, and line it up. I think of all the four-footers I've made in my apartment. I hit it firm. The ball dives away from my intended line as if it wants to do anything but go in the hole, but then, as if the hole dilated just for me, the ball catches the lip and falls in. I hear that delightful sound of the ball rattling around the inside of the cup. Eighty-nine.

I pull into the Torrance Courthouse parking lot on a blaringly bright morning. I shut off the engine, cutting off Eckhart Tolle's elfish voice mid-sentence. I take a deep breath, and say aloud, "Stay in the present moment." As I make my way toward the plain, squat courthouse, the sound of loose asphalt crunching underneath my wingtips, and the restriction of this suit, the best and last of my lawyer's wardrobe, I feel something just short of déjà vu.

I stand outside the entrance to the courthouse with dozens of others in a security line. The lady in front of me looks at the time on her cell phone with deliberate exaggeration and peers down the slow-moving line. She looks back to me for confirmation.

"Yep, this is the new normal," I say.

She grimaces, shakes her head and turns back toward the front of the line.

I want to engage with her loudly and indignantly, the way people sometimes do while waiting in lines, grumbling things like, "This is ridiculous." I want to tell her my opinions of the Patriot Act, Dick Cheney, Haliburton, the military industrial complex, the violent history of our country's intervention in foreign governments, much of which I understand at bar trivia night level, perfect for a very short conversation with a stranger. I recall Eckhart Tolle's admonitions, and I decide to keep my mouth shut. I don't want to walk into this courtroom angry. That's not the energy I want to bring. I want to walk in with the belief that a miracle is going to happen.

I recall the little chorus I made up, which I occasionally sing to myself to the tune of Michael Jackson's *Man in the Mirror*, the sappiest song I could recall.

"I'm thinkin' we can change the numbers,
I'm thinking we can make that change
to the numbers,
Yes, I'm thinking we can make the change ..."

The bailiff calls the courtroom to order. Everyone stands. Judge Von Silkman smiles tightly at me. Keri stands next to me at the defendant's table, and, on our left, at the prosecutor's table is a Deputy D.A. I've never seen before. Carmen D. Villa isn't here. Apparently, she's busy being someone else's archnemesis. The D.A. assigned to this courtroom is handling the matter. He's a nondescript affable-looking guy, harried by the stack of files on his prosecutor's table, each one, I imagine, representing a human that is likely going to prison.

"We are here for a ..." the judge says looking for someone to fill him in.

"Well, it's technically a probation status hearing, but you'll recall ..." Keri advises the judge.

"Oh yeah," Judge Von Silkman continues. "That's right. Mr. Naus, nice to see you."

"Thank you, your honor," I respond.

"I see Deputy D. Villa isn't here," the judge continues, "and well, that's unfortunate, not that I'm not happy to have you." The judge looks over at the assigned D.A.

Judge Von Silkman laughs. The assigned D.A. laughs. As he's the assigned D.A. to this courtroom, they probably spend several hours a day with each other. Hence the joke.

"So, okay. I'm quite certain, uh ... to fill you in," Judge Von Silkman says to the assigned D.A. "Mr. Naus was sentenced in my courtroom back when I was in Central. That was, uh, let's say four years ago. He's a 290 registrant. I don't believe he or society will benefit from him being registered. However, he did plead guilty, and I was obligated to accept that plea, although I never believed his intent was consistent with a sexual assault. It was clearly alcohol related and alcohol induced. Ms. McConnely?"

"Yes, your Honor," Keri responds. "That's correct. We are here to see if the D.A. will consider accepting an alternate plea *post facto,* to Change the Numbers. He's completed probation terms, paid his debt to society. He has a good job. He's an outstanding member of society, as the many letters that we've submitted reveal ..."

Keri stops and hands an extra copy of the letters to the assigned D.A. He takes them reluctantly, as if he's reached his daily paper limit.

Keri continues addressing the court. "Some of these letters are from men that Mr. Naus has helped get sober in 12-Step groups. He's completely dedicated—"

"Yes," Judge Von Silkman cuts off Keri. "This isn't contested. I mean, I'm not doubting these things. The issue is whether we can actually do what you've requested, this so-called, changing the numbers, and I have a heavy calendar, so let me just cut to the chase. I'd like to see what can be done." Judge Von Silkman then addresses the assigned D.A. "I want you to go to your superior and let them know my feelings and that I'd like to see something done about getting Mr. Naus off the registration, okay?"

"Yes, your Honor, of course," the D.A. says. "Shall we set a date?"

"There is no use for that," Judge Von Silkman snipes. "I want Ms. D. Villa here, and we don't have her calendar … but we'll get something on the calendar. Ms. McConnely, I trust, will get something on calendar pursuant to my minute order to do so. Agreed?"

"Yes, your Honor."

And just like that it's over. Keri dashes off to another courtroom, and I'm alone again. I find myself in the elevator with several dark, pant-suited attorneys and a bailiff, with my nerves dancing just under my skin, when I hear my brain demand, "Get me out of here, and get me a cigarette."

I step out onto the white concrete steps in front of the courthouse. I speak aloud. I don't care who hears me or what they think of me.

"I'm not smoking today. Tomorrow, fine, but not today."

I gaze up at the '70s-era courthouse. "There's a lot of rebar in this bad boy," I whisper to myself. I imagine all the union rebar placers who helped build this courthouse, dotted all around the hard dirt footprint of the foundation, in their orange helmets, some bent over tying the rebar at its intersections, some carrying long sticks of rebar, which bow over their shoulders and bounce with their steps. I can't see the rebar now, but it's in there. Its invisible strength holds this courthouse together. Without it, this building would crumble into a pile of rubble.

I drive home, humming "I'm thinkin' we can change the numbers …". I should be happy. Judge Von Silkman just put it on the record, again, that he doesn't think I had the intent to commit a sex crime and that he doesn't think I should be on Megan's Law List. But I don't feel happy. I'm shaky and scared.

There is tension everywhere. I feel it on the freeway. I smell it when I stand in line to buy coffee. Everything has a different tint. Inventories don't move. Full-timers become part-timers. The news is a car alarm that never stops blaring. Our beloved president, the one that bellowed about reeling in the Wall Street insiders but keeps recruiting them into his administration, is now writing the largest checks in the history of the world, not to me, or anybody I know, but to giant corporations that are, "too big to fail," like Goldman Sachs, General Motors, Chrysler, Capital One, Morgan Stanley, AIG, and dozens of others. The news is a constant cycle of well-suited, talking heads blathering about credit default swaps, derivatives, Dodd-Frank, and the Clinton and Bush financial deregulations. Banks, insurers, financial conglomerates, these people that hide within these corporations, that don't do anything of value but push money from one organ to the next, feeding invisibly, like tapeworms, they are to blame. The nameless, ubiquitous tapeworms have eaten so much that we are sick and dying. And now our beloved President of Hope, based on advice from his team of experts has decided there is only one thing to do: Feed them more. We can't let them die. They are too big to fail.

I am plenty small to fail.

I pump gas. The lady across from me is taking a gander. She looks up at the large gas-price sign and then at the pump's digital screen. She feigns exasperation, then our eyes meet, and we exchange faces to show our mutual vexation. The pump's screen is like a slot machine's payout in reverse. The price is unspeakable. I drive 550 miles a week, and the price to do so has more than doubled. My car has 190,000 miles on it. At this rate, it won't last long. I don't know what I'm going to do. The little video screen on the gas pump plays a CNN talking head. She's spewing out ghastly unemployment numbers as a nearly all-red stock ticker tape slides by below. The DOW is down again. The NASDAQ is down again. The newscaster is cut off, and CNN jumps to our weathered President of Hope standing at a podium in the White House. I wonder if he wishes he could just fly away.

There is an accident on the 10 Freeway. There is an overturned big rig with its box trailer ripped open like paper. There's a mangled motorcycle, and there's a yellow tarp 50 feet in front of it. Medics and CHP officers stand around a tarp loosely framed by chalky half burned-out flares. An ambulance passes me on the shoulder, running its siren without sound.

I'm a half-hour late to work. The boys from Dallas are here in their starched white shirts with the CIW logo on the breast. They are short men, but they walk like giants. They are here to lay down the new law. There are closed-door meetings, and I end up in one.

"Joseph, Larry here tells us you are doing good work," Ethan says, lying. "Isn't that right, Larry?"

"Oh, yeah, he's a real peach," Larry responds.

"I'm doing my best," I return the lie.

I haven't been doing my best in a while. I'm at 80 percent, tops, which is still, I smugly think to myself, 250 percent better than Larry.

"Well," Dick says. "As I'm sure you've heard, we are making some changes." Dick is a mean-eyed, short, wiry man with pale white skin and center-parted, serial killer hair. He stares at me as if he's trying to read me. I haven't heard about any changes. I've just seen these Dallas White Shirts in here a lot, and I've noticed people not coming back to work and their desks being empty and nobody really saying anything about it. At this point, I presume I'm going to be fired. It's strange, however, even for Dick and Ethan, to start off by telling me that Larry says I'm doing a good job. Dick is the one that Larry calls all the time, the one that had Ted bring me into his office and tell me not to practice law, the one Larry tells all the time that I'm trying to take his job.

"Not right away, but fairly soon, we are going to be consolidating departments..."

Ethan and Dick ham-and-egg it back and forth and occasionally allow Larry to chime in with a word or two by asking, "Isn't that right, Larry?" to which Larry responds, "You got that right," or "Sure shootin'." It's, at best, bad improv. I so badly want to say, "Just spit it out, already."

"What I'm trying to say is you don't always need charcoal to cook a steak," Dick says, and Ethan and Larry laugh. "That's probably not the best analogy, Larry," Dick says and laughs again.

They aren't even talking to me anymore. I just listen. They talk about how shitty their hotel is, how they feel just a little bad about flying business class while flying around the country laying people off.

A half-hour later, and only because lunch is looming, and Dick really wants to get to that "fish market place" again, you know, "the one you took us to last time, the one with the red garlic potatoes and free garlic bread." Larry assures them that he'll take them there, looks at his watch and says they'd better get going if they want to beat the lunch crowd. With this, Ethan turns to me, apparently recalling that I'm still one of four people in the room and need to be dealt with, and Dick offhandedly reports that I'm being promoted to Regional Contract Manager, and I'll be getting a raise.

I feel like I've been standing in front of a coiled rattlesnake for so long that I actually got bored and said, "Just bite me, already," and instead it spits up a hundred-dollar bill and slithers away. The kicker is that Larry is now the official West Coast Regional Credit Manager, and Dick and Ethan make it excruciatingly clear to me that the contracts department is within the credit department and thus, Larry is my boss, hence, I surmise, why Larry has been quietly smiling during this whole meeting or skit or whatever it is. I thank Dick and Ethan and shake their little hands. I'm not sure if Larry winked at me or if he's having eye spasms. Larry and the White Shirts rush out the door to beat the lunch crowd. Larry begins to cough. His continual cough fades away as they make their way down the hall.

When Larry and the White Shirts return from lunch and finish raving about the garlic bread, I learn all the details. I now handle all the contracts for the entire West Coast operation: Fresno, New Mexico, Colorado, Arizona, Hawaii, Washington, Oregon, San Diego, and Las Vegas. Every contract will go through me. Nobody, not even the general managers of any branch, can finalize a contract without my go-ahead. Every contract will have my signature. I'll also be in charge of all the insurance for every contract. I'll be assigned a secretary. My first thought is, "God, I hope none of our customers sees my name on these giant construction contracts and searches me on the internet."

It's been nearly three years since I was hired at CIW Rancho Rebar and just shy of a year since my promotion to regional contract manager by Dick and Ethan. My job just keeps getting easier. We work with the same 20 general contractors over and over, so I've created "master" contracts for each one, so when we get a new job with a general contractor, the project manager for the company sees that her boss has agreed to the terms in the master contract, and then she just agrees to them, usually without negotiation. I don't even read the contract terms anymore. I just feed the contract into the scanner, scan the contract, and run a software program that deconstructs pdf images into characters, and then I run a "compare documents" feature in my word processing program. It reveals every change to the boilerplate terms of the contract, which is usually, zero. Every once in a while, I catch a clever project manager trying to slip in a change on a draft contract after we've already agreed on terms. The whole process takes a half-hour, if I combine it with a trip to the breakroom for coffee and a stop by Gary's office to let him know my most recent golf swing revelation. I've also designed a spreadsheet template that allows me to select which options I want for each insurance certificate via a series of drop-down menus, so the insurance process takes me five minutes, tops. I could do 50 contracts a week with insurance certificates, which is about 45 less than what I have coming in. I refuse to be like Larry and spend most of my time pretending I'm busy by having fake meetings about non-issues or turning simple tasks into monumental ones, so I spend my free time learning other parts of the business by studying rebar specs, plan drawings, and time-lapse construction videos of our jobs, all of which I have to hide from Larry.

The Dallas White Shirts have given the marching orders to Larry, and he's sending me up to survey a dying CIW branch in Fresno that has its own contract manager, Del. He'll answer to me for a while, and then he'll be terminated. I'm not to disclose this. I've met this guy a couple times. He doesn't like me. I don't blame him. I'm sure Del's decade of dealing with Larry—playing along with Larry's strange games, none of which have anything to do with contracts—entitled Del to be the guy that gets to be the contract king when Larry dies or leaves. He really should be. He's a hard worker and knows a lot more about rebar and construction than I do. But like Larry's staff here, 10 years of interacting with Larry has infected Del with Workplace Stockholm Syndrome. Del acts as if I've slapped him in the face when I tell him to change something, anything, in a contract. He says, "Larry never had a problem with this, but okay, you're the boss." And it makes sense. His only interactions with Larry involved Larry rubber-stamping contract changes and requisite laughing each time Larry said, "Oh Del, you ole coonhound," or "What's a matter, Del? You sound as nervous as a whore in church!"

A couple weeks after my trip to Fresno, a bunch of staffers from the Fresno office, including Del, visit our office for a mandatory HR sexual harassment training that's being held at a local hotel's conference room. Larry refuses to attend, despite having been accused of harassment twice since I've been here, and many other times before. Both times, the invisible hand of Dallas intervened on Larry's behalf and there were no consequences whatsoever. This time Ted and Larry lock horns, and Ted is uncharacteristically unyielding. After I walk out of the weekly manager's meeting, I hear from the conference room, "This is crazy. Ted oversees the entire west coast and he can't tell a fucking credit manager that he has to attend a mandatory training ... fucking mandatory!" Ted demands that Larry attend the harassment training, or else. And then, the next day, Larry doesn't show up at the office. Larry's absence is the talk of the office. "He never misses a day," and "This is his life," I hear more than once. I'm told Larry has been suspended. This could be it! He's finally gone too far. I can finally take over his position and stop the insanity.

But the Monday after a three-day weekend, not only does Larry return and act as if nothing happened, he's chipper and casually reports that he's not going to the sexual harassment training. Dallas intervened again. I'm starting to wonder if the joke I've heard from a half dozen people, that Larry can do anything he wants because he's got a photo of him blowing the CEO, could actually be true.

Del's visit from CIW Fresno Rebar coincides with Larry's birthday. The days of freebies have been replaced with austerity and I'm-grateful-just-to-be-here-ness, so Larry lets everyone know he's picking up the lunch tab. There are 15 of us, mostly from the Fresno office. The only people that will go to lunch with Larry, even if he's paying, are people who are obligated to because they're in his department, which includes me.

Someone asks Larry's age as the slices of birthday cake are being cut and passed out. Larry says he's not telling and says something about The

Virgin Mary and St. Peter. I think he's gotten two of his sayings mixed up. Then people start asking about other people's ages, and the question circles the table, and it gets to me, and I report that I'm 39, and then Del is next, and he's 39 too, and one of the ladies from Fresno call him, "baby-faced," which he is, and he smiles. I'm sitting across from Larry, and for some reason look at him, and I'm rewarded. For a long moment, Larry's face registers pure hate. I'm surprised at how vicious a look it is. Is it because Del is getting attention at Larry's birthday lunch?

Several beats after the moment has passed, Larry says loudly, "Del just looks young because he's fat. Fat fills out the face."

The entire table breaks out into a harsh silence. The piped-in Mariachi music and the tinging and banging from the kitchen fills the void.

After a long pause, a secretary from Fresno says, "Oh Larry, that's not nice."

I look at Del and roll my eyes. I don't even know what I mean by this, but Del does squeeze out a brief smile in response. Then his cheeks turn red, his eyes gloss, as if he might cry. I look away. If Del was a couple pounds overweight, it wouldn't be a big deal, but he's a good hundred pounds overweight.

Larry waves his hands dismissively at the mild naysaying and says, "Oh, hush now, you bunch a' ol' ninnies. Del knows I was just joshin'." Larry looks across the table at Del, and says, "We go way back, ain't that right, Del?"

I want so badly for Del to tell him to go to hell, especially since I know that Del is already on the chopping block and so has no need to kiss Larry's ass anymore.

I drive Larry and Del back to the office. They both ignore each other by scrolling through their BlackBerry phones with great intensity. I keep thinking of my strange meeting with the White Shirts, Dick and Ethan, when I was promoted. Dick said, "And this is not to leave this room, you understand, Joseph. There are going to be some changes at the very top here. So, be glad you are on the right side of things."

A week later, Ted is gone. A week after that, it's announced that Larry and I and our staff—the credit, collections and contracts department—are moving to another location, CIW Bloomington Rebar, 10 miles further away from Los Angeles, and 15 miles away from all my allies here in the CIW Rancho Rebar office. It'll be Larry's little fiefdom.

I've been leaning on my sponsor, Francisco, more and more. I talk to him on speakerphone during my commute home. Francisco always sees the good in things first. I don't always agree with him, but just hearing his positivity has a calming influence on me. He truly believes that everything will work out. I tell him that I don't know how I'm going to handle a longer commute and being isolated with Larry and his Stockholm Syndrome Crew. He tells me to just take it one day at a time, to pray and meditate, to go to meetings. He says, it'll work itself out, it always does, God didn't take you this far to abandon you. I remind him that I don't believe in a "parking space" God that is up in the clouds dolling out bad and good consequences like a cranky dad. I believe in a God of nature, of science, of cause and effect. Francisco chuckles good-naturedly and says I might consider getting a nicer God and then repeats himself: things will work out for you if you just keep taking right actions, as if it's an undeniable fact.

I ask if killing Larry isn't a "right action" considering the emotional pain he's in and the fact that he's clearly on death's doorstep. I report, in support of my request, that I timed Larry's coughing after he came back from having a cigarette, and he coughed for over two minutes straight.

"No, Joseph, you can't kill Larry," Francisco says between titters.

I smile, envisioning Francisco's Buddha smile.

The entire office is still in shock over Ted's sudden departure and to a lesser extent, credit, collections and contracts moving to CIW-Bloomington. But there's no time for goodbyes, as the following day, it's announced that the sales department is moving to CIW-Claremont.

This is perfect. Everyone but Larry opines that contracts should be part of the sales department, not credit. I'll move to CIW-Claremont Rebar with the sales department instead of CIW-Bloomington Rebar with Larry and his crew—the equivalent of moving to a mansion in Beverly Hills instead of a trailer park in Detroit. I'll be out of Larry's hair, but he can still claim me as one of his employees, and my commute will be cut in half. And I'll get to work with Tommy and Gary, and I'll naturally learn more about sales, and eventually, I'll end up in the sales department. I'll have a job that matters. It's absolutely perfect. Francisco was right. Everything works out.

TWENTY-EIGHT

The IRS finally caught up with me. I got the letter just a week ago. It says that I didn't file for three years, and that they are going to garnish my wages immediately. Since then, I've been on the phone with them every day after work, trying to work out a payment plan. It's not easy to get through to a human voice at the IRS. It takes trial and error and great patience. Now I have the proper selections written down, 1#, 4#, 2#. They try to trick you into pressing 3# after 1#, I fell for it twice, but that ultimately leads to summary disconnection after a long, long wait.

I'm in my car in the parking lot of my new office, CIW Bloomington Rebar. I'm exhausted. I'd like to just lean the seat back and sleep until the morning, but I can't. I have a lot to do. First, the IRS. Before I start driving, I navigate through the IRS phone matrix, 1# wait, 4# wait, 2# wait, so that I can drive while I'm on hold. Hopefully, I'll get through to a person before the IRS closes in an hour or my phone drops the signal.

I've got a three-hour drive ahead of me. I'm going to the Simi Valley Psychiatric Hospital to visit a sponsee, Mikel. Mikel had been attending one of my regular meetings for several weeks. I always greeted him. I knew how he felt, not just being a newcomer in the 12-Step Rooms but being the only one in the meeting not looking so damn cool, probably the only one not working in the biz or an artist of some sort. He always wore a tie. He was built like a bag of cement, and his face was filled with red tension, as if he was mid-bench press. He asked me to sponsor him, and I agreed. I soon found out that he'd stopped drinking years before coming into the Rooms. I didn't know what to do with him. It seemed like he needed a therapist more than someone to take him through the Steps. He had a good job in the insurance business and owned a condominium unit. Mikel did the Step work I asked of him, called me daily as I asked, but when we talked, he endlessly rambled about his sister—in strange fragmented ways. I asked my sponsor, Francisco, for guidance. He told me to just do my job. Take him through the Steps. Emphasize that the Big Book says that we seek outside help for outside issues.

The last time Mikel came over, it got weird. He rambled more than usual and became agitated. It made me think of Bill Wilson's story in the Big Book, *Alcoholics Anonymous,* about an alcoholic committing suicide in his home and another lighting his couch on fire. I can't recall exactly which part of the book it's in. I should know. I read *Alcoholics Anonymous* every day for three months while I was in Chino prison. I try not to think of my time in jail at Twin Towers. There was an evil energy in there beyond anything I'd ever felt. But thoughts of Chino always remind me of Jimmy, the good Jimmy. He probably kept me from getting shanked, and he surely kept me from me being beaten. But being Jimmy's friend and cellmate was like handling a bomb. The bomb doesn't have to want to kill you to kill you. You just need to be in its presence at the wrong time.

I'm driving and still on hold with the IRS.

I recall the last time I saw Mikel, the time it got weird, weirder than usual. Mikel had been rambling again about his sister, and I suggested we get back to reading the Big Book and deal with this resentment when we got to the Fourth Step. Mikel didn't like this. My suggestion ignited something in him I'd never seen before. His eyes flared and he became a predator, and I was his prey. He jumped up off my couch, inadvertently spilling a full cup of hot coffee all over his lap, the floor and the coffee table. His coffee cup bounced off my coffee table onto the floor with a loud crack, but it didn't break. I pushed my chair back as if avoiding a wrecking ball. I must've looked terrified. His eyes stayed trained on me.

He shouted at me accusingly, "I don't think you understand what it's like, Joseph!" At that moment, I considered my options and concluded that I probably couldn't physically overtake Mikel. I considered running out of my own apartment, but I'd have to get through him to get to the door. A memory flitted through my brain: the three Vatos I'd fought in Twin Towers. Mikel seemed much more dangerous.

"Take it easy, man," I said, my voice quivering. "Hey, hey, Mikel. I'm just trying to help, man."

He stood over me frozen, as if considering what to do next. Then his eyes softened. I was so relieved, I had to suppress a nervous cackle. Mikel broke down crying, and he hugged me. He wept while he sopped up spilled coffee with paper towels. I hugged him warily, thinking that maybe I'd just witnessed an episode of Post-Traumatic Stress Disorder. After he calmed down, I walked him out to his car. I told him I'd see him at the meeting. After that, his daily calls ceased. My calls went unreturned, and he stopped attending the 12-Step meeting where we met. A couple weeks later, he called me from the payphone at the Simi Valley Psychiatric Hospital. He sounded like a broken man, but also relieved. How could I not compare myself to Mikel? I'd been arrested, declared a danger to myself and others, placed in a psychiatric facility in jail, and then sent to rehab. I too had stood in the hallway of an inpatient facility in pajamas making calls on a wall-mounted pay phone.

Just as I pass the 710 Freeway interchange, I hear a woman's voice over my mobile phone's speaker. God yes! I've finally gotten through to the IRS and can get the fear of a wage garnishment off my back.

"This is Veronica. Who's on the line?" the voice says over my phone's speaker.

"Joseph Naus, I'm calling—"

"Hello," the voice says with great irritation. "Who is on the line?"

"Joseph! Hello? I'm Joseph Naus!"

Veronica of the IRS hangs up. The line goes dead.

❖   ❖   ❖

"Larry, can I talk to you?" I ask, standing at the doorway to his office.

"Of course, child. You know I'm always here to talk. Sit down."

Larry swivels away from his computer monitor and bends down in his chair, I presume to slide his shoes on. As he rises, he begins to cough and cough. I wait and wait. I stand up to help, then begin to panic, then I ready myself to take action. I recently watched a video on CPR, so I know the new protocol, which is a lot easier than the old one. I'm ready. Larry keeps coughing and waves for me to sit down. He finally stops and sips some water.

"Lordy, Lordy. I'm going to die right here in this chair."

"Jesus, Larry, that's not funny. What'd your doctor say?"

"Oh, that ol' shyster. More pills, stop smoking, stop drinking, yada, yada."

Larry stands and opens a desk drawer and beckons me over. It's mostly full of brownish prescription bottles and half packets of cough drops. There is a red pack of cigarettes, too, my brand. Thank God I don't smoke anymore.

"Wow," I say, mostly because I think that's what he wants me to say. "You know," I continue, "quitting smoking is very hard—"

"No, it isn't," Larry interrupts. "I've done it a thousand times!" Larry laughs, and it turns into a cough, which only lasts a few moments. "Well, Joseph, I know why you're in here. Obviously, you aren't too happy with your performance review."

I hadn't even thought of my performance review. CIW has this policy where you write your own review and give it to your boss in exchange for the review your boss did of you. The first time I did it, I received perfect scores from Ted and Erik, and I'd given myself good, but not great, reviews. Larry wasn't even assigned to do a review for me because he wasn't my boss, at least not in Ted's eyes, but he did it anyway. Predictably, he gave me average marks. I completely ignored them.

Since then, because of the economic collapse, reviews were halted, but we got back on track recently, and now that Larry is my undisputable boss, he gleefully wrote me a very average review. I, in contrast, wrote myself a glowing review. Why not? I'd created the CIW contract intranet searchable database, obtained my Construction Related Insurance Certification, and I churn out contracts and insurance certificates faster than anyone could reasonably expect. I work longer hours than many of the other managers at the office, except Larry, of course. I've even learned to better mask my contempt for Larry. Short of becoming a full-fledged member of the Workplace Stockholm Syndrome Crew, I couldn't think of anything more that he could expect of me.

"Actually, no," I respond. "I'm fine with your review of me. You didn't really cite anything specific that you wanted me to improve on, but whatever it is, I'll gladly do it."

"Oh, then uh what is it?" Larry asks.

"It's about Claremont," I say.

Larry smiles, opens his drawer and carefully pries out one of the two last cough drops from a paper tube. I wish I'd laid some groundwork for my request, but what else could I have done? Should I have been more difficult, so he wouldn't want me around? Or should I have been more agreeable, so he'd want to do something nice for me?

"Yeah," Larry responds, "Tommy called me yesterday."

"He did?" I ask.

This isn't good. Larry hates Tommy at a very fundamental level because he claims Tommy called him a faggot 10 years ago.

Larry, with glee in his eyes, responds cocksure. "Yep, yessiree, bobby. I did talk to good ol' Tommy boy."

"I wasn't trying to go around you, Larry," I respond. "I just figured there was no use asking you if I could work out of Claremont if Tommy wasn't okay with it, since he's the head of sales and runs CIW Claremont now."

"That's alright. I'm used to it," Larry says. He pins his cough drop to the inside of his upper lip with his tongue, creating a bulge.

"Larry, c'mon, that's not fair," I say. "Ever since the Whitesh—I mean Dallas promoted you, I've always treated you as my boss. You ask me to write emails for you and put your name on them, and I do it without complaining. I do whatever you say with a smile. I even attend your near-daily little meetings."

Larry scrunches his face. I shouldn't have called them "little" meetings. It's hard to hide my contempt for these stupid little pow-wows.

"I do appreciate your hard work, son. Oh sorry, I mean, Joseph. You know, after all this time, you just haven't come around to my way of talkin'. I understand. Anyway, go ahead, Joseph. You were sayin' something about Claremont."

"I want to work out of Claremont," I say bluntly.

"That's what Tommy said," Larry discloses the obvious and then lifts his shoeless, socked feet up onto the corner of his desk.

I think to myself: Should I even continue? I'd thought of an alternate plan. Instead of being honest, I'd tell him that it's important that he have someone in the sales department to keep an eye out for him. Larry isn't stupid. He knows his department is mostly irrelevant, that the only part that isn't irrelevant is contracts, and even that could easily be absorbed into the sales department; that instead of being a part of the demise of Larry's department, I'd be a spy for him like he's been a spy for Dallas all these years. I'd keep up the illusion that his department has to approve all the jobs before we sign the contracts. It could work. It's exactly the type of bullshit Larry loves. But I'd have to take a deep dive into Larry's world, join the Workplace Stockholm Syndrome Crew, put on a real show, and become a double agent.

"You know Larry, there is another way to look at this," I say.

Larry appears intrigued. "Is that right?"

I mentally lick my lips, thinking, this could work, this could actually work. But then, as I'm about to disclose my inter-departmental spy mission, I suddenly feel deflated. I just can't do it. I don't want to be en-trenched in gamesmanship every day. I wish I was a lawyer again, where I'd always been judged by quantity, quality and the results of my work.

I bail out and offer something I know he couldn't care less about. "Yeah, Larry. Think of it this way, you'll get more work out of me if I spend an hour a day less fighting traffic. That's five hours of work per week, 20 hours a month. That's a lot of hours."

Larry smirks. "I know you don't like it here. And I understand you're away from Gary, Ted and Tommy—oh wait, that's right, Ted's gone—anyway, all your buddies in Rancho and Claremont—"

"It's not about that—" I defend.

"Well look. It just ain't gonna happen. Sales is moving to fancy-pants Claremont. Credit is here now in dusty ole' Bloomington. I didn't decide that, but that's the way it is. I wish I could help you."

"You could help me, if you want to," I argue. "You could allow me to work out of Claremont. Nobody would care." I feel my anger rising.

"Look, kiddo, I understand, my commute has gotten worse, too. But we need you here. Did you really think you were just going to run on over to Claremont and join the sales team? I mean we've got a good thing going here in beautiful Bloomington. ..."

Larry keeps talking, but I can't hear him, because I go under wa-ter. By "a good thing," I think to myself, Larry means his little fiefdom where he'll have no one to answer to. I watch his lips move. His smug-ness rises. My muscles flare. I could leap over his desk and choke him to death with one hand. Larry would rather hurt me than help me, even if helping me would require absolutely nothing on his part. He's reveling in his power over me. With every word, he gets more and more smug. I'll throw him through that plate glass window and follow his fall to the parking lot and beat him until the cops come and pull me off.

"... it's gonna be fine," Larry continues. "You been drivin' from Rancho to L.A. for two years. What's another 20 miles?" He doesn't expect or want an answer and keeps on talking, his Texas-twang and effeminate mannerisms revealing themselves more with every word.

Maybe the reason Larry won't let me go to Claremont is because he thinks the even-longer commute will force me to quit. He knows I won't move to the Inland Empire. I've told him so. He thinks it's only because I like Los Angeles, but the truth is I won't leave my 12-Step friends, meetings or sponsor, or Agape. I need these things. When I think of moving to the Inland Empire, I envision myself in a grungy apartment complex—the only kind that will take a registered sex offender—depressed and slowly moving toward relapses on all fronts.

"I'm not moving back!" I blurt out, interrupting Larry's rambling.

Larry, surprised, but seemingly pleased he's elicited my ire, says, "I didn't say nothin' about you movin' child."

I stare at Larry intending to eviscerate him with my laser eyes. I am engorged with anger. I don't know how I'll get my revenge, but just the thought of it fills me with renewed purpose. Larry waits for my response, but, right now, the only thing I can think of to do or say will get me fired and arrested. So I just get up and walk out.

I'm a recovered sex addict and a registered sex offender. Since Macy and I broke up over a year ago, I didn't want anything to do with sex. I have no need for it. It's just a problem. I'd just as soon detach my cock and shove it to the back of the most inaccessible cupboard, like a used blender that I'm not quite willing to donate to the Salvation Army yet. When we first began dating, Macy asked me how I viewed sex as a recovered sex addict. I had an airtight answer that I recited militaristically: My sex addiction is just like drug addiction, only with massage parlor prostitutes instead of alcohol, drunken one-night stands instead of cocaine, and street hookers instead of heroin. Relationship sex is completely different. The two things have nothing to do with each other.

My response is true, but it's not the whole truth. Macy knew that. She'd done her research, anecdotally with her pimp father and adulterous sex-addict, third ex-husband, and educationally with her study of sexual intimacy. She'd read me excerpts from Pia Mellody's books about love addiction and codependency, and David Schnarch's *Passionate Marriage* about open-eyed orgasms and his theory of "differentiation." I wasn't dismissive. I no longer believed that "making love" was only the stuff of romantic fantasy. There'd even been times when Macy and I had an emotional connection during sex. Although very rare, I'd had something similar with prior girlfriends, too.

But I just wasn't ready to "lean in." Mostly, I had sex with Macy just to keep her happy. It was fine, sometimes even good, but I felt great anxiety. If we had sex and we both came, I was relieved that I'd done my duty, that I could reset the timer before I had to perform again. I tried to pretend to myself that I didn't know our sex life wasn't enough for her. She wanted more, and I wasn't ready.

I've been single now for a long time, over a year. It's been a great relief to not have to deal with sex. But I'm lonely, and so I decide to give internet dating a try. I set up a date with a woman named Lisa. I meet Lisa at a hip Vietnamese noodle spot in Atwater Village. It has a concrete floor and a Vespa-like scooter for decoration. The walls are high and white. The entire front is glass. The staff is cool. The tables are slabs of varnished wood. They serve Mexican Coke out of a bottle. I take a table in the corner.

Lisa comes in with a bursting smile, fussing with her long shiny black hair. She wears chino shorts that are taut around her hips, a white oxford dress shirt tailored to subtly reveal serious cleavage and a pierced belly button. We hug in greeting. She smells deliciously of fruity shampoo and freshly washed laundry. I stand and pull her chair out for her and help scooch her in, awkwardly, as we are sitting at bar stools and the chairs don't cooperate, but this allows for a laugh, a recognition of the awkwardness of a first date. When I sit, she says, "Oh my God, I couldn't find parking anywhere, so I had to go into the neighborhood." And she laughs and places her hand on my forearm. Her touch sends a tingling sensation rushing through me. I ask Lisa questions, and she talks fondly about living in Vancouver, but then her face turns suddenly sour when she tells me that her mom remarried and "they thought it was best I leave." I mirror her sadness, and she responds by smiling broadly, but her eyes don't match her smile. And then for a brief moment, she even looks panicked, as if she's been found out. Also, there's this party at her work in a couple weeks that she's mentioned twice already, intimating both times that she wants me to be her date. "Well," she says. "I haven't really made many friends and, ya know, I'd like to go, ya know, girls from work will be there with their husbands and boyfriends and I don't want to be there alone. I'd be so embarrassed."

Relieved that I'm not the only one sidestepping issues, I sip my Coke, and I recite my highly edited bio: I'm sober. I used to be a lawyer. I got into some trouble. I'm rebuilding my life. Lisa does not press for details. Her eyes dart away distractedly while I talk. It's as if she's already made her mind up about me: Yes, you'll do.

Both of us seemingly pleased to have gotten past the parts of our date where we reveal that we both have some "history" our banter becomes light and quippy.

Do you spin?

Me too. It's the best, right?

This place has the best pho on the east side.

I'll be the judge of that, mister!

Ha-ha-ha.

Oh, parking in Los Angeles, so terrible!

Ha-ha-ha.

Oh yes, aren't we lucky not to live on the Westside! If you think the parking is bad here, just try Santa Monica on a Sunday night!

Ha-ha-ha.

I pay for our meal. We walk down Glendale Boulevard, and there is a magnificent rainbow in the sky out above Chevy Chase Canyon. She squeezes my hand. How can we not take this for a sign? I mean, my Lord God, it's beautiful.

"Why don't we go back to your place and watch a movie?" she says, cautiously, looking down at the sidewalk as if scanning for dropped quarters.

She follows me. Her car would be rejected by a wrecking yard during a steel shortage. Dirty frayed duct tape is crudely incorporated into the structural integrity of Lisa's right headlight, left taillight, and rear passenger window. I think about going to a junk yard for spare parts to fix it. At my apartment, she parks on a downhill spot and fights to get out of her car as gravity forces the door against her as she wobbles on her chunky-heeled open-toe sandals while trying to pull out her purse and, to my surprise, a stuffed overnight bag.

We huddle up on my futon couch. I turn on the television, ask her what she wants to watch and she says, "Let's just go to bed, okay?"

I lay panting and spent and a bit overwhelmed. I didn't expect things to progress this quickly.

"Are you alright?" Lisa asks.

"I'm fine," I say.

"Did I do something wrong? I can do whatever—"

"No, no, it was great. Amazing," I try to reassure her. "I'm just, you know, thinking. It's been a while."

I drive straight from work to the Scholl Canyon golf course in the hills of Glendale overlooking the Los Angeles skyline. Scholl's range has a sand trap at the end of it, and I take my bag of beaten balls and practice hitting into the net. It's free, and my bunker play is getting better. An hour later, I make my way to the practice green. After a couple hours, on my way back to my car, I spy an abandoned half-full tray of range balls. I dash over, my golf bag bouncing on my back, and I scoop them up before someone else does. I practice my full swing for nearly an hour, milking the time between each ball.

It's dark, and out beyond the stadium lights, the Los Angeles skyline twinkles like Oz in the distance. My back is stiff. I've been awake since 4:45 a.m., and I worked nine hours before my hour-plus commute. I came straight here to Scholl. I have to keep improving. My golf practice is the only thing in my life I have complete control of.

I lug my golf bag back down the range toward my car, and I see a flyer on the ground, blowing in the slight warm breeze. I chase it down the concrete walkway, finally catching it with my foot. It reads, "Scholl Canyon Golf Academy. $99 per month, Unlimited Golf Instruction: Video Swing Analysis, On-Course Practice, Free Range Balls Included."

God has spoken.

For the next eight months, I divide my after-work time between 12-Step meetings half the weekdays and Scholl Canyon the other half. On weekends I do both. I don't think Scholl's golf instruction program was intended to be used as I use it, signing up online for multiple classes in one day, but no one complains. There are a couple of instructors and I get to know them. They've seen my type before. There are many crazed golfers like me, but most don't stick. I see them. They come, all gung-ho, so excited, dreaming of breaking 90, but after a couple months, usually without much real improvement, they drop out. I presume they think to themselves, "Why would anyone work so hard on something that really isn't that much fun, costs money, takes a ton of time, and is nearly impossible?"

I do the drills the instructors give me, I give it everything I've got. When I can't get to Scholl Canyon, because I have to stay late at work, I stop at Empire Lakes and practice putting and chipping and occasionally find some extra cash for range balls. I'm two years into this golf thing, and I'm getting better, but not nearly as fast as I want to. One day, I'm hitting it pure and thinking I'll be shooting par soon, and the next day, I'm shanking every other ball and cursing God. I watch golf on TV. I practice my swing in the office after everyone goes home. I putt in my living room. I dream about my golf swing. I now keep a legal pad bedside, so when I wake up, I can scribble down the revelation I've received, just like I did when I was an attorney. It used to be, "Subpoena plaintiff's bank records" and now it's, "Start downswing with hips to avoid chicken wing."

My cellphone rings. But for the light sneaking past the edges of my drawn bedroom window blinds, it's still dark. My gut knows long before my brain that something is wrong. I pat bedside for my glasses and fumble with them to get them on my face. Who can this be? My grandpa is dead? My mom? My dad? Uncle Billy? No. It's her. Why is she calling at this time in the morning? I know exactly why.

"Hello," I say, exaggerating my grogginess. "What's up?"

"Joseph! I can't believe you did this to me. You are a fucking registered sex offender! I went online. I should've done it before. I'm so stupid! You are a rapist! I can't believe this. And you had sex with me!"

Lisa is hysterical.

"Whoa, whoa, look, I can explain. You don't understand, look—"

"No, you look. I can't believe it. You had sex with me!"

I begin to plead my case to her. I go through the facts and the arguments, how difficult it is to broach the subject, how I didn't expect us to have sex on the first date, how I'm innocent, how I was a victim of the D.A. As I do so, I realize why I'm doing this. It's not because I want to keep dating her, it's because I'm scared of her. I'm scared of her because the way she yells, "You had sex with me!" which is leading me to the conclusion that she thinks that I broke the law by having sex with her without telling her that I'm a registrant and for a moment, I wonder if she's right. I think of the long checklist on the last page of my sex offender registration form, and each one, in small print, is a different notice about the requirements of my sex registration. I should know them better. It's possible one says something like, "Before engaging in sexual intercourse, the registrant shall identify himself as such and must obtain notarized written authorization from the potential victim ..."

"Isn't there a law or something?" she demands.

She really does think I broke the law!

She could be working for the government. The FBI found out I was dating. There is probably already a *Huffington Post* article in the can written by a team of propagandizing FBI agents. I can see my mug shot next to Lisa's crying pretty face, with the headline, "Sex Offender Strikes Again: Why the Law Isn't Protecting Your Daughter."

"Look," I say, "there is no law against me having sex with you. And that's ... just crazy ..."

Ten minutes later, I've talked her down, and she's agreed to see me again, but she wants friends of mine to meet us for dinner, and she demands that it be a couple. Somehow, in her mind, this will prove that I'm safe. A couple hours later, I'm on the phone with Will, my former law partner, explaining the situation, now trying to convince him to bring his wife to this dinner to save me. Even as I make this desperate call to Will, who is bemused and too kind to point out the absurdity of my request, I know in my gut that this isn't right.

The phone rings, and it's Lisa again. My heart pounds. I calmed her down, but she might have freaked out again. Maybe she called the police.

I take a deep breath and answer my phone.

"Hi Lisa, is everything alright? Are you at work?"

"I'm actually parked right outside," she responds.

"Oh, oh. You are? Uh ... well, c'mon in," I say, trying to disguise that my blood pressure is rocketing.

Lisa is in the driveway when I open the door, her face all scrunched up. She hugs me. Now she's on my couch crying. She apologizes. I feel relieved. She tells me that she is bipolar and on heavy medication. She speaks too fast for full comprehension. She disjointedly rambles about her childhood. Then divorce and remarriage. I'm not sure if it was her divorce or her parents or both. She pulls out a bottle of lithium from her giant Louis Vuitton bag. She shows me the label and rattles it. I tell her I don't know anything about bipolar disorder, but I did take medication for depression, and I think it probably saved my life. I prepare PG Tips tea for her and listen, but between the cadence of her speech and the chatter in my head, I take in very little, and my discomfort grows.

Suddenly she declares, "I'm fine!" and then blows her nose into a paper towel. "I guess the real reason I was so upset was because I'd be so embarrassed if people from my work found out my boyfriend is a registered sex offender. We'll have to keep that secret."

"Actually, I'm not a registered sex offender," I say, mildly taking a stand. "I'm going to stop saying that. Language is important. I'm a registrant. I didn't commit a sex crime, and so I'm not a sex offender, registered or otherwise. I'm someone who has been forced to register, a registrant."

"Whatever … like it matters how you say it," she says, does not pause and continues at a blistering pace.

Lisa explains to me how she was able to ascertain that I am a registrant. She spent all night researching me on the internet and had an investigative break that led her to a social media site. That lead her to the State Bar website.

"I didn't lie about anything," I respond.

"You purposefully didn't tell me your last name," Lisa says flatly. "But really what you should have done is used a fake last name." She pauses and ponders, "That's what we'll do. We'll have to think of a good name, something common, like Johnson or Smith."

Lisa gets up and tells me she needs to go to her car to get her overnight bag. She ignores me when I ask why she isn't at work. We are on completely different tracks. I'm very excited by the idea of her leaving my apartment. I follow her to the door and hand over her giant purse.

"I'm not sure if this is going to work, Lisa ... you know ... I'm sorry we rushed into sex, but you know," I say. Lisa registers shock and then it appears as if she's trying to pull all her features into the center of her face. I'm not sure whether she is going to explode with tears or anger. Within seconds the answer is clear. Anger, definitely anger.

TWENTY-NINE

I can't afford therapy with Kamella anymore. I'd have to give up Scholl Canyon golf instruction or sell my CIW stock in order to pay her, and I'm not willing to do either. And the call I'm about to make is free. This little plastic business card I'm holding represents the emergency mental health services that are part of my CIW health benefits package. The card has a toll-free number and some small print. I read the small print. It ensures confidentiality. I sit in the parking lot of CIW about to embark on another 55-mile commute. My offer of compromise is still pending with the IRS. Soon, I'll have to start paying them monthly, too. My dream of working in Claremont is dashed. My days at CIW mostly involve doing my job, which takes a few hours at most, then pretending to work while fantasizing about schemes to destroy Larry. My odometer is about to flip to 170,000. I'm always tired. For the first time ever, I've fallen asleep in public. I fell completely asleep in a 12-Step meeting. I'm spinning and lifting, but I'm still getting fat because I can't stop binge-eating donuts, street-vendor burritos, French fries, entire pizzas, and pints of ice cream. Despite my constant practice, I've peaked in golf, and I can't break 80. Macy is gone for good. Internet dating was such a disaster that I'm recommitted to a life of left-hand-and-lotion celibacy.

I can't keep this up, and yet there is nothing I'm willing to stop doing: not golf, work, commute, or 12-Step meetings. I'm in a race to death with Larry. One of us is going to die first. If it's him, I'll get a promotion and a raise. It won't be big enough to buy a house, not in Los Angeles. But I'll have a nicer car and more responsibility. I'll run a mostly irrelevant department, and I'll be the one left with the choice of disclosing the ridiculousness of the department or keeping my job. Maybe at some point my criminal history will be so far behind me that people won't care. No, that's bullshit. They'll always care. The older I get, the creepier I'll seem.

"Thank you for calling. Please recite the number on the bottom right of your card."

I do so. The sterile voice of the operator tells me that the number only identifies my employer, not me individually, so I can retain my anonymity and they are still able to tell me what mental health services I qualify for. I briefly tell her my reason for calling. She listens without interrupting until I say, "That's basically it."

I'm a little disappointed that she does not react, but I'm impressed by her training.

"Do you have a plan to hurt yourself or others?" she asks, with laudable plainness.

"You know, that's the same exact question the lady asked me back when I was arrested for attempted murder."

"It's a standard question. It helps us assess how we can help you."

"I understand. No, I'm not going to hurt myself or anyone else," I respond, speculating that she knows that I know that my response may or may not be true because if I report that I plan on hurting myself, and have a plan for doing so in the immediate future, she's obligated to involve emergency services, and thus, if I really wanted to kill myself, I wouldn't tell her so. Of course, I've made a deal with God not to kill myself and to stay sober and help others get and stay sober, and I'm not in enough pain to break my promise, not yet. That's why I'm calling. I don't want my mental state to get any worse. Meetings, meditation, prayer, it's good, but it's not enough right now. I need more.

The operator puts me on hold while researching my employee medical coverage options. A string quartet, Vivaldi, I believe, plays softly under the pre-recorded woman's voice, a mental health public service announcement: "Spend time with family, friends and pets; exercise, especially in a group setting ..."

I have several good days, days where I heed the advice of Reverend Beckwith and Eckart Tolle, most specifically, to focus only on the moment I am in. Ironically, this contentedness is anchored by my knowledge that I'll be meeting with a psych at Kaiser in a couple days.

Kaiser Sunset is a series of squatty buildings on Sunset Boulevard just east of Vermont. The big blue Scientology building stands defiantly across from the main Kaiser campus building. There are protesters outside carrying signs urging the retraction of Scientology's federal tax-exempt status. I remember their strange golf course out in Hemet. It was one of the first times I'd ever played golf, and I'd lost so many balls I ran out. It was at the huge Scientology campus where they film their movies. There were beautifully painted giant studio lot buildings. In the pro shop were photos of Tom Cruise and John Travolta in a glass cabinet. Men on Enduro motorcycles with assault rifles strapped to their backs patrolled the grounds. There were security cameras affixed to the posts of the high razor-ribboned fences that separated the golf course from the film lot. On the tee box of one hole that ran along the border of the film lot, we'd discovered that the camera moved to follow us.

I have a late appointment, and everyone who works here is gone. I feel as if I shouldn't be here. I ride the elevator up alone and walk down an elbow of hallway. Sunset's traffic is muted outside through the glass but visible down below. I envision a black Town Car with tinted windows, several Enduro motorcycles buzz around it aggressively, guarding Scientology royalty.

A young man appears from behind a door, and I follow him from the lobby to a tiny little office with a view of an alley. He asks me to tell him why I'm here.

"I'll keep it short," I say and I relay my story. It takes a few minutes. He listens and writes and adjusts his body forward during the good parts. I stop. I look down. He reminds me of Al Madrigal, and I can't tell what ethnicity he is, and I wonder if that is a racist thing to think.

"So yeah, that's my story, been a tough several years, and I'm basically at the end of my rope, you know."

He takes off his glasses, squints his eyes, then rubs them and pinches his nose. He re-glasses and shakes his head and says, "God damn, man. That is ... wow."

I like this guy. He's telling it like it is. It's refreshing.

"Yeah, wow, right?" I respond.

"That's a horror story. Jesus Christ," he says.

I tuck my chin, widen my eyes, breathe in and chuckle at his response.

"I mean, what can I say?" he says. "Who wouldn't be depressed? You're living with all that and driving a hundred miles a day and dealing with a jerk boss and barely able to pay your bills. I'd probably feel suicidal, too."

"Well, you know ... I'm not going to do it, I just feel horrible. I mean—it's not like there aren't a ton of people that have it worse."

Why did I say that? What am I doing? Did he draw that out of me?

"Look," he says. "You've got six of these sessions, and we can talk. And I can help you with some strategy stuff, but it sounds like you've already got a program. You said you are active in the Program, right?"

"Yeah."

"You got a sponsor?"

"Yeah, of course," I say and contemplate how he knows about sponsorship. Was 12-step stuff part of his training or is he in a Program, too?

"You want a referral to a psychiatrist? You'd have no problem getting anti-depressants. You been on any SSRIs?"

"Yeah, I don't want that shit again."

"I didn't think so," he announces, as if winning a guessing game.

"Alrighty," I say as I lift myself out of the chair by pressing down on the armrests. "I guess there isn't a whole lot to say."

He stands, too.

"Look, Joseph, I'd use the tools that helped you survive to this point."

I hug him, and he does not resist. I'm surprised at how un-awkward it feels. I walk to my car. He's right. What am I doing? When I get back to my apartment, I call Francisco and ask him if we can start going through the Steps again. I've always believed that since Bill Wilson never wrote about or recommended going through the Steps multiple times, I shouldn't do so, that the Tenth Step—which is a mini Fourth Step—was all that was needed. Of course, I don't really do Tenth Steps. But I've always obtained relief from praying and meditating. I need to get in the Steps. I need to find some newcomers to help. I need to stop feeling sorry for myself. What happened to me? The Kaiser therapist was right on, like a no-nonsense angel pointing me in the right direction. I've been doing the very thing I used to criticize others for: acting as if the Program is only going to meetings; not having any commitments at the meetings; not introducing myself to newcomers at every meeting, whether I want to or not. I haven't been on a Hospitals & Institutions panel since I started working at CIW. I used to do one every month. I used to pick guys up at rehabs and sober livings and take them to meetings.

Bloomington is a place for truck drivers to stop and gas up their trucks and not much else. Every day I drive here, CIW Bloomington Rebar, and I wait in my office for Larry to buzz my phone or send some email, "Come in my office. Important!" Nearly every day, he calls his staff into his office. He rambles. He tries to involve us in a game that exists only because he makes it up. He's successfully expanding a department that does nothing. Dallas keeps authorizing new hires. And now we have six people in here. The new hires come into my office, dazed, with questions, just like I had for Ted when I was first hired. Some are competent professionals. Some come from good companies. The Great Recession has left a lot of talented people out of work. They are not accustomed to Larry's clown-play, but they are desperate for work. They look exasperated and ask me, "Is Larry for real?" and "But what is the point of doing this if …?" I tell these new hires the truth.

"Well if it appears that issuing credit consistent with a traditional buy-sell transaction process doesn't make sense on construction projects where payment flows from the project owner down according to payment completion and has no connection to direct customer creditworthiness, and you've inquired as to why that is, and you've been offered no reasonable explanation, then what does that tell you?"

I use the Socratic method so my words can't be used against me. I know from experience that Larry will turn some of them, and they'll join his Workplace Stockholm Syndrome Crew. It's not their fault. I might have done so, too, if things hadn't started the way they did. But ever since we moved to Bloomington, I just can't shake the burning anger I have for him. I think of Larry all the time. I can't forgive him for not letting me go to Claremont.

I consider getting a motel one or two nights a week. It'd practically pay for itself just in gas, but I never do. It's just not quite far enough to justify the hassle and, missing my meetings and not going to Scholl Canyon to practice, but I have to accept that the drive is breaking me down. I can only listen to Reverend Beckwith and Eckhart Tolle so many times, and I feel more and more disconnected from their teachings of serenity and acceptance. I'll be serene and accept Larry when he's dead.

It's 5:40 p.m., and I'm here at the office by myself. I've been here 11 hours. I'm too tired to go to Scholl Canyon tonight. I turn off the ever-present fluorescent lights. I grab the seven-iron I keep in my office, and I practice my swing. It's cool in here and strangely peaceful. The clubhead brushes the grey office carpet. The club feels good in my hand. I take it back smoothly and unwind. How many practice swings does it take to become a master? How many years? Ten? Twenty? Is it too late for me? Maybe, maybe not, but either way, I won't quit until I'm dead. And even then they're going to have to cremate me with this seven-iron, because I'll never let it go.

Larry left early in a coughing fit. Would it be so bad if he died? As far as I can tell, he does nothing but make other peoples' lives miserable through his constant gamesmanship. There'd be a funeral and people would play sad, but they'd know the truth. The world will be better without him.

Jesus, Joseph. What a God dang horrible thing to think, I say to myself as I line up my seven-iron behind an imaginary golf ball.

I walk to Larry's office to shut the door before I leave, and I notice that his secret file drawer, the one he locks even when he goes to the bathroom, is slightly open and the key is in the lock. He must've forgotten about it when he was leaving in his coughing fit. There is nobody here, not in the whole building.

I carefully slide the drawer open and thumb through the manila file folder tabs. One is marked JWN. I take the manila folders on either side of it and turn them sideways to mark it, and I pull it out. The thought occurs to me that I should wear gloves, that I might leave fingerprints. I run to the window and look out at the empty parking lot. My heart races. I feel just like I did when I used to get up late at night and clandestinely watch porn channels at my aunt and uncle's house when they had satellite television in the '80s.

I pull the file out and sit cross-legged on the floor, but then think again. I think I'll bring the file into my office just in case Larry comes back. But then what if he notices the drawer is open and then checks it and sees the file is missing? He'll know I took it. I decide to stand up by the window so I can see any car coming into the parking lot.

I open the file like a book, and page through it. It's my file alright. Larry has a dossier on me, like he's a spy. There are pages from my criminal background check, printouts from the State Bar website. But mostly it's emails. There are emails from and to me, some to and from

Ted and Erik. They are diplomatic. I remember them. They were from when I was first hired and are more reflective of my befuddlement than anything else. How did Larry get these? Did Erik or Ted give them to him? No, that doesn't make sense. They wrote things that they wouldn't want him to see either. Nothing too bad, "Larry's a character," and "Just ignore him." Did Marshall in IT give them to him? Did Connie in HR give them to him? I recall the receptionist that was fired last year during a little scandal where she and a married guy in shipping were emailing each other sexual emails. Her temp status was not made permanent, and he went on vacation or sabbatical or something. Obviously, emails are monitored. I presumed this, but I didn't think Larry would have access to them.

What does this mean? It means Dallas knows everything about me. That's no surprise, but somehow my merit has prevailed thus far. If they wanted to fire me, they could have. They didn't. They promoted me. So far, I've survived The Great Recession longer than many employees that were here years before me.

The intranet contracts site I created is a hit. I have general managers calling me about it, congratulating me, saying it's about time. The insurance certificates have never been smoother. There is no reason to think I won't take Larry's spot as soon as he retires or dies. If they were going to get rid of me, they would have done so already. That hateful little man Dick, Larry's greatest ally, one of the White Shirts, doesn't even fly out here anymore.

The sound of a door shutting on the first floor of the office startles me. I rush to Larry's office and reinsert the JWN dossier, shut the metal drawer and close Larry's office door behind me.

The shop manager appears in the stairwell.

"I was just locking up, but you're still here, so ... uh, okay, good-night," he says.

❖   ❖   ❖

It's Saturday morning. I'm in the airy art studio in the back of my sponsor's house. We are framed in on three sides by rolls of colorful fabrics, boxes of uncovered throw pillows, a long built-in desk with two sleek Apple iMac computers and a large industrial fabric printer. There is a bookshelf filled with art books, most of them on the subject of pattern designs; my favorites are *Houndstooth, Volumes 1-3*. I usually comment on the houndstooth volumes, joke about how much bigger volume one is than two and three or tell Francisco that it reminds me of the interior of the 1968 Camaro RS I stupidly bought when I got my first lawyer job. But today I'm preoccupied with the subject of our emergency sponsor-sponsee meeting.

"I fucking hate Larry. It's that simple," I confide. "He's a menace to everyone around him. He's incompetent. He's a fucking liar, too. It's gotten so bad that I can't stop thinking about him. I'll be in a meeting, and I'll realize I'm not hearing a word anyone is saying because I'm grinding my teeth, thinking about how much I hate Larry."

"So tell me how you feel about Larry, Joseph," Francisco jokes.

I swivel back and forth in Francisco's pink plastic office chair. I appreciate Francisco's levity, but I'm not able to join in. I clench my jaw, and I can feel thoughts of Larry pulsing between my temples.

Francisco, adjusting to my mood, gains gravity. "He's an asshole, I get it," Francisco concedes. "But you know, justified resentments are the hardest to deal with. It's because we feel we deserve to have the resentment."

"Yeah, I know," I respond, dryly.

Francisco paraphrases an infamous line from the Big Book. "Remember, resentments are the luxury of non-alcoholics. For us, they can be deadly, because they can fester and lead to relapse."

"It's not fair," I plead, huffing. "I wish he'd just go away! I can't believe I have to put up with this shit!"

I hear myself speak, and my words and tone surprise me. They are the words of a petulant child. The sound of my own voice, hearing how distressed I am, almost as if I'm listening to someone else, leads me to an emotional release. I close my eyes, and I feel my foot-stomping anger dissolve into a defeated sadness.

"Why does it have to be like this?" I ask but expect no answer. I begin to cry.

"It's alright," Francisco says, leaning in to me as I dab my eyes with the sleeve of my t-shirt. Francisco hugs me tightly. He's barrel-shaped, tall as me, and kind to the core. It's like getting a hug from the Coca-Cola polar bear.

When Francisco took me through the Steps, my second time doing them, he told me to write my Fourth Step resentment list without intellectually filtering it. He told me to write it as a petulant child would. There was something freeing and revealing about doing it that way. It cut to the raw emotion of my resentments. It's how I feel right now about my resentment against Larry. It's like when I was five or six years old, and my mom would make me clean my room, and I'd writhe on my bed, kicking, twisting, and yelling in anger, "I hate you! I hate you! I hope you die!" and then I'd cry for 15 minutes like a wailing siren, and then I'd feel sad for a while, and then I'd get over it. I'm just not at the getting-over it part yet.

I gather myself and sit back in my chair, only a little embarrassed.

"I get this job," I tell Francisco. "A complete miracle. I work hard, I do a good job, everyone likes me, and how am I rewarded? With this maniac-of-a-boss who should have been fired 10 times over and yet keeps getting promoted."

I get out my notebook and tell Francisco, in bullet points, all my Larry resentments: the gossiping, the game-playing, the incompetence, taking credit for my work, harassing me, and mostly, not letting me work out of the Claremont office. Francisco mostly just listens, nodding occasionally, and chimes in at the most egregious acts, "Oh that sucks" and "Jesus, really?" Then we move on to "my part." This is where the rubber meets the road, and while I'd prefer that Larry's balls were squeezed between said rubber and said road, I must instead read my list of the ways I've been an asshole to Larry. It's the genius in this part of the Fourth and Fifth Step. It doesn't matter what Larry has done to me, all I'm to consider is where I've wronged him. There are no scales of justice when performing a Fourth and Fifth Step, or Tenth Step—a mini-Fourth and Fifth Step—as I'm doing today with Francisco. Staying with the road analogy—apropos, considering how much time I spend driving—I'm to only look at my side of the street, because that's the only side of the street I can clean up.

"Well," I say, prompted by my list. "I've always lorded over him that I'm smarter than he is. I do it subtly, but I usually revel in opportunities to make him look stupid, which happens on a near-daily basis."

"Okay, good. Next," Francisco says.

"I've purposefully instilled fear in him. Here he is in a job he's been doing for decades, and I come along with the support of Ted and Erik and, uh, you know, I didn't exactly hide the fact that I was there to take his job."

"Okay, yep, go on."

"I've definitely gossiped about him," I admit, and then I feel my receding anger rise back up, and I go off script. "But that prick has gossiped, straight-up lied ..." Seeing Francisco's disapproving facial expression, I stop and sigh.

"Yeah, just your part," Francisco instructs.

"Yep, okay, you're right. I've gossiped about him. I definitely shouldn't have talked about the story he told me about his son committing suicide, whether it's true or not, with Tommy at the manager's retreat."

"Anything else?" Francisco asks.

"One more. I, uh, kind of looked into his secure file cabinet when he left it open."

"Oh," Francisco says with raised eyebrows. "I haven't heard about this."

We talk about my resentments and "my part" and, as is almost always the case, how it all comes back to fear—fear that I won't be able to take care of myself, fear that I won't get what I want and what I think I deserve. The antidote to fear is faith. More God, less Joseph. Go back to the Third Step. Pray and meditate. Ask for God's guidance. All the usual suspects. It feels good to know I'm just another alcoholic with a resentment against his asshole boss.

"God has a plan for you," Francisco says, matter-of-factly. "I know your resentments at Larry are going to get resolved—same with the State Bar, same with that ridiculous stupid sex-offender list they've got you on. It'll all work out."

Francisco speaks with such confidence it's as if he's seen my future. I feel a flash of anger, and I want to chastise him for so flippantly giving me false hope. I want to tell him, "Don't you understand? The sex offender list is permanent!" But then I look at his kind eyes, and I think of how unconditionally he has loved me, and my anger melts, and for just a moment, against all reason, I believe him.

"Amazing things happen in the Program," Francisco continues. "You're a living example of that."

"Can't argue with you there," I reply.

"Okay, now. Let's wrap this up. You know the drill. Go home, pray and meditate, and then from this day on, you know what you have to do."

I do know, and it's not going to be easy.

I recall a couple weeks ago, I got a call from a sponsee, Max, who's working at Home Depot cutting lumber. He's got a business degree from Tulane and a law degree, too, but this is the only job he's been able to get. Max tells me his boss is an asshole, that the prick always rides him over total bullshit. Max was on the phone with me, he was in the breakroom, huffing with anger, about to quit his job. I told him I could relate. I told him about my prick boss, Larry. Then I told him that 12-Steppers don't quit jobs in anger. We pray, we meditate, we consult the Big Book, we talk to our fellows, and we get guidance from our sponsors. I told him that he did the right thing by calling before he did anything rash. I told him, "This is where God has you right now. You need this job to support yourself. Do the best you can, and in your free time look for a better job." Then I told him the same thing Francisco is about to tell me. "Pray for your asshole boss. Pray that he gets everything that you want for yourself. Treat him like a newcomer. Be of service to him." I told him, straight out of the Big Book, to remember that holding onto a resentment is like drinking poison and expecting the other person to die. Sometimes it feels hokey saying the things I say to sponsees like Max. I never thought I'd hear myself say, "This is where God has you right now," unless it was a punchline or an imitation of one of the bumper-sticker, megachurch Christians that populate the Inland Empire. But there is something about sponsorship in the Program. It's a sacrosanct duty. It turns hopeless addicts into Big Book-thumping spiritualists.

Francisco instructs me as expected, "Pray for Larry every night, sincerely. Pray for him every time you feel resentful toward him—all day if you have to. Pray that he gets everything you want for yourself—health, happiness, friends, money. And then at work, you have to treat him exactly as you would a newcomer. From what you've told me about him, he very well might be an active addict. But it doesn't matter. It takes two to fight, and you aren't to fight with him anymore. Your job is to be of service to him no matter what he does. That doesn't mean you don't stand up for yourself, but don't retaliate."

I sigh deeply at the thought of what seems an impossible task.

"God is your employer," Francisco says. "You've tried fighting Larry. It hasn't worked. You do your job as best you can, and you be of service to Larry, just like you would a newcomer. Let God take care of the rest."

"You sure you want to go out, Joseph?" the rough-faced Griffith Park golf starter asks.

I lean into the window. "I'm playing today."

"Suit yourself, but it's supposed to start comin' down hard. We aren't even lettin' carts out on the course."

"Only pussies play in golf carts," I say, knowing he's a walker too, because we've teed off together so early that our first shots were hit in the dark.

He laughs gruffly.

I have no rain gear, just a Griffith Park Golf logo baseball cap, a cotton sweater and cotton pants. I do have wet-weather black golf gloves. The course is all mine. Anyone ahead of me is trying to finish up. Nobody in their right mind would tee off now, not under this grey-going-black sky. It's already drizzling. But, I've long ago made a deal with God that I won't stop playing golf in the middle of a round just because of a little lightning. Dying with a seven-iron in my hand in the fairway is the perfect way to go. Just dig a bigger than usual divot, put me in, and don't forget to cover me up with sand, so the next golfer doesn't have to play his ball out of a divot.

I'm two under par at the turn. Two under through nine holes!

I tee my ball up on hole Number 10, a short par-four. I try not to, but I think, "I'm two-under through nine, how *can't* I break 80?" I place the ball on the tee, and a thought makes me back off: I shouldn't be thinking about breaking 80, I should be thinking about shooting par, 72. I'm two under through nine holes! If I do the same on the back as on the front, I'll shoot a PGA-esque 68!

My confidence has never been higher. I swing my driver as hard as I possibly can. Ten minutes later, I finally find my ball lying in the middle of the fairway, the wrong fairway, right next to the 5 Freeway. The cars stream slowly along, headlights on, over the wet tarmac. I wonder how many commuters see me and what they think. Insane? Lucky? It takes me two shots to get my ball back in the correct fairway. I walk to Hole

11, in shock as much as anger. A quadruple bogey, a snowman on my card after playing a perfect nine holes!

A wave of dark thoughts rolls through me. This is how it goes for me. I work hard. I perform well, really well, impressively well. But then the loser in me comes out and says, "This is not for you, Joseph. Kids like you don't get the good things in life." And then I agree. I must agree. Because that's when I throw a grenade into the soup. It doesn't matter what it is, career, relationships, sports, you'll find a way to repeat the pattern. You always do. Did you think this would change just because you aren't smoking and drinking yourself to death anymore?

What would Reverend Beckwith tell me to do? Eckhart Tolle? Tito? Francisco? They may not know it, but they are my fathers. My fathers would tell me not to fight the dark voice. They'd tell me to accept it, to shine the light on it. They'd all say it in their own ways, but they'd tell me to love myself, to let God in. I look out over the narrow tree-lined fairway. I shiver. That's not me anymore. I'm not a loser. I'll just keep trying until I succeed. That's what not-losers do.

I'm damp through to my boxers. Number 11 is a tough hole. The disaster is playing itself out in my mind. As far as I'm concerned, it's already happened. I'm going to blow up, I'm going to hit horrible shots. I'm going to get angry, and then it's going to get worse. I can already see myself walking from Hole 18, past the clubhouse to the parking lot, a steady stream of rain rolling off my cap, obscuring my anger-crumpled face. I'll be muttering to myself.

No, no, no. Fuck all that loser-story bullshit. Fuck all that, not because "it's just golf" and therefore not a big deal. It's a big deal to me, and no one else needs to understand that but me. No, fuck that, because golf is my practice. I control my mind, and my mind controls my body. I can choose which thoughts I think. I am going to break 80.

I fade a weak drive 200 yards into the right rough. I stomp through puddles and mushy grass fairway. I pull a four-iron. The wind blows rain into my eyes. I take a swing and rip through the rough, hit my ball thick and leave it 20 yards short of the green. Bogey. Three-over through 11 holes, on track for a 75.

And so it goes for the next five holes, bogey after bogey. By Hole 17, I'm soaked no differently than if I had jumped in a pool. It's raining furiously. There are puddles all over the fairway and on the greens. I need to go one-over total on Hole 17 and Hole 18 to shoot 79. They are easy holes, but I want this so bad, and I can't pretend I don't.

The dark voice in my head is back. You're a loser. All the positive affirmations, all the golf practice, all the 12-Step meetings, all the Step work, Agape services and classes, all the prayer and meditation, it doesn't matter. You were born to losers, and you're a loser. You'll blow up right before you succeed, just like you always do.

No. No. No. It's different now, because I don't quit, no matter what. And my life matters, because I love, and I help others. I don't do the things I used to do, and I'm not who I used to be. I never was.

Now a word comes to my mind, and it's followed by a calm that makes its way through me. "Larry." Larry, my enemy. Larry, the asshole. I've been praying for Larry, praying and praying, since I met with Francisco a couple months ago. At first it was cursory, but then I started imagining Larry receiving everything I want for myself: health, money, friends, respect, and love. It got easier and easier, until sometimes I enjoyed my Larry-prayers. I'd think of Larry spending time with his friends, some I'd make up. I'd see him being praised at work in a big meeting full of Dallas White Shirts. I'd see Larry in the doctor's office, and the doctor telling him his cough has cleared up. And then the prayers became more ephemeral. They've been morphing into meditations, and I get that feeling I used to get when I first got sober, back when my life was a hurricane of feces, and I'd float above and observe myself. Now I deeply understand—feel—that Larry and I are players in the same game, that we are connected, we are parts of the whole.

"What's up Larry?" I say loudly through the darting rain. I look around. I can smell the mud. It's raining so hard, there is a curtain of water rolling off the brim of my baseball hat. I skim it with my gloved hand. There's no one around to see me talking to myself, or worse, to my asshole boss who isn't here. I hear a rumble of thunder northwest over Burbank.

Larry becomes my imaginary caddie. "Hey, Kiddo, you got this. It's a wide-open fairway. You just need to hit a nice baby-fade with your driver. Easy as a two-dollar whore."

"Thanks, Larry. I couldn't agree more."

My golf ball flies low and right, and lands on the right side of the fairway. I slog through the mud. My ball has come to rest in a puddle, or as it's referred to in the *Rules of Golf*, "casual water." I move my ball a yard back and right to a little knoll in the fairway where the water hasn't puddled, "closest point of relief, no closer to the hole." The wind gusts and pulls at my hat. I take it off and stash it in my bag. The rain pelts my face.

I take a short practice swing, and then address my ball. I hit it fat. Mud splatters my face. A rumble of thunder, closer than the last, follows, as if on cue.

I spread the mud on my face with my drenched sleeve, and I knock my contact lens out of my right eye. Fine. I can't see anyway. My ball lands on the edge of the green 30 yards from the hole. The green has so many puddles that I can't possibly putt the ball to the hole. I grab a wedge. I take a few practice swings. One doesn't normally hit a chip shot with a wedge off a putting green. One could be kicked off a course for taking a divot on a putting green. But this is no ordinary round and no ordinary conditions. It's Saturday at 3 p.m. and it's nearly dark, and water is dumping from the sky, and the wind is pushing it sideways, right into my face. I'm in Los Angeles, at Griffith Park, Harding Golf Course, my favorite golf course, all by myself, about to break 80 for the first time.

I widen my stance to stable myself against the wind and swing my wedge. I catch the ball thin, and it skates across the entire green, hydroplaning over puddles and then trickling past the flag and over the green. I two-putt and pull my ball out of the water-filled cup.

Hole 18. Just like when I broke 90 several months ago, I need to par this par-five hole.

"Whaddaya think, Larry?" I ask my imaginary caddie.

"This is an easy par-five, Honey Child. It doesn't even require three good shots. You can play half-steam, just like you do at work. You got this, boo."

A rumble of thunder reverberates through the air. Parrots squawk from the zoo. I can hear the peeling of rain from the slow line of cars making their way through Griffith Park, just behind me.

My tee shot flies right up the middle. I march up the inclined fairway, squishing with each step. My second shot flies right down the center of the fairway. I leave myself 130 yards uphill to the green. I take a smooth swing with a nine-iron and clip the ball off the turf with just a spray of water. It lands in the dead center of the green, leaving me a downhill putt of 25 feet. The green is sloped severely from back to front, so it's not pooling water.

On the green, I kneel down and see the imaginary line my ball should take from where it lies to the hole. I take a practice swing, and then I let it go. My putter meets the ball right in the sweet spot. My ball rolls true, at just the right pace, end over end, and it breaks just as it should, snaking down and right. It rolls past the hole to 18 inches. I stand over this little kick-in putt, a putt I wouldn't even consider missing under any other circumstances. But this is for 79. Anything can happen. I've seen pros miss 18-inch putts. I line it up, and I hit the ball into the center of the cup.

I walk off the 18-green onto the walkway between the practice putting greens and the old white adobe clubhouse. A small brass plaque mounted on the wall reveals it was built by the WPA in the '30s, during the Great Depression, 80 years before this Great Recession. My vision is blurry, adding a romantic hue to the scene. There are no other golfers.

An aproned man walks hurriedly just ahead of me, under the awning alongside the pro shop, toward the restaurant entry.

I giggle. I'm soaked. I'm not sure I've ever been happier. I recall highlights of my round, chuckle about how insane I'd have looked to anyone who heard me talking to myself over the last four hours. Seventy-nine. I broke 80. I did it.

I sit on the wood bench under the clubhouse awning, admiring the storm. A grounds crewman pulls up in a utility cart, looks at me and shakes his head in bemusement, then rushes over to the practice putting green and extracts the mini flags from the holes. He wears a bright yellow hardhat with matching rain poncho and rubber boots. He lays the mini flags in the back of his cart's bed and speeds away.

The idea of smoking a cigarette pops into my head. I love smoking alone, in the cold, with a view of something—the ocean, the sky, the city, the rain—especially after something tremendous has happened. I haven't had this thought in a while. I'm coming up on two years off the cigs, and the greatest thing about it is that I hardly ever think of it. That's the real miracle. "Fuck that," I think. I'm not going back. I'll stop by Café Tropical and get a café mocha on my way home. I'll just sit there under the little umbrella outside my cozy apartment and sip on my mocha and watch the rain and replay every glorious shot of my first time scoring in the 70s.

I drive home very carefully. Given the weather and my missing contact lens, it's a both-hands-on-the-steering-wheel kind of trip. I take Riverside Avenue, which runs beside the 5 Freeway, now a sea of red brake lights south and white headlights north and pounding rain. Waiting at a stop light, two full cycles now, it occurs to me that the two most difficult things I've ever accomplished in my life are quitting smoking and breaking 80.

"Imagine that," I say to myself very loudly. I'm still so giddy that I break out into feverish laughter every few blocks.

THIRTY

On Tuesday, I wake up in a deep peace. It's still dark out. I'm sleep-deprived, but I'm surging with a clean, still energy. I drive to the office. The drive is so smooth, it's like I'm on a monorail. I listen to one of Reverend Beckwith's sermons on my car's cassette player. I remember this Sunday sermon a couple months ago. It was as if he was in a God-induced trance, even more than usual. I don't even know what he said, not in any detail, just the usual, "God is all that there is," "God is my source," "We need to remember who we are and whose we are!" We congregants were all mesmerized. That's why I bought the tape. I had to hear it again.

When it comes to spiritual experiences, mine are typically of the "educational variety" and not the "burning bush" kind. But this thing with Larry is a miracle. It was like a cannonball being shot through parchment paper. My resentment is gone. God damn gone. The burning in my chest, that grinding in my jaw, the constant niggling thoughts of his smirking face, all gone. It's all blowing Larry's mind. It's not as if I didn't do my work before or didn't do what he told me to do, it's just that now I'm eager to help and I've given up on judging him. The department is what it is, and I'm there making a paycheck, so I might as well make the best of it. When I take over, I'll make changes, but until then, I've got one job: Be of service to Larry.

"Joseph," Larry yells across the office. I used to ignore him when he did this, and when I did finally respond, I'd cast a mile of shade, but now I get up, smiling, really smiling. I don't even have to fake it. It's genuine.

"What can I do for you, Larry?"

Larry scrunches his face in suspicion. Larry is still suspect of my attitude change. He's trying to find the angle. Yesterday, I left to go to lunch and I forgot my keys. I ran back up the steps, and there was Larry and my secretary, Lydia. I heard her say, "I don't know, Larry. I really don't," and when I got to my door, they both became quiet. Larry stumbled over his words, trying to explain why they were in my office. I pretended nothing was out of the ordinary. I just said, "Sorry to interrupt—forgot my keys."

"I need you to help me respond to this," Larry says, and hands me a printed email.

Now that Larry has been promoted to the regional level of management, his inability to write has become a problem. Now he has to communicate with people at corporate, competent people who don't think Larry's way of doing things is quaint. Larry accidentally forwarded me an email from a corporate director that read, "In the future, please correspond with me in basic proper English. I don't have time to re-write your emails before forwarding them to someone who has requested information. Thanks." I printed that one out for my "Larry dossier." That was before my new policy of service, just after I found that Larry had kept a dossier on me. I figured we both could play spy games. But I've since shredded my Larry dossier.

"No problem, Larry. How 'bout I look over the email, massage it a little, and then send it?"

"The email needs to come from me, Joseph," Larry says defensively.

"Of course. I meant 'send it back to you.' I'll just, uh, punch it up a little and send it back to you. Don't worry. My name won't be anywhere on it," I reply with genuine lightheartedness.

Larry appears confused. I walk away. He forwards the email. It's one of his usual hack jobs. Reading it, I recall being at lunch with Randy from shipping and a couple guys from sales back when we were at the Rancho office. "Larry is pissed at me again," Randy from shipping started, in the same tone one would start a take-my-wife joke. "I got one of those Larry emails. You know the ones, Dear Randy, *dot-dot-dot*, I'm really concerned about something that isn't my business and doesn't matter, *dot-dot-dot*, do it my way, *dot-dot-dot*, or I'm going to tell Dallas on you *dot-dot-dot*." The laughter was uproarious.

The thought makes me feel a little sad for Larry. I imagine myself defending him. "We shouldn't talk shit about Larry. He actually has an incredible memory. He's just *dot-dot-dot* ..." And then I realize that over the last two-plus years of working with Larry, every time I try to give Larry the benefit of the doubt, try to justify his behavior, try to be nice to him, he does something even more cunning. I have no reason to doubt he'll do it again. But I have to keep my side of the street clear. I must understand what's going on here. I'm not trying to become friends with Larry or to justify his behavior. I'm here to be of service to him for selfish reasons. My policy of service and non-resistance is for me. Larry is just the beneficiary. I'm an addict. A festering resentment can kill me.

At first, Larry flexes his muscles and does things like schedule meetings late on Friday so that I will have to work 12 hours or sit in traffic for three hours. Now that he knows I won't fight with him no matter what, he's getting more and more bold. He used to hide it when he took credit for things I've done, now he flaunts it. But after a couple weeks of this, he seems to have become bored with me. He's pushed my buttons, and I no longer respond. He even approaches me directly.

"What's going on with you, son? It's like you lost your piss or something, not that I'm complainin'."

"Nothing, I'm just doing my job, Larry. Can I help you with something?"

Larry is still an asshole, but he's directed his anger away from me, mostly toward corporate, which, since the Economic Crisis, has become a thorn in his side, wanting reports that he doesn't know how to prepare, using computer programs he doesn't know how to use. To Larry's great objection—listening to him complain about it was as much fun as

I've had at work since before the annual golf tournament was canceled—one of his new superiors in Dallas insisted that Larry complete an on-line class to learn a basic spreadsheet program. Larry has also started confiding in me about his own economic downturn. Like so many others at CIW, he had a great deal of company stock in his retirement portfolio. What was once the relative size of a grapefruit was now the size of a grape. On top of that, he tells me, "My house is worth a third less than what it was five years ago! God damn varmints! I bet those sons-a-bitches at corporate, in their mansions and Mercedes, are still getting bonuses and raises!"

I tell no one of my rain-soaked victory, except my buddy Phil, a 12-Stepper and expert golfer who loves to gamble on the golf course. It's a perfect sunny day at Griffith Park, and he and I are playing a putting game called "7s," which he almost always wins.

"Tees up?" Phil asks me, after I casually mention that I shot a 79.

"Yeah, dude, tees were up. It was pouring rain," I say defensively. "They always move the tees up when the course is wet because the ball doesn't roll out. There were literally puddles on the greens."

"Ball in hand?" Phil asks while stroking a long downhill putt, pretending not to bait me.

"Yeah, Phil. I mean, at the end of the round, I had to move the ball from standing water on nearly every fairway after Hole 12."

"You mean casual water?" he asks.

"Yes, whatever," I respond.

"I thought that was only on the PGA? Pretty sure I'm right, actually," Phil says dismissively.

I argue with him, but the truth is I'm not convinced my 79 was really legit. Or maybe I believe it was legit, but not repeatable. I've only played a full round once since, and I shot an 84. I'm particularly vulnerable right now, as the last time I practiced at Scholl, one of the coaches took slow motion video during one of the classes. Seeing my swing in slow motion felt the same as when my dentist showed me X-rays of my impacted molars. All I could do was gasp. How could I practice so much and still have the same swing faults? My swing was a classic over-the-top move. It was exactly what Ben Hogan tried to get golfers not to do. I was, once again, the example of how to turn a lot of hard work into a God-forsaken disaster. I'd felt nauseous. All this practice, and all I was doing was perfecting a shitty swing.

I end up playing with Phil and his buddies in their regular money game. One of their usual foursome went missing. They are not happy about me joining them, as I can't afford to bet as they do, but I do put $20 on the line. Both of Phil's buddies are even better than he is, and they never play unless money is on the line.

After nine holes, I'm again two under par. But this time, I don't fall to pieces on the back nine. I play it safe, and I end up shooting a 75. I even make a little money.

Afterward, I sit on the same bench I sat on a few weeks earlier in the pouring rain. Only today is a perfect Los Angeles winter day, high 70s with a nice little breeze, and that unmistakable Los Angeles blue-yellow light that makes the greens richer and shade blacker. The course is busy. Milling around is the usual contingency of Korean men and women in their head-to-toe branded Korean golf gear; old muni-heads with thinning hair, their gruff lo-fi pull carts, worn bags and clubs; and a group of serious scratch golfers, with their gleaming precision chrome irons, looking like surgical instruments, neatly ordered and protruding out of golf bags with their names embroidered on the front pocket. Group numbers and tee times are called out over the crackling loudspeaker.

I feel calm. For just a moment, I feel like there is nothing else I should be doing right now. I can breathe. I just shot my lowest score ever, a 75. I reminisce: It has been less than three years since I got serious about this game. I've often embarrassed myself on the course, not by my performance, but by my behavior. It might surprise someone who witnessed one of my tirades, but I did the best I could to control myself. And, most importantly, I didn't quit. But I know the truth. My round today is the best it's going to get. Sure, I might sink a few long putts and get lucky and shoot a par-72, but I know that I don't have the tools to consistently score low. My game is a perfected maladjustment. Given my size, I should be crushing the ball, not carrying it to 220 yards max and hoping it rolls out to a barely respectable 240. It's not about distance, it's about having a mechanically sound swing. Like alcohol is to an alcoholic, lack of distance to a golfer is only a symptom of a disease. Ben Hogan wrote about "effortless power," that a correctly executed swing is a great pleasure. My swing is not a great pleasure. It's "effort*full*" and "power*less*."

It's back to the drawing board for me. I'm going to start over. I have to go deep. I have to lean in. I have to address my defects, take an axe to the root of them. I'll need help. I know it'll be a long and sometimes painful journey, but there is nothing else for me. I made a promise to myself. I can't live with these defects. I'll spend my remaining days rooting them out if that's what it takes. And one of these days, I'm going to sit on this bench after shooting in the 60s and think back on this moment. Maybe it'll take five, 10, 15 years, maybe more, but that's what I'm going to do.

The rough-faced Griffith Park starter stops in front of me. "Howdya hit 'em today?"

I couldn't recall his name on the day I shot 79 when he was in the starter's booth and warned me about the rain, and I still can't, even though we've played a round together. I look in vain for a name tag.

"Oh man—" I start in, excited to pump my ego and tell him I shot a 75. But then I just can't. I can feel how sick I'm going to feel immediately after bragging. Just this once, I can keep my mouth shut. Instead I say, "It's beautiful out there. This is why we live in Southern California, right?"

He chuckles, pulls a pack of cigarettes from his breast pocket, turns away and looks out over the course. He turns back to me and says, "Damn right. I grew up in Detroit. You can't even imagine." He lifts his unlit cigarette into his mouth and walks off.

D.A. D. Villa is here. The judge is here. Keri is here. I am here. It's starting to feel real. This can really happen. Why shouldn't I believe?

"He seems like he's in a good mood," I whisper to Keri about Judge Von Silkman. We sit in the audience waiting for my case to be called. We are here once again, in an attempt to Change the Numbers. I sing my Change the Numbers song in my head to calm my nerves.

> "I'm thinkin' we can change the numbers,
> I'm thinking we can make that change
> to the numbers…"

It's magic. Take all that nasty stuff and simply wipe it away with the stroke of the judge's pen; replace it with something more socially palatable than Assault with Intent to Commit Rape. I don't need to be a registrant. The judge said so. Judges get what they want. I've been good. I played ball. I'm tired of worrying about people searching my name on the internet. It's time to let me have a fresh start, get my Bar license back. I need to make some real money. I owe a lot of corporations and government entities a lot of money. I'm just barely paying the minimum payments. Gas prices are going up. I can't even afford to play twilight golf but once a month. I sunk every dollar I had saved into CIW stock when it hit bottom. I figured it either has to go up, or else it'll go out of business. If it goes out of business, I'm out of a job anyway, and the least of my worries will be a bad investment.

"People v. Naus," Judge Von Silkman's court clerk calls out.

"It looks like we have everyone here," Judge Von Silkman says. "Good. So, Ms. D. Villa, are we going to be able to get something done?"

"I'm sorry, your Honor ..." D.A. D. Villa responds.

That's all I need to hear to know the outcome. Things turn surreal while I listen to Judge Von Silkman.

"And just for the record, I don't think that what happened that night is something that Mr. Naus should be registering for the rest of his life. It was an anomaly. It was an aberration. It was a fugue state. It was a blackout state which I'm familiar with. And he's not a sexual predator. He's not a sexual—He's not somebody who's going to be sexually assaulting people or molesting people or anything like that. He had no clue what he was doing. But that's the best I can do is to state that on the record ..."

Everything in me sinks.

Like Toru in Haruki Murakami's *The Wind-Up Bird Chronicle,* I sit at the bottom of the well without a ladder, without a flashlight. It's like before, before I made the plea deal to go spend the summer of 2005 in Chino prison. I was completely at the mercy of this woman, D.A. D. Villa, a woman I've now been praying for nightly for over five years. But she still won't let me go. She won't drop the rope ladder. She's going to leave me here for dead.

I'm in that place again, just like five years ago when I was at my own bail hearing. I can see everything normally, but my thinking slows like I'm drunk, and my hearing is filtered as if I'm underwater.

I hear Keri arguing to the judge. I say something. I'm not sure exactly what, but I sound like a petulant child, "But you promised!" I look at Keri and then Judge Von Silkman, and realize whatever I said, I went too far. D. Villa argues that even if her superior did agree to Change the Numbers, she's not sure it would take me off the federal or state registered sex offender list. All three of them go back and forth, discussing legal intricacies. Judge Von Silkman grows impatient with Keri's arguments and begins to side with D.A. D. Villa. I suddenly feel drowsy. The muscles in my legs go weak, and I wobble a bit. My jaw and eyelids feel so heavy they could just slide off my face. Oh God, please, everyone just shut up. I just want to plop down into my chair, lay my head down on the desk and go to sleep.

"I'm sorry, Mr. Naus," Judge Von Silkman says.

I gather myself and respond as cheerfully as possible, wanting to make amends for my petulant outburst, "Thank you for your time, your Honor."

Judge Von Silkman addresses D.A. D. Villa and Keri generally, "If there is nothing else, counsel?"

"No, your Honor," Keri and D. Villa both respond, nearly simultaneously.

I can't say anything to Keri. It takes all the power I have to move, to walk to my car. I think about smoking. I can see a pack of Marlboro Red 100's. I can see a Jack and Coke with ice in a sweaty glass. I took the day off from work for this hearing. I could go home, walk to the liquor store and buy a bottle of Jack Daniels, a liter of Coke, some ice, a couple packs of cigarettes. I could sit on my little secluded patio and drink. I'd have to call in sick the next day. I'm not sure I could stop, and if I was able to go to work the day after next, I'd surely still be drunk from the night before. Nobody would have to know. But could I stop? I think of a line that I always say when I share my story at a 12-Step meeting, "If I could drink like a normal person, I'd drink all day every day." That line always gets a huge laugh, because they understand exactly what I mean. They understand that it's true.

I get in my car. I sit behind the steering wheel, and I pray hard. I pray like I did when I was in prison. You just got to get me through this, God. I believe in God now, it's just not the God I hear so much about, the one with the magical son. This one is different. It's the gravity that makes the water drip, the invisible force that binds cells together. It's impersonal, but at least it's real. One day at a time. Hell, one moment at a time. That's it. I can get through this. I'm not drinking, and I'm not smoking.

Just for today. I've still got a golf range token left. I can go practice my swing at the Griffith Park driving range. I call my sponsor on speaker phone as I drive. He tells me he's sorry about my court hearing, but he still believes I'll eventually get off Megan's Law List and get my Bar license back. He says he loves me. He tells me I'm going to be alright. He insists I go to a meeting today.

I cuss, yell and stomp my way through a bucket of balls, by myself at the very furthest bay at a thankfully-empty Griffith Park Golf Range. I go to a noon meeting. After the meeting, I confide in a 12-Step friend I've known for several years now. He knows that I'm registered. He was at my sentencing hearing five years ago. I tell him what happened. He hugs me. He tells me that it's going to be alright. He reminds me that I've been through worse. He tells me that he's here for me. I believe him. I go to another 12-Step meeting. I go home. I pray. I meditate. I In-N-Out Burger. I Ben & Jerry's. I watch *Scrubs*. I go to bed.

THIRTY-ONE

I sit in one of several rows of folding chairs in the rebar shop, behind the office here in Bloomington. It's a mammoth tin shed-like structure with a roof, three-stories high. It's a state-of-the-art rebar packaging plant with enormous German-made tools bolted to the ground, for cutting, bending, binding and ultimately loading sticks of rebar onto truck beds where it will be shipped to job sites throughout Southern California.

All the brass is here from the local shops, including Erik from Rancho, and several guys from Dallas, a couple I know from my training in Dallas on the SAP computer system, a few I don't know at all. They all sit behind a line of folding tables, facing us, the audience.

I got a call from Erik less than an hour ago. After I got off the phone, I rushed to finish the contract on one of the rare big private jobs we've landed since the Great Recession started, over two years ago. I signed it, scanned it, and emailed it out, with an insurance certificate, exactly one minute before I was supposed to be down here, in this giant shed.

Erik's call was unexpected.

He said he was on his way over to my office in Bloomington from Rancho. He said he was leading a caravan of rental cars loaded with a bunch of brass from Dallas who flew in last night.

"Joseph, nobody else knows..." Erik said, with a grimness in his voice I'd never heard before. "And I'm not supposed to tell you, but because we're friends, and, uh ... you don't deserve this, man..."

My fellow co-workers, mostly shop workers, mill about, presumably assuming this is some type of corporate *rah rah* meeting or another training seminar. Some, the ones seated, know that something isn't quite right. But most are casually enjoying the break from work and the coffee and donuts.

In a softened Texas twang and wearing a politician's pantsuit, the Head Corporate HR lady, clears her throat, and begins.

"Ladies and gentlemen, please take your seats." She waits a few moments for people to sit and then continues. "Because of the unfortunate financial downturn ..."

"The unfortunate financial downturn," I repeat in my mind. "That's an interesting way to put it."

"... we will be laying many of you off today. On behalf of the entire CIW family, I want to say that I wish this wasn't necessary."

People gasp. A man in blue navy work clothes stands with his arms out and pivots, looking around as if this is a Pentecostal church. A murmur rises into something more. The woman seated next to me begins crying, and it quickly turns into wailing. I've seen her in the parking lot. The man next to her, an older diminutive man with deep brown skin, wraps his arm around her. She tilts her head onto his shoulder and looks up at him as he offers her a dirty red shop rag. I can't see her face. His forearms are a circuit of thick steel cables, honed from years of gripping rebar.

The Dallas HR Queen shifts uncomfortably at the commotion her announcement draws. Her eyes scan. Her apologetic tone is replaced with an intimidating one as she announces how things will progress from this point forward. She says CIW is offering severance packages. When your name is called, please come up to the table and get your packet and look it over. If you accept it, sign it, and you will be given a check right now. If not, then you are to gather your things and leave the premises.

There are outbursts of shock and anger, and another lady begins to cry loudly. And the man next to me leans over, after hearing his name, rises and says to all of us, "I've been working here for over 20 years." I watch him walk down the aisle to receive his manila envelope.

I think of the CEO's email a couple years ago, and how he was foregoing a part of his salary because of the financial crisis. His stock options have since doubled and are worth $10 million, enough to pay every salary in this giant shed for two years, easy.

Some of the men who flew in from Texas are standing near the exits, stoic, with their arms crossed, like security. I ask myself, oh my God, were they really anticipating some type of violent response from us?

One of the secretaries from our department goes to the crying woman and consoles her. I can hear her say, "I have kids. This can't be happening—"

"Joseph Naus," the lady calls my name. It reminds me of prison and jail. They were always calling my name, and I was always sheepishly responding, really just wanting to be left alone. I'm full of emotion. I'm angry. I'm shocked at how this is being handled, although I do understand that there are very specific legal requirements with mass layoffs, and I'm also somewhat proud to be included with the blue-collar workers. I don't deserve better. At least these people actually did something. They touched rebar. They bent it and cut it and got it ready to go in buildings. I was just pushing paper for no good reason and making two or three times as much money as they were.

"Joseph, I'm sorry," Erik says, seated behind the table with all the other brass. "You know I fought for you," he says under his breath.

"Thanks, man," I say and shake his hand vigorously. After working with him for three years, I'm no longer shocked by his catcher's mitt hand. I think of the time we drove to Las Vegas and back in one day to negotiate a job. We ate at the Rio Casino and I watched nervously, before we left, as he played $500-a-hand blackjack.

It occurs to me that I no longer have to deal with Larry, that I don't have to drive a hundred miles a day. These thoughts mix with so many others. I no longer have health insurance. I no longer have an income. My fellow terminated employees mill around with their manila envelopes, consoling each other, a few tearful, many on their cell phones, talking to their wives and husbands, I suppose. I have no one to call. I could call Macy or Keri, my mom, or even Francisco, but I don't have to. My firing isn't going to affect their lives directly. It's just me.

I sit back down and open my manila folder. The offer is surprisingly adequate, four months' salary. I sign the form and pick up my check. I begin to walk to my car. I knew what was happening. I already put my single banker's box of stuff in my car, and I have my keys and wallet, but something stops me. I suddenly become very angry. I go up to my office, because no one is stopping me. By this time, some of the brass is in the conference room next to my now-former office. Erik, Dick and several other guys from Dallas are standing around, looking at a piece of paper with names on it.

"Joseph," Dick says. "We're really sorry."

My face is hot. The room is silent as they wait to see what I'm going to do. I peek out of the room to see Larry through the glass wall of his office, hiding. I shout into the conference room loud enough so Larry can hear me. "You chose that fucking idiot over me? I put up with that motherfucker for three years. No matter what bullshit he pulled, you guys never did anything. You even promoted him, and now you get rid of me!"

Erik half smiles at me. I know he agrees wholeheartedly but he can't say anything.

Dick says, "Joseph, look, this came down from the top of the executive suite ..."

I ignore him and walk out.

My drive home is glorious. There is no traffic. I'm so freed by the reality that I don't have to get up tomorrow and do the commute again, deal with Larry again, sit in an office chair for 10 hours again, try to muster up the energy for an irrelevant job again, that the joy is drowning out the fear of not having a job and how that is going to work financially. All I can think of is how splendid my week is going to be. I'm going to go to a coffee shop and sit in it all day and read, I'm going to go to Griffith Park in the middle of the day, when it's empty, and practice my chipping and putting all damn day. I'm going to go to Keri's condo in downtown Los Angeles while she's at work, and I'm going to work out in the little chic gym and then swim in the rooftop pool, lay out, and then walk her dog. I'm going to go to the Geffen Art Museum and the Los Angeles MoMA and stare at moody Degas oil paintings at the Norton Simon. I'm going to hike in Griffith Park and start running again. My corporate gym membership is gone, so I'll start doing those P90X workouts on DVD my golfing buddy gave me, get rid of these 30 extra pounds of fat I've picked up. I'm going to 12-Step meetings every damn night, and get my daily meditation practice back on track, too.

I'll be just fine.

EPILOGUE

I'm at Chango, my favorite little coffee shop in Echo Park. This is the west coast epicenter of the modern beatnik. I do not fit in. I'm not wearing anything ironic, although my navy blue CIW-Rancho Rebar hoodie may be perceived as such. And I'm not wearing skinny jeans, for one, because I'm not skinny anymore. I tap away on my laptop's keyboard, trying to get a few pages down before the battery dies. I'm the only one of the many laptop writers in here, presumably all wildly successful screenwriters, without a sleek white Apple laptop, not because I'm a contrarian but because I can't afford one. There's a line at the cash register. Coffee smells waft about. Lauren Hill of the Fugees sings in the background, through the café's mounted speakers from a barista's iPod playlist. Above me is Chango's signature piece: a large stretched canvas, a black-on-white portrait painting of Biggie Small's face, layered with ribbons of musical scales. Street noises spike and wane when the front door opens and closes. The barista pounds a commercial portafilter against the espresso machine, and the cash register drawer jangles.

A friend from the Program I haven't seen for a couple years walks in. He doesn't notice me at first, and I find myself trying to get his attention without disturbing the other dozen laptoppers. I'm unsuccessful, so I holler out. "Mikey, what's up?"

Mikey looks up, as do several laptoppers, annoyed at the interruption.

"Hey man," Mikey mouths from across the café. He motions that he's going to get his coffee before joining me.

Seeing Mikey reminds me of all my dead 12-Step friends. It's not unlike the AIDS epidemic. The gentrification of this neighborhood and adjoining Silver Lake was started by gays in the '80s. I've heard the stories. One minute, they're healthy, the next they're dead, ravaged by a ruthless disease. Funerals every other weekend. Nobody was able to stop it. It's still like that now in the 12-Step Rooms, probably has been even since the days of Bill Wilson. In *Alcoholics Anonymous*, Bill writes that an alcoholic hanged himself in him and his wife, Lois', home.

But that's how it is if you stay clean and sober. People come in, and you become friends. Sometimes you become good friends, because you have this thing in common, but then some of them go out, and some of them make it, and you see them at the grocery store, maybe buying some wine, as if it's no biggie, they got it licked, like when I saw Peter at Trader Joe's, and then later they die in an accident that you know deep down happened because they were getting high. And then one of your fellows gets married and moves to Austin, and they seem so happy on their social media posts, and then you find out they overdosed in a hotel room after a fight with their wife. And you cry, and people say sad and nice things, and then nothing. And that's how it goes. One day they're in a 12-Step meeting, and the next day they're dead, not at 80 years old from old age, but 20, 30, and 40 years old from overdosing on pills, booze or junk, or they straight-up suicide. That's the way it is with us.

Mikey sits down across from me, takes a sip through the nipple of his to-go cup. "Hey, man, it's good to see you," he says with a sincerity that instantly shifts my sad reminiscing into a deep gratitude—as we are fellow disaster survivors.

Mikey is one of the men that Trenton and I befriended when Mikey first came in the Rooms. Mikey was perma-depressed, a serious junkie and pill-head, who chased it all with booze. Now he's shining and smiling voraciously.

"It's good to see you, too," I respond.

"I haven't seen you in so long," Mikey says.

"I know, man," I reply. "I'm sorry I haven't called. I had that dang job that just took over my life."

"Had?" Mikey says and raises his eyebrows.

"Yeah, I just got laid off," I report.

"Sorry, man. That sucks."

"I'm actually fine."

Mikey nods.

I lean in a little across the table so no one else can hear, especially the cute hipster girl sitting next to us. "I mean, you know, I'm fine considering I'm a two-strike felon, on the sex offender list, a disbarred lawyer with $200,000 in debt and, uh, like, you know, no income."

Mikey and I both laugh heartily above the ambient rap music, now a B-side A Tribe Called Quest track. Mikey reminds me of what I love about recovered addicts.

"Well, you look pretty damn stoked," Mikey says.

"How 'bout you?" I ask.

"I'm a fucking nurse," Mikey declares proudly. He stands up a little, revealing mint-green scrub bottoms.

"Oh shit! I didn't even notice those. Whoa."

I feel a deep joy at hearing this news.

For a few moments, we just sit there grinning and nodding like happy fools.

"Amazing, right?" Mikey says.

"Dude," I say. "When you came in to the Rooms, you were strung-out, homeless, or like, couch surfing, right? What's it been—like, five, six years later, and now you're a nurse?"

"Yeah, man. You used to pick me up and take me to Meetings with that other dude. What was his name? ... With the crazy hair—" Mikey says, holding his hands up as if he's holding a globe on his head.

"Trenton," I say.

"Yeah, Trenton," Mikey says, and repeats the name, as if recalling him, "Trenton ... good dude. Helped me out a lot."

Mikey doesn't ask about Trenton, so I don't say anything.

I take a sip of my coffee. I'm at once filled with joy for Mikey but reliving the pain of losing Trenton. Some get the gift, some get the tragedy. Mikey's facial expression flattens as he apparently senses my change in mood after the mention of Trenton.

I purposefully reset. I sit up tall and smile. I feel as if this meeting with Mikey is something more than a chance meeting.

"So," Mikey says, breaking the silence. "What are you working on?" He points to my laptop and yellow legal pad.

"Oh yeah," I respond coyly. "Well, since you asked, now that I've got some time, I've decided to write a memoir about my story."

"Well, it is one hell of a story," Mikey says.

Mikey's phone chimes. He looks down and reads a text. "I gotta go, man. It's great to see you, Joseph." He stands up, readying himself to leave.

"You too, Mikey. A nurse. Wow, I'm so happy for you."

"Thanks, man. I'm glad you're still sober, too. And don't worry about your money sitch. God's your employer."

We stand, shake hands and hug. He pushes in his chair and starts away.

I open my laptop and prepare to get back to writing.

"Hey, Joseph," I hear Mikey say. I look up at him. He has a look of severe curiosity. "What are you going to call your book?"

"I think I'm going to call it *Straight Pepper Diet*."

An excerpt from Joseph W. Naus's first memoir

Straight Pepper Diet
One (Prologue)

I'm sitting in my office at Yi & Naus, the two-man law firm, my partner Will and I started last year. I have no less than twenty phone calls to return, a dozen letters to write, and several motions to draft, but I've been staring out the window at the traffic passing by, several stories below, for nearly an hour. In my chest is a feeling of dread. This feeling varies in strength, but it never completely disappears. Today it's strong. Today, it took every bit of self-discipline I could muster just to drive into the office. As I stare downward, I keep thinking, do other people feel this shitty?

I can't let anyone know the way I feel. They'd think I was insane, or at best, clinically depressed. I'd be committed to an insane asylum like my grandma was, or I'd have to spend the rest of my life in a shrink's office zonked out on Valium talking about my feelings and walking around with a mannequin's smile. I'd lose everything. It's much better to conquer this on my own, just as I've done with everything else in my life. I'll try harder. I'll pull myself up by my bootstraps. I'm tough.

I hear Will's wingtips tapping on the hallway floor. He's heading toward my office.

"Hey champ," Will says.

I take a deep breath, force a smile, and swivel around in my chair.

"How was court? Did we win?" I ask.

"Kind of ..." Will replies.

"You know, Will, at Yi & Naus, victory is the only acceptable result," I kid.

Will chuckles but doesn't comment. The crease between his eyes reveals that he has something on his mind—I presume a warning or a reminder or something along those lines.

"Joseph, remember—tomorrow at 7:00 a.m., Brookside, Course Number One. Dr. Lee, could not be more important."

"I got it. I *totally* got it." I hold up my mobile phone. "It's even in here."

"Do you need a wake-up call?" Will asks.

"No, I'm good, dude. Really," I say reassuringly.

"Okay. I'll see you there." Will seems satisfied with my commitment to the gravity of tomorrow's meeting and breaks a smile. "Get there a little early and warm up that hor-rific swing of yours."

Will and I are a good team. He is extremely practical, and knows how to run a law office. I'm not, and I don't. Will likes to stay in the office doing transactional work. I'd rather be trying cases in front of a judge and jury every day. Law is business to Will. I practice law, because it's who I am. Will couldn't care less about being in the newspaper. I love seeing my name in print. It's proof of my success.

Last month I landed two cases from a friend I used to work with at Thomas & Colbert, who now works as in-house counsel at a Fortune 500 company. Among a dozen other cases, I represent a couple real estate investment trusts that are a constant source of business. Will has a few good clients, too, including two financial conglomerates who pay us a retainer that covers our entire monthly overhead. If things continue this way, we'll move to a bigger office, hire an associate attorney, and soon I'll be the rainmaking trial lawyer I've always wanted to be. Surely then my dread will finally go away.

The guy we're meeting tomorrow, Dr. Lee, a retired surgeon, is our biggest individual client. He owns a ton of property in Los Angeles, and he's rich, not first-class-plane-seat-rich but private-jet-rich. He's flying in from Singapore to visit his business interests and to meet me, the new litigation wunderkind who is handling most of his cases. I've dreamt of client meetings like this since I was first at Pepperdine Law, ten years ago. It's incredible: I'm meeting at a golf course with a client that pays me hundreds of dollars an hour to do what I love to do. I know how to handle this meeting. After I shank my tee shot into the water hazard, I'll refrain from throwing my golf bag in the lake, and, instead, brush it off and charm Dr. Lee with the story about how last week I showed up with the Los Angeles County Sheriff and a locksmith and evicted his tenants from the largest Chinese restaurant in Chinatown, and how I didn't know what to do with the lobsters in the tank, and how I had to turn off all the gas, because the sheriff threw out the kitchen staff while the burners were still going. Then I'll tell him about the deposition I took on one of his cases in San Francisco, and how I crucified the cross-defendant. Charming Dr. Lee will be easy. All I have to do is suit up and show up.

It's just past 8:00 p.m.; I've gotten nothing done at the office, and I'm driving back home to Santa Monica. It's been nearly two years since my drunk driving accident in Riverside, when I was working for Thomas & Colbert, and I still feel a little sketchy driving. I look over my shoulder and check the rearview and side mirrors over and over before changing lanes like I'm OCD. Sometimes I have to simply abort the mission and stay in my lane, even if it means missing an off-ramp or two. It doesn't make sense. There were no other vehicles involved in my accident. It happened because I was drunk out of my mind and tried to take a turn in an SUV at eighty-five miles per hour. But this fact doesn't stop me from breaking into a cold sweat every time I see a cop, or from panicking every time I'm approaching a yellow light at an intersection.

It isn't only fear of cops, Vehicular OCD, and a criminal record that I acquired after my drunk driving accident. Something far more disturbing has been with me since. It's the knowledge that there are two of me. There is the Joseph that lives life and does things, and then there is this other Joseph that constantly narrates my dread. The dread is shot-out nerves, reaching out, anticipating things going wrong, *terribly wrong*. It lives in my chest, and on full blast it radiates from the back of my eyes through my forehead and pulsates down my shoulders to my fingertips. I used to *feel* the dread, but now it comes with a narrator. No matter the subject of its diatribe, its basic message is the same: *You Are Fucked.* Sometimes there is a reason, and sometimes there isn't. The only time the narration stops is when I really lose myself in work, which has become exceedingly rare, or, when I'm fucking or drinking, preferably in combination. That's when the real relief comes. I used to mistake the relief as bliss, but now I know it's just a lack of pain—a temporary muzzle on the dread's narrator. When I'm done drinking and fucking, when I wake up, it comes right back at full volume, as if it's been saving up, waiting for me to wake up so it can lay into me. I so badly want it to stop. Sometimes, when I'm by myself at home or in the office, or sometimes even in the car, I shout out loud, *Shut the fuck up, and leave me alone!* And then I wonder if that makes me crazy.

Tonight, as with every other weeknight, I pull into the Chevron on Pico and buy a pack of Marlboro Red 100s and a lighter. I've wanted to quit smoking since I started. Smoking doesn't stop the dread, but it feels good and lowers the volume, and, even if it didn't, I'd still smoke, because I'm completely addicted. I can't go a night without smoking. Nevertheless, I throw away a lighter every night just after I declare that I will never smoke again, and that I'm serious this time. The clerk at the Chevron, a middle-aged Indian man with a kind smile, who I presume owns the station, pretends he doesn't notice the oddity of my buying a new lighter every night, yet he no longer asks me what color lighter I want. He knows I want the crayon-red Bic. If he doesn't have that color, I have to go somewhere else.

I drive through the Taco Bell on Pico, as I do nearly every night. The dread's narrator is clear and loud. Even my Snoop Dogg CD can't drown him out.

You're such a loser. You shouldn't even be eating fast food.

A half-hour later, I'm post-tacos, standing on my lanai, still in my suit. I'm chain-smoking and thinking. My neighbor passes by for the second time. I'm embarrassed. I avoid eye contact.

She thinks you're a maniac, a freak, standing out here chain-smoking all night. What's the matter with you?

I know. I feel like shit. This is the last night. As soon as I'm done with this pack, I'll never smoke again. I'll even throw away the lighter. I mean it this time.

Uh-huh. Yeah right.

Look, I graduated from law school and passed the California Bar Exam on the first try. I can fucking quit smoking if I want to. Tonight is the last night. Period.

Uh-huh. Yeah right.

Fuck you, if you don't believe me.

The sincerity of my declaration brings the sobering memory of what it feels like when I crave a cigarette and try not to smoke. I'm usually able to hold out for about an hour before I find myself standing on the lanai with a Marlboro Red 100 in my hand, hating myself … again.

God, I wish I could just feel good.

You know what? I want to go to the Liquid Kitty and drink Jack and Cokes at the end of the bar. That's what I want to do. I can stop and get another pack of cigarettes on my way. I haven't even thrown away my lighter yet.

That's a terrible idea. It's almost ten, and I have to be up at the crack of dawn to meet Will and Dr. Lee at Brookside Golf Course. Even if I go to bed now, I won't get eight hours of sleep.

But, it'd be a nice little walk. I'll just have a couple … a few, Jack and Cokes, and I'll be in bed by midnight.

I remember the last time I was going to try and only drink a few, a month ago at Ryan's bachelor party in Las Vegas. I ended up disappearing for nearly two days, and then I woke up, and I couldn't remember where I'd been. I had a pocket full of bank withdrawal receipts, adding up to nearly five grand, and a half-smudged telephone number written in lipstick across my back. I'm not even supposed to be drinking. That was part of the plea bargain on my DUI. I'm supposed to start AA and drunk driving school by the end of next week.

Yeah, that's right. I can drink tomorrow. I just need to finish this pack of cigarettes and go to bed. Just get to bed. Tomorrow, I can drive straight home from the golf course and go to a bar to celebrate my first day smoke free. I only have one cigarette left. I wish I had four or five. I'm going to make this last one count. I go in the kitchen, full of pricey unused stainless steel appliances, and mix myself a strong Jack and Coke.

The Liquid Kitty is dark, hiply curated, and the bartenders serve uniformly eye-watering strong drinks. I've only been here for an hour, and I am four Jack and Cokes in, and I'm not close to where I need to be. *M-something*, but not Mary, has ropy brown curly hair that is making me want to touch it. She's talking to me and sitting next to me at the end of the bar waiting for her drink. She works at an architectural firm in Century City, *Something & Something*. That's about all I hear over the music. She takes her soup bowl-sized chocolate martini and returns back to her gaggle of girlfriends. I drink another and tip five dollars. The gaggle leaves, and M-something leaves with them. She looks back at me and smiles, and then she's gone. She's a nice one, a sleeper, like Larisa, the twenty-one-year-old I just broke up with.

That tip was my last five bucks. Thank God I accidentally brought my ATM card in my summer jacket, even though I'd thought I'd only brought forty dollars to make sure I didn't stay too long. Forty dollars is not enough. I drink another. Now I'm where I want to be—in the warm, gooey, alcohol-induced, sweet spot. I smoke another. I drink, smoke, drink, and smoke. It's just me in here now, the sexy bartender, and a couple extras. She's nice to me but doesn't—*does not*—want to fuck me. I checked to make sure the last ... *whatever day* it was I was here last ... the day before yesterday? I could be such a great boyfriend to her. *She's so hot.* I drink, smoke, drink, and smoke. I could do this forever. She's *such a good bartender. I totally love her.* I can't remember her name. I knew it two drinks ago. Nick Cave or maybe Tom Waits plays on the jukebox, or maybe one of those other guys you have to be cooler than I am to appreciate. The guy she'll sleep with tonight, he'll be skinny with dark, perfectly disheveled hair, and he'll have tattoos up his arms. He probably has the entire Nick Cave and Tom Waits collection. *Fuck that guy.*

Things are going fuzzy and black and loud and jagged. I've been cut off from here before, maybe not the last time, but two times before that. I'm trying to stay mellow so she'll keep serving me. I order another and another. How many? Maybe nine or something like that, not a dozen. I've always been good with numbers, although things get a little fuzzy in the neighborhood of geometry. I think I just said that out loud, but I'm not sure.

Everything goes black.

Black pavement, street lights, cars, the neon Taco Bell sign, the liquor store, the 10 Freeway underpass at Pico, the red neon of the porn shop. Visions streak by, and my feet thud numbly under me. I'm running wild. The cool summer night. My heart beats hard, and my lungs groan from inhaling two packs of cigarettes in a few hours.

I stopped somewhere on the way, and now I'm pounding on the door to the Oriental massage parlor. There's no back door; bad configuration. My vision is blurred. I can see if I close one eye. Things are not real. It's like a dream, but I can feel the warm summer air. Colors are snapping in my peripheral. Light and sound dart in an out of silence and shadows.

Again, everything goes black.

And then I'm back in the dream world. Now, I'm in a small dark motel room. It's factory-loud. It has to do with the Oriental massage parlor. A man is yelling. *Jesus Christ! Whoa!* I'm fighting, but it's as if I'm watching myself. I try to shut him down. I try to contain an angry screaming man. I'm naked, and my cock is hard. *Whoa!* I'm in trouble, and I need to get out of here. I was in the massage parlor bathroom. Now an Asian man swings wildly at me. He rocks me, and I see stars, flashing colors. I grab him and put him in a choke hold. Elbow –V to Adam's apple; cinch it in tight. He tries to scream, but he's losing air.

Shut the fuck up! I hear. It's me. I yelled that.

We are interlocked, flying around the little room. He's half my size. It's dark, and there is an industrial fan sounding like a prop plane. He won't shut up, but if I keep squeezing, I'll accidentally kill him on purpose.

Shut the fuck up, or I'm going to kill you! I yell again.

I let go. He gasps for air and wrestles with the front door.

I grab my clothes and back away from him into the bathroom. I lunge and fall out the bathroom window. I'm in a little alleyway between the building and a cinderblock wall. I climb clumsily, all angles. I'm out on the street, hopping, trying to get my pants on. I'm shirtless. I have no shoes. I'm on 32nd and Pico. I was in the massage parlor. There is Der Wienerschnitzel with its bright yellow lights.

Here comes the Asian man, and now he has a friend. They're pissed. One has a skateboard. One has a bat. I'm standing in the front lawn of a tidy little house across the street. They've cornered me.

They're yelling at me. I'm trying to get away. Screaming words are going back and forth. I can't understand what they are saying, and they don't seem to understand what I'm saying. This is not a dream and is getting more real every moment. I just want to get away. They won't let me go. I'm spinning; red and blue spots are floating in my vision. I think some of the lights are real, some aren't. I'm not sure which. My arms and legs are moving so slowly. My brain is telling my arms to move. They don't listen until a few moments later.

Thwack! Asian Man slams the deck of his skateboard right down on my head like I'm a giant tent stake he's trying to drive into the turf.

There are stars again. I concuss to blackness and then come back. I can't move. Like a cartoon character, he just hit me as hard as he can with a skateboard that is almost as big as he is, but I don't feel it, not at all.

Thud. Asian Man's friend hits me with the bat in my right arm. I heard it, but the feeling was as if my arm was wrapped by a giant pillow. I turn to the Asian Man, and he's yelling at me, something about Hawaii.

I try to reason with them, because I can't really see, and I can't really feel, and I can't really speak. I'm telling them about Hawaii and Volkswagens and fraternal brotherhood. They don't understand. I know what I'm saying, but it doesn't make sense.

Please just let me go! I yell.

I watch from somewhere just outside of me as they continue to beat me.

Thwack! with the bat.

Crack! with the skateboard.

The fifth or sixth strike to my head with the skateboard makes a new sound. Something gave way. All three of us react. The little Asian man looks concerned and backs off a bit, skateboard cocked above his head.

I want to go home now. I should have never left. I need to go home and sleep. I'm going to die if he doesn't stop. I try to move toward the street so I can run away, but they won't let me.

Asian Man does a little bullfighter parry. I'm the bull. Then again with the chopping motion.

Crack!

I'm gonna die.

I don't know if I just said that, but I know he realizes it and is thinking about whether he wants to kill me.

Thud! This one lands on my shoulder. Did he break my arm?

I gather all my will and decide to throw a kick. The thought passes my brain and travels down to my hapless limb, and the Asian man casually steps back as I fall. I'm a tranquilized bear. He's laughing, and his friend says something, something about stopping my beating.

Thwack!

Seriously man, you better stop.

I lunge toward the street while pulling up my jeans. I fall and drag my leg against the asphalt. It bleeds like a broken catsup bottle. I rise and hear sirens coming from all around, helicopter, *chop-chop-chop-chop*. I look back. People are gathering toward Pico. I'm running, barefoot and shirtless. I dive into a bush near the porch of someone's sweet little home.

Police show in force. They shine their spotlight. I don't want to get shot.

I'm here, I yell.

I stand and raise my hands in the air. They go berserk. Guns drawn, screaming. Get down, turn around! Handcuffs and pats and yelling and loud radios and spinning colors, as in my head when I was just in that dark room with the angry Asian man, spinning around like a fat palsied ballerina. The radios—loud and squawking: crackle, static, pop.

Stretcher, ambulance, and then blackness.

My contacts feel as if they've been transformed into miniature potato chips, fused to my corneas. My whole body buzzes from massive quantities of nicotine. My kidneys are pulsating, trying to escape through my back. My mouth is gummy from dehydration, and I am desperately thirsty. This is the all-too-familiar physical sensation I feel upon waking from a night of drinking. I know from experience that this is just the starting point. The real pain comes when my brain begins functioning. I want to go back to sleep before this happens.

Too late.

The realization that I've probably blown an appointment vacuums out my lungs. I try to regain my breath, and I'm hit with it. I was supposed to meet Will and Dr. Lee at Brookside. We have a 7:00 a.m. tee time. *Fuck!* Dr. Lee flew in from Singapore the night before last. *Jesus Christ!* I brace myself to open my aching eyes so I can see the alarm clock. Maybe things are okay. Maybe it's still early. I haven't heard my cell phone or my alarm clock. I take a deep breath and swing my legs around, while I pry open my eyes. My right leg slams into something hard. My ankle blurts out with pain. My wrist is held back, and I hear metal slide on metal. My vision is fuzzy, but I can tell it's dark outside and the lights are on in this room, very on. A firm hand presses down on my shoulder, easing me back into bed.

"Take it easy."

My eyes focus. There is a young uniformed police officer standing over me.

"Take it easy," he repeats. "There is nothing you can do right now."

Fuck. This is not my room and not my bed. It's a hospital bed. There is a cop standing over me, and I have an IV in my arm. *Very Fuck.*

I sit up, mouth agape, searching my memory for an explanation. It pours in like a horror montage: The Liquid Kitty; the front door of the massage parlor on Pico; a dark room with a loud industrial hum; swinging fists, struggling with someone in the dark, angry yelling; flashing red, green, and blue lights; sirens, cops, black handguns, *Get down!*, handcuffs; ambulance. It all had something to do with the Oriental massage parlor by my house.

I don't remember being with one of the girls. I remember the girl at the bar with the shiny hair, but she left with her friends. Nothing makes any sense. It wouldn't have been open after the Liquid Kitty closed. I know better than to go to a massage parlor at night. I've been to dozens of massage parlors, hundreds of times. I've never been late at night. But I must have.

The young cop says something, but I can't hear what he says through the blaring in my head. He has kind eyes. He leaves for just a moment and returns with a tall thin lady doctor, like one from a medical soap opera. She has a shiny instrument with a trigger. I'm sorry she has had to wake up to deal with me. She's probably married and has kids and lives in Beverly Hills. I picture her in bed with her husband when her pager sounds. He stirs and she kisses him, and she gets up and checks the number. It's a medical emergency, sure enough. She tells him, "Go back to sleep, honey; I'll be back soon."

She applies alcohol to my head with an oversized Q-tip. She has the fingers of a pianist. She holds the gun to my head.

"This is going to hurt, so brace yourself."

I grip the bed railings tightly and clench my jaw.

Chikew! The brassy sound echoes off the hard-lit sterile white walls. She stands back and observes me. She looks bewildered at my lack of reaction.

A memory pops. It was the two Asian guys in the front yard across from the massage parlor. They were yelling at me and taking turns whacking me. I remember thinking to myself that I should be feeling something; that if he kept hitting me he would kill me.

"That didn't hurt?" the doctor asks, rhetorically.

It didn't. She does it again and again. Each time the loud, brassy sound ricochets off the walls offending what should be the quietest time of the night. She is stapling my scalp back together, but the procedure is no more painful than a haircut. I open my eyes. She looks at me again. She's puzzled at my lack of pain, and she is disgusted by me. She is disgusted by me, because I'm disgusting. *You're right, Lady Doctor, and I'm sorry.*

It turns out I'm not in a hospital, just a medical room in the police station. The doctor finishes, and the cop takes me to use the phone. After my drunk driving accident, I never thought I'd have another "one phone call", but here I am, in the Santa Monica Police Station, in the same building where I had my first law school moot court competition ten years earlier. I've handled several cases in this building; I even know a couple of the judges.

I call Keri, my ex-girlfriend/criminal defense attorney, and after a disheartening number of rings, she finally picks up.

"Keri, Oh, you picked up," I say, relieved. "Thank God. Uh ... I'm in trouble, and I need you to come bail me out."

"Joseph ... *serious?* Are you drunk?"

"Yes, I'm drunk and no, I mean yes, I'm serious."

"Where are you?"

"Santa Monica jail."

Keri sighs deeply into the receiver. It's the sound of exasperated disappointment that I became so familiar with during our tumultuous relationship and during her handling of my felony DUI case.

"What are you being charged with?"

"I uh ... I ... well, don't know exactly ... probably ... uh ... solicitation?"

"Solicitation of what?"

"Uh ..." I realize there is no good way to say it, so I just say it, "prostitution."

"Prostitution?"—She sighs again, louder this time. "Joseph, *really?*"

"Well, I don't know, really. It could be anything. I was *really* wasted. Actually, I still am. I don't remember much. You'll find out when you get here. Just hurry up, and bail me out, okay?"

I'm taken to a holding cell. I'm by myself. There is a big steel door, and I stare at it wondering who will come through it. It's been at least two hours, and still no Keri. I shiver as cold alcohol and nicotine-laced sweat leaches out of my pores. A merciful lady cop brings me an itchy, gray, wool blanket and gives me a tight smile, as if she's looking at a rabid dog that used to be a cute family pet but now must be put down. The blanket doesn't stop me from shivering. As I sober up I begin to feel the gravity of my predicament. I'm in jail, and I'm probably in trouble again. *How embarrassing.* Pain radiates through to my back. I squeeze my arms tightly against my stomach to contain the pain. I wait and wait, but still no Keri. Maybe she's decided to let me sit in here a while to teach me a lesson. I should have told her that I need to get out as soon as possible so I can call Will and tell him I'm sick and can't make it to meet him and Dr. Lee—if it's not already too late.

I recall some mental snapshots of the night but nothing new. I'm starting to feel crawly. This is what happens after I binge drink. I need another drink so I can come down easy. I wish Keri would come get me out of here. I need a cold beer right away. I just want to shut my eyes and wake up in my bed. I shut my eyes, but I start to see a kaleidoscope of ants in red, and blue flashes of light. God, I just want to be in my bed. I wish I'd not gone out drinking. Just this once, I wish I'd done the right thing.

Keri finally arrives. The lady cop takes me to a visiting booth. Plexiglas separates Keri and me. She looks scared. Her full lips are white, and her eucalyptus-colored eyes washed gray. She holds her mouth tight.

"Goddamn, Keri, what took you so long?" I ask through the telephone receiver.

"I was meeting with the detectives. You wouldn't believe what I had to do to see you. They didn't want to let me see you."

"What? Why? I figured you were dealing with bail."

Keri is acting odd, even for this situation. She should be mad at me for waking her up, not to mention for getting arrested again after she finally settled my drunk driving case. There is something else, something grave; she looks like she used to look when we lived together in law school, and I'd hold her in the middle of the night after she'd woken up from a nightmare.

"What's the deal, Keri? When do I get out of here?"

She stares right at me, then down, then into my eyes again. I know that move. She's about to cry, but this time she doesn't. Instead, she shuts her eyes for a long moment. When she opens her eyes, she has her lawyer mask on.

"You don't understand," Keri says. "Don't say anything to anyone." She speaks with a slow solemnity that makes me realize that she must be right. Suddenly, things have become terribly serious.

"Keri, what am I being charged with?"

She takes a deep breath in through her teeth and then blows it out hard.

"You are being charged with Attempted Murder."

Acknowledgments

To fans of *Straight Pepper Diet*. Thank you for buying it, reading it, reviewing it, and recommending it. Thank you to so many people that reached out to me on my website and on social media. I'm so grateful. Many of you said you wanted me to write a follow-up because you wanted to know what happened next. Well, here it is. I so hope you enjoy it. I tried my best to become a better writer.

To my beautiful wife, Theresa Saso, who supported me through the often emotionally grueling, multi-year process of creating this memoir. She also contributed to every aspect of its creation: story editing, copy editing, engineering and editing the recording of the audio version, cover design, promotion, book design, administrating vendors, and website design and maintenance.

To my mom, a real American hero. She died from the effects of nicotine addiction in her 50s just like Grandma. I still can't believe I can't call you anymore.

To Sheri, a mother, and Buddy, a father. Thank you for rescuing me.

To Grandpa, who even found a way to rescue me in death.

To Tracy M., a great spiritualist, teacher and mother.

To Kelly C. Quinn, Esq. a magnificent lawyer and true friend.

To The Quinn Family, especially Christine. I can't thank you enough for what you did for me.

To my story editor extraordinaire, Allison Palmer.

To Catherine Palmer who copy edited this text with such great care.

To Vincent Jones, for your friendship and expertise.

To Scott, Esq. and Tom, Esq. for putting up with me on the golf course, among other kindnesses.

To Bill at "CIW." Thanks for taking a chance on me. To Gregg, Adam, Chris S., Chris L., Tony and Christine at "CIW." Thanks for making the unbearable bearable. To "Larry," a great antagonist. I hope you are alive and happy.

To Grace Kallis, Esq. Thanks for being a baller-Hollywood-agent-shark. To Sean Clement. Thanks for showing me how a pro behaves.

To Ahiah CSL and Agape International Spiritual Center, sanctuaries of love. To Reverend Michael Bernard Beckwith, Rickie Byars, Reverend Michael Bernard Lattimore, Reverend Scott Olson, Alfajiri McDonald, Caroline Fitzgerald and Reverend Cheryl Ward. These are teachers and spiritual guides, holding a space for Love, no matter what the external world looks like.

To the podcasters that graciously host stories of addiction and recovery, including mine, Rich Roll (The Rich Roll Podcast), Anna David (Afterpartypod) Omar Pinto (The Recovery Revolution Podcast) and Shane Ramer (Sober Guy Podcast).

To Kjeld and Jenny of à bloc café in Highland Park, Los Angeles.

To Nina Daly, Esq. for your hard work and friendship.

To Heidi Ferrer of girltomom.com. Thanks for getting the ball rolling. To Nick Guthe for helping me believe that I am a writer.

To Francis. Thank you for always being there for me.

To Aunt Vicki and Uncle Frank for your love and support when I needed it so much.

To Sarah and Andrew for talking story with me over wonderful family dinners.

About the Author

As of 2020, Joseph W. Naus lives in Los Angeles with his wife, Theresa and cat, Bogey. He's still clean, sober, "abstinent" and "smober" and an active 12-Stepper. Joseph has yet to secure his status as a PGA Tour pro. And he continues to write. *On Death, Four Short Stories* (memoir) is slated for release late 2020. To be notified of future publications, please sign up at www.josephwnaus.com

CPSIA information can be obtained
at www.ICGtesting.com
Printed in the USA
FSHW021547290120
66588FS

9 780986 283314